D1187673

Metacognition, Cognition, and Human Performance

VOLUME 1
Theoretical Perspectives

Metacognition, Cognition, and Human Performance

VOLUME 1
Theoretical Perspectives

Edited by

D. L. Forrest-Pressley
Department of Psychology
Children's Psychiatric Research Institute
Ontario, Canada

G. E. MacKinnon
Department of Psychology
University of Waterloo
Ontario, Canada

T. Gary Waller
Department of Psychology
University of Waterloo
Ontario, Canada

1985

ACADEMIC PRESS, INC.

(Harcourt Brace Jovanovich, Publishers)

Orlando   San Diego   New York   London
Toronto   Montreal   Sydney   Tokyo

ACADEMIC PRESS, INC.
Orlando, Florida 32887

United Kingdom Edition published by
ACADEMIC PRESS INC. (LONDON) LTD.
24-28 Oval Road, London NW1 7DX

LIBRARY OF CONGRESS CATALOGING IN PUBLICATION DATA

Main entry under title:

Metacognition, cognition, and human performance.

    Includes indexes.
    Contents: v. 1. Theoretical perspectives — v.2.
Instructional practices.
    1. Metacognition.   2. Cognition.   3. Cognition in
children.   4. Performance.   5. Learning, Psychology of.
I. Forrest-Pressley, Donna-Lynn.   II. MacKinnon, G. E.
III. Waller, Gary T.   [DNLM: 1. Cognition—in infancy &
childhood.   2. Psychomotor Performance—in infancy &
childhood.   3. Child Development.   WS 105.5.C7]
BF311.M4487   1985   153   84-21688
ISBN 0-12-262301-0 (v. 1 : alk. paper)
ISBN 0-12-262302-9 (v. 2 : alk. paper)

PRINTED IN THE UNITED STATES OF AMERICA

85 86 87 88   9 8 7 6 5 4 3 2 1

Contents

3
Developmental Trends in the Metamemory–Memory Behavior Relationship: An Integrative Review
Wolfgang Schneider

4
Children's Metamemory and the Teaching of Memory Strategies
Michael Pressley, John G. Borkowski, and Julie O'Sullivan

5
How Do We Know When We Don't Understand? Standards for Evaluating Text Comprehension
Linda Baker

6

A Metacognitive Framework for the Development of First and Second Language Skills

Ellen Bialystok and Ellen Bouchard Ryan

7

The Role of Metacognition in Contemporary Theories of Cognitive Development

Steven R. Yussen

Contributors

Numbers in parentheses indicate the pages on which the authors' contributions begin.

Linda Baker (155), Department of Psychology, University of Maryland Baltimore County, Catonsville, Maryland 21228

Ellen Bialystok (207), Department of Psychology, York University, Downsview, Ontario M3J 1P3, Canada

John G. Borkowski (111), Department of Psychology, University of Notre Dame, Notre Dame, Indiana 46556

Jeanne Day (33), Department of Psychology, University of Notre Dame, Notre Dame, Indiana 46556

Lucia A. French (33), Center for the Study of Psychological Development, Graduate School of Education and Human Development, University of Rochester, Rochester, New York 14627

Lynda Hall (33), Department of Psychology, University of Notre Dame, Notre Dame, Indiana 46556

Julie O'Sullivan (111), Department of Psychology, University of Western Ontario, London, Ontario N6A 5L2, Canada

Michael Pressley (111), Department of Psychology, University of Western Ontario, London, Ontario N6A 5L2, Canada

Ellen Bouchard Ryan (207), Department of Psychiatry, McMaster University, Hamilton, Ontario L8N 3Z5, Canada

Wolfgang Schneider (57), Max-Planck-Institut für Psychologische Forschung, D–8000 München 40, Federal Republic of Germany

Henry Wellman (1), Center for Human Growth and Development, University of Michigan, Ann Arbor, Michigan 48109

Steven R. Yussen (253), Wisconsin Center for Education Research, School of Education, University of Wisconsin, Madison, Wisconsin 53706

Preface

It has been only a decade or so since Ann Brown, John Flavell, Lila Gleitman, Ellen Markman, Ignatius Mattingly, and others first made us conscious of metacognition and particularly of its relevance to the field of child development. Not surprisingly, the "instant fame" enjoyed by metacognition in the 1970s and 1980s has not been without difficulty and genuine concern. Many researchers quickly discerned, and even became discouraged by, the imprecision of the construct, the lack of testable theory in the area, and a host of important but unanswered questions. Some of these questions are, for example, How does metacognition originate? What factors affect its development? How are metacognitive knowledge and monitoring skill acquired? How does such knowledge affect the use of a specific strategy in the execution of a skill? Does recent research on metacognition speak coherently to the ways in which we teach and remediate young learners? These were just some of the questions that we posed to our authors. After reading their replies, we can only say that we are more than pleased with the quality of their answers and with the directions they suggest for future work.

The book starts at the logical beginning of the various issues facing us. In the first chapter, Henry Wellman attempts to answer the question of how metacognition originates and how it develops. Wellman argues that the origins of metacognition derive from the child's early acquisition of the conceptual distinction between internal mental phenomena and external material objects and behaviors. In becoming aware of the existence of the mental world, the child, in effect, constructs a theory of mind. Such a theory, Wellman suggests, is crucial in the development of a concept of reality and is a fundamental building block of ontological knowledge. While Wellman argues that metacognition exerts subtle but powerful influences on much of conceptual development, he cautions against exaggerated claims for the practical utility of metacognitive knowledge in enhancing the execution of any particular skill.

In Chapter 2, Jeanne Day, Lucia French, and Lynda Hall also address the origin of metacognition. These authors emphasize the importance of social factors in the development of both cognitive and metacognitive competence. Day et al. review studies that provide detailed, historical descriptions of the interaction between adults and young children in a variety of naturalistic settings. They conclude from these studies that metacognition emerges as the *regulation* of problem solving and of other cognitive and linguistic activities shifts from the adult to the child.

The practical utility of metacognitive knowledge is examined by Wolfgang Schneider in Chapter 3. Schneider analyzes the literature on the relationship between metamemory and memory behavior. If metamemory has little or no relation to memory behavior, then there would be little reason to worry about many of the broader theoretical issues or implications for training effective learning strategies. Schneider presents a comprehensive and analytical summary of research on (1) use of memory knowledge in monitoring tasks, (2) memory knowledge and the use of various strategies, and (3) training of strategy use. Using a meta-analysis procedure, Schneider presents evidence that there is indeed a strong relationship between metamemory and memory behavior. Therefore, metacognitive knowledge, at least as far as memory is concerned, would appear to have considerable practical utility.

In the next chapter, Michael Pressley, John Borkowski, and Julie O'Sullivan propose a model to explain the relationship between metamemory and memory strategy use. They suggest that there are two types of important knowledge: first, metamemory about strategies and, second, specific strategy knowledge. Pressley et al. discuss how metacognitions are acquired and what the role of metacognition is in instruction. The authors outline metamemory acquisition procedures (MAPS) and deal with the thorny issue of transfer in training situations.

In Chapter 5, Linda Baker deals with the monitoring of skill execution and specifically with the monitoring of ongoing comprehension during reading. Baker points out that comprehension monitoring involves two major component activities: evaluating how well one understands what one reads and regulating what one does while reading *after* one has evaluated one's understanding. Baker focuses on the evaluation of ongoing comprehension and provides an overall framework for conceptualizing the different kinds of criteria that readers use to evaluate their understanding. The sophisticated comprehension monitor, Baker argues, employs multiple criteria in evaluating his understanding of text. Readers may differ, however, as a function of age, experience, and other factors, in their ability to employ particular criteria. A reader may be proficient in evaluating his understanding of individual words in a text and yet fail to evaluate adequately his appreciation of the text's internal consistency. Baker discusses what is known (and what is yet to be learned) about the complex factors that determine the facility with which various criteria can be used and points out the kind of research that will be necessary to meet the goal of improving readers' abilities "to decide for themselves when they understand and when they do not."

Ellen Bialystok and Ellen Ryan, in Chapter 6, develop a framework to account for the development of first- and second-language skills. This framework draws on the notion of metacognition as conscious knowledge and on current thinking on the nature of comprehension monitoring. Bialystok and Ryan suggest that language skills, like other cognitive skills, have two dimensions—analyzed knowledge and cognitive control—both of which influence skill acquisition. The authors suggest that the sequence of skill acquisition can be explained by the interaction between these two dimensions. Bialystok and Ryan illustrate their model with examples from recent studies on conversation, reading–writing, and metalinguistics.

The volume concludes with a critique by Steven Yussen of metacognition as a theoretical construct and of its role in current theories of cognitive development. Yussen points out that the use of the term *metacognition* has been highly variable and that much of current theory has been shaped largely by use of a particular framework (i.e., the solving of well-defined problems) for studying cognition and by a focus on childhood. As a result, Yussen argues, many of our current conceptualizations of metacognition have restrictive explanatory power and limited realistic practical utility. Yussen urges that researchers begin to extend the construct of metacognition beyond the currently popular information-processing paradigm to other theoretical perspectives and that they begin to investigate, in both children and adults, the acquisition of metacognitive knowledge in situations and contexts that go beyond the solving of clearly defined problems.

While the theoretical issues surrounding metacognition obviously are not completely settled in this book, these chapters both solidify what we know and point to new directions for theory as well as empirical work. Volume 2 deals with the implication of metacognition in the field of education and provides several illustrations of how the concept has been employed in the development of instructional programs.

Contents of Volume 2

CHAPTER 1

The Origins of Metacognition*

Henry M. Wellman

Introduction

The term *metacognition* has increasingly been employed to refer to a person's cognition about cognition, that is, the person's knowledge of cognitive processes and states such as memory, attention, knowledge, conjecture, illusion. Of interest here is not *how* does the person execute these processes but *what* do they know and believe about these processes? The premise behind research in this domain is that persons are not only organisms who cognize about objects, events, and behaviors, but importantly they also cognize about cognition itself. They form and hold conceptions about how the mind works, about which mental problems are hard, which easy, about their own mental states and processes.

This brief introduction to metacognition, and even considerable knowledge of the literature on the topic, provokes a number of questions. What, exactly, is metacognition? Which aspects of metacognition are acquired at what time? Of what use or practical application is an individual's metacognitive knowledge? How should this special type of cognition best be studied? In this chapter, I take for granted that metacognition exists in adults, that it develops in children, that such conceptions can be ingeniously studied, and that an understanding of one's own and others' cognition is instrumental both in certain cognitive performances and in a

*Preparation of this chapter was supported by a Spencer Fellowship from the National Academy of Education.

1

further understanding of the social world of self and others (see Wellman, 1983; 1985). I wish to consider different and prior questions: Where does metacognition come from? Why and how does it first develop?

Two different though complementary sorts of answers can be considered to these questions. These should be briefly distinguished because they are often confused. One sort of answer focuses on mechanisms. That is, it would attempt to specify or even model those types of external experiences and internal processes of acquisition that cause children to acquire initially and to amend developmentally their metacognitive concepts. A second sort of answer concentrates on origins. This would attempt to specify not the detailed mechanisms of acquisition but the earliest glimmerings of this sort of concept and the earlier-yet precursors from whence metacognition springs. As the title states, this chapter is concerned more with origins than with initial mechanisms.

A search for the origins of some developmental attainment is conditioned by the assumptions or knowledge one has about the nature of that attainment. In this regard I argue that the child's metacognitive knowledge is not some one cognitive "item"; there is not some singular developmental acquisition reasonably labeled metacognition. Analysis of the knowledge about cognition possessed by naive adults, findings addressing the conceptions of children, as well as logical thought about the topic, indicate that a person's knowledge about the mental world encompasses a large number of interwoven concepts and insights. Many universally acquired, as well as many individually different, understandings about cognition are logically part and parcel of a person's metacognition. For these reasons the phrase *theory of mind* (Bretherton & Beeghly, 1982; Wellman, 1985) seems specially useful to refer to a person's metacognition. The term *theory* appropriately suggests a large number of related propositions, facts, and implications. Theories, further, typically have an evolution or development of their own. Acquiring metacognition is thus quite a complex and extended process because it involves acquisition of a multifaceted theory of mind.

As partial elaboration of this characterization, consider briefly the variety of knowledge and concepts that might constitute a complete theory of mind. When I attempt to consider this issue I can identify at least five different but overlapping sets of knowledge that form a person's metacognition (Wellman, 1985).

1. **Existence.** In the first instance, the person must know that thoughts and internal mental states exist, that they are not the same as external acts or events. Take for example, concepts such as lies, hunches, guesses, and pretending. All of these are based on some notion of the

difference between a mental state and external behavior. I can know that one thing is true, but say or act as if it is not. That is, I can lie or pretend. I can be completely ignorant of the correct answer on a test, but pick the correct choice by a lucky guess. Mental states exist, independent of external behavior of physical events.

2. **Distinct Processes.** Humans engage in many cognitive processes. They can remember or forget, they can visualize images, they can dream, they can reason, they can concentrate or daydream, they can conjecture and guess. That is, there are a variety of distinct mental acts, and a reasonably comprehensive theory of mind must distinguish between different mental acts and capture the distinctive features of different mental processes (e.g., the differences between guessing and knowing, between dreaming and daydreaming).

3. **Integration.** While there are numerous possible distinctions among different mental acts, all mental processes are also similar and related. In some sense there is only one mind. For example, adults typically believe that all mental processes similarly reside in the brain or mind (Johnson & Wellman, 1982); remove the brain and all, not some, disappear. We know that thinking, dreaming, and imagining are all internal invisible events, yet, different from other internal invisible events, such as digesting food or the heart pumping blood. The similarities and interactions between different mental processes must be encompassed in a theory of the mind.

4. **Variables.** Any one mental performance is influenced by a number of other factors or variables. In remembering, for example, how much one can remember depends on how hard the task is, the nature of the items, and the memory strategies used. Long lists are harder to remember than short; meaningful items (English words) are easier to remember than meaningless ones (e.g., Russian words); writing yourself a note is often more effective than "brute force" memory. A theory of mind must incorporate knowledge about a host of such variables that influence different acts of cognition, and about their specific effects.

5. **Cognitive Monitoring.** Finally, humans are often able to "read" their own mental states, or monitor their ongoing cognitive processes. Even children often know when they know something and when not (Wellman, 1977; Cultice, Somerville, & Wellman, 1983), when they understand and when not (Markman, 1977, 1979), when they are fantasizing, dreaming, imagining, and when not (Johnson & Raye, 1981). Cognitive monitoring refers to abilities to accurately assess the state of information within one's own cognitive system. This knowledge of the contents of one's mind is part of the person's moment-by-moment understanding of his or her cognition and thus part of his or her conception of cognition itself.

In sum, a theory of mind encompasses many distinctions and insights. No single acquisition or insight seems definitive or criterial. In the rest of this chapter, however, I focus primarily on the first conception outlined above, namely, knowledge of the existence of the mental world. When do children become aware that the mental world exists independent of the external world of observable behaviors and events? An answer to this question is fundamental to uncovering the origins of knowledge about cognition.

Early Awareness of the Existence of the Mental World

Consider the following claim: An awareness of the existence of the mental world (a conceptual distinction between internal, mental phenomena and external material objects and behaviors) is a formative and early acquisition, acquired by 2-year-olds. Such a claim directly contradicts what may be termed the classic view. This view originated with Piaget (1929), who asked children questions like, "What is *thinking?*" and "What are *dreams?*" and then concluded:

> We have traced three distinct stages, the first of which is easily distinguishable from the other two . . . . During this first stage children believe that thinking is "with the mouth." Thought is identified with the voice. Nothing takes place either *in* the head or *in* the body. Naturally, thought is confused with the things themselves . . . . There is nothing subjective in the act of thinking. The average age for children of this (first) stage is 6. (Piaget, 1929, p. 38).

I term this classic view the *externalization hypothesis*. The assertion is that young children are not aware of internal, invisible mental events and processes and so they understand and produce statements that appear to be about mental phenomena, but that are actually about related external observable behavioral or physical phenomena instead. For example, "Thinking is talking; dreams are motion pictures you see while asleep."[1]

There are reasons to suspect the evidence on which Piaget based his

[1]Piaget's claim is actually somewhat more complex than this. He believed that young children understand no distinction between subjective and objective, physical and psychic, internal and external experiences or things, as adults do. Thus they could be seen to both (1) identify internal events with external ones (realism), and (2) interpret external objects as conscious, or physical events as motivated (animism). For a contemporary proposal of the externalization hypothesis, see Misciones, Marvin, O'Brien, and Greenburg (1978).

version of the externalization hypothesis. If trying to diagnose the early origins of some conception, then asking young children open ended questions (such as, "What are dreams?") presents numerous problems of interpretation. These problems revolve around the children's possible (mis)conceptions of the question and their (mis)conceptions of or inability to comply with the requirements of an appropriate answer (Bullock, Gelman & Baillargeon, 1982; Donaldson, 1978; Wellman, 1985). In our research into the origins of a theory of mind, my collaborators and I have avoided Piagetian interviews and have focused instead on the child's developing understanding of mental terms—terms like *remember, know, guess,* and *dream.* We have exploited children's developing language competence as a window to their conceptual knowledge. An example of this research, an early investigation of young children's understanding of *remember* and *forget* (Wellman & Johnson, 1979), makes the approach clear.

Consider first, adults' use of the mental verbs *remember* and *forget.* The diagram in Table 1 captures some of the major distinctions required. There are two factors involved, titled Previous Knowledge and Present Performance. If I *remember* something, I must have known about it previously and I must correctly retrieve the information now. If I knew about it earlier, but cannot retrieve it correctly now, then I have not remembered, I have *forgotten.* If I have no previous knowledge, then regardless of my performance now I cannot have remembered or forgotten.

Our method with children was to make up scenarios capturing the four situations of Table 1 and to ask the child to judge if the character remembered or forgot. For example, for the situation in the upper left of that table (correct present performance, previous knowledge present), a toy character was depicted who saw his coat put in one of two closets. Then, later, the character came back and chose the correct closet as the one containing his coat. The child subject was asked, did the character remember? Adults would say yes. Did he forget? No. Contrast that sce-

Table 1

Use of Remember *and* Forget

| | Present performance | | | |
| | Correct | | Incorrect | |
Previous knowledge	Remember?	Forget?	Remember?	Forget?
Present	Yes	No	No	Yes
Absent	No	No	No	No

nario with the other three situations. For example, a scenario based on
the lower left cell of Table 1 (correct present performance, previous knowledge absent) depicted that a friend put the character's coat in one of two
closets while he was *not* watching. Later when the character needed his
coat, he went to the correct closet and found it. In this case, because the
character just guesssed correctly he should be judged as neither remembering nor forgetting.

When children were tested on their use of these verbs in all the relevant situations, only a small number of patterns of response appeared.
One possible pattern for judgments about remembering is what could be
called the Adult pattern, the pattern I have just been explicating and shown
schematically in Table 2. A second pattern is termed a Performance pattern in Table 2. Here the child says, "yes the character remembers," whenever the character makes a correct performance choice, regardless of his
knowledge state.

The bottom portion of Table 2 shows the percentage of children at
different ages who respond with these different patterns. As is clear there,
first, 3-year-olds do not reveal a discriminate understanding of these verbs
at all, under these conditions. They just answer *yes* to every question in
every situation. Second, 4-year-olds answer on the basis of external performance, regardless of differences in internal knowledge. Finally, older
children progressively acquire an adult-like meaning of the terms.

These results show a pattern of acquisition that Piaget might have
been pleased with, where the first understanding of a mental term is based
on external behavioral performance rather than internal mental states.
Young children, the 4-year-olds in the Wellman and Johnson research, appear to understand mental terms not in regard to mental phenomena but
in regard to external aspects of behavior, specifically the correctness or
incorrectness of performance. This can be shown when the child must
judge someone else's behavior, as in the preceding research, and when
judging his or her own behavior (Misciones, Marvin, O'Brien & Greenburg, 1978). Yet there are several reasons to look more closely at the externalization hypothesis and these tests. Most importantly, internal, mental
states are by their very nature internal and invisible, which makes them
potentially less salient in many situations than external events. It is possible, therefore, that the child may have a fundamental understanding of
these less salient mental states, but this understanding may go undetected
because in many situations mental factors are obscured by a multitude of
more obvious external factors.

In a subsequent study (Johnson & Wellman, 1980) therefore, we devised a situation where some mental state was made reasonably salient for
the child, before studying his or her judgements. Once this was accom-

Table 2

Patterns of Performance for Remember *Judgments*

Adult pattern			Performance pattern		
	Performance			Performance	
Knowledge	Correct	Incorrect	Knowledge	Correct	Incorrect
Present	Yes	No	Present	Yes	No
Absent	No	No	Absent	Yes	No

	% of Subjects			
Age in years	Adult pattern	Performance pattern	All-yes responses	Other
3	0	13	75	12
4	10	70	0	20
5	70	10	0	20
7	80	10	0	10

plished the goal once again was to contrast mental versus behavioral states and then observe which of these factors would account for children's judgments. We tackled this by investigating children's understanding of the terms *remember, know,* and *guess.* The design of this study is presented in Table 3. The idea was to devise different situations, carefully created to involve contrasting factors, and to get the child to judge his or her own behavior in these situations using the terms *remember, know,* and *guess.* The factors we included were those of Previous Knowledge, Present Knowledge, and Present Performance. For example, in the Remember condition, as depicted in Table 3, the child saw an item hidden in one of two containers. Then, after a very brief delay, the child found the item. At this point, he or she was asked, "Did you *remember?*" "Did you *know?*" or "Did you *guess* where the item was?" For each of the knowledge conditions, there was a similar task but one location was transparent. The child did not see the item hidden (i.e., he or she was provided with no previous knowledge) but could know where it was either by looking, or by inferring from where it was not (different types of present knowledge). After children pointed correctly at the correct location (on the basis of their present knowledge) they were asked whether they knew, they remembered, or they guessed the object's position. In the guessing conditions, the child did not see where the object was hidden, and could not know where it was hidden, but made a choice anyway. We manipulated

Table 3
Remember, Know, Guess

Conditions	Previous knowledge	Present knowledge	Performance	Stimuli	Judgments		
					Remember?	Know?	Guess?
Remember	Present	Absent	+	◥◣	Yes	Yes	No
Trick	Present	Absent	−	◢◣	Yes	Yes	No
Know: present sight	Absent	Present	+	◁•	No	Yes	No
Know: inference	Absent	Present	+	◁◣	No	Yes	No
Guess right	Absent	Absent	+	◣◣	No	No	Yes
Guess wrong	Absent	Absent	−	◢◥	No	No	Yes
Remember	Present	Absent	Absent	◢◣	Yes	Yes	No
Guess	Absent	Absent	Absent	◢◥	No	No	Yes

this choice in the guessing situations with trick boxes so that the child was correct half the time, and incorrect the other half.

This research had two related goals. One was to see when children discriminated among distinct mental processes, especially the processes of knowing, remembering, and guessing. As can be seen in Table 3, questions about these three processes provide a unique set of contrastive judgments across the various situations. Thus, we could study the child's developing understanding of distinct processes and the informational conditions that define them. The other goal was to see if young children could refer to their mental states, in addition to their overt performances. For this question, which addresses knowledge of the existence of mental states, the central condition is the trick condition. In the trick condition, as shown in Table 3, the child sees the item hidden, but we manipulate it so that when he or she in fact chooses that location the item is in the other location instead. This is a very provocative situation: The child knows where the item ought to be, but he or she performs incorrectly nonetheless. Will the child use mental verbs in this situation to refer to his or her knowledge or instead to refer only to overt behavior?

The data of interest involve three contrasting conditions that are isolated in Table 4. Note that across these three conditions, two are identical in mental state, but differ in performance (remember vs. trick). Conversely, a different pair are identical in performance, but differ in mental state (trick vs. guess wrong). If children answer on the basis of external performance, they ought to say they know or remember in the remember condition but not in the trick or guess wrong conditions; external performance is correct in the remember condition and incorrect in the others. On the other hand, if children answer on the basis of internal mental state they should say they know or remember in both the remember and trick conditions, but not in the guess wrong condition. This is because previous knowledge is present in both the remember and trick conditions even though these conditions differ in correctness of performance. Table 4

Table 4

Percentage of Yes Judgments to the Know Question

Conditions	Previous knowledge	Present knowledge	Performance	Know? (Age in years) 4	5	6	9
Remember	P	A	+	93	93	100	100
Trick	P	A	−	73	80	100	100
Guess wrong	A	A	−	27	33	6	0

shows the percentage of *know* judgments for the various conditions: the percentage of times the children asserted yes when asked "Did you know where it was?" As is clear in Table 4, the remember and trick conditions were judged similarly ("I knew where it was"). That is, in the salient trick condition, mental verbs were in fact used by the children to refer to their own internal knowledge, not to the correctness of their overt performance.

This pattern, as well as other aspects of the data, strongly suggest that young children do understand that internal mental states exist. Such states are different from external behaviors and they can be referred to via mental verbs. Young children do not necessarily externalize the mental world. Similar conclusions are mandated by a series of studies investigating children's conceptions of the brain and mind (Johnson & Wellman, 1982). In those investigations, it was clear that 4- and 5-year-olds did *not* merely identify the brain or mind with the external head—as would be expected by an externalization hypothesis (e.g., Broughton, 1978). Instead, they associated prototypic mental activities, such as remembering, with an internal brain or mind, but associated other acts, like wiggling your toes, with external body organs like the feet. In addition they associated together a number of different mental activities—activities such as remembering, dreaming, and guessing—as internal mental acts.

The preceding demonstrations of preschoolers' awareness of the existence of the mental world, as well as other recent work by other investigators (e.g., Wimmer & Perner, 1983), present the same dilemma. Namely, while evidence of mental conceptions is clear for 4-year-olds, the evidence from 3-year-olds is typically uninterpretable. It is not the case that these younger children give evidence of externalized conceptions. Instead, they typically answer all questions yes or no, or give random answers, and one can not tell what, if anything, they are thinking.

It seems clear, however, that the origins of mental conceptions must arise in 2- or 3-year-olds. In the preceding studies, 4-year-olds appear to know so much about the mental world that this knowledge must possess some previous history. Moreover, interest in the younger child's concepts of mind is further aroused because young children use mental verbs. Verbs like *remember, think* and *know,* appear in spontaneous speech before 2½ years of age (Limber, 1973).

Since young children use these verbs, why not investigate early concepts of mind in their natural language productions? However, obstacles arise in any attempt to use natural language data as an index of children's theories of mind. Suppose I suggest that because children use conventional mental terms—words like *remember, know, dream*—that they must necessarily possess some understanding of the mental world that these terms refer to. This claim presents several problems that exemplify the difficulties in using natural speech to explore conceptions of mind.

The first problem is that even adult use of mental terms often has no mental significance—that is, the terms are used for many functions, not simply for referring to mental states and processes. For example, consider utterances such as "That was an interesting program, you know." "You know" in this case functions as a pause filler not a reference to knowledge. Similarly there are utterances like "Know what? I hate this," where the mental term, or expression, functions simply to introduce new information or to get the listener's attention. Adults also will say things like, "I think it is time to wash your hands for dinner" as a device to soften an indirect command. In short, even in adult speech the presence of mental terms is no guarantee of true reference to the mental states of self and others, that is, mental reference.

The second difficulty is this. Suppose an adult produces the sentence, "I didn't know that today was your birthday." In this case a listener might plausibly assume that the speaker is referring to his or her internal knowledge (knowing or not knowing about a birthday). This is plausible because in numerous situations, we know that adults use such verbs to distinguish between action and cognition (e.g., deliberate versus accidental acts), to attempt to deceive others about their own cognition, to distinguish abstract from physical objects (e.g., an idea versus a rock) as well as other everyday demonstrations of an understanding of the existence of the mental world. However, if a young child said that same sentence we have no assurance that he or she means this sort of thing at all. The child may be referring to lack of knowledge ("I didn't know"), but he or she may be referring only to some reasonably correlated behavioral event, such as not having a present. This obvious possibility is why in our earlier studies we resorted to specially contrasting tasks and situations, in order to distinguish *mental* from *behavioral* reference.

In short, the utility of a study of children's naturally occurring use of mental terms depends on methods for confidently ruling out conversational uses of mental terms, and confidently identifying at least some paradigmatic instances of true mental reference. In a recent investigation we have overcome these difficulties (Shatz, Wellman, & Silber, 1983). Our solution to the first problem—nonmental, conversational use of mental terms—was to devise a conservative version of a rating procedure used earlier by Gelman and Shatz (1977) for identifying conversational functions. Our rating procedure (see the following discussion and Shatz, Wellman, & Silber, 1983) allowed us to distinguish potential mental uses of mental terms from conversational uses of such terms. The solution to the second problem was provided by the children themselves. In carefully scrutinizing children's utterances we found that they at times said things like, "It's not real, I was only pretending." We termed these sorts of statements *constrastives* because in such utterances the child explicitly contrasts his or her mental use of a mental term with some potential behavioral or physical misuse. In "It's *not* real, I was only *pretending*," the child spontaneously distinguishes his or her mental act—pretending—from some external, physical reference by stating that it is not real. The presence of a substantial number of constrastives in the child's speech would provide essential evidence that the child distinguishes mental from objective reference, at least at times.

The data for this research came from two sources: from one child, Abe, for whom we had extensive transcripts from age 2 years, 4 months (2:4) old until he was 4 years old; and from 30 other children sampled longitudinally in the last half of their third year. For Abe, about 5% of his utterances contained some sort of mental term (e.g., *remember, dream, idea, brain*). Of all these mental terms, 96% were mental verbs, so the primary analyses focused on just the mental verbs such as *know, think, mean, remember, guess, pretend,* and *dream.*

There were eight distinct categories in the coding scheme devised to categorize uses of mental verbs into various different functions. These categories included seven categories of nonmental uses, such as those exemplified earlier, as well as the category of primary interest, termed *mental state.* To be coded as mental state, an utterance had to be judged most plausibly referring to some mental state or process, such as dreaming, or remembering. A child was credited with this type of use only if both a careful reading and analysis of the utterance and its context supported this, *and* if all of the other possible interpretations were ruled out. As indicated, this system alone, while a strict one, is still less than perfect in that behavioral reference could be mistakenly coded as mental reference, that is, mental state—hence the special importance of further identifying, within the category of mental state utterances, instances of constrastives. To be coded as a constrastive, all criteria for coding an utterance as mental state were applied and then in addition the child had to distinguish, in his or her expanded discourse, a mental interpretation of the term with some potential behavioral or physical misinterpretation. Several examples of constrastives will clarify this phenomena: "I was just dreaming" (said to discount a realistic interpretation of an event). "I thought this was a crocodile; now I know it's an alligator." "Not for real, I was pretending" (see Table 7 in the next section for more detailed examples).

Table 5 shows the occurrence, for Abe, of mental verb utterances (any utterance with a mental verb), mental-state utterances (rated as previously explained) and constrastives. As is clear there, mental state utterances occur in all time periods. The first mental verb utterances coded as mental state occurred when the child was 2:8. Mental-state utterances increased as the child became older, both in absolute number and more importantly

Table 5

Abe's Utterances

	Age period			
	2:4–2:8	2:9–3:1	3:2–3:6	3:7–3:11
Total utterances	5973	9416	7913	6858
Proportion of total utterances that contain a mental verb	.01(83)[a]	.04(387)	.06(473)	.08(540)
Proportion of mental verb utterances classed as mental state	.04(3)	.23(79)	.28(118)	.42(208)
Proportion of mental state utterances that are contrastives	.67(2)	.20(16)	.31(36)	.20(41)

[a]Numbers in parentheses are the total utterances.

as a proportion of the child's mental verb utterances. Contrastive mental utterances remained a fairly stable fraction of the mental-state utterances, about 20%. These data for Abe were replicated when we analyzed the utterances of the 30 other children who were approximately the same age as Abe was in his first time period.

The fact that in all of this data about 20% or more of the utterances coded as mental state were also identifiable as contrastives provides sound evidence that, in general, some sizable portion of early mental utterances represent true mental reference, not mistaken behavioral reference. Contrastive utterances clearly distinguish reference to mental processes from behavioral or physical ones, and thus indicate an essential realization of the existence of the mental world. These constrastive uses of mental terms occurred concomitantly with the child's earliest mental-state utterances and together these occurred quite early, in the second half of the third year. In short, in their natural speech, very young children evidence an understanding of the existence of the mental world distinct from the external world of physical and behavioral occurrences.

An early understanding of the distinction between mental states versus physical or behavioral events does not mean that the child's theory of mind is fully formed or adult like. This early origin however provides an essential basis for the child's further theorizing about the nature of distinct mental processes, the variables influencing mental performance, the possibility of attempts to read and control such processes. In addition it provides an essential ingredient for the understanding of behavior of self and others, including such powerful constructs as intention, belief, intelligence, deception, meaning, and ultimately congition in all its myriad forms.

Precursors and Larger Conceptions

Imagine the early knowledge discussed in the previous section as occupying a small regular region in a two-dimensional space. The vertical dimension of this space corresponds to age or development. Thus, the locus of the focal set on this dimension would refer to the developmental timing of the acquired knowledge, in this case from 2½ to 4½ years. The horizontal dimension would refer to an ordering of all possible conceptions and knowledge. Here, early knowledge of the mental world would appear in relation to other conceptions, these conceptions being more closely related psychologically the closer they lie along the horizontal axis. Within this context I wish to expand the focus of discussion over that in the previous section both vertically (ages considered) and horizontally (topics considered). Specifically, I wish to discuss two intimately related topics: (1) the precursors to the child's early concepts of mind, as well as (2) the larger conceptual "kin" that bracket, determine, and illuminate these concepts of cognition. The two topics are indeed related because the best place to prospect for precursors are among early developing, logically associated conceptual bedfellows.

Along the horizontal axis, early conceptions of the mental world can be seen as lying between, or at the overlap of, two sorts of larger conceptual networks. On one hand there is knowledge of the social world, especially the child's concepts of persons. On the other hand there is knowledge of the basic categories of things—ontological knowledge (Keil, 1979), especially the child's conception of real versus abstract things.

Early Metacognition and Person Concepts

It is persons who, typically, have minds. Mental processes and states, such as thoughts and beliefs, are part of a larger set of internal psychological processes and states—including emotions, motives, abilities—that we use in order to understand human behavior and to interact with others. In this sense it is easy to argue that concepts of mind must develop early; they are fundamentally necessary to an understanding of persons and an understanding of persons has a rich early development in infancy (see Lamb & Sherrod, 1981).

Relationships between understanding persons and understanding internal mental states have been postulated by many (see Tagiuri, 1969). Recently, however, Bretherton (Bretherton & Beeghly, 1982; Bretherton, McNew, Beeghly-Smith, 1981) has offered an analysis of how early explicit mental concepts may evolve from other forms of person knowledge. Understanding her proposal rests on understanding two distinctions. One is a distinction between an implicit and an explicit theory of mind. The other is a distinction between cognitive states and processes (mental states narrowly construed, such as knowing, thinking, pretending, dreaming) and other internal psychological states (perceptual, affective, and physiological states, such as hearing, feeling angry, and feeling hungry).

According to Bretherton, an early implicit theory of mind can be seen as required by any form of intentional communication. Because intentional communication requires sharing meanings, and meanings are intrasubjective psychological states, then intentional communication demonstrates an implicit theory of mind. This is because the communicator acts "as if" he or she appreciates that others are *psychologically* similar to him or her, in that they can share (possess, amend) meanings. Intentional communication is thought to appear at the end of the first year of infancy (Bretherton et al. 1981).

Recognition of the psychological status of self and others begins implicitly, but it becomes more and more explicit in the next 2 years. This is revealed in the child's use of verbal expressions of perception, physiology, affect, and cognition to attribute internal states to others. The early use of mental verbs documented in the previous section of this chapter is thus the culmination of certain aspects of the infant's struggle to understand persons, self, and others. As regards the appearance of a more obvious, explicit theory of mind, Bretherton and Beeghly (1982) present data, based on diary records of language acquisition, that use of words for perceptual, physiological, and affective states (e.g., *see, hungry, happy*) developmentally precede similar expressions of mental or cognitive states and processes (e.g., *know*). This data is based essentially on the occurrence of such words in the child's speech, and as argued earlier, mere occurrence does not ensure that the child means something like the adult would mean by such expressions. Nonetheless these data make a preliminary case for the claim that understanding of mental states appears after an earlier understanding of other nonmental but internal personal states.

Bretherton's proposals are intriguing, because they offer a plausible set of precursors to an early theory of mind, and do so by exploiting the relations of concepts of cognition to the wider domain of conceptions of persons. This analysis is by no means the only one possible or probable, however. Indeed my aim in this section is to provide an alternate proposal for understanding early metacognition. The analysis offered here also delineates precursors of a theory of mind by exploring its relationship to a larger cognitive endeavor. It is different, however, in that it exploits a different larger conceptual domain, namely conceptions of reality. This analysis is complementary to one concentrating on early social cognition as the infrastructure for metacognition. There is no reason at present to believe that one, but not the other, of these larger conceptual domains provides *the* developmental precursors for a theory of mind.

Early Metacognition and Conceptions of Reality

Where does the early development of a theory of mind, charted in this chapter, come from? I argue that the child's early struggle to construct a conception of the mental world is part and parcel of the child's rarely investigated struggle with a larger epistemological question: What is real and what is not? That is, a conception of mind is inseparable from a larger conception of reality. This claim represents something of a return to Piaget's early concerns (Piaget, 1929). His investigations of children's concepts of dreams and thinking were an attempt to understand what he saw as the young child's realism. The details of the present proposal, derived as they are from a more contemporary appreciation of the competencies of very young children, differ from Piaget's conclusions.

More specifically, the claim is this. For the child, reality is an ill-defined notion consisting of a central core containing entities that are prototypically "real." These prototypic real things contrast with several other kinds of entities that are "not real." One of these related "not-realities" is that of the mental world; an understanding of the mental world develops in concert with an understanding of reality itself. Two sorts of data can be marshalled as preliminary support for such a claim. However, these depend in the first instance on an intuitive analysis of adult notions about reality. Based on this analysis, suggestive evidence about young children's conception of reality and its relation to their understanding of mind can be seen in their talk about real and not-real phenomena.

The Adult's Naive Ideas about Reality

Reality is, of course, a very complex notion (Austin, 1962). Yet adults manage to communicate about the world in ways that implicitly categorize the objects of their communication into various categories of reality. An intuitive analysis of everyday adult notions of one aspect of reality is offered here—what I call the reality–mentality distinction. This distinction concerns the difference between a real, physical object and its mental counterpart—a real chair versus an imagined chair, for example. The analysis I offer concerning this distinction is not meant to be philosophically definitive. It is not my goal to specify the necessary and sufficient conditions for believing that something is real rather than mental. Nor is it necessary to resolve the classification of ambiguous, marginal cases or even to outline a definitive logic for doing so. It suffices to concentrate on clear examples of real entities and not-real, mental entities and to capture in part how adults distinguish and communicate about these things. This provides the background for considering children's early thoughts about similar things.

In some sense everything is real. Even dreams, for example, are real; they are real dreams. However, the objects that inhabit dreams have an acknowledged different reality state than the objects of everyday perception.[2] The contrasts between unquestionably real objects, and other less-real entities serve to anchor our notions of reality. Unquestionable, prototypic, real entities include especially three-dimensional living and nonliving objects such as rocks, books, chairs, people, animals, walls, and so forth. These objects can be seen, touched, manipulated, shown to others. Real entities also impede certain other acts. For example, they can not be walked through, they can not be wished away, they can not occupy the exact same space as another real object. Palpable objects are the prototypic stuff of reality. Several classes of not-real entities can be defined by contrast. That is, they can be tested on certain criteria that are possessed by obviously real objects. If tested, they are found wanting in various characteristics, and thus are classed as not real.

The primary criterion or characteristic of real entities is the one just indicated: real objects occupy space, can be seen, touched, smelled, and dealt with in certain ways. That is, they afford behavioral–sensory evidence or contact. While primary, such a criterion is usually not definitive, because some not-real entities (e.g., dreamed-of objects) phenomenally *seem* to yield behavioral–sensory evidence. They can still be classified as not real, however ("it wasn't real, it was just a dream"), because they fail certain other tests.

One important other test is a requirement of *convergent* behavioral-sensory evidence. Unquestionably real objects afford many behavioral-sensory contacts that converge on a similar experience of the object. A chair

[2]Obviously, different cultures can define differently what they consider real and not real. Thus, the precise issue is not whether things are real or not but what sorts of reality status they possess. Even in cultures where dream objects are "real," presumably they can be distinguished, along the lines of the present analysis, as different ontological entities from everyday chairs or rocks. In our culture, and this chapter, such distinctions are captured by terming different sorts of things real and not real.

looks like it is there, feels like it is there, can be sat on like it is there, and so forth. Consider as a contrast illusions, such as a mirage in the desert. The mirage of an oasis may seem to be real at first. However, if you change your vantage point, or attempt to throw a rock into it, or try to drink from it, these different sorts of behavioral–sensory experiences, these different tests, quickly reveal an illusion. The real object (e.g., a pool of water, not a mirage) affords convergent—or "orderly and coherent" (Kennick, 1967)—evidence.

While it is a relatively simply matter to note that real things provide converging evidence of their realness, and not-real things (e.g., illusions) do not, it is a difficult matter to specify exactly what logic we use in dealing with this evidence and what kinds of convergence we require. For example, what if I possess only partial evidence (because my experience of the object is limited)? How do I categorize the target object or how do I decide that I possess insufficient evidence to do so? Or, what if I possess clearly contradictory evidence? How do I resolve evidential contradictions? Fortunately, it is not necessary here to talk at length about the logic of convergence that determines our judgments of reality, or that allows categorization of difficult ambiguous cases. It is sufficient to note that (1) clear cases of real entities afford much converging behavioral-sensory evidence, (2) clear cases of not-real, mental entities do not offer it, though at first they might appear to, and (3) unclear cases exist that perplex us or that are dealt with only by special societal conventions.

Behavioral–sensory evidence and the convergence of different samples of such evidence are not the only obvious criteria used in judging reality. For example, dream objects are classified as not real because, while seemingly real to me they are not similarly experienced by other independent observers. Thus, they are different from real, physical objects in that they do not have the same sort of public existence. An object is clearly real if all can potentially see or touch it, but not if only one person can. Prototypic real things have generally unquestioned public existences, or at least the potential for public acknowledgement if presented or demonstrated in the correct fashion.[3] Thus, speaking precisely, we know that dreaming as a phenomenon is real since most people dream (i.e., dreams have public existence of a sort); dream objects, however, are not real in the way that physical objects are, since they do not possess public existence.

---

[3]What procedures constitute correct public demonstration of an entity or phenomena? This is a difficult question for many objects. Witness the scientific edifice necessary to establish atoms as real, but the ether as not. Again, the existence of cases requiring special (and possibly culturally different) societal conventions does not invalidate the overwhelming number of everyday clear cases.

The objects of dreams also are not real because they have inconsistent rather than *consistent existence*. My house is consistently there, consistently real day by day. Dream objects on the other hand are there one evening but not the next, mirages are there one moment but gone the next.[4] Their existence is less temporally consistent and more ephemeral, thereby calling into question and eventually contradicting their reality. Importantly, most not-real, mental entities, such as mental images, are present only when one is thinking of them, that is, actively representing them. Real objects continue to exist whether or not they are also presently an object of cognition.

These four interrelated criteria—behavioral–sensory evidence, convergent evidence, public existence, and consistent existence—are essential for the adult diagnosis and understanding of reality in the sense of distinguishing the real from the mental. There may also be other criteria (Aggernaes & Haugsted, 1976). At the least, some of the criteria I have delineated have interesting special corollaries. For example, if an experience is associated only with some *special state* it is less likely to be real in the unquestionable, prototypic sense of that word. Sensory experiences occurring within states such as sleeping, severe deprivation, and drunkenness are suspect. Wakeful, aware, unimpeded cognition counts more as evidence of an object's reality. It seems to me that such impeded-cognition experiences are suspect because they may eventually prove to have little consistency and little publicness. Thus, this test is, at least arguably, a corollary of the requirements of consistency and publicness.

Again, while clear cases of real and not-real entities exist that consistently conform to criteria of behavioral-sensory evidence, convergence, consistency and publicness, this does not specify how we reason about marginal or unclear cases. For example, a lifelike nightmare that recurs, or an obsessive hallucination, might seem to be real on the basis of sensory experiences as well as consistency. In this case, lack of publicness is usually taken as the telling flaw. Obviously, not every entity is unambiguously either real or not real, certainly not at first experience. However, the point here is that we possess a prototypic notion, and a set of tests or requirements, as well as an (unspecified) logic for evaluating these tests, which allow us to classify things as real and not real. Further, these tests and their logic are sufficient to deal with the vast majority of everyday experiences. Indeed, whether an entity is real or not is usually compellingly

---

[4]Clearly, material things can also come and go in existence (e.g. be constructed and destroyed) and mental phenomena can recur consistently (e.g., an obsession). However, the timing, frequency causes, nature, and residual products of coming into and out of existence are characteristically and predictably different for real vs mental entities (e.g., growing and eating a tomatoe vs. dreaming of a tomatoe).

clear, despite the philosophical and psychological insight legitimately to be gained from careful consideration of marginal, difficult examples. Because of this, a preliminary analysis of the present sort proves useful in considering children's conceptions of reality, at least for clear cases.

Notice in the preceding examples that notions about reality, based on clear prototypic cases, are as central to an understanding of not-real things as to an understanding of real things. This is apparent in adult speech. Not-real entities are typically defined by contrasting them with real ones. Dreams are not real, hallucinations are not real. Further, in describing not-real things, we typically describe them with a vocabulary of real things and then simply qualify them as being like that, but not quite or "not really." Dreams *are* like motion pictures, but not really. Consider in this regard the widespread use of mental metaphors. We possess few words to describe mental phenomena themselves. Instead we typically describe them as like real, external phenomena then qualify that description. Mental talk metaphorically borrows descriptions of real objects to describe mental states (Lakof & Johnson, 1980). "I can't quite *grasp* that." "That's just a *rough* idea." "His ideas are all *foggy* to me, they're just not *clear*." William James was correct, at least for the naive adult, when he said that our vocabulary for talking of the mind is based on our vocabulary for talking about real objects. "Language was originally made by men who were not psychologists, and most men today employ almost exclusively the vocabulary of outward things" (1890/1950, p. 194).

To summarize, a preliminary analysis of naive adult conception about reality suggests that notions of reality are (1) ordered around a central core of clearly real physical objects, with (2) not-real phenomena of various kinds defined contrastively with this core. In particular, not-real mental entities contrast by failing tests of behavioral-sensory evidence, convergence, publicness, and consistency (and possibly others) in certain reasonably clear ways. Some ability to distinguish real and not-real things—or more precisely, to distinguish different categories of reality for various objects of cognition—is central to much of the everyday commonsense reasoning of adults, even though such distinctions may depend on potentially irreconcilable (but most often converging) criteria, and even though marginal, difficult to classify cases also exist.

The Young Child's Understanding of Reality

Conceptions of reality are not just the province of adults. Late in infancy, or soon thereafter, the child begins to appreciate the distinction between real and not-real things and some of the bases for this distinction. The child at this time begins to distinguish a variety of not-real entities that contrast with his or her developing notions of prototypic real objects. There are a limited set of these conceptual contrasts, one of which is the category of mental entities. Thus, a concept of the existence of the mental world, hand in hand with several other not-real categories, stems from and is influenced by early developing conceptions of reality. In short, the origins of an understanding of the mental world are to be found, in part, by contrast to a conception of the real world.

Unfortunately, except for Piaget's early claims concerning the realism of preschool children, and perhaps because of Piaget's pessimistic conclusions here, little research has tackled the topic of children's developing conceptions of reality (see however, Aggernaest Haugsted, 1976; Morrison & Gardner, 1978; Flavell, Flavell, & Green, 1983). Research with very young children 1-, 2-, and 3-year-olds is particularly rare. However, the data from our study of children's spontaneous use of mental terms also provided some revealing evidence on this larger topic. One source of evidence here involves the content of the contrastive utterances described earlier. What sorts of things do young children talk of in these utterances? A second sort of evidence stems from the fact that at times even young children need to resort to arguments about the reality of phenomena. These instances, where the child has to persuade or convince another as to the reality of some object, provide preliminary information about the child's conceptions of the nature and organization of real and not-real things.

An extended sampling of some of the focal child's (Abe's) contrastive utterances (including some that do not involve mental verb use) is provided in Table 6. Recall that contrastives distinguish mental phenomena from physical phenomena and mental states from behavioral acts and states. Close scrutiny of Abe's contrastive statements reveals two things of note. First, many of these utterances are explicitly marked by the disclaimer that "it's not so," "it's not true," and especially "it's not real." Thus, children, like adults, contrastively define mental phenomena as not real. See for instance, Examples 5, 8, 14, 15, and 18.

Second, while contrastives typically employ mental verbs, actually the things that were defined by the child as not real in such utterances include instances of four distinguishable types: mental states, pretense or tricks, false appearances or illusions, and fictional objects especially fictional characters. These different categories overlap and interpenetrate in the child's talk and conception. For example, tricks often depend on illusions of some sort. Most importantly *all* of these phenomena are mental in the sense that they all depend on some distinction between mental representations and real things themselves. Tricks and illusions depend on mistaken, deceptive beliefs; pretend play depends on suspension of certain beliefs and knowledge; fictional objects only exist in imagination or by the

Table 6

Types of Contrastives

Mental states

1.	Child:	The people thought Dracula was mean but he was nice.	
2.	Child:	I was really mad, and I thought Greggy ripped it all up. 'Cept he said, "I didn't rip it, someone else did."	
3.	Child:	I thought there wasn't any socks [in the drawer], but when I looked I saw them. I didn't know you got 'em.	

4. Child: Joey's mother knows our name.   Mother: Does she?
   Child: Yeah.   Mother: What does she think our name is?

   Child: Appel   Mother: Appel's not our name.
   Child: That's what she thinks our name is.

5.   Father: Let me use your scissors. They're not too small.

   Child: I thought so 'cept they weren't.
6.   Mother: We're going to a wedding today.

   Child: I don't wanna go ... They would think I'm not there.

                                             Mother: What?

   Child: They would think you had not a kid.

                                             Mother: Why would they think that if you came?

   Child: No, they would think that if I didn't come.

Pretense and tricks

7. Child: First I'm gonna drink my hot chocolate ... poop, poop. I pooped in my hot chocolate. (laughs) I was teasing.

                                             Mother: What a relief.

   Child: I was teasing you. I was pretending, 'cept you didn't know that.
8.   Father: I made it up.

   Child: Then it must not be true.

                                             Father: Why?

   Child: Because you said you made it up. I know when you make something up it's not true. It's just pretend.

Table 6 (*Continued*)

Pretense and tricks

9.
	Mother: How come you punched her?
Child: It was part of the game.	
	Mother: I hope you weren't being mean.
Child: I wasn't. We laughed. It was just a silly game. We laughed and talked and punched.	

10.
	Mother: If someone said, "your name's goofy," would they think your name was goofy.
Child: No, they would be tricking me. They would say, "Hi Abe, we tricked you."	

11.
	Father: Did you have any dreams last night?
Child: No. I didn't have any dreams at all.	
	Father: Oh.
Child: I didn't. 'Cept I tricked you.	
	Father: You tricked me?
Child: Uh huh. I did have dreams.	

12. Child: Do you know what I fixed for myself?

	Mother: What?
Child: I fixed you for myself.	
	Mother: For lunch?
Child: Yes . . . I couldn't fix you. You're a people. I tricked you.	

False appearances and illusions

13. Child: Daddy, do you remember when I was teasing you with that string coming out?

	Father: Uh huh. That mustard thing (squeeze bottle).
Child: Yeah. I squished it but it didn't really have mustard. It really had a string in it. It really was a string.	

14. Child: He's not real. He's just a toy.

15. Child: I'll show you where the fire that wasn't real was.

	Father: Where the what?
Child: Where the fire was.	
	Father: How come you didn't think it was real?
Child: It's in the pages.	
	Father: Oh, it's just a picture.

(*Continued*)

Table 6 (*Continued*)

Fictional Objects

16. Child: How do you think Santa could
            sneak into the house? He has *real*
            sneaky toes or slippers. Quiet
            shoes. Santa Claus has *real* magic
            powers.
17. Child: Mommy, in real life there were di-
            nosaurs. Right?
18. Child: "Is Robin Hood real?"

        Father: We saw a movie about him.

    Child: No, is Robin Hood real here?
19. Child: Hey, Daddy. How do you think
            those Indians keep their hair up?
            (talking about Mohawk hair cuts)

        Father: I don't know.

    Child: Is that in true life that they could
            do that?
20. Child: Mom, remember that one dog that
            was just this big? (a story about a
            very small dog)

        Mother: Yeah.

    Child: Dad, do you believe a dog could be
            that big?

---

pretense of an actor or writer. Nonetheless, one gets the distinct feeling that the child treats these sorts of nonrealities as fairly different types of things. Each has its core instances that separately contrast with prototypically real physical objects. Thus, early conceptions of the mental world form part of a collection of other phenomena that relate to each other by being on one side of a fuzzy but fundamental distinction—the distinction between reality and nonreality.

Young children not only speak contrastively, they also at times offer explicit arguments about reality. David Estes, Laura McClosky, and I have examined Abe's transcripts for naturally occurring arguments of this sort. Table 7 presents a sampling of these. Close scrutiny of these arguments is quite informative; examination of the arguments in that table makes it clear that the child in this age range (2 through 4 years) is actively dealing with the classification of various sorts of things as to their reality. Further, it seems that the kinds of evidence that this child seeks for formulating his classifications or that he gives when trying to convince another include the four sorts mentioned earlier: behavioral–sensory evidence, converging evidence, public existence, and consistent existence. For example, in Ar-

Table 7

A Sample of Abe's Arguments about Reality

1.	Child:	I was gonna play with it and then I saw a crack in it. And then I feeled it and I feeled there was a bump and so it was breaked. I could tell it breaked.	
2.	Child:	This is wheat bread . . . Do you know this is wheat bread because it's made from wheat?	
			Father: Yep, I know that.
	Child:	I didn't know that.	
			Father: Then how come you told me.
	Child:	Because I tasted it.	
			Father: You didn't know until you tasted it?
	Child:	No. I thought it wasn't wheat bread.	
3.			Father: What's under there?
	Child:	A mouse	
			Father: A Mouse?
	Child:	Yeah. Do you want to see if it's really a mouse?	
4.	Child:	Dad, you are not coming. I could see you. You are not coming; you are looking at the tape recorder.	
5.	Child:	I have one face.	
			Father: You have how many faces?
	Child:	One.	
			Father: Really?
	Child:	Yes.	
			Father: When you cry do you have the same face as when you laugh.
	Child:	Yeah. They just *look* different.	
6.	(Child says he threw his spear through a wall)		
			Father: Wow, will Mommy be mad.
	Child:	It really didn't go through a wall. Let's really trick her, O.K.? And don't tell her I'm tricking, O.K.? We'll trick her and she'll really think that I threw my sword through the wall and landed here. But, Dad, tell Mommy my spear went through the wall.	
			Father: How come you want me to tell Mommy that?
	Child:	Because she won't believe me.	

(Continued)

Table 7 (*Continued*)

7.	Child:	Did you see the clouds?		
			Father:	That was smoke left over from the fireworks.
	Child:	You thought that but I thought they was clouds.		
8.	Child:	Let's go outside.		
			Father:	It's wet outside.
	Child:	I'll look out and see if its raining. I don't see any rain.		
9.	Child:	I can't see anything. Wait a second. Look through this. Now can you see anything?		
			Father:	No.
	Child:	That's what I mean.		
10.	Child:	I heard something.		
			Father:	What do you think it is?
	Child:	I'm going to look and see what it is.		
11.	Child:	We saw a big ape 'cept it had sharp teeth.		
			Father:	Real sharp like mine?
	Child:	No, not sharper than yours. They were just plastic sharp. The rest of him was plastic.		
			Father:	A plastic ape.
	Child:	He wasn't real.		

guments 1, 2, 3, 4, 8, 9, 10, the child acknowledges that real entities afford various forms of behavioral contact, that not-real entities do not, and that arguments about reality can be based on this point. Similarly, in cases of doubt converging evidence of reality status is appealed to, as in Arguments 1, 2, and 10. Further, real entities are explicitly expected to appear real to all reasonable persons; thus evidence about public existence is discussed and evaluated, as in Arguments 6, 7, and 9. Finally, the child's recognition of the need or use of claims concerning consistent existence is evident, as in Argument 5, although such arguments are comparatively rare.

Enough arguments about reality exist in these transcripts to demonstrate an early fundamental ability to distinguish real and not-real entities, and to emphasize the child's active reasoning about these ontological categories. However, too few exist to reveal much about the details of the child's logic. There are some hints, however. As for most adults, visual evidence is considered stronger evidence than merely someone else's verbal assertion (see Examples 3 and 8). In addition, other tests such as tasting

(Example 2) and feeling (Example 1) are needed at times to validate vision. On the other hand, verbal assertions can be compared and evaluated on the basis of the authority of the speaker making the claim as well as the number of different claimants (Example 6).

The child, even at this young age, makes clear distinctions among numerous not-real things, and seldom mistakes the reality status of clear cases of real things such as rocks, trees, houses, or real people he has seen and known. Even so, it is also true that some things provide difficulty to the child when it comes to classifying specific instances as real or not real. This is not surprising, because under the preceding analysis, ambiguous, unclear examples occur even for adults. Three sorts of things appear as signally troublesome for Abe in these transcripts. First are fictional objects. The instances under this heading in Table 6 include several examples of false and uncertain classifications. The trouble here seems likely to be that the child must depend solely on verbal reports with little or no resort to converging behavioral–sensory evidence. Consider the difference between dragons and dinosaurs (Morrison & Gardner, 1978); the key distinction here is that in one case the animals once lived (so we are told) and in the other they never did so (so we are told). Similarly, consider fictional and real story characters: Is Tom Sawyer fiction or biography, and how can one tell?

Another sometimes difficult instance concerns dream objects. Phenomenal salience can be hard to overcome in specific instances even when one knows dreams as a class to be not real; ask any adult about their most lifelike dream.

A final difficult case concerns invisible things. A good example here is air. Is invisible, intangible, unsmellable stuff like air real, and if so how so? This is a difficult categorization task for the child. It is probably the case that, as Piaget (1929) seems to suggest, the child's understanding of air becomes a prototypic instance of an invisible but real substance, which then figures into his other conceptions of invisible and intangible things by analogy. Abe at least explicitly suggests this:

Child: Daddy, there's just one thing that's invisible and do you know what that is?
Father: What is it?
Child: Air. There's no more things that are invisible 'cept air.

A strong implication of the preceding analysis and data is that children's early ability to distinguish real from not-real things must be limited to certain innumerable, but familiar instances that are clear cases. That is, the entity in question presents a consistent picture across tests of behavioral–sensory contact, convergence, publicness, and consistency. It is not surprising under this analysis that previous research has demonstrated confusions on the part of even older children about reality when the objects of classification have concerned difficult cases, such as dreams (Keil, 1979; Kohlberg, 1969; Piaget, 1929) and fictional characters (Morrison & Gardner, 1978). The same child, while troubled (as adults are) by difficult cases, understands much of the distinction between reality and not-reality as it applies to clear converging cases.

Finally, it is important to note that the focus here concerns the origins of the child's understanding of reality. There is every reason to believe that in spite of an early achieved distinction between real and not-real objects, much remains to be acquired—just as an early understanding of mental verbs only begins the process of metacognitive development. Specifically, to say that the child has an early understanding of reality is not to say that she or he has a full understanding of the reality versus not-reality distinction or its place in a full classification of ontological categories (see Keil, 1979; Flavell, Flavell & Green, 1983). The claim here is simply that in certain essential and significant ways the child understands the not-real nature of a variety of things and formulates an understanding of mental phenomena within that larger understanding.

It is possible to characterize the distinction of interest in this section—that between reality and its contrasts—as a distinction between *being* and *seeming*. Things are not always what they seem; dream objects are not real though they seem like it, the stick in the water is not bent though it seems to be at first glance. Acceptance of a distinction between being and seeming has strong implications for one's theory of cognition. If things always *were* what they *seemed*, cognition would be direct and simple, a form of naive realism. If being and seeming are different, however, one must consider the mechanism that produces beliefs, thoughts, and appearances, as distinct from the world of physical things. That is, one must consider what accounts for, what causes the difference between how things are (being) and how we construe them (seeming). In this section I have claimed that young children distinguish being and seeming; they are not realists. Further, an appreciation of the distinction between being and seeming requires, and forms part of the basis for, the child's theory of mind. Because things often are not what they seem, because thoughts and beliefs may be purposefully or accidentally different from what is so, some conception of what mediates these differences is necessary. That is, a conception of the mind becomes necessary. In short, at an early age children simultaneously begin to wrestle with two inseparable issues: The difference between being and seeming, and the construction of a theory of mind.

Conclusions

An understanding of the origins of metacognition can be based on one axiom and three supportable propositions. The axiom is definitional, asserting that metacognition consists of a large multifaceted theory of mind. The three propositions are, first, that very young children, 2- and 3-year-olds, grasp the existence of the mental world, the realm of mental states and processes marked off from that of physical objects or behavioral acts. Second, children of this age and younger also understand much about the distinction between reality and not reality. They are easily able to distinguish, in certain clear cases, real from not-real things, being from seeming. Third, development of an understanding of mind and an understanding of reality are intertwined. A distinction between being and seeming requires some theory of mind and an early understanding of mind stems in part from contrasting that category of experience with reality.

The support for the first proposition—that certain essential aspects of knowledge about the internal mental world are early understood—comes from a series of research, reviewed in this chapter, exploring the acquisition of mental verbs in young children. The support for the second and third propositions is less abundant, less experimental, and more preliminary. It rests on an analysis of concepts of reality in adults and the presence of obvious communication about reality in the speech of young children. Assuming that the child examined here is minimally representative, then very young children distinguish several categories of clearly not-real things from a central set of real things and do so on the basis of several reasonable criteria or tests. The arguments in this part of the chapter are offered as a plausible hypothesis, consistent with preliminary evidence, and worthy of further research.

In sum, children's knowledge about the mental world and about reality have an early and rich beginning. While Piaget clearly underestimated the early origins of understanding of these two domains, he was, I believe, correct in insisting that the child's understanding of the one is strongly tied to the other. An early understanding of the mental world depends in part on an understanding of the real world.

Many, at times exaggerated, claims have been advanced for the importance of metacognitive knowledge (see Wellman, 1983). In general, these claims stress the practical utility of knowledge about cognition for the execution of various problem-solving performances—for example, knowledge about memory for remembering, knowledge about language for speaking or reading. I doubt that the early metacognitive knowledge characterized in this chapter has much direct bearing on the child's use of various cognitive strategies to enhance the outcome of specific cognitive performances. Nevertheless, it may be more important still. The category of mind is a fundamental category of human cognition. As argued in this chapter it is intimately a part of understanding both the social world of self and others and the physical world of objects. As such as it is a fundamental building block of ontological knowledge—the child's developing conception of the basic categories of existence, the objects of the world in the sense of objects of knowledge. In this role, metacognition exerts a series of subtle, powerful influences on much of concept development. If this speculation proves true, research into the child's early developing knowledge of the mind will prove necessary for any general account of cognitive development.

References

Aggernaes, A. & Haugsted, R. Experienced reality in 3- to 6-year-old children: A study of direct reality testing. *Journal of Child Psychology and Psychiatry*, 1976, *17*, 323–335.

Austin, J. L. *Sense and sensibilia*. London: Oxford University Press, 1962.

Bretherton, I. & Beeghly, M. Talking about internal states: The acquisition of a theory of mind. *Developmental Psychology*, 1982, *18*, 906–921.

Bretherton, I., McNew, S., & Beeghly-Smith, M. Early person knowledge as expressed in gestural and verbal communication: When do infants acquire a "theory of mind"? In M. Lamb & L. Sherrod (Eds.), *Social cognition in infancy*. Hillsdale, NJ: Erlbaum, 1981.

Broughton, J. Development of concepts of self, mind, reality and knowledge. In W. Damon (Ed.) *New directions for child development*. San Francisco: Jossey–Bass, 1978.

Bullock, M., Gelman, R., & Baillargeon, R. The development of causal reasoning. In W. J. Friedman (Ed.), *The developmental psychology of time*. New York: Academic Press, 1982.

Cultice, J. C., Somerville, S. C., & Wellman, H. M. Preschoolers memory monitoring: Feeling of knowing judgments. *Child Development*, 1983, *54*,1480–1486.

Donaldson, M. *Children's minds*. Glasgow: William Collins & Sons, 1978.

Flavell, J. H., Flavell, E. R., & Green, F. L. Development of the appearance–reality distinction. *Cognitive Psychology*, 1983, *15*, 95–120.

Gelman, R., & Shatz, M. Appropriate speech adjustments: The operation of conversational constraints on talk to two-year-olds. In M. Lewis & L. Rosenblum (Eds.), *Interaction, conversation, and the development of language*. New York: Wiley, 1977.

James, W. *The principles of psychology*. New York: Dover Publications, 1950. (Originally published 1890.)

Johnson, C. N. & Wellman, H. M. Children's developing understanding of mental verbs: Remember, know, and guess. *Child Development*, 1980, *51*, 1095–1102.

Johnson, C. N. & Wellman, H. M. Children's developing conceptions of the mind and brain. *Child Development*, 1982, *53*, 222–234.

Johnson, M. K., & Raye, C. L. Reality monitoring. *Psychological Review*, 1981, *88*, 67–85.

Keil, F. *Semantic and conceptual development*. Cambridge, MA: Harvard University Press, 1979.

Kennick, W. E. Appearance and reality. In P. Edwards (Ed.), *The encyclopedia of philosophy*. New York: Macmillan, 1967.

Kohlberg, L. Stage and sequence: The cognitive-developmental approach to socialization. In D. A. Goslin (Ed.), *Handbook of socialization theory and research*. New York: Rand McNally, 1969.

Lakoff, G. & Johnson, M. *Metaphors we live by*. Chicago: University of Chicago Press, 1980.

Lamb, M. E. & Sherrod, L. R. *Infant social cognition: Theoretical and empirical considerations*. Hillsdale, NJ: Erlbaum, 1981.

Limber, J. The genesis of complex sentences. In T. E. Moore (Ed.), *Cognitive development and the acquisition of language*. New York: Academic Press, 1973.

Markman, E. M. Realizing you don't understand: A preliminary investigation. *Child Development*, 1977, 48, 986–992.

Markman, E. M. Realizing that you don't understand: Elementary school children's awareness of inconsistencies. *Child Development*, 1979, 50, 643–655.

Misciones, J. L., Marvin, R. S., O'Brien, R. G., & Greenburg, M. T. A developmental study of preschool children's understanding of the words "know" and "guess." *Child Development*, 1978, 48, 1107–1113.

Morrison, P., & Gardner, H. Dragons and dinosaurs: The child's capacity to differentiate fantasy from reality. *Child Development*, 1978, 49, 642–648.

Piaget, J. *The child's conception of the world*. London: Routledge and Kegan Paul, 1929.

Shatz, M., Wellman, H. M., & Silber, S. The acquisition of mental verbs: A systematic investigation of the first reference to mental state. *Cognition*, 1983, 14, 301–321.

Tagiuri, R. Person perception. In G. Lindzey & E. Aronson (Eds.), *The handbook of social psychology* (Vol. 3). Reading, MA: Addison–Wesley, 1969.

Wellman, H. M. Tip of the tongue and feeling of knowing experiences: A developmental study of memory monitoring. *Child Development*, 1977, 48, 13–21.

Wellman, H. M. Metamemory revisited. In M. T. H. Chi (Ed.), *Contributions to human development: Trends in memory development* Vol. 2. Basel, Switzerland: S. Karger, 1983.

Wellman, H. M. A child's theory of mind: The development of conceptions of cognition. In S. R. Yussen (Ed.), *The growth of reflection*. New York: Academic Press, 1985.

Wellman, H. M., & Johnson, C. N. Understanding mental processes: A developmental study of *remember* and *forget*. *Child Development*, 1979, 50, 79–88.

Wimmer, H., & Perner, J. Beliefs about beliefs: Representation and constraining function of wrong beliefs in young children's understanding of deception. *Cognition*, 1983, 13, 103–128.

CHAPTER 2

Social Influences
on Cognitive Development*

Jeanne D. Day, Lucia A. French, and Lynda K. Hall

Introduction

Development takes place within a sociocultural milieu. This is so obvious that it has become virtually transparent, and there has been a tendency to talk about cognitive development as if it occurred either spontaneously and independently (a maturational view), or as a result of individual interaction with the physical environment (a common interpretation of Piaget's view). The major premise of this chapter is that cognitive skills initially emerge in, and subsequently develop within, social contexts. Social contexts provide children with opportunities to acquire and share knowledge, to display competencies, and to learn and practice new skills.

The social world is ubiquitous for the young child, who is largely reliant upon others. Four points can be made regarding the role that the social world assumes in cognitive growth. First, cognitive abilities are socially transmitted. Adults and older peers pass on the knowledge and skills required in their culture to children. Second, cognitive abilities are socially constrained. Children employ skills in social interactions that they cannot use when working in isolation. Third, nascent cognitive abilities are socially nurtured. Adults and more expert peers allow children to practice

*Preparation of this manuscript was supported, in part, by NIH training grant (HD–07184).

33

new skills by assuming responsibility for other aspects of children's activities. In other words, they find ways to reduce the cognitive workload for children. Fourth, independent use of new cognitive abilities is socially encouraged. Adults and more expert peers take on less of the workload for children as they demonstrate increasing competence. This view of the social origins of cognitive development is congruent with Vygotsky's (1978) cultural–historical theory of the genesis of higher mental functions.

Since the mid-1970s, three separate subfields within the general domain of early cognitive development have evolved, which, despite quite independent origins, share striking parallels in that they characterize the young child's emerging cognitive competencies as resulting, in large part, from social factors. These three subfields include the emphasis upon mother–child interaction in language learning (Bruner, 1981; Nelson, 1973; Snow, 1979). Nelson's (1978) discussion of the young child's generalized event representations (scripts), and various investigators' discussion of learning in terms of Vygotsky's theory of cognitive development. Although the precise formulation of how social interaction promotes cognitive growth varies across these domains, their shared emphasis on the social milieu as the driving force behind cognitive development is striking and quite at odds with the standard approach of studying cognitive growth without reference to the social context.

What follows is divided into five sections. The first describes Vygotsky's theory of cognitive development in general terms. The second examines some research addressing novice–expert interactions in the context of particular tasks, and discusses how such interactions may enhance or inhibit cognitive development. We then discuss more recent research emphasizing the interactive basis of language acquisition. This is followed by a discussion of the ways in which children's event knowledge supports both social interaction and the display of cognitive and linguistic abilities. Finally, in the conclusion, we discuss interrelationships among the different topics presented and consider general implications of the position that cognitive abilities are largely social in origin.

Vygotsky's Theory of Cognitive Development

Vygotsky (1978) claims that all higher psychological functions develop in social interaction. He argues that adults and more capable peers mediate the child's experiences. They organize the environment (e.g., by making some objects available and others not), interpret and give meaning to events, direct attention to relevant dimensions of experience, provide ways to cope with the environment, and regulate ongoing problem-solving efforts. In other words, adults supply the child with culturally appropriate means of understanding, which become part of the child's individual psychological functioning.

The claim that children learn from others is in no way unique. Three important components of Vygotsky's theory, however, do offer novel perspectives on the origins of cognitive development. First, in addition to the widely accepted view that *knowledge* is socially transmitted, Vygotsky claims that *cognitive processes* are transmitted through social interaction. Joint participation in an activity permits cognitive processes to be displayed, shared, and practiced, so that the child is able to modify her or his current mode of functioning. Second, the adult or more capable peer lightens the cognitive "workload" for the learner by taking responsibility for some parts of a task while the child concentrates on one subcomponent. In current terminology, the expert assumes metacognitive control of the situation, monitoring the novice's activities to see that they are appropriate for the task, goal-directed, and completed successfully. The expert's metacognitive control is essential in that the novice can gain awareness of and control over mental processes only after those processes have been used and practiced (Vygotsky, 1962). Moreover, in fulfilling the executive function, the expert has a chance to model important metacognitive processes for the child. We offer some illustrations of these activities later. Third, Vygotsky takes an unusual perspective on the relationship between learning and development. Piaget assumed that the child could only learn those things that were congruent with already established developmental levels; this is akin to the "readiness" notion familiar to educators. From Piaget's perspective then, development preceded, permitted, and limited learning. Vygotsky took the reverse perspective, claiming that learning preceded, and indeed enabled, development. The basis for this claim was Vygotsky's observation of a distinction between the levels of cognitive ability that children can display independently and in collaboration with adults or more capable peers. He claimed that the skills children could display independently reflected "completed" development, whereas skills children were able to demonstrate only in socially supported contexts were in the process of being learned and only later would become internalized and reflected in the child's independent activity. This distinction is similar to the distinction educators make between level of mastery and level of instruction. Vygotsky referred to the distance between the abilities displayed independently and with social support as the zone of proximal development, and claimed that this zone is created by learning. Children acquire new abilities and use their embryonic ones in settings that are socially supportive. Without those social supports the child's activity is not sufficiently monitored or regulated to allow proximal skills to be introduced and practiced.

The concept of the zone of proximal development has obvious mental testing implications. For example, if we have knowledge of a child's zone of proximal development for a particular skill, we can predict how that child will independently utilize that skill in the near future. (More complete discussions of these implications can be found in Brown & French, 1979; Day, 1983; Luria, 1928, 1961; Vygotsky, 1929, 1978; and Wozniak, 1975.) However, Vygotsky's (1978) discussion of the relationship between learning and development also has important instructional ramifications. Maximally effective instruction occurs within the child's zone of proximal development. Instruction directed at the level of completed development can, of course, increase the child's knowledge base, but will have minimal effect upon her or his cognitive ability. Instruction directed beyond the proximal level will tend to be incomprehensible to the child and thus will affect neither knowledge nor cognitive ability. The most effective teaching is therefore, somewhat, but not too much, in advance of development.[1] Such instruction involves the novice working with more capable others on challenging tasks she could not solve independently. The more able participants model appropriate problem-solving behaviors, present new approaches to the problem, and encourage the novice to use her or his embryonic skills by assuming responsibility for some parts of the task. As novices develop the abilities required, they should receive less assistance and solve more of the problem independently. Simultaneously, of course, they will encounter yet more challenging tasks on which they will continue to receive help. Effective teaching–learning transactions thus establish successive zones of proximal development.

Vygotsky's (1978) claim that psychological processes appear first on an interpersonal level and only later on an intrapersonal plane emphasizes the dynamic nature of cognitive development. Cognitive abilities are neither magically generated in social isolation, nor innately given, nor passively assimilated. Rather, nascent skills emerge and are refined as children actively participate in supportive contexts that are structured by others. The next three sections present evidence relevant to the socialization of cognition. Although much of the research to be described was not motivated by Vygotskian theory, all of the studies examine social factors that may influence cognitive development.

---

[1]This position, under the label "the problem of the match" was also developed by J. McVicar Hunt (1961) quite independently from Vygotsky.

Acquisition of Cognitive Skills

Since Hunt (1961) argued that human intellectual capacity was malleable and Bloom (1964) identified the preschool years as highly important to children's intellectual development, investigators have sought to describe the early experiences conducive to cognitive growth. Toward this end, they have assessed several dimensions of children's home environments and correlated these measures with children's intellectual performance in standardized tests or achievement in school. *Nonsocial* aspects of the child's home (e.g., the number of magazines and books available to the child) as well as social factors (e.g., quantity of maternal stimulation or contingency of maternal response) have been studied and found to relate to the child's cognitive abilities (e.g., Bradley & Caldwell, 1976a, 1976b, 1977, 1978; Bradley, Caldwell, & Elardo, 1979; Caldwell, 1968; Clarke-Stewart, 1973; Cohen & Beckwith, 1979; Lewis & Goldberg, 1969; Wachs, 1976; Yarrow, Pedersen, & Rubenstein, 1977). In addition, researchers have observed mother–child dyads as the mothers taught their children how to solve novel tasks and correlated maternal teaching style with child competence (e.g., Bee, 1967; Bee, Van Egeren, Streissguth, Nyman, & Leckie, 1969; Bing, 1963; Hess & Shipman, 1965, 1967). For example, Hess and Shipman (1965, 1967) observed mothers as they helped their 4-year-old children solve specific tasks (e.g., copying an etch-a-sketch design, sorting toys). They identified three styles of maternal behavior that appeared to be related to the child's cognitive functioning. Mothers who used an imperative–normative orientation offered the child little or no justification for their requests or commands. The language with which they communicated was limited and condensed with much of the meaning implied rather than expressly stated. This orientation was correlated with poor performance by their children on the Stanford-Binet test, on conceptual sorting tasks, and with the tendency to give nonverbal rather than verbal responses. In contrast, mothers who adopted either a subjective or a cognitive–rational orientation used more elaborated response styles. They tended to offer individualized justifications for their requests or commands and used particular, differentiated, and precise language. Mothers who used the elaborated orientations a greater portion of the time tended to have children who were more verbal and who performed better on intellectual tasks.

The assumption underlying research like Hess and Shipman's is that cognitive abilities are socially influenced. Unfortunately however, such research does not illuminate the processes by which interpersonal activities come to affect individual cognition. One problem is that the analysis of the interaction is too global. The descriptions of maternal interactive styles provided by Hess and Shipman (1965, 1967), for example, do not enumerate the particular skills, strategies or problem-solving techniques that mothers present to help their children learn to solve the tasks. In other words, the content of the mother–child interaction is not described fully enough to permit inferences about what the child actually learns. Second, the tasks that mothers are asked to help their children on are not necessarily ones that the mothers would normally teach. Some mothers may not know a variety of strategies for the task at hand, and others may not find the chosen activity to be significant in any way. Third, the outcome measure (performance on standardized tests) is also too global. Because researchers in this area are primarily interested in examining group differences, they do not attempt to trace the genesis and subsequent development of any particular skill or strategy. They do not assess how children function independently after interacting with their parents, what children learn to do with assistance that they cannot do alone, or how well children transfer their learning to other situations. Fourth, considerable emphasis is placed on the parents' behaviors, and relatively little attention is given to the children's activities. Thus, the direction of causality is obscured. Parents who use elaborated interactive styles may foster their children's cognitive growth, or cognitively advanced children may demand more elaborated responses from their parents. A historical analysis of a particular cognitive skill (Wertsch & Stone, 1978) would provide more information regarding the specific roles of parent and child in the interaction.

One way to determine how interpersonal activities become intrapersonal psychological processes is to study teaching–learning transactions. An adult or more capable peer would be asked to help a child solve a novel problem. The content, form, and style of the tutor's explanations and/or demonstrations would be analyzed, as would the child's responses, requests for help, and so forth. Ideally, this transaction would occur in a familiar social context, to facilitate displays of competence on the child's part and, presumably, better teaching on the tutor's part. Moreover, the problem would be one the child could encounter in his or her everyday environment and would be one with which the tutor was familiar. Finally, the adult (or peer) would be someone with whom the child might normally interact, for example, a parent, teacher, or sibling. Prior to and following instruction, the child would be asked to work on the problem without assistance, thus providing a measure of the effectiveness of training. In addition, maintenance and generalization measures would be taken to assess the effectiveness of the intervention.

Although no one has conducted the study just described in its entirety, several investigations designed from the perspective of Vygotskian theory have begun to explore the relevant issues (e.g., Gardner & Rogoff,

1982; Wertsch, 1979; Wertsch, McNamee, Budwig, & McLane, 1980). Each of these studies provide detailed descriptions of the context of interaction between mothers and their children. Gardner and Rogoff, for example, describe how a mother assists her 8-year-old son prepare for a memory test. The child's task is to remember the organization of 18 household items so that he can arrange them in a predetermined order on six shelves in a simulated kitchen. The mother assists the child by classifying the items both taxonomically (according to categories) and schematically (providing temporal, logical, or causal connections among items), by modeling a rehearsal strategy, and by providing metamemorial information relevant to the task. Thus, Gardner and Rogoff provide excellent examples of the types of cognitive skills that parents can introduce in interaction with their children.

The Wertsch studies focus on the development of self-regulatory skills in preschoolers as they work on a jigsaw puzzle with their mothers. Wertsch (1979) identifies four levels of interaction as regulation of the problem-solving process shifts from mother to child. At the first level, the child's understanding of the task is quite limited, and communication between mother and child is difficult. Children often do not perceive the relationship between the mother's prompts or instructions and the task situation. Thus, regulation of the child's activity by the mother is almost nonexistent. By the second level, however, children realize that the adult's instructions are related to the task in some way. Still, the full connection between speech and activity is not always evident to children, so that they may have difficulty making appropriate inferences from their mothers' instructions. For example, children may not realize that directions from their mothers in the form of questions can provide information about the task solution. This lack of realization on the part of the child requires the mother to put her directions in a more explicit form, such as an imperative statement.

When the child reaches the third level, she or he is able to make inferences from parental instructions, and thus is able to interpret nonexplicit statements in a meaningful way. The problem-solving activity is still primarily social, but the child has begun to regulate more personal activity as she or he has begun to more adequately understand the task and the solution process. This transition from mother-regulation to the child's self-regulation continues as the child proceeds to the fourth, most advanced level. At this point the child regulates her or his own activity. Notably, the child often utters a monologue as she or he solves the task, so that self-regulation is observable.

The documentation of each of these levels supports the notion that parents initially regulate their child's problem-solving behavior and cede this regulation as the child's competence grows. For example, on the jig-saw puzzle task, Wertsch et al. (1980) found a developmental progression of parental regulation in groups of 2½, 3½, and 4½-year-old children, with the youngest children receiving the most control and support from their mothers. These mothers obviously had some awareness of their child's developmental level, and they adjusted their degree of control over the child's behavior accordingly. To the extent that mothers (or other adults) share this awareness with the child and encourage the child to adopt plan-ning, monitoring, and other regulatory strategies, they may enhance the child's developing metacognition (Wertsch et al., 1980). Thus, metacog-nitive processes, like other higher psychological functions, have social origins.

Gardner and Rogoff (1982) and Wertsch (1979; Wertsch et al., 1980) contribute substantially to our understanding of the socialization of cog-nition. They document how strategic problem-solving activities can be car-ried out by children in collaboration with adults. They provide examples of the kinds of skills and strategies adults can describe to children, of the ways adults share task responsibility and behavior regulation, and of the gradual ceding of problem-solving responsibility to the child. Teachers (Gearhart & Newman, 1980; Hood, McDermott, & Cole, 1980; Petitto, 1983) and peers (Cazden, 1981; Cazden, Cox, Dickinson, Steinberg, & Stone, 1979; Ellis & Rogoff, 1982) appear to engage in similar activities. For example, Cazden et al. (1979) describe several teaching–learning trans-actions. These transactions begin as the teacher helps one of her grade school students learn to complete a somewhat challenging worksheet as-signment. At first the teacher is quite explicit and directive; she clarifies the goals of the task and makes sure that each step is completed success-fully. The teacher becomes less directive as the student comes to under-stand the task until finally, she asks the student to show a few classmates how to fill in the worksheet. Although students vary in the ease with which they adopt the tutor role and in their ability to gain and hold their class-mates' attention, most do succeed in communicating the goals and pro-cedures involved in the task. In fact, their instructions tend to be elaborated and detailed initially and to become less so as their classmates understand the task. Thus, students who tutor provide metacognitive control that they gradually cede as their classmates become more competent on the task.

In teaching environments, therefore, adults and more-capable peers can describe, demonstrate, and explain strategies relevant to task comple-tion. In addition, they can monitor and regulate the learner's problem-solving efforts, keeping them goal-directed. However, the externalization of cognitive skills and the transition from other- to self-regulation might only occur in formal settings where the explicitly stated goal is to teach cognitive skills. Teaching–learning transactions in informal, "everyday" settings might be quite different. The next two sections, the first on language acquisition and the second on event knowledge, contain data that suggest that even in less-structured settings adults do externalize culturally available skills, do monitor and regulate children's use of those skills, and do relinquish control as children demonstrate increasing competence. Moreover, children display surprising levels of cognitive and linguistic competence in familiar settings with familiar people.

The Interactive Basis of Language Acquisition

Various investigators focus on different aspects of the language learning process, depending upon their definition of language. Those who define language as a set of syntactic rules have focused on the acquisition of syntax; those who define language as a means of referring have focused on the acquisition of semantic knowledge; those who define language as a communicative system have focused on the development of communicative competence. Language is clearly all of these things, and any complete account of language acquisition must consider all of them. From the mother's and child's perspectives, however, it appears that the overriding goal that spurs language acquisition is the desire to communicate (e.g., Bruner, 1981).

Early research on children's language acquisition (e.g., Brown, 1973) focused almost exclusively on the child's productions. Interest in mothers' speech was limited primarily to correlating the frequency of certain syntactic forms in a mother's speech to their occurrence in her child's speech, and to observing the effect of different sorts of feedback, such as expansions and corrections, on acquisition. Gradually, however, the focus shifted, and currently a high proportion of research on language acquisition focuses on the communicative exchanges in which the child engages.

According to Snow (1979), there have been three stages in the study of mothers' speech to language-learning children. The first stage focused upon syntactic features of the mothers' speech. The impetus for these investigations was the general assumption, fostered by Chomsky (e.g., Miller & Chomsky, 1963), that the language to which young children were exposed was syntactically ill-formed, and so provided unsuitable input for the learning of syntactic rules. These investigations revealed that the language mothers use when talking to young children is syntactically simple, well-formed, and highly repetitive. The second stage focused on the semantic content of mothers' speech, and revealed that it tends to be highly restricted. As Snow (1979) points out, "Mothers limit their utterances to the present tense, to concrete nouns, to comments on what the child is doing and on what is happening around the child" (p. 370). Restricting linguistic reference to those things about which the child already has extralinguistic knowledge obviously contributes to the child's "cracking" of the linguistic code (e.g., Macnamara, 1972). As noted here subsequently, Lucariello (1983) found 2-year-olds engaging in displaced reference when talking with their mothers. Rather than initially occurring in play settings (the context in which most samples of mother–child speech have been collected), displaced reference first emerges during joint participation in routine activities, about which young children have a great deal of extralinguistic knowledge.

The third stage in the study of mothers' speech to young children addressed the question of *how* mothers keep their speech finely adjusted to their children's syntactic and semantic level. The answer to this question seems to be that mothers do not "talk at" but rather "talk with" their children. Children simply do not attend to language that they cannot understand, and mothers correspondingly adjust their speech so that the child is attentive. Furthermore, children often introduce topics, which mothers pick up and elaborate on. Snow (1979) suggests that although the mother clearly has much more linguistic knowledge than the child, the child to a large extent controls the linguistic interaction through level of attentiveness and the selection of "conversational" topics.

Even before infants begin talking, mothers converse with them. For example, if an infant sneezes, a mother might say "Oh, what a big noise you can make!" or "Ahh, do you have a tickle in your nose?" Snow (1979) suggests that by interpreting the child's behavior as if it had communicative intent, the mother is actually teaching the child that he or she is capable of communicating.

The fine adjustments mothers make to their young children's communicative competency is illustrated by Bruner's (1981; Ninio & Bruner, 1978) longitudinal research. Bruner studied two mother–infant dyads during the first 2 years of the infants' lives, and traced the ontogenesis of communicative interactions from the very early attention-getting methods adopted by mothers through the development of ritualized labeling games. Bruner (1981) notes:

> Semantically, syntactically, lexically, intonationally, in terms of sentence length and complexity, parents get down to the level on which their children are operating and move ahead with them at a rate that shows remarkable sensitivity to their child's progress (p. 160).

Bruner began observing one mother–infant dyad when the infant (Jonathan) was 3 months old. At that time, the mother established joint attention to objects in two ways. While in eye-to-eye contact with the infant, she would interpose an object between them. Alternatively, she would select an object in the child's line of regard and move it toward the child. In both variations, the mother used a distinctive intonation pattern to verbally signal her attempt to attract the child's attention. Later, the mother was able to attract the child's attention through the use of routinized verbalizations (such as the child's name) having a distinctive intonation pattern. Once the children were able to reach, they were able to give, rather than simply to receive, signals about objects. Toward the end of the first year, the infants began both pointing to objects and producing phonologically consistent forms (PCFs) to indicate reference to particular objects. The children's ability to refer, through pointing and verbal labeling, led to more complex communicative interactions. Bruner (1981) illustrates these with reference to Ninio and Bruner's (1978) detailed analysis of the interaction between Jonathan and his mother in a book-reading context over the period between Jonathan's first and second birthdays. Within this context, the mother adjusted her behavior to the nature of the task and Jonathan's apparent competence, and continually readjusted it as his competence grew. Bruner reports that the mother relied upon four primary utterance types, which virtually always occurred in the same order, thereby establishing a fixed format or script that could support the child's interpretation of the task. These utterance types were (1) an attentional vocative, such as "Look"; (2) a query, such as "What's that?"; (3) a label, such as "That's an X", and (4) a feedback statement such as "Yes, that's an X".

Jonathan and his mother began playing this game before Jonathan was able to point or to produce PCFs, and therefore, before he could respond to the queries. Once Jonathan began producing any vocalization to the queries, his mother would not provide a label until he vocalized. Later, when Jonathan began producing PCFs, his mother held out for the appropriate "label" if she believed he knew it. At this point, the mother varied the intonation pattern of the query, using falling intonation if she expected Jonathan to label the picture, and rising intonation if she did not believe he knew the appropriate label. When the child produced appropriate labels, his mother skipped her labeling turn, and moved directly to the feedback utterance.

Within these mundane mother–infant interactions, which take place thousands of times every day, there are some important insights to be gained about how the child acquires language. The mother–child interactions described by Bruner (1981), Snow (1979) and others are primarily social and communicative. The mother establishes routinized communicative contexts, the structure of which the child quickly comes to understand. The child has a particular role in these contexts, which changes as the mother reevaluates his or her communicative skills. At a fairly primitive level, the mother may simply interpret burps, sneezes, and random vocalizations as if they were intended to convey meanings. At a fairly advanced level, the mother may insist that the child produce the appropriate label for a picture they are viewing together. The child's failures to respond keep the sensitive mother from demanding more than the child can contribute, and the mother's demands challenge the child to contribute as much as he or she can. As the child masters the components of the various communicative contexts, the mother may introduce more complex variations. For example, once the child consistently labels a particular picture, the mother will comment on what is happening in the picture, then later, demand that the child describe what is happening. The child is thereby led, through graduated stages of complexity, to achieve communicative competence.

Bruner accepts the possibility of an innate language acquisition device (LAD) that generates and tests hypotheses about syntactic structures. He suggests however that rather than operating upon undifferentiated speech, the LAD requires input of a certain sort. Specifically, Bruner suggests that the LAD necessarily requires speech that is communicative, that refers to extralinguistic knowledge, and that is carefully calibrated to the child's emerging competencies. In short, Bruner suggests that the basic phenomenon of adjusting input language to the child's level of competency (which he refers to as LAS, or Language Assistance System) is a universal preadapted species-specific system, which is necessary for language acquisition. While others might argue about whether such finely adjusted input is necessary and innate (e.g., see Nelson, in press), there can be little doubt that it provides an optimal context for language acquisition. Because the major function of language is communication, the ideal context for acquisition would seem to be one that is structured in such a way that the child can comprehend the linguistic and extralinguistic input, and the mother can interpret the child's responses as having communicative intent. Burner's detailed analysis of how mothers facilitate language acquisition is strikingly similar to the view of cognitive development proposed by Vygotsky (1978) and elaborated by Wertsch (1979) and others.

Event Knowledge: Socially Acquired and Socially Shared

The structured communicative formats, such as "book-reading", on which Bruner has focused in his study of language acquisition, are one type of "script." This section considers scripts more generally, illustrating how scripts support the display of cognitive and linguistic abilities, as well as permit assumptions of shared knowledge, thereby supporting social interaction.

Nelson (1978; Nelson & Gruendel, 1981) employs the concept of scripts or "generalized event representations" or describe children's schematic knowledge of routine events. These representations include a specification of the event's temporal–causal structure, its obligatory and optional components, and the props and roles commonly associated with the event. Scripts are acquired quite readily. Even very young children seem to construct schematic representations of an event after one or two opportunities to participate in it (Nelson, 1980). In addition, young children's basic event knowledge is very similar to that of adults' in terms of both its schematic structure and its consistency across time and individuals (Nelson, 1978).[2] Such event representations constitute one of the child's earliest and most stable forms of knowledge about the world and form "basic building blocks" for subsequent cognitive development (Nelson and Gruendel, 1981). That scripts are acquired rapidly suggests that the very young child is somehow specially attuned to make sense of activities in which she or he participates. That scripts have a schematic structure from very early on allows the child to extend scripted knowledge to novel experiences.[3] That is, the schematic representation, unlike a concrete representation, permits the incorporation of new information about a particular type of event, and thus allows for continual elaboration and refinement of event knowledge.

Unlike much of the other knowledge young children acquire (for example, knowledge about word meanings, the spatial layout of their homes, and preferred means of interacting with the family pet), scripts necessitate and provide the basis for knowledge about temporal and logical relationships. By their very nature, generalized event representations contain information about temporal and logical relationships. For example, our knowledge about eating at a restaurant includes knowing that seeing a menu enables ordering, which enables obtaining food, which enables eating.

Scripts also constitute a very important form of social knowledge. While individuals undoubtedly have some idiosyncratic and private scripts, many scripts reflect knowledge widely shared within the culture. This is

---

[2]By this we mean that the representation in both cases seems to be schematic, to contain information about optional and necessary components, and to have a temporal–causal organization. Clearly, adults and older children have more complete, and thus more complex, knowledge about many events.

[3]It also indicates that very young children are capable of generalization and abstraction—cognitive abilities not usually attributed to them except in the domain of language acquisition.

true for scripts about events generally enacted in private settings (e.g., brushing one's teeth), as well as for those about events enacted in social settings (e.g., eating at a restaurant). The ability to assume that scripted knowledge is shared by others has profound effects on dialogue and social interaction.

The interrelationships among scripts, language, and cognition have been considered from several perspectives. Children's descriptions of scripted events (in response to questions such as "What happens when you eat at a restaurant?") reveal surprisingly advanced cognitive and linguistic abilities (French, 1981, 1983; French & Nelson, 1981, 1982, 1983). Mother–child conversations employ more sophisticated linguistic forms in scripted than in play-based settings (Lucariello, 1983; Lucariello & Nelson, 1982). Child–child conversations based on scripted knowledge are not egocentric (Nelson, Gruendel, 1979) and are maintained over a greater number of discourse turns than are conversations not based on scripted knowledge (Nelson , Seidman, 1983; Seidman, 1983).

French and Nelson (1982) found that 3- to 5-year-old children's descriptions of their generalized event representations revealed various linguistic abilities, including facility with temporally and spatially displaced reference, timeless verbs, and relational terms (e.g., *before, after, because, so, or,* and *but*), which previous investigators had concluded were not within the capacity of children of this age. The event descriptions also revealed cognitive abilities not usually attributed to children of this age. The structure of the descriptions reflected the temporal structure of the events being described, providing the strongest evidence to date that young children can construct representations of temporal structure, maintain such representations over time, and recall them at will. There were also indications in some of the descriptions that the children could move bidirectionally within these representations, as in the following examples:

> She gots something out to bake muffins with. But first, she has to buy some things for muffins. (Age 2 years, 11 months [2:11])
>
> Make the dough. And then you put it in the oven. But before you put it in the oven, you make the cookie shapes and then you put it in the oven. And then when the bell rings, you take out the cookies. (Age 4:7).

The abilities to construct and move bidirectionally within a temporal representation are ones that Piaget (1969) claims constitute temporal reversibility, a cognitive operation he claims first emerges during the period of concrete operations, that is, around age 6 or 7 years.

The appropriate use of the aforementioned relational terms indicates an understanding of the logical relationships expressed by these terms. None of these logical relationships have traditionally been considered to be understood by preschoolers. In some cases, such as for the adversative relationship expressed by *but*, there has been no position taken on whether preschoolers understand the relationship (although, see Kail, 1980; Kail & Weissenborn, 1980). In other cases, for example for the causal relationships expressed by *because* and *so*, and temporal relationships, the Piagetian position has been that the understanding of the relationship is beyond the capability of preschoolers. Thus while French and Nelson's data are of varying degrees of relevance for the different terms, they are consistent in demonstrating the presence, at a very early age, of an understanding of the logical relationships considered to be essential components of human cognition.

Preschoolers' descriptions of scripted events indicate that scripted knowledge is well established, complexly represented, and readily accessible. The fact that the abilities displayed in describing scripts are not readily apparent in other settings designed to assess preschoolers' cognitive and linguistic abilities (e.g., spontaneous speech during free-play and experimental tasks) suggests that scripts hold a privileged position in young children's early cognitive development. That is, children may be especially able to "make sense of" temporally–causally structured events in which they participate. For the young child, such events are virtually always initially social, even those that adults consider private, such as bathing and brushing one's teeth. Observations of children talking with their mothers (while participating in scripted activities and engaging in peer play based on scripted knowledge) reveal that scripts facilitate social interaction, which in turn facilitates cognitive and linguistic development.

Lucariello (1983; Lucariello & Nelson, 1982) recorded mother–child dyads (children 2:0 to 2:5) interacting in three contexts: a routine, scripted context such as bathing or eating lunch, a standard free-play context with assorted toys, and a fantasy-play context with an unfamiliar castle. Although such standard variables as mean length of utterance and proportion of mother to child utterances did not vary across the three contexts, some important semantic, syntactic, and discourse features did. Temporally and spatially displaced reference occurred in the children's speech in the scripted contexts, but not in either of the play contexts. Apparently, children's complex knowledge of scripted activities supports their early references to things not present in the immediately perceptible environment (e.g., negotiations with their mother about what to eat for lunch). Although no substantial differences were found in the number of questions mothers posed across the three contexts, the children were significantly better at answering questions in the scripted contexts, and the questions posed in the scripted contexts were more likely to genuinely seek information from the child rather than display the child's knowledge or direct the child's attention. These findings indicate that in the course of conversations during routine interactions, mothers encourage their children to independently use previously acquired knowledge. In the unscripted settings, mothers may ask display and attention-directing questions in order to assist the children in reviewing and organizing information about the situation.

Lucariello and Nelson (1982) offer three overlapping explanations for the finding that the linguistic competencies exhibited by young children vary substantially across contexts, with the most advanced skills apparently being demonstrated in scripted contexts. First, children's knowledge about routine events provides the basis, in terms of content, for their productions. Second, scripts represent a primary source of shared knowledge between mother and child, and shared knowledge is a necessary prerequisite for genuine conversation. Finally, the fact that scripted activities are well understood by children means that they do not need to devote a great deal of cognitive effort to monitoring the ongoing activities and so can devote more cognitive effort to verbal communication. Apparently the fact that their knowledge about routine events is shared, and that the child's knowledge about these events is complex, allows the mother to introduce more advanced language during joint participation in routine settings, and supports the child's ability to understand, respond to, and eventually adopt such language use.

Piaget's characterization of young children's speech is egocentric referred in part to the phenomenon of *collective monologues*, in which children observe conversational turn-taking conventions, but violate contingency conventions. Nelson and Gruendel (1979) suggest that such collective monologues occur when children are not talking about a topic familiar to each, that is, when they do not have shared knowledge, and thus lack the basis for contingent responding. Compared to adults and older children, young children are relatively unskilled at those conversational ploys that test their listener's knowledge and fill in the gaps necessary to allow the establishment of shared reference. However, when young children are discussing familiar, scripted events, their speech is decidedly not egocentric (Nelson & Gruendel, 1979; Seidman, 1983), indicating that discourse context and content are critical components in accounting for the young child's display of communicative competence. For example, Nelson and Gruendel (1979) report a (pretend) telephone conversation between two 4-year-olds playing at being a married couple negotiating what to have for dinner. Seidman (1983; Nelson & Seidman, 1983) also found that while children talk of many things during peer play, their ability to maintain dialogue over successive turns is affected by their conversational topic, with longer dialogues occurring when the children are engaging in script-based play. Scripts appear to form an ideal basis for both mother–child and child–child conversations. By talking about those things for which they have shared knowledge, young children can maintain social interaction and develop their conversational, perspective-taking, and negotiation skills. The skills developed in this conversational context are undoubtedly eventually transferred to contexts where shared knowledge must be established rather than assumed.

Conclusion

In this chapter, we have argued that cognitive growth is highly dependent on social interaction. This argument is intended to apply to growth in both cognitive and metacognitive domains. As Brown, Bransford, Ferrara and Campione (1983) have pointed out, metacognition is a fuzzy concept encompassing a number of distinguishable phenomena (e.g., planning ahead, monitoring, self-questioning, self-correcting). One major unresolved issue concerns where to draw the line between cognition and metacognition. Another source of confusion is whether conscious reflection is necessary for the attribution of metacognition. Although any attempt to resolve these disputes is beyond the scope of this chapter, we do feel comfortable with the view that self-regulation, whether consciously carried out or not, is an indication of metacognition activity. One of Vygotsky's (1978) major interests was in children's increasing ability to direct and control their cognitive behavior, and he argued that such self-regulation reflects the gradual internalization of the means by which adults and more knowledgeable others have previously organized and directed the child's behavior.

Within the domains we have reviewed, the influence of social interaction upon metacognitive skills can be seen most clearly in the microgenetic analyses of the teaching–learning process (Gardner & Rogoff, 1982; Petitto, 1983; Wertsch, 1979). In addition to assuming executive control of a learning interaction, the teacher often models the problem-solving *process*. For example, the mothers observed by Wertsch (1979) typically used questions rather than directives to guide their child's puzzle-completion attempts. Questions serve to direct and organize the learners' activity at a given moment. Such questions *also* model for the learner important components of metacognition (e.g., "Does that look right?" "What should we do next?"). In learning to complete puzzles independently, the child internalizes these metacognitive queries. One of the nicest aspects of Wertsch's research is that children were observed actually asking these questions of themselves aloud.

Metacognitive activity is not always explicitly modeled for learners; the children who have passed the age at which they talk aloud to themselves during the course of problem solving may not give clear-cut evidence of engaging in metacognitive activity. However, even when metacognitive activity is not directly modeled for the child, the social interactions that take place in learning environments often are conducive to the *induction* of metacognitive skills. A teacher might respond to a child who gave an answer "9" to the problem, "5 − 4 = _____" by asking "How did you get that answer?" "What does this sign mean?" "If you only start out with five, and take something away, could you end up with *more* than five?" In the course of such a dialogue, the child would learn more than that he or she had made an error. The child would learn something specific about how to solve and check a subtraction problem and would perhaps induce some general metacognitive skills (checking, monitoring, asking whether an answer makes sense) that would be applicable outside the confines of subtraction problems.

One theme that has been implicit throughout our discussion of the social basis of cognitive development has been that the social agents from whom the child learns have goals (which may not be consciously articulated). These goals are both general and specific. At a general level, the adult's goal is for the child to achieve competence, that is, to become able to perform independently. This general goal leads the adult to relinquish control over various aspects of a task as the child attains the ability to assume control. At a more specific level, the adult has a representation of the end point to be achieved—that is, of the higher-order goal of a specific activity. As Nelson and Gruendel (1981), Petitto (1983), and Snow (1979) point out, the child may not initially share or even understand the adult's higher-order goal. The infant who acquires a bath-taking script probably does not have personal hygiene as a goal. The grade-school child does not know enough about mathematics to set the goal of learning long-division. However, in many cases, as illustrated in Petitto's (1983) observations of the teaching of long-division and Connor's (1983) observations of the teaching of a solitaire game, the adult guides and interprets the child's actions according to the adult's understanding of the overall goal of the activity. That is, the adult will respond to the child's behavior as if it were in fact goal-directed. This phenomenon can be seen in mother–child communicative (Bruner, 1981; Snow, 1979) and puzzle-completion (Wertsch, 1979) interactions as well. The adult's attribution of goals to the child— which the child may in fact not have—enables the child to acquire skills in the context of their functional significance and eventually to adopt the goal as her or his own (Petitto, 1983).

Olson (1976) presented two views of intelligence that provide a useful framework within which to discuss the social nature of cognitive development. Humans are both biological and cultural creatures. From a primarily biological perspective, the individual's need is to adapt to nature, and adaptive intelligence is seen as mediating between the individual and nature. From a primarily cultural perspective, adaptive intelligence is seen as mediating between the individual and the culture, with the culture mediating between the individual and nature: "the culture has already 'worked up' procedures for dealing with the natural environment, these procedures being embodied in the artifacts, institutions, conventions, and technologies of that culture" (Olson, 1976, p. 190). Olson makes a compelling case that the cultural model is the more accurate, because the culture to a large extent arranges, controls, and provides the interpretation for the individual's interactions with nature.

When considering the young child, however, we can argue for the superiority of a third model (much like that proposed by Nelson, 1973, in discussing language acquisition) in which other people mediate between the child and the culture. Just as the culture organizes one's interactions with nature, parents (and other significant people in the child's environment) organize the child's interactions with the culture. Other people determine, both directly and indirectly, the aspects of the culture to which the child will be exposed at a given time. They arrange and control the child's interactions with the culture, and provide the child with the means to interpret those interactions.

In social interactions—in contrast to interaction with "nature" or "the culture"—the child behaves intelligently, as do others with whom the child interacts. Intelligence can therefore be seen as residing in the social interaction itself rather than simply in individual minds. Just as the psychologist is best able to study intelligence when it is manifested as overt behavior in response to tasks the psychologist understands, the child is best able to acquire intelligence when it is socially displayed in response to situations the child understands.

Throughout this chapter, we have argued that other people have a profound influence on young children's cognitive development. In the introduction, we made four points regarding the role of social interaction in cognitive growth: Cognitive abilities are (1) socially transmitted, (2) socially constrained, (3) socially nurtured, and (4) socially encouraged. These points were drawn from Vygotsky's theory of cognitive development, and we have described data collected by Wertsch (1979) and others that support these points quite well. Substituting "linguistic" for "cognitive" in the preceding points yields claims that fit current views of the interactive basis of language acquisition almost perfectly.

The relationship of scripts to these four points is less apparent, because the acquisition of scripts seems to be a direct outcome of participation in activities rather than a form of learning that benefits from carefully adjusted input from others. However, adjusted input is adjusted in relation to *something*, namely, what the other knows the child knows. In the preceding model, in which social agents mediate between the child and the culture, scripted knowledge could be considered to be one form of already acquired cultural knowledge. Because it is something the child already knows, it does not need to be arranged and presented in a carefully organized manner. Rather, it has, from a Vygotskian perspective, the status of completed development, and so can form the basis for interactions within the child's zone of proximal development. For example, within the mother–child book-reading interactions discussed by Ninio and Bruner (1978), the child's ability to quickly understand the (ever-changing) structure of this interactional framework (i.e., to acquire a book-reading script) allowed the mother to use it as a setting within which to make increasingly complex communicative demands.

Shared knowledge of some sort, whether or not it takes the form of shared scripts, seems essential for the types of carefully adjusted input that characterize interactive learning. Extensive shared knowledge enables the tutor to judge, and to capitalize on, what the child already knows. If there is a mismatch between what the child and tutor know, then the tutor may be unable to establish an interaction that is meaningful to the child. Thus, it would seem that the success of instructional interactions will be jointly determined by the child's individual characteristics (e.g., IQ, anxiety level, preexisting knowledge), the nature and context of the learning interaction, and the extent of shared knowledge between the tutor and child.

These factors affect the outcome of assessment, as well as instructional, interactions. This is apparent both in experiments designed to assess cognitive development and in intelligence-testing situations. In many assessment situations, cognitive failures or incompetencies may best be understood as instances in which a cognitive ability is inadequately elicited or insufficiently supported. However, assessment is often carried out with an implicit assumption that the existence or nonexistence of cognitive abilities is an absolute state, and that, if they exist, they will be used. This assumption leads investigators and testers to conclude—often erroneously—that when the child does not use an ability in a setting in which its use would be appropriate, the child simply does not have the ability at all.

If, instead, cognitive abilities are recognized as being socially constrained and contextually bound, a clearer conception of their development can be formulated. Experimenters, testers, teachers, and parents can arrange the environment and interactive context so that the young child appears competent or incompetent. Many investigators (e.g., Brown, 1976; DeLoache, 1980; Donaldson, 1978; French & Nelson, 1982; Gelman, 1978) have recently provided striking illustrations of young children displaying cognitive abilities previously thought to be outside their range of competencies. Those occasions on which the child demonstrates seemingly surprising levels of ability are those for which the social agent has taken care to arrange the task demands and social environment so that they are familiar and/or meaningful to the child. Currently, a great deal of research is directed toward simplifying and clarifying experimental tasks to discover what cognitive abilities the preschooler can display within maximally supportive contexts (see Donaldson, 1978; Gelman, 1978; and Gerlman & Baillargeon, 1983 and for selective reviews of this research).

The growing realization that contextual and social factors have substantial effects on the acquisition and display of cognitive abilities is having an impact on the way investigators go about studying cognitive development. In the early 1980s, there has been concern with adopting more naturalistic measures of cognitive abilities (DeLoache, 1980), with explicating the effects of familiarity upon performance (Bremner, 1982), with tapping into the child's mental representations of her or his world (Nelson & Gruendel, 1981), and with observing learning as it takes place within social interactions (Brown, 1982; Hall & Day, 1982; Ninio & Bruner, 1978; Petitto, 1983). These approaches are yielding a much more detailed depiction of the course of cognitive development than the relatively simple stage models of the past. However, the process of development is undoubtedly exceedingly complex and multiply determined, and adequate accounts are unlikely to be parsimonious.

References

Bee, H. L. Parent–child interaction and distractibility in 9 year old children. *Merrill–Palmer Quarterly*, 1967, *13*, 175–190.

Bee, H. L., Van Egeren, L. F., Streissguth, A. P., Nyman, B. A., & Leckie, S. L. Social class differences in maternal teaching strategies and speech patterns. *Developmental Psychology*, 1969, *1*, 726–734.

Bing, E. Effect of childrearing practices on development of differential cognitive abilities. *Child Development*, 1963, *34*, 631–645.

Bloom, B. S. *Stability and change in human characteristics.* New York: Wiley, 1964.

Bradley, R. H., & Caldwell, B. M. Early home environment and changes in mental test performance in children from 6 to 36 months. *Developmental Psychology,* 1976, *12*, 93–97. (a)

Bradley, R. H., & Caldwell, B. M. The relation of infants' home-environments to mental test performance at fifty-four months: A follow-up study. *Child Development*, 1976, *47*, 1172–1174. (b)

Bradley, R. H., & Caldwell, B. M. Home observation for measurement of the environment: A validation study of screening efficiency. *American Journal of Mental Deficiency*, 1977, *81*, 417–420.

Bradley, R. H., & Caldwell, B. M. Screening the environment. *American Journal of Orthopsychiatry*, 1978, *48*, 114–130.

Bradley, R. H., Caldwell, B. M., & Elardo, R. Home environment and cognitive development in the first 2 years: A cross-lagged panel analysis. *Developmental Psychology*, 1979, *15*, 246–250.

Bremner, J. G. *The infant's environment and development of early knowledge.* Paper presented at the Annual Conference of the Developmental Section of the British Psychological Society, Durham, 1982.

Brown, A. L. Learning and development: The problems of compatibility, access, and induction. *Human Development*, 1982, *25*, 89–115.

Brown, A. L., Bransford, J. D., Ferrara, R. A., & Campione, J. C. Learning, remembering and understanding. In P. H. Mussen (Ed.), *Handbook of child psychology* (vol. 3): *Cognitive development.* (4th ed.) New York: Wiley, 1983.

Brown, A. L., & French L. The zone of potential development: Implications for intelligence testing in the year 2000. *Intelligence*, 1979, *3*, 253–271.

Brown, R. *A first language: The early stages.* Cambridge, MA: Harvard University Press, 1973.

Bruner, J. S. The social context of language acquisition. *Language and Communication*, 1981, *1*, 155–178.

Caldwell, B. M. On designing supplementary environments for early child development. *BAEYC reports.* Boston Association for the Education of Young Children. October 1968, pp. 1–11.

Cazden, C. B. Performance before competence: Assistance to child discourse in the zone of proximal development. *The Quarterly Newsletter of the Laboratory of Comparative Human Cognition*, 1981, *3*, 5–8.

Cazden, C. B., Cox, M., Dickinson, D., Steinberg, Z., & Stone, C. "You all gonna hafta listen": Peer teaching in a primary classroom. In W. A. Collins (Ed.), *The Minnesota Symposia on Child Psychology* (Vol. 12). Hillsdale, NJ: Erlbaum, 1979.

Clarke-Stewart, K. A. Interactions between mothers and their young children: Characteristics and consequences. *Monographs of the Society for Research in Child Development*, 1973, *38*, (Serial No. 153).

Cohen, S. E., & Beckwith, L. Preterm infant interaction with the caregiver in the first year of life and competence at age two. *Child Development*, 1979, *50*, 767–776.

Connor, A. *An investigation of the transition from other regulation to self regulation in a six year old child.* Unpublished mansucript, University of Rochester, Rochester, NY, 1983.

Day, J. D. The zone of proximal development. In M. Pressley & J. Levin (Eds.), *Cognitive strategy research: Psychological foundations.* New York: Springer–Verlag, 1983.

DeLoache, J. S. Naturalistic studies of memory for object location in very young children. *New Directions for Child Development*, 1980, *10*, 17–32.

Donaldson, M. *Children's Minds.* New York: W. W. Norton & Company, 1978.

Ellis, S., & Rogoff, B. The strategies and efficacy of child versus adult teachers. *Child Development*, 1982, *53*, 730–735.

French, L. A. *But of course preschoolers understand the meaning of 'but'!* Paper presented at the Sixth Annual Boston University Conference on Language Development, October 1981.

French, L. A. *Language in scripts*. Paper presented at the Biennial Meeting of the Society for Research in Child Development, Detroit, April 1983.

French, L. A., & Nelson, K. Temporal knowledge expressed in preschoolers' descriptions of familiar activities. *Papers and Reports on Child Language Development*, 1981, *20*, 61–69.

French, L. A., & Nelson, K. Taking away the supportive context: Preschoolers talk about the "then-and-there." *The Quarterly Newsletter of the Laboratory of Comparative Human Cognition*, 1982, *40*, 1–6.

French, L. A., & Nelson, K. *Ifs, ors, and buts about preschoolers' understanding of relational terms*. Unpublished manuscript, University of Rochester, Rochester, NY: 1983.

Gardner, W., & Rogoff, B. The role of instruction in memory development: Some methodological choices. *The Quarterly Newsletter of the Laboratory of Comparative Human Cognition*, 1982, *4*, 6–12.

Gearhart, M., & Newman, D. Learning to draw a picture: The social context of an individual activity. *Discourse Processes*, 1980, *3*, 169–184.

Gelman, R. Cognitive development. *Annual Review of Psychology*, 1978, *29*, 297–332.

Gelman, R., & Baillargeon, R. A. Review of some Piagetian concepts. In P. H. Mussen (Ed.) *Handbook of child psychology* (Vol. 3): *Cognitive development* (4th ed.) New York: Wiley, 1983.

Hall, L. K., & Day, J. D. *A comparison of the zone of proximal development in learning disabled, mentally retarded, and normal children*. Paper presented at the meetings of the American Educational Research Association, New York, 1982.

Hess, R. D., & Shipman, V. C. Early experience and the specialization of cognitive modes in children. *Child Development*, 1965, *36*, 869–886.

Hess, R. D., & Shipman, V. C. Cognitive elements in maternal behavior. In J. P. Hill (Ed.), *Minnesota symposia on child psychology* (Vol. 1). Minneapolis: University of Minnesota Press, 1967.

Hood, L., McDermott, R., & Cole, M. "Let's try to make it a good day": Some not so simple ways. *Discourse Processes*, 1980, *3*, 155–168.

Hunt, J. McV. *Intelligence and experience*. New York: Ronald Press, 1961.

Kail, M. Etude génétique des présupposes de certains morphèmes grammaticaux. Un exemple: Mais. *Approaches du language, Publications de la Sorbonne, serie études* (Tome 16) Paris, 1980.

Kail, M., & Weissenborn, J. *A developmental cross-linguistic study of the processing of lexical presuppositions: French 'mais' and German 'aber' vs. 'sondern'*. Paper presented at the Fifth Annual Boston University Conference on Language Development, Boston, 1980.

Lewis, M., & Goldberg, S. Perceptual–cognitive development in infancy: A generalized expectancy model as a function of the mother–infant interaction. *Merrill–Palmer Quarterly*, 1969, *15*, 81–100.

Lucariello, J. *Context and conversations*. Paper presented at the Biennial Meetings of the Society for Research in Child Development, Detroit, 1983.

Lucariello, J., & Nelson, K. *Situational variation in mother–child interaction*. Paper presented at the Third International Conference on Infant Studies, Austin, TX, 1982.

Luria, A. The problem of the cultural development of the child. *Journal of Genetic Psychology*, 1928, *36*, 493–506.

Luria, A. R. An objective approach to the study of the abnormal child. *American Journal of Orthopsychiatry*, 1961, *31*, 1–14.

Macnamara, J. Cognitive basis of language learning in infants. *Psychological Review*, 1972, *79*, 1–13.

Miller, G., & Chomsky, N. Finitary models of language users. In R. Luce, R. Bush, & E.

Galanter (Eds.), *Handbook of mathematical psychology* (Vol. 2). New York: Wiley, 1963.

Nelson, K. Structure and strategy in learning to talk. *Monographs of the Society for Research in Child Develo* 1973, 38,(1–2, Serial No. 149).

Nelson, K. H   en represent knowledge of their world in and out of language. In R. Si   *ren's thinking: What develops?* Hillsdale, NJ: Erlbaum, 1978.

Nelson, K. *Ch   ldren's scripts for familiar events.* Paper presented at the Annual Mee ican Psychological Association, Montreal, 1980.

Nelson, K. *Mak   tic development in early childhood.* New York: Academic Press, in pr

Nelson, K., & Gru   ning it's lunchtime: A scriptal view of children's dialogues. *Discourse Pro   73–94.

Nelson, K., & Grue   neralized event representations: Basic building blocks of cognitive devel   4. Lamb & A. L. Brown (Eds.), *Advances in developmental psychology,* (Vol   illsdale, NJ: Erlbaum, 1981.

Nelson, K., & Seidman, S. *Playing with scripts,* Unpublished manuscript, 1983.

Ninio, A., & Bruner, J. S. The achievement and antecedents of labelling. *Journal of Child Language,* 1978, 5, 1–15.

Olson, D. R. Culture, technology, and intellect. In L. B. Resnick (Ed.), *The nature of intelligence.* Hillsdale, NJ: Erlbaum, 1976.

Petitto, A. L. *Long division of labor: In support of an interactive theory of learning.* Unpublished manuscript, University of Rochester, Rochester, NY, 1983.

Piaget, J. *The Child's Conception of Time.* London: Routledge and Kegan Paul, 1969.

Seidman, S. *Eventful play: Preschoolers' scripts for pretense.* Paper presented at the Biennial Meetings of the Society for Research in Child Development, Detroit, 1983.

Snow, C. E. Conversations with children. In P. Fletcher & M. Garmon (Eds.), *Language acquisition.* New York: Cambridge University Press, 1979.

Vygotsky, L. S. The problem of the cultural development of the child. *Journal of Genetic Psychology,* 1929, 36, 415–434.

Vygotsky, L. S. *Thought and language.* (E. Haufman & G. Vakar, Eds. & Trans.), Cambridge, MA: MIT Press, 1962.

Vygotsky, L. *Mind in society: The development of higher psychological processes.* M. Cole, V. John-Steiner, S. Scritmer, E. Souberman (Eds.), Cambridge, MA: Harvard University Press, 1978.

Wachs, T. Utilization of a Piagetian approach in the investigation of early experience effects: A research strategy and some illustrative data. *Merrill–Palmer Quarterly,* 1976, 22, 11–30.

Wertsch, J. V. From social interaction to higher psychological processes: A clarification and application of Vygotsky's theory. *Human Development,* 1979, 22, 1–22.

Wertsch, J., McNamee, G., Budwig, N., & McLane, J. The adult–child dyad as a problem-solving system. *Child Development,* 1980, 51, 1215–1221.

Wertsch, J. V., & Stone, C. A. Microgenesis as a tool for developmental analysis. *The Quarterly Newsletter of the Laboratory of Comparative Human Cognition,* 1978, 2, 15–18.

Wozniak, R. H. Psychology and education of the learning disabled child in the Soviet Union. In W. Cruickshank & D. P. Hallahan (Eds.), *Perceptual and learning disabilities in children* (Vol. 1): *Psychoeducational practices.* Syracuse: Syracuse University Press, 1975.

Yarrow, L. J., Pedersen, F. A., & Rubenstein, J. Mother–infant interaction and development in infancy. In P. H. Leiderman, S. R. Tulkin, & A. Rosenfeld (Eds.) *Culture and infancy: Variations in the human experience.* New York: Academic Press, 1977.

CHAPTER 3

Developmental Trends in the
Metamemory–Memory Behavior
Relationship: An Integrative Review*

Wolfgang Schneider

Introduction

Since the beginning of the 1970s, increasing attention has been directed toward the development of children's awareness of their own memory. This phenomenon has been termed *metamemory* by John Flavell (1971), who broadly defined it as the individual's potentially verbalizable knowledge concerning any aspect of information storage and retrieval. Whereas the interest in metamemory development has been growing rapidly since then, documenting the construct's general usefulness in a wide area of different memory situations, there are at least two critical points that deserve special consideration: (1) the conceptualization of the construct and (2) its status as a predictor of actual memory behavior. While the latter is the topic of the present chapter and is discussed in more detail, we first concentrate on some problems related to the definition of metamemory.

The first taxonomy of classes of memory knowledge was provided in the metamemory interview study by Kreutzer, Leonard, and Flavell (1975).

*This manuscript was prepared during a stay at the Department of Psychology, Stanford University, which was made possible by a grant from the Stiftung Volkswagenwerk, Hannover, Federal Republic of Germany.

57

Subsequently, Flavell and Wellman (1977) offered a more systematic and elaborated attempt to classify different types or contents of metamemory. Although alternative conceptualizations have been presented (see Chi, 1983), and more extended and general models of metacognition have been developed since (see Flavell, 1978, 1979, 1981; Kluwe, 1982), the classification scheme of Flavell and Wellman has been used in the majority of empirical studies concerned with the development of metamemory. According to this taxonomy, a distinction between two types of memory knowledge can be made: (1) the *sensitivity* category refers to the child's knowledge that some situations require intentional mnemonic behavior and others not; (2) the *variable* category refers to the knowledge that performance in a memory situation is influenced by a number of factors or variables. Within the latter type of metamemory, the person, task, and strategy variables are differentiated. In brief, the *person category* concerns the knowledge about one's own general memory limitations and capacities as well as the ability to monitor concrete experiences in a memory task (here-and-now-memory monitoring). *Task variables* refer to the awareness that task demands or properties of input information can influence memory performance. *Strategy variables* correspond to the individual's knowledge of storage and retrieval strategies.

It should be noted that this taxonomy of metamemory was not intended to be exhaustive, and the authors pointed out that they did not attempt to define the concept precisely. In their review articles, Cavanaugh and Perlmutter (1982) and Wellman (1983) emphasized that the vagueness of the metamemory conceptualization seems to be responsible for some of the inherent problems: as is typical of ill-defined concepts, there is agreement with regard to the central instances, but the underlying disagreement of current approaches to metamemory becomes obvious when more detailed analyses of the phenomenon are considered. Thus, while most definitions of metamemory include long-term knowledge about task demands, strategy, and person variables (as well as knowledge about one's own current memory states), it is uncertain and questionable (see Cavanaugh & Perlmutter, 1982) whether the conceptualization should also include the use of memory knowledge (i.e., the translation of memory knowledge into efficient executive processes). With other words, the problem is if metamemory should be considered a mixture of what Chi (1983) has called *declarative* knowledge (i.e., factual and verbalizable knowledge about memory) and *procedural* knowledge (i.e., knowledge about production rules). As a consequence, investigators should state explicitly and in more detail the instances they subsume under the concept of metamemory in order to eliminate possible sources of confusion.

A second problem in connection with metamemory, and the one of primary interest in the present article, concerns the role it plays in the determination of actual memory behavior. As Brown (1978) stated, one of the most convincing arguments in favor of studying metamemory was that there must be a close relationship between the individual's knowledge of memory and her or his performance in different memory tasks. Similarly, Hagen (1975) in his commentary on the Kreutzer et al. (1975) interview study emphasized the need for research demonstrating the applicability, generality, and validity of the metamemory interview data. The possibility of predicting and explaining memory behavior attracted most investigators of metamemory and stimulated empirical research.

On the other hand, Flavell and Wellman (1977; Flavell, 1978; Wellman, 1983) pointed out that although conceptual analysis of the problem is necessary to understand whether, when, and how metamemory and memory behavior *might* be related, they argued that one cannot expect to find a strong connection between memory knowledge and memory activity. That is, there is no reason to assume that a strong metamemory–memory behavior relationship should be found regardless of subjects' age or task demands. On the contrary, various examples were given demonstrating that under certain circumstances (e.g., lack of motivation, problems with effort allocation) a strong relationship is rather unlikely. Although the authors do believe that metamemory will have a substantial impact on memory behavior when the motivational factors are favorable, their analyses indicate that this relationship and its developmental changes are complicated subjects.

In view of this theoretical complexity, it should be interesting to look at the existing empirical evidence of the metamemory–memory behavior relationship. At first glance, the results seem discouraging. Mainly relying on the negative findings of the often-cited studies by Kelly, Scholnick, Travers, and Johnson (1976) and by Salatas and Flavell (1976), several more recent articles have concluded that the empirical evidence for a close tie between metamemory and memory behavior is notably lacking (e.g., Brown, Bransford, Ferrara, & Campione, 1983; Chi, in press). In a more extended evaluation including about a dozen empirical studies, Cavanaugh and Perlmutter (1982) also found that the majority of these have yielded moderate or low correlations between children's declarable knowledge of memory and their performance on certain memory tasks.

In contrast, Wellman (1983) cited several investigations reporting more substantial links between metamemory and memory behavior. A closer examination of the possible reasons for this discrepancy reveals that while Wellman concentrates on the memory *monitoring* literature, Cavanaugh and Perlmutter focus mainly on investigations concerned with the development of *organizational strategies*. Thus, the strength of the relationship between memory knowledge and memory behavior may partly depend on the type of knowledge and behavior studied. Studies referring to the dynamic aspect of the person variable of the Flavell and Wellman taxonomy (here-and-now memory monitoring) appear to show a more positive relationship, whereas those concentrating on the task or strategy variable (importance of organizational strategies) in most cases fail to show a metamemory–memory behavior connection. This conclusion is tentative, however, because these two reviews are clearly not exhaustive, as indicated by their surprisingly small overlap in cited research. These articles mainly concentrated on conceptual problems, and the metamemory–memory behavior relation was only one of several interesting points they discussed. Thus, a more exhaustive review appears to be necessary to get a more reliable answer to the question how metamemory and memory behavior are related.

From a theoretical point of view, there is no reason to expect to find a single, uniform relation between memory knowledge and memory behavior. Most of the empirical investigations have been developmental in nature, assessing the connection between memory knowledge and actual memory performance in different age groups and for different tasks. Consequently, it is the purpose of the present article to evaluate both the developmental pattern of the metamemory to memory behavior link and the dependence of this link on selected task variables.

As noted earlier, the somewhat fuzzy conceptualization of metamemory makes it necessary to give an explicit description of the measures accepted as characteristics of the construct in the present review. In the present review, studies were judged to empirically assess the metamemory–memory behavior relationship when they include either verbal or nonverbal measures of memory knowledge and related them to separate measures of memory activity. Data from interviews and questionnaires are typical verbal measures of metamemory found in studies concerned with organizational strategies, whereas different kinds of judgment (e.g., feeling of knowing, performance prediction, judgment of recall readiness) are typically used in studies analyzing memory monitoring. In addition to these verbal reports, more indirect nonverbal measures are also accepted when they appeared to indicate metamnemonic activities. Examples include the underlining of text units judged as important for understanding and reproducing prose and reaction time measures indicating memory search processes, the latter showing a high correlation with (verbal) feeling of knowing judgments (cf. Moore & Haith, 1979; for a more detailed discussion see Cavanaugh & Perlmutter, 1982).

Interestingly, the selection of measures used to assess metamemory appears to depend on the category of metamemory (e.g., knowledge of person variables versus knowledge of task demands) under investigation.

Memory monitoring studies generally used more indirect, derived metamemory indicators, compared with the verbal measures found in studies concerned with knowledge of task variables. Furthermore, the latter allows a more differential assessment of the metamemory-memory behavior relationship, because different forms of memory behavior (e.g., strategy use during information storage and information retrieval as well as amount of recall) could be related to memory knowledge. In contrast, memory monitoring studies simply assessed the correspondence between knowledge and memory performance. In view of these apparent differences between the two major types of metamemory-memory behavior relations, an attempt will be made in the present study to describe the different task requirements in terms of the complexity of skills or cognitive processes involved. It is hypothesized that the main differences in developmental patterns found for different types of metamemory-memory behavior relationship are due to different levels of memory tasks difficulty. Consequently, as a variety of experimental settings are encountered in investigations into both major types of relationship, it is further assumed that within-type differences in developmental patterns will be larger than between-type differences.

According to the preceding selection criteria, approximately 50 studies were found assessing the metamemory–memory behavior relation. Our classification of the research is evident in the organization of the review. In the first major section, studies analyzing memory monitoring are considered. Although alternative categorizations seem possible, two types of studies are distinguished with regard to the kind of memory monitoring process analyzed. In investigations assessing performance prediction, judgments were made *prior* to study. Thus, estimations of performance are required in advance of the actual memory task (mostly in the span prediction paradigm).

The second type of studies focused on what Brown et al. (1983) and Wellman (1983) have labeled *effort and attention allocation strategies*. While these studies investigate different memory situations (e.g., retrieval vs study effort) and differ with respect to the degree of complexity of the judgment required, in all the studies of the second type the knowledge of the *current* state of one's own memory determines memory performance.

The second section is devoted to studies concerned with the child's knowledge of organizational and elaborational strategies and their use in actual memory tasks. While most of these studies focused on the use of clustering strategies, a few studies assessed children's knowledge of various elaborational strategies that could be used in paired associate tasks.

The third major section covers studies that include a training period. These training and intervention studies were first developed to establish memory strategies and test metamnemonic activities in educable mentally retarded children (see Brown, 1978). But in later studies, this experimental design was found to be useful in the analysis of the metamemory–memory behavior relationship in normal populations. As Borkowski, Reid, and Kurtz (1984) pointed out, the somewhat unsatisfying empirical evidence for this relationship from studies employing the free-recall learning paradigm might be due to the fact that preexisting and well-established organizational strategies can be used. These function automatically, so there may be no need to activate metamnemonic knowledge in this type of situation. Training studies normally include a strategy transfer task, which requires a decision about whether to use, to modify, or to abandon a previously learned strategy. This transfer paradigm may provide a more favorable context for the appearance of a connection between metamemory and memory performance.

Finally, a statistical procedure for summarizing research findings is presented in the fourth section. The traditional method of literature review has been repeatedly criticized for lack of analytical precision as a result of the idiosyncracies of the reviewer's perspective or neglect of important information in the primary data (see Cooper, 1979; Cooper & Rosenthal, 1980). Procedures of numerically combining the results of independent studies, labeled *meta-analysis* by Glass (1976, 1978; Glass, McGaw & Smith, 1981), were used to provide a quality control for the literary review presented in the first three sections. Although these statistical procedures have been suggested as an alternative to the narrative review, it should be noted that the present metaanalysis of correlational studies faced some problems that seem to restrict its general value. Although the guidelines given by Glass (1978) helped to overcome the difficulty of converting a variety of summary statistics (e.g., phi coefficients, contingency coefficients, t values) into product–moment correlation coefficients, there remained several studies that did not contain statistical information of the kind that could be used for this type of transformation. As a consequence, the intended quality control could not be secured for all parts of the literary review. Thus, the metaanalysis was considered to supplement and not to replace the traditional procedure.

The Use of Memory Knowledge in Memory Monitoring Tasks

Performance Prediction

Studies concerning the metamemory–memory behavior relationship have been confined to a limited number of experimental tasks and procedures. A considerable proportion of these studies concentrated on the performance prediction paradigm, particularly the memory span prediction task. Recall that the metamemory–memory behavior relationship usually has been assessed by comparing children's judgments with their actual memory performance. But here, the relationship between these two measures (i.e., prediction accuracy) is regarded as a measure of *metamemory*. Consequently, no independent measure of memory is available in these studies. Nevertheless, several investigators tried to connect children's metamemory with selected indicators of memory behavior by comparing prediction accuracy with the amount of recall. Interestingly, only a few authors explained why these two variables should be expected to be highly correlated; but generally, it was speculated that proficient memorizers should also be more aware of their memory capacities and limitations. Before these attempts are discussed in more detail, a short survey of the numerous developmental studies of memory-span prediction is given to determine the developmental pattern of metamemory for this type of task.

Memory Span in Serial Recall Tasks

In the classical study of span prediction, Flavell, Friedrichs, and Hoyt (1970) asked preschool children, kindergarteners, second and fourth graders to predict their immediate memory span. Successively longer sequences of pictures showing familiar objects were briefly presented to the child, who had to indicate whether she or he could recall them in correct serial order. The prediction process continued until the subject judged the series of pictures too long to reproduce or until a series of 10 pictures had been presented. Next, the child's actual memory span was assessed using the same procedure. The main result was that the two youngest groups tended to considerably overestimate their memory ability: more than half of them predicted a span of 10 items, while fewer than one fourth of the older children did so. Although mean predicted span was higher than mean actual span at each grade level, the difference was considerably smaller for the two older groups as a result of both an increase in actual span and a decrease in their predicted span. According to these results, only children of about 7 years and older seem to be able to assess their memory span limitations accurately. It is worth noting, however, that about one third of the younger children could predict their own span with surprising skill. In a replication of this part of Flavell et al.'s (1970) study with kindergarteners, Markman (1973) got results very similar to those of Flavell et al.: about one half of the 5-year-old children made unrealistic predictions, judging that they could recall all 10 items in serial order.

Subsequent investigations attempted to discover why young children have difficulties in monitoring their memory by either using additional procedures or modifying the original one. According to one hypothesis, the abstractness of the memory task might have caused the inaccurate predictions of young children. Indeed, a series of experiments have shown that preschoolers and kindergarteners can accurately predict their performance on simple motor tasks (see Markman, 1973). Similarly, young children benefited considerably when the prediction task was presented in a meaningful context such as a board game (see Justice & Bray, 1974) or a simulated shopping situation (Wippich, 1981).

A second hypothesis assumed that young children's difficulties in predicting memory span were due to their lack of experience in thinking about their own memory. But here, the empirical evidence is somewhat equivocal. While some studies demonstrated that kindergarteners could benefit from training trials (Markman, 1973) or feedback and experience with the memory task (Chi, 1978; Justice & Bray, 1979; Moynahan, 1976; Wippich, 1981), the results of other studies do not support the conclusion that lack of experience causes young children's difficulties. For example, Yussen and Levy (1975) and Wippich (1980) replicated the findings of Flavell et al. (1970), despite the fact that they provided opportunity for the children to experience the difficulty of the memory task either by reversing the sequence of the estimation procedure (Yussen & Levy, 1975) or by assessing the actual memory span first (Wippich, 1980).

All in all, these findings indicate that preschoolers have enormous difficulties with the unfamiliar-span prediction task. They apparently do not benefit from actual experience with serial recall unless specific prompts are given. On the other hand, there exists some empirical evidence indicating that preschoolers do possess the metamnemonic abilities to handle this problem when task conditions are favorable.

Another series of investigations focused on predictions of the *content* of future recall rather than the amount of recallable stimuli. It was assumed that predictions on an item-by-item basis could provide a more sensitive measure of developmental differences in children's awareness of their own retrieval limitations. In particular, it seemed possible that the unrealistic overpredictions of young children obtained in the span prediction task were due to their difficulties in discriminating memorizable from nonmemorizable stimulus items. This hypothesis can easily be tested by using signal detection analysis, especially its parameter d', which indicates the distinctiveness in the distributions of memorizable and nonmemorizable items (the greater the ability to correctly predict which stimuli will or will not be remembered, the greater d').

While Kelly, Scholnick, Travers, and Johnson (1976) and Monroe and Lange (1977) found that the rate of correct predictions of recall (i.e., hits) was rather high even for preschoolers and kindergarteners, Worden and Sladewski-Awig (1982) pointed out that neither of these two studies examined response bias as a second possible source of estimation inaccuracy, varying independently of d'. The author's assumption was that sensitivity for memorizable and nonmemorizable items may be as good in preschool children as in older children, but that their poorer performance in prediction of future recall could be due to a more liberal response bias (i.e., a greater proportion of hits and false alarms). In their study, kindergarteners, second, fourth, and sixth graders were nearly equally accurate in discriminating between recallable and nonrecallable picture stimuli. Additional analyses of response bias, however, supported the authors' hypothesis that younger children responded more liberally, obviously using weak signals to predict correct recall. Thus, the younger children's aforementioned overprediction of serial recall seemed to be mainly due to their increased false alarm rates, a result also found in the Kelly et al. study.

Taken together, these findings from studies investigating children's predictions of the content of recallable stimuli can explain the reasons for young children's bad metamemory in this task. They indicate that preschooler's metamemory concerning the prediction of serial recall is generally not well developed. On the other hand, young elementary school children demonstrate accurate memory knowledge independent of the type of span-prediction procedure.

But how does metamemory influence the amount of recall in this memory task? One of the most-cited studies (Kelly et al., 1976) concluded that no relationship between prediction accuracy and memory performance could be found. A closer examination of the experimental design, however, showed that it differed in several aspects from the aforementioned traditional span prediction tasks. In this study, the subjects (kindergarteners, first, and fourth graders) did not have to retrieve the items themselves, only their spatial locations. Because the recall test was nonverbal (children had to replace the items in serial order) and the list-estimation procedure included feedback, the prediction task was considerably simplified, providing optimal conditions for the younger children. Consequently, the authors failed to detect age differences in prediction accuracy, which was rather high at each grade level (.75 in average). On the other hand, fourth graders recalled significantly more than the younger children. As metamemory was nearly equally high across all age groups regardless of the number of items actually recalled, the correlation between metamemory and recall was necessarily nonsignificant. There seems to be reason to believe that the nonsignificant relation between metamemory and memory performance was due to a ceiling effect in the prediction task. The connection between knowledge and behavior may be different when analyzed separately for each age group, instead of across age groups as done by Kelly et al. (1976).

Empirical support for this possibility comes from two investigations that compared the prediction of serial recall versus recognition (Levin, Yussen, DeRose, & Pressley, 1977; Yussen & Berman, 1981). As Levin et al. (1977) emphasized, it has been demonstrated in several studies that recognition memory is high for both children and adults (see Brown, 1975). Older children and even adults, however, do not seem to be aware of the enormous capacity of their recognition memory. Thus, the authors assumed that, in contrast to the prediction for serial recall, no significant age differences should be expected on the recognition task; the usually high predictions of younger children should correspond more closely with their actual recognition performance, while the incomplete awareness of the older subjects might result in an underestimation of their recognition capacity. This hypothesis was empirically confirmed for all groups of subjects (first graders, third graders, and college students) in their sample. More important, while in the recall condition, high correlations between prediction accuracy and actual performance were obtained even for the youngest children, this relationship turned out to be rather weak for all groups in the recognition condition. Yussen and Berman (1981) were able to replicate and generalize these findings for groups of first, third, and fifth graders. Again, the correlations between metamemory and memory performance were high for both recall problems (i.e., recall for word lists and sentence lists), but only weak for the two corresponding recognition tasks, regardless of age. Similarly, Wippich (1981) reported significant negative correlations between the amount of overestimation and the amount of recall when memory span prediction was assessed in the simulated shopping situation. Interestingly, no relationship could be found when the kindergarteners in this study were presented with the traditional (laboratory) type of span-prediction task.

In sum, these results confirm the speculation that proficient memorizers are more aware of their memory and its limitations when prediction of serial recall is considered. This is true even for very young children (kindergarteners) provided that the task is presented in a meaningful context. On the other hand, it also has been shown that these conclusions cannot be generalized to different classes of memory problems. There is strong evidence that the relationship between metamemory and memory performance in a recognition task is generally modest even for adolescents and adults.

Prediction of Recall for Differently Structured Lists

Many studies have demonstrated that even young children usually show an increase in recall when they are asked to learn items from categorizable word lists, compared with their performance on lists with un-related items (see Tenney, 1975). Several studies investigated children's spontaneous awareness of this fact by using the memory prediction para-digm. In a study by Moynahan (1973), first, third, and fifth graders were required to predict the relative ease of free recall for pairs of categorized and noncategorized picture lists. Children were first asked why they thought the chosen list was easier to remember and then asked to recall the lists. Here, metamemory (i.e., awareness of the facilitative effect of categorization) was assumed to particularly improve children's recall of categorizable lists, compared with their performance on unrelated lists. Thus, the difference between subjects' recall of clusterable and nonclus-terable lists was chosen as the performance measure and related to pre-diction accuracy. Moynahan found that subjects generally recalled more from categorized lists than from noncategorized lists, and that recall in-creased with age. When asked to explain their choice, third and fifth grad-ers more frequently referred to the categorical characteristics than first graders. A similar age trend was found for prediction accuracy, but it must be emphasized that first graders' scores still were significantly above chance expectation. But, although the correlations between prediction accuracy and recall performance were positive for all tasks and grades, none reached significance.

Yussen, Levin, Berman, and Palm (1979), using a similar design, in-cluded picture lists organized according to physical (shape) categories, in addition to lists containing semantic or random categories. On the meta-memory task, first, third, and fifth graders had to predict which of the three lists would be easiest to remember. For recall, subjects were first asked to sort the items according to one of the three categories, and then were required to name the pictures after they had been covered. Children at all grade levels judged the semantic organization to be significantly eas-ier than random organization, but only the oldest subjects also rated se-mantic organization more effective than physical categorization. With regard to recall, children in the semantic sorting condition were superior to all other subjects. Similar to the findings of Moynahan (1973), no sig-nificant correlations between metamemory (i.e., prediction) and actual memory performance were detected, although several of these were highly positive.

The results of these two studies are consistent with those usually re-ported in span prediction studies. Spontaneous awareness of the impact of different list organizations on ease of retrieval is found even in the youngest age groups. The metamemory–memory behavior relationship, however, is considerably more modest than that found in the span-pre-diction tasks. Although this might be partly due to the rather crude metamemory measures used in the studies of Moynahan (1973) and Yussen et al. (1979), the requirements (i.e., the identification of list properties combined with the awareness of their implications for recall) appear to be more difficult for younger children, compared with the requirements of the span prediction tasks. Empirical support for this assumption comes from the observation that first graders usually did well in the span-prediction tasks, but had considerable problems when required to predict recall for differently structured lists.

Effort and Attention Allocation Strategies for Rote Memory Tasks

All studies discussed up to this point have assessed children's general knowledge about the properties of their own memory, its capacities, and its limitations. In contrast, a considerable body of research concentrated on what Flavell and Wellman (1977) have called "here-and-now memory monitoring"—that is, the ability to assess the transient processes and to interpret the current state of memory.

Allocation of Study Effort

In the study–time apportionment task introduced by Masur, McIntyre, and Flavell (1973), first and third graders, together with college students, were given lists of pictures to learn in a multitrial, free-recall task. In all trials but the first, subjects were allowed to select half of the items for extra study. Planfulness in this task was defined as (1) *attention* allocation—that is, awareness of the current state of the to-be-retrieved items, and more important, (2) study *effort* allocation—that is, the distribution of study time in such a way that the previously not-recalled difficult items got the most attention. Both third graders and college students did select previously missed items for further study, whereas first graders appeared to select randomly, thus demonstrating poor metamemory. When the metamemory–memory behavior relationship was considered, it turned out that use of the appropriate strategy increased memory performance only for college students. Third graders seemed to benefit only slightly from the more sophisticated strategy.

Bisanz, Vesonder, and Voss (1978) used paired-associate lists to study the development of what they called the "two-state discrimination–utilization strategy." According to their hypothesis, an effective acquisition strategy based on memory monitoring consists of (1) discrimination of recalled and missed items, and (2) the effective distribution of study time and/or effort—that is, greater processing effort for the previously missed items. The authors found that the discrimination–utilization strategy used by fifth graders and college students could not be detected in their youngest subjects (first and third graders). While the studies of Masur et al. (1973) and Bisanz et al. (1978) corroborated the findings of Berch and Evans (1973) that younger children are capable of distinguishing recalled from missed items, their results indicated a time lag between when children are able to identify missed items correctly and when they select these items for additional study. According to Brown (1978), the major difficulty of the study-time apportionment task has to do with the problem that the previously recalled items have to be maintained in memory while the previously missed items are selected for further study. As the subject is likely to forget the items already recalled if she or he does not work with them during the extra study time period, two activities have to be coordinated to cope with the task demands: (1) concentrating on the previously missed items, and (2) repeating the previously remembered items. Thus, the poor memory performance of first graders and also third graders in this task could be partly due to their difficulties in using appropriate rehearsal strategies. In contrast, fifth graders apparently not only know what activities have to be selected for this kind of task, but also do use these strategies efficiently.

On the other hand, Rogoff, Newcombe, and Kagan (1974) demonstrated that effort-allocation strategies of young elementary school children can be effective when recognition memory tasks are used. When asked to study pictures for a memory task, 8-year-old children adjusted their inspection times according to the length of the delay period (a few minutes, a day, or a week) between inspection and test. In contrast, 4- and 6-year-olds did not show longer inspection times when longer delays were announced. Furthermore, a significant negative correlation between the number of recognition errors and inspection time was detected, indicating the efficiency of strategic behavior.

In sum, knowledge about the successful use of effort-allocation strategies in the study-time apportionment paradigm seems to develop rather late in childhood. In case of free recall or paired-associate learning tasks, successful performance apparently results only if a discrimination–utilization strategy is combined with continuous rehearsal activities. It has been shown that children at age 10 years and above are able to master this complex problem, but for younger children a close relationship between metamemory (i.e., strategy awareness) and memory performance has not been found. When an easier recognition task is used instead, 8-year-old children also can show some planfulness, but younger subjects in general fail to understand the task demands.

Allocation of Retrieval Effort: Feeling-of-Knowing Experiences

A different set of investigations concentrated on children's knowledge of retrieval effort allocation strategies. Most of them dealt with the well-known everyday tip-of-the-tongue experience and the related feeling-of-knowing state. In both of these phenomena the subject fails to recall something, but still knows that she or he knows it. The tip-of-the-tongue experience reflects the subject's knowledge that an item not currently re-called is imminently recallable, while the feeling-of-knowing experience reflects the knowledge that an unrecalled item is recognizable. In two stud-ies by Wellman (1977; 1979) it was assumed that metamemory (i.e., knowl-edge about the recallability or recognizability of items) is likely to influence the subject's strategic memory search behavior (i.e., increased retrieval ef-fort), which in turn should positively affect memory performance.

Wellman (1977) studied both phenomena in kindergarteners, first, and third grade children. Each subject was presented with three sets of pic-tures varying in ease of naming. If the child could not name a stimulus the child was asked if (1) she or he had ever seen the item before ("seen" judgment), or if (2) she or he could recognize the item among a set of alternatives (feeling-of-knowing judgment). Subsequently, a recognition test was given, and the child rated her or his confidence in the choice. The results indicated that the ability to monitor the states of unrecalled items significantly increased with age. The accuracy of "seen" judgments was greater than feeling-of-knowing accuracy in the two youngest age groups, but for the third graders, feeling-of-knowing judgments were the better predictors of subsequent name recognition. Thus, in this age group a rather close connection between metamemory and memory perfor-mance could be found. Although the younger children had relevant in-formation in their memories, they obviously did not use it when making the feeling-of-knowing judgments. On the other hand, older subjects were more frequently found to experience the tip-of-the-tongue phenomenon, demonstrating some of the emotional reactions (e.g., agitation or frustra-tion) well-known from similar experiments with adults.

In an attempt to analyze these data more exhaustively, Wellman (1979) additionally examined the relationship between children's feeling-of-know-ing judgments and their actual retrieval effort. Indications of retrieval effort were inferred from transcriptions of tape recordings of the children's com-ments and vocalizations like attempting to name the items, asking for re-trieval time, affirming retrieval possibility, and so forth. The hypothesis was that judging an item as known should lead to an increased retrieval effort; judging it as not known, however, should result in less effort. This assumption was confirmed for all age groups: although the correspondence between metamemory and this type of memory behavior was closer for the older children, kindergarteners also significantly related retrieval effort to feeling-of-knowing judgments in the predicted manner. Thus, apparently, children's often inaccurate perception of their knowledge seemed to determine their search behavior more than what they actually knew.

Similar results were found in a study by Posnansky (1978). Here, kindergarteners and third graders were asked to remember picture stimuli grouped in categories of different size. Children were either given category size information, were required to estimate category size, or did not get any information about the true category size. The interval between the last word produced in a given category and the first word produced in the next category during recall was considered an indicator of systematic search behavior guided by the knowledge about the actual category size. Posnansky found that those kindergarteners and third graders who had estimated the category size first used their estimates to guide recall. That is, significant negative correlations between intercategory pause time and percentage of category recalled were found for both age groups. Even more important, length of intercategory interval correlated more highly with children's estimates of category size than with true category size. Thus it was the child's own estimate of category size (i.e., metamemory) that closely corresponded with search efforts for kindergarteners as well as for third graders.

Finally, Brown and Lawton (1977) analyzed the feeling-of-knowing experience in educable retarded (EMR) children of three varying ability levels (mental ages [MA] = 6, 8, and 10 years). Younger children were not able to predict the accessibility of items in memory, but could judge the correctness of their recognition response *after* it had been made (see the corresponding findings for very young children by Berch & Evans, 1973). In contrast, educable retarded children with MAs of 8 years and above were able to predict recognition accuracy when recall failed.

In sum, the results obtained using the feeling-of-knowing paradigm indicate that children at age 8 years and above are accurate when asked to estimate the retrievability of items that are not recallable at the moment. For these subjects, metamemory (i.e., awareness of the current state of information in memory) was closely related both to retrieval effort and memory performance. Although the evidence for younger children is not so clear-cut, it appears that they do possess information relevant for the solution of this task. Thus, although in the two studies by Wellman (1977; 1979) kindergarteners' metamemory (i.e., feeling-of-knowing experience) did not strongly affect their memory performance, it was closely related to their retrieval effort. According to Brown and Lawton (1977), monitoring of retrieval effort seems to be somewhat easier than monitoring of attention allocation of study effort: their EMR children with MAs of 8 years were capable of correctly estimating the current state of items in the feeling-of-knowing task, but failed when asked to predict recall readiness or to apportion their study time efficiently.

Effort and Attention Allocation Strategies for Prose Materials

The studies described so far have in common that they investigated children's memory monitoring skills by using rote-learning laboratory materials. This procedure has been criticized by several researchers who emphasized that such knowledge has only a limited range of applicability (see Brown, 1978). As a consequence, a number of more recent studies assessed children's knowledge of skills extremely useful in their everyday school life experiences, namely, study-monitoring abilities when text processing (memory for prose) was required. According to Baker and Brown (1981), this area of research deals with "reading for remembering," as opposed to the comprehension monitoring literature focusing on "reading for meaning." Reading for remembering not only involves all activities necessary for comprehension monitoring, but also includes several study-monitoring skills. The research concerning the development of study-monitoring abilities particularly concentrated on skills such as (1) focusing on the main ideas of texts, and (2) making use of the logical structure of the material (or prose organization).

Sensitivity to the Main Idea of Text Passages

Most of the investigations in this field have been carried out by Ann Brown and her colleagues (Brown & Smiley, 1977, 1978; Brown, Smiley, Day, Townsend, & Lawton, 1977; Brown, Smiley, & Lawton, 1978). The authors used rather complicated procedures to assess children's knowledge about central issues of text passages. Prior to the outset of the studies, the verbal materials (Japanese folk stories) were divided into linguistic subunits, and independent groups of college students rated the structural importance of these idea units for the main theme of the stories using a 4-point scale. The resulting four levels of importance of information were regarded as a quasi-objective measure that was compared with the ratings of the experimental subjects. Thus, children's sensitivity to the constituent units of texts was chosen as a measure of metamemory. It was hypothesized that those children concentrating on the main events of a story during study should also show the same organization in recall, that is, they should reproduce the most important events but exclude nonessential details. Metamemory here was inferred from a behavioral measure; subjects had to indicate (i.e., cross out with pencils of different colors) successively higher levels of importance. With regard to recall, a rating procedure was used to determine the number of idea units reproduced by the subjects.

By comparing the importance ratings of their subjects with the quasi-objective measure, Brown and Smiley (1977) found that metamemory (i.e., sensitivity to importance units) developed gradually over the entire age range studied. While third graders made no distinction among levels of importance, fifth graders differentiated the most important units from the remaining three categories. Seventh graders showed greater sensitivity, distinguishing the two upper and the two lower levels, but had difficulties in distinguishing the medium levels. In contrast, college students could distinguish every level of importance, thus demonstrating the reliability of the measurement procedure. Importance level was highly significant in determining recall. Interesting enough, recall was determined by the structural importance of the text units for all age groups (see also Brown et al., 1977), but only children at age 12 years and above showed some awareness of the essential organizing features of texts. As these children also recalled significantly more idea units of the story, a rather close metamemory–memory behavior relationship for this task was assumed to develop by Grade 7. In contrast to the results obtained for the development of monitoring skills in rote-memory tasks, here the development of metamemory lagged behind memory performance. That is, although younger children were not aware of the important structural units of the texts, they still favored these important units in recall.

In a subsequent study (Brown & Smiley, 1978), the authors tested the hypothesis that the more mature readers would use their better knowledge about the crucial elements of texts when extra study time was provided. As in the aforementioned study by Masur et al. (1973), strategic effort-allocation was chosen here as a measure of metamemory. It was assumed that the older students should benefit from increased study time because they were aware of the fact that selective attention should be given to the central ideas of the story. As expected, most fifth-grade children did not improve their recall with the extra study time, but children from seventh grade up benefitted considerably, improving their recall particularly on the two most important levels of information. A closer examination of children's study activities showed that spontaneous underliners represented the superior group at each age level. But while fifth graders isolated only the most important units and consequently improved their recall of these units only, spontaneous underliners in the seventh- and eighth-grade samples showed a greater sensitivity to the two most important levels; their recall patterns resembled those of adults. Thus, Brown and Smiley (1978) concluded that most of the younger children in their sample could not use extra time efficiently because they did not know the important elements of texts. On the other hand, older students tended to show more strategic behavior, paying attention to the main ideas of the stories. Here again, a close connection between metamemory and recall was not found before Grade 7. But, as already mentioned, it should not be overlooked that also a certain proportion of fifth graders spontaneously used adequate strategies favoring the important elements of the stories.

In another related study, Brown et al. (1978) modified the procedure used by Brown and Smiley (1977, 1978), in that half of the subjects were asked to select retrieval cues they judged important to recall the stories instead of rating the importance of text units. Fifth graders did not differentiate between these two task demands, but older children (seventh and eight graders) tended to choose lower importance levels when selecting retrieval cues, compared with their selection of main ideas. According to Brown et al. (1978), the latter finding proves the existence of a rather sophisticated retrieval plan in older children, who seem to anticipate that the less central facts will provide most difficulties when recall is attempted. Not surprisingly, this fine sensitivity to the demands of gist-recall tasks is a skill that develops very late in childhood, and even older high school students have problems using a flexible retrieval strategy. Although these results appear to indicate that the ability to select the main ideas of a text passage (i.e., sufficient metamemory) cannot be found in elementary school children, Brown and her colleagues repeatedly emphasized that the problems experienced by their younger subjects could be the result either of the length of the passage to be rated, the complexity of the material or the difficulty of the rating procedure itself, which might have masked young children's sensitivity to the task.

Some support for this assumption comes from a study by Yussen, Matthews, Buss, and Kane (1980), who examined children's metacognitive awareness of important text units in rather simple and short prose passages, compared with the stories used by Brown and her co-workers. Perhaps more important, the authors referred to an explicit theory of story structure (i.e., the formal story grammar used by Stein & Glenn, 1979) to test their hypothesis that children's knowledge of text units relevant for recall develops during the elementary school years. According to this grammar, the initiating event, the character's action, and the result of the action can be considered basic categories of simple stories, and there is a greater probability of them being recalled than all others. As predicted, these key categories of the stories were recalled significantly better than other categories regardless of age, but it turned out that the youngest children (second graders) were not aware of the salience of the basic categories. When asked to select the most critical elements in the stories, they randomly chose among basic and unimportant categories. In contrast, fourth graders were more likely to identify the parts of the stories that were most important. Furthermore, modest support for a significant metamemory–memory behavior relationship was only found for the older children, indicating that the more knowledgeable children were also better at recalling the stories.

Knowledge about the Effect of Prose Organization

Finally, several further studies concentrated on another aspect of metamemory, namely, children's sensitivity to different text structures. Danner (1976) investigated children's understanding of prose organization and its effect on their recall by using short descriptive passages differing in logical structure. In topically well-organized passages, each paragraph dealt with one topic, whereas in disorganized versions, sentences from different topics were mixed together. Children in Grades 2, 4, and 6 were required to recall both types of passages. In addition, they were asked which task was the more difficult one and why. It turned out that passage organization affected the amount of recall and its structure (clustering) in children from all age groups, but only the older subjects (fourth and sixth graders) could explain how the passages differed. The younger children were able to detect that the disorganized passages were more difficult, and they also did quite well when asked to describe the main topics of the paragraphs, but they obviously were not aware of the relationship between organization and recall. Again, these findings suggest that the awareness of the facilitative effects of topical organization on recall considerably lags behind the age at which the organization itself has a significant effect. This result also illustrates the effects of task difficulty. Although the prose material used by Danner consisted of very short and simple sentences, the task to judge the difficulty of differently organized prose passages seems to be more complex, compared with the task to judge the difficulty of categorized or uncategorized word lists (cf. Moynahan, 1973). Thus, as Brown (1978) stated, a child knowing a lot about organization, when the basis of that organization is taxonomic categorization, may know little or nothing about the organizational principles underlying text materials.

On the other hand, knowledge about the impact of the logical structure of prose passages appears to be well developed by Grade 6, as Elliott (1980) demonstrated. In his study, the effects of two types of textual organization called "adversative" and "attribution" were examined. While in an adversative top-level structure, a favored view is related to an opposing view; in an attribution passage, the ideas are all related to a superordinate topic, but not necessarily to each other. It is assumed that the more loose organization of ideas in an attribution structure can explain the fact that in earlier studies, recall for this type of organization was reported to be more difficult. The two short passages used by Elliott covered the same content but differed in top-level structure. Sixth graders and college students were required to read and immediately recall the passages and, in addition, were given a metacognitive questionnaire focusing on a comparison of the two versions of experimental passages. Furthermore, subjects were individually interviewed about their awareness of more general characteristics of texts, learners, and study situations. Highly significant relationships between metamemory scores and recall were found for both age groups. Although the adversative structure facilitated college students' recall more than that of sixth graders, the younger subjects, too, seemed to be aware of the effect of organization.

In sum, investigations of effort and attention allocation when studying texts have shown that this skill develops rather late in childhood. As Brown et al. (1983) point out, adequately judging one's mastery of the gist of texts requires that one first distinguish between important and unimportant segments of the passage, then concentrate on the central elements of texts and, as they become well known, shift to less important segments. The research done by Brown and her colleagues shows that young school children are not aware of this complex strategy. Although older elementary school children and even high school students had some problems using strategy knowledge in the experimental paradigm developed by Brown et al., further investigations with easier tasks and procedures showed that advanced elementary school children do possess efficient study-monitoring abilities. In contrast, children younger than 10 years of age appear to be unaware of the organizational principles underlying text materials, irrespective of their task difficulty.

This survey of the memory-monitoring literature has shown that a wide variety of experimental tasks have been used to analyze the relationship between children's memory knowledge and their memory performance. As expected, the results do not represent a uniform developmental pattern of the relationship, but strongly suggest that different levels of task difficulty seem to be mainly responsible for the heterogeneous findings. The results differ systematically according to the complexity of skills–processes involved in the tasks. A rather close connection between metamemory and memory behavior is found even in kindergarteners and young elementary school children when task requirements do not overload working memory—that is, when either the recallability or the recognizability of single items or limited item sets is tested. This seems to be true for most studies concerning the prediction of amount and composition of future recall as well as for studies assessing children's retrieval-effort allocation strategies (e.g., feeling-of-knowing experiences). On the other hand, when either supraspan lists are presented, or a combination of complex strategies (e.g., self-testing, rehearsal) is required to cope with the task demands, significant relationships between metamemory and memory performance are only found in advanced elementary school children. Examples of these more difficult task requirements include attention-allocation strategies and study-effort allocation strategies (e.g., study-time apportionment) for rote-memory tasks as well as for prose materials.

Memory Knowledge and the Use of Organizational Strategies

With regard to the task variable of metamemory in the taxonomy of Flavell and Wellman (1977), most investigations into the metamemory–memory behavior relationship dealt with children's knowledge of the importance for recallability of the relationship among stimulus items, thereby assessing the impact of children's knowledge about the categorical structure of item lists on subsequent recall. Thus, here metamemory was defined as children's verbalizable knowledge of the role of organization in recall. Most of these studies had in common that subjects were provided with a sort-recall task: they usually were first encouraged or forced to establish input organization by sorting the items into personally meaningful or predefined groupings, and then were asked to freely recall the items. Thus, metamemory could be related to different forms of memory behavior: (1) strategic sorting behavior as a measure of input organization, (2) clustering or categorization during recall as a measure of output organization, and (3) the amount of recall as an indicator of memory performance.

It should be noted that the relationships among children's input organization, output organization, and memory performance has been analyzed in many developmental studies during the 1970s (cf., e.g., Kobasigawa, 1977; Lange, 1978; Moely, 1977), but only a few of them also assessed children's verbalization knowledge of the role of organization recall. In brief, the majority of these previous studies demonstrated that younger subjects (6- to 8-year-old children) did not spontaneously engage in sorting activities, but could increase their recall when required to do so. In contrast, most children at Grade 4 and above spontaneously used their abilities to sort items into categories when asked to prepare for future recall. In view of these "production deficiencies" in the use of category organization among young children, it is worth noting that they apparently do know about the impact of organizational principles on recall, as can be concluded from the interview data obtained by Kreutzer et al. (1975) and Moynahan (1973). Similarly, even the majority of the mentally retarded children in the sample of Eyde and Altman (1978) were able to recognize adaptive behavior (i.e., the categorization of items) in this task, but here again only the older and higher-ability children spontaneously used the categorization strategy in preparing for recall.

More recent investigations into the metamemory–memory behavior relationship are characterized by their common attempt to analyze the sources of children's organization failures. Consequently, most of them have concentrated on the effects of task manipulation that might increase children's spontaneous use of recall organization. Modifications of the aforementioned traditional sort-recall task mainly included variations of (1) the kind of instructions given before or during the presentation of the item lists, and (2) the interrelationship among stimuli to be recalled. Further, some more-recent investigations focused specifically on the connection between domain-specific knowledge and the awareness of the functional relationship between the means and goals in this kind of memory task.

The Impact of Instruction

In the often-cited study by Salatas and Flavell (1976), a sort-recall task including three study-test trials was used to analyze the ability to distinguish between perceiving and memorizing in first-grade children. Subjects in the experimental condition were instructed to remember a set of clusterable picture stimuli in a free-recall task, whereas control subjects were asked to look at the items and received an unexpected recall test. As expected, recall was significantly higher for the remember condition, compared to the look group. The attempt at trying to remember in the experimental group also led to significantly more correct answers in a subsequent metamemory test, which addressed children's knowledge of the facilitative effect of categorization. But surprisingly, metamemory was not related to sorting behavior during the study trials, and it also could not predict children's strategic behavior in a retest given 6 weeks later. Subjects who had not categorized during study were as likely as categorizers to say that grouping of the items would facilitate recall. Thus, the authors concluded that there was no evidence that memory knowledge was a necessary condition for actual strategy use.

This assumption was tested in a study by Wimmer and Tornquist

(1980), who also used a sort-recall task to compare the metamemory–memory behavior relationship for first graders, fourth graders, and high school students. The metamemory questions corresponded to those given by Salatas and Flavell (1976), but were presented either before (i.e., awareness condition) or after the memory task (control condition). Metamemory turned out to be a necessary condition for strategic behavior in this study, as almost all subjects showing strategic behavior also explicitly stated their knowledge about the efficiency of categorical item grouping. Further, metamemory was significantly related to strategy use when the data were aggregated across age and experimental conditions. But a closer examination of the data reveals that this effect is primarily due to the inclusion of the 10- and 17-year-old subjects, who generally were aware of the facilitative effect of clustering and did use it efficiently in the memory task. In contrast, only about 50% of the first graders (the same proportion as found by Salatas & Flavell) showed adequate memory knowledge, and fewer than half of these knowledgeable children also used the clustering strategy *after* the metamemory interview had been presented. On the other hand, no strategy users could be found in this age group when the memory task was given *prior* to the metamemory interview. This result sharply contrasts with the findings of Salatas and Flavell (1976) showing that about half of the first graders spontaneously used clustering sorting strategies in this experimental condition. Although differences in task materials (27 items from 9 categories in the Wimmer & Tornquist study, 16 items from 4 categories in the study by Salatas & Flavell) might have contributed to the discrepant findings, they certainly cannot totally explain the different patterns of results. Nevertheless, both studies demonstrated that (1) knowledge of the facilitative effect of stimulus grouping is not well developed in first graders, and (2) metamemory does not relate to strategy use in this age group. In addition, the results obtained by Wimmer and Tornquist suggest that a rather close relationship between knowledge and behavior in this type of memory task does exist for children of age 10 years and above, given that categorizable items are used in the task. Corsale and Ornstein (1980) have shown that when semantically unrelated stimuli are chosen instead, a stable metamemory–memory behavior relationship emerges even later in childhood. In their study, third and seventh graders were assigned to one of three instructional conditions. Meaning-instructed subjects were told to sort the picture stimuli into groups that "go together," but were not informed of a subsequent recall test, while recall-instructed subjects were asked to sort the items in a way that would help to remember them. A third group received a combination of both instructions. As predicted, instructional manipulations had no effect on the recall of seventh graders, showing that these older children had learned to ad-

79

tive organizational strategies when the goal was to remem-
ther hand, the recall-instructed third graders remembered
ess than all other experimental groups. Apparently, these
dren did not know what it means to prepare for recall when
hip among stimuli is not as obvious as in the usual sort-recall
task wい. ighly familiar, clusterable items. Further, although a subsequent metamemory interview indicated that all subjects were aware of the
fact that organized materials are easier to remember, the third graders
obviously did not know *when* an organizational strategy should be used
(i.e., if it is appropriate when a few or many things have to be remembered).

Effects of Task Properties

The preceding three studies have in common that they examined the
relationship between metamemory and memory behavior by using a single
task and only two or three *task-specific* metamemory questions. Flavell and
Wellman (1977) have suggested that *general* memory knowledge should be
a crucial factor in understanding how metamemory is related to memory
behavior. If it is true that metamemory is necessary for effective memory
behavior, a similar relation between knowledge and strategic behavior
should be obtained across several related memory tasks.

These problems were addressed in a study by Cavanaugh and Borkowski (1980), which is undoubtedly one of the most comprehensive investigations ever done in this area. Kindergarteners, first, third, and fifth
graders were presented with all 14 metamemory subtests of the extensive
interview developed by Kreutzer et al. (1975), before they received three
related memory tasks (sort-recall, cognitive cueing, alphabet search). While
in the traditional sort-recall task the children were told to do anything with
the items that might be useful to remember them, in the cognitive cuing
task children were required to sort the stimuli into boxes with the cue
pictures that remained visible during recall. Finally, an alphabet-search
task required subjects to write down randomly presented letters before
they were presented with an unexpected recall task. Partial correlations
controlling for age revealed rather modest but consistent correlations between metamemory and measures of recall, input organization, and output organization. Thus, it appeared that the metamemory–memory
behavior relationship seemed to be broadly based across several domains
of memory knowledge and several memory tasks. But when the data were
analyzed for developmental trends, the number of significant correlations
dropped considerably; specific memory knowledge was significantly re-

lated to memory behavior only for the oldest age group (fifth graders). In contrast, strong developmental trends could be found for the degree of consistency of memory behavior in the three recall tasks. While none of the intercorrelations for the kindergarteners reached significance, all were significant for the fifth graders. By using a contingency analysis similar to that of Salatas and Flavell (1976) and Wimmer and Tornquist (1980), the authors further tested the hypothesis that metamemory is a necessary condition for efficient memory behavior. In contrast to the findings of Wimmer and Tornquist, subjects with low metamemory and high strategy-use scores were frequently observed regardless of the metamemory subtest actually chosen. Similarly, no support was found for the assumption that a close metamemory–memory behavior relationship can only be detected if task-specific and general knowledge components are considered simultaneously. The metamemory subtests involving task-specific knowledge proved to be the best predictors of memory behavior. In view of their failure to find predictable patterns among the significant metamemory–memory behavior correlations, Cavanaugh and Borkowski (1980) concluded that "it appears that fresh conceptual analysis of the metamemory side of the metamemory–memory relationship is needed, especially as regards the aspects of knowledge that *ought* to be involved. Such reanalysis must be accompanied by further refinement of metamemory assessment methods" (p. 450).

With regard to the metamemory assessment problem, interesting results were obtained in a study by Best and Ornstein (1979). The authors examined the hypothesis that experience with taxonomic materials facilitates and enhances (in a learning-set sense) memory performance in sort-recall tasks with semantically unrelated items. Third and sixth graders were first either given three trials of sort-recall with semantically associated stimuli or presented with semantically unrelated picture lists. In the test phase, subjects in both conditions were given two sort-recall tasks with unrelated items to find out if the different previous experiences could influence children's strategic behavior. After the memory tasks, metamemory was assessed with a comprehensive battery of questions derived from previous investigations. In addition to this traditional procedure, a behavioral measure of metamemory was used: subjects had to instruct first graders concerning performance on the sort-recall task, telling them the strategies most useful to remember the items. It was assumed that the subjects would be more explicit in the information provided when the "pupils" are considerably younger. With regard to memory performance, it turned out that prior experience with categorized or uncategorized material influenced sorting behavior and recall of third graders in the expected manner, but did not affect memory behavior of sixth graders, who used adequate organizational strategies irrespective of prior experience (cf. the similar findings by Corsale & Ornstein, 1980). As in the study by Cavanaugh and Borkowski (1980), data from the metamemory interview did not significantly correlate with memory performance of third graders, and the connection was also modest for sixth graders (Best, personal-communication, February 1982). Although the pattern of correlations was not consistent, it turned out that in general the behavioral metamemory measure was more closely related to recall. Interesting enough, the two metamemory measures had little relationship to each other. This finding seems to shed some doubts on the validity of the interview data, especially for younger children. Although the reliability of the metamemory interview of Kreutzer et al. (1975) has been repeatedly demonstrated (cf. Cavanaugh & Borkowski, 1980; Kurtz, Reid, Borkowski, & Cavanaugh, 1982), peer tutoring as a behavioral measure of metamemory appears to be more sensitive to children's actual knowledge. In a similar study, Best (1981) replicated the finding that categorical experience induced the children (third graders) to use organizational strategies and increased their recall of subsequently presented unrelated items lists. But it was also shown that a *simulated* peer tutoring task (children were asked to pretend that the experimenter was a first grader to whom they had to explain the strategy) turned out to be a weak indicator of children's metamemory. According to Best, children had enormous difficulties in pretending that the experimenter was a first grader.

The Impact of Children's Knowledge Base
and Their Perceptions of the Task

While the preceding studies demonstrated young children's production deficiencies in a variety of experimental conditions, the question why children did not use their strategy knowledge still remains open, and there is also no satisfactory explanation of why and how children learn to overcome production deficiencies (see Paris, 1978; Paris & Lindauer, 1982). Some recent studies (Corsale, 1981; Bjorklund & Zeman, 1982) have addressed this point, either concentrating on the role of knowledge base (i.e., stimulus familiarity) or measuring children's perceived value of the strategy used in this type of task.

As for the impact of children's familiarity with the particular content area, studies have shown that sophisticated organizational strategies are spontaneously used and age differences in recall and clustering are sharply reduced when the memory task minimizes age differences in knowledge base.

For example, Corsale (1981) found that third graders spontaneously organized stimuli in a sort-recall task with high-salient (i.e., prototypical) items regardless of the kind of instruction used, that is, they sorted the items taxonomically whether instructions emphasized meaningful groupings or only the recall of items. When low-salient items were used instead, spontaneous use of categorization (combined with better recall) was observed only for children instructed to group for meaning. In contrast, kindergarteners did not benefit from recall instructions. Thus, the level of categorical salience of items usually chosen in sort-recall tasks seems to be at least partly responsible for young elementary school children's production deficiencies. But this explanation cannot account for the problems of kindergarteners, who did not spontaneously engage in strategic behavior even when they knew the basic category structures.

Bjorklund and Zeman (1982) contrasted the traditional sort-recall task with a "class-recall" task, where children had to remember the names of their classmates. A series of experiments was conducted to test the assumption that young children's production deficiencies can be explained by developmental differences in knowledge base. Indeed, while significant age differences were obtained for recall and clustering behavior in the sort-recall task, memory performance of the first, third, and fifth graders in the study was comparably high in class-recall. When metamemory (i.e., children's awareness of the strategies they used to recall the names of their classmates) was related to memory performance, it turned out that strategy awareness was generally poor for children of all age groups despite high levels of recall. Only fifth graders showed some increase in memory performance and strategy awareness when the metamemory questions were presented prior to the memory task, provided they had some time to prepare for the task. Most of the younger children apparently entered the task without a definite retrieval plan, but occasionally discovered an effective grouping strategy (e.g., considering seating arrangements, reading groups, gender, or race) during their retrieval attempts.

Further interesting evidence concerning the nature of young children's production deficiencies came from studies investigating children's perceived value of strategies useable in the sort-recall task. Thus, Justice (1981) asked preschoolers, kindergarteners, and second graders to judge the mnemonic effectiveness of four different memory strategies (i.e., grouping, repeating, naming, and looking) for a given sort-recall task. To assess the metamemory–memory behavior relationship, strategies chosen as optimal by the children were compared with those actually adopted on the memory task. While half of the second graders adopted the strategy chosen as optimal, only 20% of the preschool and 15% of the kindergarteners did so. Furthermore, second graders preferred the more complex and sophisticated strategies (i.e., grouping and rehearsal) both in judgment and actual behavior. On the other hand, the younger subjects rated the ineffective looking strategy as optimal and actually used naming strategies on the memory tasks. Thus, as the utility of the complex strategies was not apparent to the younger children, they chose other means they were familiar with and that they believed to be effective.

A similar phenomenon was observed in a study by Cox and Paris (1979). Here, fourth graders, young adults, and the elderly were presented with a random list of categorically related words and instructed either to recall the items after studying (the remember condition), to generate as many memory strategies as possible before the study of items (the generate condition), or to learn the lists by conceptually grouping the items (the instruct condition). After the memory task, subjects were asked to (1) report the strategies used, (2) rank order strategies in terms of perceived effectiveness, and (3) indicate which strategies would be used by them as a future study activity on similar tasks. Although correspondence between the generated strategies (metamemory) and those actually used (memory behavior) was high for all age groups, there were interesting age differences in the types of strategies preferred. While college students and elderly subjects relied on categorization, most fourth graders rather consistently used rehearsal and rated it higher than other strategies. Even those children instructed to categorize during study thought rehearsal to be the most effective strategy and also reported that they would use rehearsal as a future study activity. Thus, the brief practice with a more sophisticated strategy did not change children's belief about the effectiveness of certain mnemonic techniques in producing better memory performance. They apparently did not understand the importance of categorization as a mnemonic operation facilitating recall. Interestingly, although both fourth graders and elderly showed poorer results in the remember condition, compared with their recall in the instruct condition, only the elderly subjects benefitted from the generate condition. Thus, production deficiencies of children and elderly appear superficially similar, but reflect underlying qualitative differences in task understanding. The poorer performance of the elderly under remember instructions seem to be due to a lack of self-testing and familiarity with the task; in contrast to the fourth graders, they knew about the facilitative effect of categorization and had easy access to this strategy after a prompt was given in the generate condition. As in this study the subject's evaluations of means and goals relevant for the task were taken into account; it was possible to find out different sources of a superficially similar memory difficulty.

To summarize, a consistent and rather close connection between metamemory and memory behavior in the traditional sort-recall task with categorizable stimulus material seems to emerge rather late in childhood. Children younger than 10 years old did not systematically relate their knowledge to adequate strategic behavior in the memory task without additional prompts or highly associated stimulus lists. Although even second graders knew that semantically organized lists are easier to remember than unrelated lists, they usually were unaware of the importance of categorization strategies for facilitation of recall and preferred to rely on familiar strategies (e.g., rehearsal) that proved to be less effective.

The Status of Output Organization in the Sort-Recall Task

The discussion of the metamemory–memory behavior relationship in the sort-recall task so far has focused on sorting behavior (input organization) as an indicator of strategy use (i.e., memory behavior). Clustering during recall (output organization) has also been considered as a possible indicator of strategic behavior (as discussed previously). Although some of the aforementioned studies reported moderate to high correlations between clustering and recall, it has been repeatedly questioned whether clustering always indicates deliberately chosen retrieval strategies. Thus Neimark, Slotnick, and Ulrich (1971) stated that in their study, clustering per se was insufficient evidence of deliberate organizing, and Corsale (1981) emphasized that for young children, use of category structure during retrieval was related neither to sorting behavior nor to level of recall, particularly when high-salient items were used. This result can be accounted for by Lange's (1978) assumption that highly associated items automatically elicit one another's recall. Thus here the associativity among items results in what seems to be a sophisticated categorization strategy. A tenuous relationship between clustering and recall was also found in a study by Kee and Bell (1981), who additionally pointed out that organization during recall was no source of developmental differences in free-recall learning. In contrast, organization at study turned out to be at least a partial source of developmental differences in the recall performance of second graders, sixth graders, and college students. All in all, these findings seem to justify the decision to focus on input organization as an indicator of strategic behavior in the sort-recall task.

Memory Knowledge and Use of Strategies in Paired-Associate Learning Tasks

The results of the few studies analyzing children's knowledge and spontaneous use of organizational strategies in a paired-associate task (Pressley and Levin, 1977; Waters, 1982) suggest that here the metamemory–memory behavior relationship is much clearer, compared with the findings for the sort-recall task (see Brown et al., 1983). It should be considered, however, that both studies differed from the majority of the preceding sort-recall studies in that they used samples of advanced elementary school and high school children.

In the study by Pressley and Levin (1977), children's awareness of the strategies used in a paired-associate task was chosen as an indicator of metamemory. Subjects reported the strategies used immediately after the presentation of a list of paired-associate items, and on the basis of their reports they were classified as rehearsers, elaborators, or mixed-strategy users. As predicted, there was a change in strategy use during adolescence: the proportion of those subjects relying on at least some elaboration significantly increased between Grades 5 and 9, whereas the proportion of rehearsers decreased between these two grade levels. Perhaps more interesting, when analyzing the memory performance it turned out that the effect of the strategy used was significant, indicating that elaborators recalled most and rehearsers least at all age levels. Furthermore, fifth graders who reported elaborating outperformed ninth graders who did not report using the more sophisticated strategy. Thus, here the strategy used by the subjects was a better predictor of performance than the age of subjects, a result rarely found in studies using younger samples and different memory tasks.

Waters (1982) also analyzed the relationship between reported strategy use and memory performance in a paired-associate learning task, but additionally assessed which of four possible strategies (i.e., reading carefully, rehearsal, and visual and verbal elaboration) was judged most effective by the eight and tenth graders of her sample. Metamemory was significantly related to both strategy use and memory performance in both age groups, and again subjects who used either verbal or visual elaboration more often tended to recall more word pairs. But even eighth and tenth graders' metamemory seemed to benefit from task experience, as shown by a comparison with control subjects who received only the metamemory questions. After the recall test, most experimental subjects identified elaboration as the most effective strategy, but only one-fourth of the eighth graders and one third of the tenth graders in the control group did so. This finding indicates that knowledge about the facilitative effect of elaboration strategies in paired-associate tasks appears to emerge later in childhood than knowledge about the effects of clustering strategies in sort-recall tasks. On the other hand, Moynahan (1978) demonstrated that even first graders can successfully be taught to effectively use some form of elaboration (i.e., physical interaction strategies) in a paired-associate task when recognition is assessed instead of recall. Here, most of the young children correctly rated this strategy as better than a rehearsal strategy, and also

spontaneously used it on another paired-associate recognit
apparently it takes a long time until knowledge about elabor:
taneously verbalizable and usable in paired-associate recall ta

In sum, the studies reviewed in this section indicate th
organizational strategies in categorization or paired-associate ta,   ᷄ ᷄on-
cerned, a close metamemory–memory behavior relationship emerges
rather late in childhood. As for the sort-recall task, children younger than
10 years only spontaneously engage in sorting activities when high-salient
items are presented and usually prefer to rely on familiar rote-learning
strategies (e.g., rehearsal). Similar to the more complex memory-monitoring procedures the task involves learning of supraspan lists, and successful
performance requires the combination of rather complex skills. As Neimark et al. (1971) stated, in order to cope with the task, an exhaustive
organization for efficient encoding of each item has to be combined with
the ability to keep track of "readout"—that is, to now what has been recalled and what is still missing. Younger children appear to be unaware of
both requirements, and there is evidence that they sometimes discover
organizational strategies only as a result of retrieval attempts (see Bjorklund & Hock, 1982). On the other hand, it appears that the traditional
metamemory interview leads to an underestimation of younger children's
actual knowledge. Thus, it seems possible that the metamemory–memory
behavior connection might be stronger when behavioral measures of
knowledge are used.

Training of Strategy Use

As already mentioned, tests of maintenance and generalization of
strategies might be contexts in which metamemory and memory behavior
are closely related. Because in a transfer situation, decisions are required
about whether or how to use a newly acquired strategy, in a (slightly) modified task arrangement, it was assumed that the metamemory–memory behavior connection would be more apparent in intervention studies (cf.
Borkowski & Cavanaugh, 1979; Borkowski, Reid, & Kurtz, 1984). Several
recent studies have concentrated on this hypothesis by training either
memory monitoring skills or the use of organizational strategies in sort-
recall tasks.

Training in Memory Monitoring

Brown, Campione, and their colleagues (Brown & Barclay, 1976;
Brown & Campione, 1977; Brown, Campione, & Barclay, 1979; Brown,

Campione & Murphy, 1977) conducted several studies to assess the effects of specific mnemonic skills on the educable retarded children. These studies differed with respect to the trained strategies but were similar in design. They all included a pretest to assess baseline behavior, some days of strategy training, and two or three prompted or unprompted posttests assessing maintenance and (in some cases) generalization of the strategy in question. Furthermore, all studies were directly comparable in that two groups of subjects (children of MAs 6 and 8 years) were always considered in the analysis. Uniform results were obtained for maintenance—that is, a successful implementation of a mnemonic skill. In general, both groups of subjects responded to training and improved their monitoring skills during the training procedure, but only the older children showed the same level of skill on subsequent posttests, irrespective of the type of memory monitoring strategy under investigation. Interestingly enough, this was true for rather simple task requirements like span estimation (Brown, Campione, & Murphy, 1977) as well as for more complicated ones like recall readiness (Brown, Barclay, 1976; Brown, Campione, & Barclay, 1979), and study time apportionment (Brown & Campione, 1977). Although evidence of maintenance of older subjects was generally encouraging, Brown et al. (1977) did not succeed in effecting transfer of strategic behavior in the memory-span estimation task to new situations, where either the task format was slightly changed or numbers were used instead of pictures. Thus, training for one specific skill or task did not generalize to highly similar tasks. In other words, metamemory was not related to subsequent strategy use when rather task-specific strategies had been taught.

Consequently, Brown et al. (1979) concentrated their effort on the training of more general skills. Training of general self-testing strategies like rehearsal or anticipation proved to be very effective in the older age group. Improved recall readiness was detectable even 1 year after training, replicating, and extending the results obtained by Brown and Barclay (1976). But more important, training recall readiness on a list-learning task transferred to quite a different task, namely, preparing for gist recall of prose passages. Children trained in the preceding two self-testing strategies recalled significantly more idea units at each level of importance than the control subjects. Thus it was shown that even educable retarded children (MA = 8 years) are able to transfer a memory monitoring strategy to a quite dissimilar recall readiness task. Because they failed to effect generalization in much simpler tasks (e.g., memory-span prediction) when attempting to train children in task-specific mnemonics, the authors have good reason to attribute their success in this study to the fact that a more general problem-solving routine was trained. This finding corroborates Belmont, Butterfield, and Ferretti's conclusion (1980) that generalization can be observed only when some aspect of self-monitoring strategy is taught.

Training in the Use of Organizational Strategies

Even more recently, several investigations have been conducted to assess the relationship between metamemory and maintenance as well as successful transfer of organizational strategies in paired-associate and sort-recall learning tasks. Although these training studies differed in many procedural details, they all have in common a focus on strategy training in young children between ages 7 and 9 years.

Organizational Strategies in Paired-Associate (PA) Learning Tasks

Two related studies by John Borkowski and his colleagues (Kendall, Borkowski, & Cavanaugh, 1980; Kurtz et al., 1982) analyzed the relationship between metamemory and successful strategy transfer in PA tasks.

In the study by Kendall et al. (1980), mentally retarded children (MA = 6:9 years) were trained in a four-step interrogative strategy considered as helpful for PA learning. Children were instructed to (1) associate a relationship between the PA items; (2) ask why the two items are together; (3) elaborate on characteristics of the items; and (4) use these elaborations to answer the "why" question generated in Step 2. A battery of metamemory questions (mainly from the Kreutzer et al., 1975, interview study) was given before the training procedure and after the strategy generalization task. Children in the experimental condition were taught to use the interrogative strategy during four training sessions and were tested in long-term retention of the final training list, strategy maintenance, and strategy generalization. Children in the interrogative control condition received no strategy instructions and established a baseline for training effects. A second control group participated only in the two metamemory interviews. It turned out that recall was significantly better for experimental children than for control children across all training sessions and in the tests of maintenance and generalization. Thus, the interrogative strategy was maintained and successfully transferred to the generalization task. While no significant correlations were found between metamemory pretest and recall, metamemory pretest was significantly related to quality of elaborations at generalization. On the other hand, metamemory posttest significantly correlated with recall in the later training sessions as well as with recall in the long-term retention test, maintenance, and generalization tasks. In addition, a significant relationship between metamemory posttest and quality of elaborations (i.e., strategy use) was found. Thus, here the importance of metamemory for effective strategy use during maintenance and generalization was shown even for young educable retarded children. It should be noted, however, that strategy transfer was assessed for what Kendall et al. (1980) called a "near" generalization task, which was only slightly changed in that triads of items were used instead of pairs.

A similar study with normal second graders was conducted by Kurtz et al. (1982). Major changes in design concerned the omission of the long-term retention test and the metamemory posttest. Thus, only a (interrogative) control group was compared with the experimental children. With respect to experimental–control differences in recall, the results were similar to those of Kendall et al. (1980). But in contrast, (pretest) metamemory was significantly related to strategy use and memory performance in both maintenance and generalization. Interestingly enough, the correlation between metamemory and strategy use in maintenance remained significant even when the effect of IQ was partialled out. Furthermore, metamemory was a better predictor of strategy use during maintenance and generalization than the IQ measure. In sum, the results of both training studies showed the importance of metamemory in strategy maintenance and transfer, thus confirming the assumption of the authors that good metamemory seems to be a prerequisite for strategy generalization in PA tasks (see also Moynahan, 1978). Nevertheless, the data were not completely consistent with those of Kendall et al., in that pretest metamemory proved to be an efficient predictor of memory behavior only for the normal children in Kurtz et al. (1982). On the other hand, educable retarded children did not enter the task with appropriate knowledge but did benefit considerably from the extensive training program.

Organizational Strategies in Free-Recall Learning Tasks

Most investigations concerned with the training of organizational strategies used the aforementioned sort-recall paradigm. But before the results of these studies are discussed in more detail, two studies are considered first, which also concentrated on free recall or word lists or picture lists. Here, however, children were instructed to use simple rehearsal (Kramer & Engle, 1981) or cumulative rehearsal (Cavanaugh & Borkowski, 1979) within chunks or clusters instead of sorting items during the study phase. While metamemory and memory performance (i.e., recall) were assessed in the same way as in the sort-recall studies, memory behavior (i.e., strategy use) was inferred from exposure durations of the final stimulus within each cluster or chunk—considerably longer than that of the preceding items.

In the study by Cavanaugh and Borkowski (1979), task-specific measures of metamemory were used to find out if (1) metamemory can predict children's level of strategy use and (2) successful strategy training can in turn influence metamemory. Consequently, pre- and posttests of metamemory were used. Children in the experimental condition were provided with two training sessions and instructed to use cumulative rehearsal within clusters of items. Half of them received feedback on the value of the cumulative clustering strategy following the maintenance task, which was given 2 weeks after the last training session. While an uninstructed control group participated in all sessions, a second control group only received the two metamemory tests to control for the possible effects of noninstructed free-recall learning on metamemory. No generalization task was given in this study. As for maintenance, the results showed that correct strategy use was found for the experimental subjects but not for the control group. Children who maintained the cumulative rehearsal strategy also recalled significantly more than those experimental subjects who did not do so and the control children. More important for the present review, significant correlations were detected between pretest metamemory and both strategy use and recall in the maintenance task. Additionally, strategy use at maintenance was significantly related to metamemory assessed 3 weeks after the maintenance test. Comparisons of the pretest–posttest metamemory scores yielded a significant improvement only for the experimental children in the feedback condition, thus underlining the importance of awareness induction in this task.

While these results supported the view of Borkowski et al. (1984) that training studies provide a more favorable context for a close metamemory–memory behavior relationship, Kramer and Engle (1981) were not equally successful in demonstrating the effectiveness of rehearsal training and strategy awareness for strategy use and memory performance in their generalization tasks. In this study, normal and retarded children of equivalent developmental age (MA = 8 years) were trained in a rehearsal strategy in order to recall relatively unrelated picture stimuli. Two days of training were followed by an immediate and a delayed posttest, both including a maintenance free-recall task and two generalization tasks (i.e., a serial-position probe test and a picture-recognition task). Subjects were assigned to four treatment groups, according to the systematic variation of training conditions (i.e., rehearsal and strategy awareness training). While all subjects received metamemory questions following the training and posttest sessions, only subjects in the strategy-awareness condition got feedback on the value of strategy use. When recall and strategy use on the maintenance tests were analyzed, it turned out that rehearsal training (but not strategy-awareness training) improved performance on the two posttests.

With regard to the two generalization tasks, no strategy transfer was observed for the serial-recall probe, and there was only weak evidence for strategy transfer on the recognition task. Moreover, although some of the correlations were rather high, metamemory was neither significantly related to memory behavior (i.e., strategy use) nor to memory performance on the maintenance and generalization tasks. Thus, this study provided no support for the notion that a high level of metamemory is necessarily related to good memory performance in this type of task. The authors attributed their failure to induce generalization to the fact that the subjects were made aware of the utility of a particular strategy but were not trained in more general self-checking strategies (see also Brown et al., 1979). But there might still be other reasons for the negative results. It is by no means obvious that subjects should transfer the strategy of repeating stimuli in sets of four-item chunks to a task dealing with serial recall of only 8 digits, particularly when the findings concerning children's prediction of their own memory span for digits (see preceding section) are taken into account. Moreover, the recognition task seems to be inappropriate as a generalization measure because a ceiling effect was reported for all treatment groups. That is, due to the enormous capacity of recognition memory all subjects were performing almost without error. Thus, there is good reason to assume that the selection of inappropriate generalization tasks may have contributed to the negative findings in this study.

When training studies using sort-recall tasks are considered instead, the pattern of results seems to be more clear-cut. One of the first studies combining strategy training in a sort-recall task with the assessment of children's knowledge about the usefulness of mnemonic strategies was conducted by Ringel and Springer (1980). Here, first, third and fifth graders were assigned either to an uninstructed control group or to three experimental groups instructed to use a semantically based sorting strategy. Two of these experimental groups additionally received feedback telling them about their improvement and the cause–effect relationship between strategy use and improvement in performance. Following the test of strategy maintenance on a new sort-recall task, each child was presented with a variety of metamemory questions. Unfortunately, the investigation did not systematically relate metamemory to memory performance and strategy use in the maintenance task. But when the three task-specific metamemory items were considered, it turned out that third grade experimental subjects in the two feedback conditions who maintained the strategy gave more correct answers than the instruction-only and control subjects. All experimental subjects in fifth grade, however, maintained the sorting strategy *and* showed better metamemory than the control children. In contrast, first graders' metamemory scores did not vary as a function of experimental condition. Thus, only for the two older age groups was there a close relationship between metamemory and memory behavior.

More direct evidence concerning the important role of metamemory in strategy acquisition, maintenance, and generalization in sort-recall tasks was reported by Borkowski, Peck, Reid, and Kurtz (1983). In their study, two similar experiments were conducted to explore the connections between young children's cognitive tempo (i.e., impulsivity–reflectivity), metamemory, and strategic behavior on multiple tasks. As in the preceding study by Cavanaugh and Borkowski (1980), sort-recall, alphabet-search, and cognitive-cuing tasks were used, but the design differed in so far as the traditional sort-recall procedure and the alphabet-search task were used to assess strategy acquisition and maintenance, while the cognitive-cuing task was chosen to assess strategy generalization. In other words, the purpose of these experiments was to assess the combined effect of clustering-rehearsal strategy training (on a sort-recall task) and an exhaustive search-strategy training (on an alphabet search task) on memory behavior and performance in a related task that required subjects to sort stimuli into boxes with cue pictures remaining visible during recall. The main differences between the two experiments concerned the position of the meta-memory interview, which was given either before or after the training procedure. Moreover, two training periods instead of one were given in the second study. When metamemory was assessed after training (Study 1), significant correlations were found between metamemory and strategy use in the maintenance and generalization tasks. Both input and output strategies contributed to the significant correlations, and perhaps more important, the correlations changed only slightly when cognitive tempo (impulsivity) or verbal ability were partialled out. As the second experiment demonstrated, a different pattern of results was obtained when metamemory was assessed before the training sessions. Metamemory did not correlate with strategy use at transfer in the first generalization task, but was significantly related to transfer after the second training period had been completed. Again, the correlation remained significant when cognitive tempo was partialled out. Thus, both experiments showed that children who successfully maintained and generalized experimenter-induced strategies also had higher levels of metamemory. Moreover, although metamemory was significantly correlated with cognitive style, it proved to be a better predictor of memory behavior than impulsivity–reflectivity. These results demonstrate the importance of metamemory as a mediator or causal link in the process of strategy maintenance and generalization.

Further support for this assumption comes from a study by Paris, Newman, and McVey (1982). The authors tried to show that strategy train-

To summarize, most of the training studies described in this section confirmed the assumption that the level of metamemory predicts strategy use and memory performance in maintenance and generalization tasks when organizational strategies are under investigation. The relationship between metamemory, memory behavior, and memory performance turned out to be much stronger in the transfer paradigm than in the free-recall paradigm discussed earlier. Consequently, this pattern of results confirms the view of Borkowski, Reid, and Kurtz (1984) that the transfer paradigm provides a more favorable context for the appearance of the metamemory–memory behavior relationship because it requires a decision about whether to use or to abandon a previously learned strategy. Interesting enough, the results obtained by John Borkowski and his colleagues have also shown that metamemory proves to be a better predictor of memory behavior than related concepts like IQ and cognitive style. Furthermore, the findings reported by Borkowski et al. (1984) appear to confirm the "bidirectional hypothesis" with regard to the link between metamemory and memory behavior discussed by Brown (1978) and Flavell (1978). That is, it has been repeatedly shown that the availability of an appropriate strategy *combined with an understanding of its value* leads to successful strategy transfer, which in turn adds to metacognitive knowledge. But it should be mentioned that the demonstration of a close metamemory–memory behavior relationship has been restricted to "near" generalization tasks (see Borkowski & Cavanaugh, 1979) that are very similar to the training situation. The only "far" generalization task—that is, the serial probe recall task used by Kramer and Engle (1981), which differed in such aspects as structure and content, failed to document strategy transfer. Although this task appears to be inappropriate for the aforementioned reasons, the question of whether metamemory is also closely related to strategy transfer in "far" generalization tasks still remain open.

As Pressley, Borkowski, and O'Sullivan (Chapter 4, this volume) have pointed out, most of the training studies discussed so far did not include a self-testing component. According to their findings, the training of procedural knowledge for acquiring specific strategy knowledge—referred to as Metamemory Acquisition Procedures (MAPs) by Pressley et al.—seems to be extremely effective in facilitating transfer. MAPs include memory monitoring processes such as comparing performance after using different strategies (to detect relative strategy efficacy) or self-testing (to evaluate the usefulness of a new strategy). First empirical results given by Pressley et al. (Chapter 4, this volume) demonstrate that children as young as 7 to 8 years of age can possess memory knowledge about relative strategy efficacy *and* use this information to direct subsequent cognitive activity. Teaching MAPs obviously enhances both strategy awareness and strategy usage and may facilitate transfer in "far" generalization tasks.

Meta-analysis of the Correlational Findings

As already mentioned, a statistical procedure for summarizing research findings (i.e., meta-analysis) was additionally chosen to supplement and provide a quality control of the conclusions drawn in the traditional review of research. With regard to the preceding correlation studies, such an approach intuitively makes sense when the relationship between sample size and statistical significance of results is taken into account. For example, consider the case that due to the complex experimental design of many of the preceding studies, a correlation of about .35 between metamemory and memory behavior may fail to reach statistical significance because of small sample size. Undoubtedly, this nonsignificant finding will be taken as negative evidence for the assumed relationship. But on the other hand, when the same correlation coefficient is obtained after ten or more similar studies have been statistically integrated, the conclusion that there is no significant relationship between the two variables in question is no longer justified. As this result is now based on a rather large sample size, it has to be assumed that not only a statistically significant but also a practically relevant relationship was found.

Given the obvious advantage of this procedure of recording the findings of studies in quantitative terms, one is nevertheless confronted with several problems when attempting to extract from each study the statistics needed for combining the results (see Cooper, 1979). The main problem of the present meta-analysis was the fact that several studies had to be omitted from analysis because they did not report any statistics convertable into correlation coefficients. Many other experimental reports contained summary measures like t or F statistics, chi-square, and nonparametric statistics. But here, the guidelines given by Glass (1978) and Glass et al. (1981) proved very helpful in converting these statistics into Pearson correlation coefficients (the guidelines for converting various summary statistics into product–moment correlations used in the present meta-analysis are listed in the appendix).

A second problem faced in the meta-analysis is related to the fact that its basic unit, namely the *study*, is a vaguely specified concept. As Glass (1978) stated, it may represent "anything from an afternoon dalliance with a dozen subjects to an enormous field trial lasting months" (p. 355). As a consequence, the difficulty encountered when statistics from the various metamemory studies were collected was that some articles reported coefficients for several dependent variables (i.e., memory tasks), whereas others concentrated only on a single measure. Moreover, several studies reported results from a series of independent experiments. Although in that case, alternative courses of action are open to the reviewer, the units of analysis chosen here were correlations between metamemory and memory behavior obtained in independent experiments.

With regard to the statistical combination (aggregation) of the correlation coefficients, analysis was carried out in the metric of $r(xy)$, that is, in terms of the familiar product–moment correlation scale. Although it is frequently recommended that the correlations should be squared, averaged, and the square root taken rather than averaged directly, Glass et al. (1981) demonstrated that this choice seldom makes a practical difference.

All in all, 47 correlations were collected or reconstructed by using the preceding strategy. Nearly 50% of the studies reported statistics that had to be converted into correlation coefficients (an overview of all studies included in the meta-analysis is presented in the appendix).[1] Taken together, the correlations between metamemory and memory behavior averaged .41 with a standard deviation of about .18. Thus, the average quantitative relationship was considerably above what was generally assumed to be the strength of association of these two variables. When the correlations were classified by the type of study–memory task and age group (see Table 1), it was shown that the pattern of correlations by and large corroborates the conclusions drawn in the narrative review. Although developmental trends were found for the correlations between metamemory and memory monitoring, the strength of association was remarkable even for preschoolers and kindergarteners. On the other hand, the connection was only modest for younger children when knowledge about organizational strategies in sort-recall tasks was considered. Furthermore, as concluded from the literary review, the association was much stronger for training studies dealing with organizational strategies. Unfortunately, only few age-specific correlations were available here because most researchers in this field collapsed their data across the different age groups to assess the relationship between the two variables. When the correlation between metamemory and strategy use was compared with that between metamemory and memory performance in the studies concerned with organizational strategies, it turned out that the strength of association was higher for the former in both sort-recall studies (.27 vs. .23) and training studies (.42 vs. .33).

In sum, the meta-analytical findings confirmed the assumption that different patterns of correlations can be found for different classes of memory tasks and strategies, and that developmental trends are demon-

[1] The number of age-specific correlations does not equal the number reported for the average correlation both because of this fact and because the age-specific correlations were averaged within each study before the results of the experiments were statistically combined.

Table 1

Correlations between Metamemory and Memory Behavior–Performance Classified by Type of Study and Grade Level[a]

			Grade			
Group	P/K[b]	1/2	3/4	5/6	7+	Average
Memory monitoring (rote memory tasks)	.39 (4)	.48 (6)	.52 (6)	.55 (5)	.59 (2)	.45 (11)
Memory monitoring (prose materials)	—	—	—	.55 (3)	.54 (2)	.57 (3)
Organizational strategies (clustering)	—	.21 (1)	.21 (2)	.46 (3)	—	.25 (13)
Organizational strategies (paired-associate)	—	—	—	—	.52 (2)	.64 (3)
Training studies (organizational strategies)	—	.43 (7)	.28 (7)	—	—	.38 (16)

[a]Numbers in parentheses indicate the number of correlation coefficients available for the analysis.

[b]P, preschool; K, kindergarten.

Given that a strategy is a constructed means–goals relationship (cf. Cox strable for the metamemory–memory behavior relationship within each paradigm. On the other hand, most of the numerical values obtained for the different relationships were surprisingly high. A mean correlation of .41 between metamemory and memory behavior–performance based on the data of several hundred subjects clearly contradicts the conclusion conveyed in most reviews of the field that only a weak link between the two variables has been found. Rather, the quantitative integration of the empirical findings does indicate that metamemory is substantially related to memory behavior and performance. Thus, meta-analysis of metamemory studies led to a conclusion similar to that drawn by Gage (1978) when discussing meta-analysis of empirical research on teaching: "Considered as clusters, the studies acquire sufficient power to dispel the false impression created when the statistical significance of weak single studies is taken seriously" (p. 30).

Summary and Conclusion

The detailed survey of the empirical evidence for the metamemory–memory behavior relationship presented in this article was stimulated by the apparently discrepant conclusions of the review articles by Cavanaugh and Perlmutter (1982) and Wellman (1983). Thus, it is reasonable to ask which of the two views of the relationship proved to be more adequate. The answer is rather simple: the conclusions of both articles were correct with regard to the particular sample of metamemory studies on which they concentrated. That is, most studies assessing the link between metamemory and memory behavior in sort-recall tasks (reviewed by Cavanaugh & Perlmutter, 1982) revealed only weak to moderate relationships even in advanced elementary school children. On the contrary, the pattern of results was generally more positive when memory monitoring tasks were considered instead (as done by Wellman, 1983). Here, considerably more significant relationships between memory knowledge and memory performance were reported, and it was found that occasionally even preschoolers and kindergarteners were capable of efficiently relating metamemory to memory behavior. As a rule of thumb, positive relationships between these two variables were detected for younger children when the memory task required recall or recognition of either single items or small items sets. On the other hand, only weak relationships at best were found for younger subjects when (1) the task was to recall supraspan item lists and (2) a combination of complex strategies was necessary to cope with the task demands.

Neither of these reviews included the results of studies analyzing the metamemory–memory behavior relationship for organizational strategies in paired-associate learning tasks or for several types of intervention programs (i.e., studies investigating the maintenance and generalization of instructed strategies), all of which contributed substantially to the overall positive pattern of results. Taken together, the empirical findings support Wellman's assertion that gloom about weak relationships between metamemory and memory behavior is unwarranted. As the metanalysis of empirical results demonstrates, there is a significant and substantial relationship. Moreover, metamemory predicts memory behavior better than such related concepts as intelligence and cognitive style (cf. Borkowski et al., 1983).

This overall result is all the more impressive in view of the fact that a variety of both methodological and theoretical problems were detected in most studies. The most obvious shortcomings concerned the assessment of metamemory and the lack of explicit theoretical models dealing with the metamemory–memory behavior relationship. As the solution of both types of problems appears to be essential for future progress in metamemory research, particularly for the evaluation of the metamemory–memory behavior relationship, this point should be discussed in more detail.

First of all, as for the methodological problem the most important point concerns the question *how* (i.e., what measures should be used) and *when* (i.e., before, during, or after memory activity) metamemory should be assessed. As already mentioned, in the studies discussed so far the type of metamemory assessment varied systematically with the category of metamemory under investigation. That is, memory monitoring studies mainly used verbal or nonverbal measures concurrent with a memory activity, whereas investigations into the use of organizational strategies relied on verbal measures (i.e., interview questions) given either before or after memory performance. At first glance, the general empirical finding that the concurrent, mainly nonverbal and high-inference metamemory measures proved to be better predictors of memory behavior than the low-inference, independent verbal reports may seem surprising. Nevertheless, it corroborates the results of the thorough, theoretical analysis of the various metamemory measures done by Cavanaugh and Perlmutter (1982), which showed that "in general, concurrent measures are preferable to independent measures, and nonverbal ones (e.g., comparative judgments) are less problematic than those based on verbal reports" (p. 20). Thus, there is good reason to assume that the weak results found in metamemory studies dealing with organizational strategies are at least partly due to the particularly poor metamemory assessment method used in this paradigm. Indeed, as Kurtz et al. (1982) demonstrated, many of these studies did not adequately address the issue of reliability, by using only two or three interview questions (mostly from the Kreutzer et al. interview study). It was shown that an acceptable level of reliability could only be obtained when scores of the various subtests of the Kreutzer et al. interview were pooled to yield a composite score. But as for the aforementioned "how" question, it does not seem to be sufficient to increase only reliability of the interview measure. Because almost all measures of metamemory have their specific limitations and drawbacks (see, for a detailed discussion, Cavanaugh & Perlmutter, 1982; Meichenbaum, Burland, Gruson, & Cameron, in press), a multimethod assessment approach providing converging measures of metamemory is needed to minimize the conceptual and methodological shortcomings of the individual techniques.

With regard to the "when" question, it is very surprising that this problem has been neglected by most metamemory researchers. Even if the often-cited problem connected with the veridicality of postexperimental verbal reports is left out for the moment (see for a more detailed discussion Brown et al., 1983; Cavanaugh & Perlmutter, 1982; Ericsson & Simon, 1980), it may be argued that the retrospective assessment of metamemory leads to an overestimation of long-term, stable memory knowledge. Given the aforementioned bidirectionality hypothesis, experience with a memory task will lead to an increase in postperformance metamemory scores, but nothing is known about the durability of the effect.

That is, we do not know how much of the knowledge acquired in the actual memory situation will actually be transferred to long-term memory. In the case of preexperimental interviews, an underestimation of the "true" metamemory capacity seems to be more probable, especially for younger subjects. As mentioned earlier, making predictions in advance of an actual memory activity appears to be a very difficult task for young children. Yet, most of the subtests of the Kreutzer et al. (1975) interview require children to imagine possible scenarios and to consider how they might act in them (see Brown et al., 1983). This hypothesis of a metamemory overestimation in postexperimental interviews and a metamemory underestimation in preexperimental verbal reports has not yet been systematically tested. Nevertheless, the metanalytical data do show that the "when" question is of empirical importance: whereas the correlation between preexperimental metamemory and memory behavior averaged .25, the relationship was considerably higher (.54) for postexperimental metamemory interviews. Again, a multimethod assessment approach should help to solve or at least minimize this problem.

A second main problem concerns the lack of sophisticated theoretical models leading to an understanding of whether, when, and how metamemory and memory behavior might be related in different age groups and for different tasks. Many of the examples given by Flavell (1978) and Wellman (1983) to describe possible settings when metamemory and memory behavior might not be related do not refer to situations typically found in the empirical investigations into the phenomenon. That is, most of the empirical situations were designed to stimulate conscious, strategic memory activities, and there was also reason to assume that metamemory would influence memory behavior if the former occurred. Consequently, the assumption of a positive relationship between metamemory and memory behavior seems plausible for a wide range of memory-monitoring tasks as well as for memory tasks dealing with organizational strategies. On the other hand, it is not equally easy to maintain that the relationship between metamemory and memory performance (e.g., number of items recalled) should be similarly tight. Although efficient strategy use may improve memory performance in many situations, here the influence of other important variables like memory capacity or information-processing speed should be taken into account and controlled to provide an adequate test of the hypothesis.

With regard to developmental trends in the metamemory–memory behavior relationship, the influence of task characteristics also has to be considered. Negative findings have usually been attributed to production deficiencies of the younger subjects. When children's deficits were on the memory behavior side (as was the case in most studies dealing with rote memory tasks), it proved very helpful to assess the children's belief about the task-specific means–goals relationship in order to explain the empirical findings (see Cox & Paris, 1979; Wellman, 1977). Interestingly, when the identical empirical fact (i.e., no metamemory–memory behavior relationship) was found in studies dealing with prose materials, this was mainly due to deficits on the metamemory side. That is, younger subjects were not aware of the most important text units but automatically reproduced these key categories during recall. These findings seem to indicate that task-oriented theoretical models are necessary to explain developmental trends in the metamemory–memory behavior relationship. On the other hand, it also may be interesting to see if the more general and sophisticated models of knowledge behavior relationships already developed in other areas (e.g., the attitude–behavior connection in social psychology) can be used to form testable hypotheses about the nature of metamemory–memory behavior relationships (see the suggestions by Cavanaugh & Perlmutter, 1982; Wellman, 1983).

A last crucial point is the fact that empirical evidence about the metamemory–memory behavior relationship is restricted to cross-sectional studies mostly using age groups as units of analysis. Given the large within-group variances reported in several studies (see Brown & Smiley, 1978; Pressley & Levin, 1977) and the assumption that understanding of intraindividual change is necessary to truly understand interindividual differences (see Baltes, Reese, & Nesselroade, 1977), longitudinal studies are also needed. So far, there appears to be only one study that systematically analyzes the metamemory–memory behavior relationship in a (long-term) longitudinal design, combining single-case studies with the traditional age-group assessments (Knopf, Körkel, Schneider, Vogel, Weinert, & Wetzel, 1981). But mainly due to both time-consuming assessment methods and large sample size, results are not yet available.

To conclude, a comprehensive analysis of the empirical evidence of the metamemory–memory behavior relationship yields a complex but generally more positive pattern than recently assumed in the literature. Nevertheless, a variety of methodological and conceptual problems restrict both reliability and validity of the findings. But because remedial procedures seem to be available, there is hope that the metamemory concept may prove even more efficient in predicting memory behavior and will find its place in theories of cognitive development and intelligence.

Acknowledgment

I am especially grateful to John Flavell for encouraging me to work on this project and for many hours of discussion on this topic. Thanks are further due to John Borkowski, John Cavanaugh, Joachim Körkel, Vonnie McLoyd, Harriet Mischel, Michael Pressley, Marjorie Taylor, Franz Weinert, and Heinz Wimmer for helpful comments on earlier versions of the article.

Appendix

To make the meta-analytical procedure used in this study clearer and replicable, a listing of the statistical conversions applied to the data is given in Tables A1 and A2. It should be noted that Table A1 only contains the conversion rules

Table A1

Guidelines for Converting Various Summary Statistics into Product–Moment Correlations

Reported statistic	Transformation to r_{xy}
(1) Point-biserial correlation, r_{pb}	$r_{xy} = r_{pb} \sqrt{n_1 n_2}\ un$ (u = ordinate of unit normal distribution n = total sample size)
(2) $t = \dfrac{\overline{X}_1 - \overline{X}_2}{\sqrt{s^2 \left(\dfrac{1}{n_1} + \dfrac{1}{n_2} \right)}}$	$r_{pb} = \sqrt{\dfrac{t^2}{t^2 + (n_1 + n_2 - 2)}}$ then convert r_{pb} to r_{xy} via (1)
(3) $F = MS_b/MS_w$ for $J = 2$ groups	$\sqrt{F} = |t|$ then proceed via (2) above
(4) $F = MS_b/MS_w$ for $J > 2$ groups	Collapse J groups to 2 then proceed via (3) above
(5) χ^2 only (i.e., no frequencies reported) for a contingency table	$r_{xy} \cong P = \left(\dfrac{\chi^2}{\chi^2 + n} \right)^{1/2}$
(6) 2 × 2 contingency table	Calculate tetrachoric r_{xy} from tables

Table A2

Correlations between Metamemory and Memory Behavior-Performance Classified by Study and Grade Level[a]

Studies classified by type	Grade					
	P/K	1/2	3/4	5/6	7+	Average
Memory monitoring (rote memory)						
Bisanz et al. (1978)	—	.24	.23	.39	.55	.35
Brown & Lawton (1977)	—	—	—	—	—	.65
Kelly et al. (1976)	—	—	—	—	—	.12 (2)

(Continued)

Table A2 (*Continued*)

Studies classified by type	Grade					
	P/K	1/2	3/4	5/6	7+	Average
Levin et al. (1977)	—	.65	—	.69	.62	.65
Posnansky (1978)	.64	—	.51	—	—	.57
Rogoff et al. (1974)	—	—	—	—	—	.34
Wellman (1977)	.19	.35	.60	—	—	.36
Wippich (1981)	.45	—	—	—	—	.45
Worden & Sladewski-Awig (1982)	.29	.33	.32	.26	—	.30
Yussen & Berman (1981)	—	.64	.73	.70	—	.69 (2)
Memory monitoring (prose materials)						
Brown & Smiley (1978)	—	—	—	.33	.53	.43
Elliott (1980)	—	—	—	.76	.54	.71
Yussen et al. (1980)	—	—	—	.57	—	.57
Organizational strategies (clustering)						
Best & Ornstein (1979)	—	—	.21	.36	—	.26
Cavanaugh & Borkowski (1980)	—	—	—	—	—	.12 (6)
Justice (1979)	—	—	—	—	—	.32
Salatas & Flavell (1976)	—	.21	—	—	—	.21
Wimmer & Tornquist (1980)	—	—	—	—	—	.44
Bjorklund & Zeman (1982)	—	—	—	.65	—	.32 (3)
Organizational strategies (paired associate)						
Waters (1982)	—	—	—	—	.52	.52
Pressley & Levin (1977)	—	—	—	—	.52	.52
Moynahan (1978)	—	—	—	—	—	.88
Training studies (organizational strategies)						
Borkowski et al. (1983)	—	—	—	—	—	.53 (2)
Cavanaugh & Borkowski (1979)	—	—	.38	—	—	.38 (4)
Kendall et al. (1980)	—	.53	—	—	—	.53 (2)
Kurtz et al. (1982)	—	.37	—	—	—	.37 (4)
Paris et al. (1982)	—	.37	—	—	—	.37
Kramer & Engle (1981)	—	—	.19	—	—	.19 (3)

[a]Numbers in parentheses indicate the number of correlation coefficients available for analysis.

used in this study; a more comprehensive listing of possible guidelines can be found in Glass, McGaw, & Smith (1981, pp. 149 and 150).

Furthermore, a more detailed overview of the results of meta-analysis is given in Table A2, presenting the specific correlation coefficients obtained for each study included in the meta-analysis.

References

Baker, L., & Brown, A. L. Metacognition and the reading process. In D. Pearson (Ed.), *A handbook of reading research*. New York: Plenum, 1981.

Baltes, P. B., Reese, H. W., & Nesselroade, J. R. *Life-span developmental psychology: Introduction to research methods*. Belmont, CA: Wadsworth, 1977.

Belmont, J. M., Butterfield, E. C., & Ferretti, R. P. *To secure transfer of training, instruct self-management skills*. Paper presented at the annual meeting of the American Educational Research Association, Boston, 1980.

Berch, D. B., & Evans, R. C. Decision processes in children's recognition memory. *Journal of Experimental Child Psychology*, 1973, 16, 148–164.

Best, D. L. *Inducing children to generate organizational strategies: A comparison with explicit training procedures*. Paper presented at the biennial meeting of the Society for Research in Child Development, Boston, April 1981.

Best, D. L., & Ornstein, P. A. *Children's generation and communication of organizational strategies*. Paper presented at the biennial meeting of the Society for Research in Child Development, San Francisco, March 1979.

Bisanz, G. L., Vesonder, G. T., & Voss, J. T. Knowledge of one's own responding and the relation of such knowledge to learning: A developmental study. *Journal of Experimental Child Psychology*, 1978, 25, 116–128.

Bjorklund, D. F., & Hock, H. S. Age differences in the temporal locus of memory organization in children's recall. *Journal of Experimental Child Psychology*, 1982, 33, 347–362.

Bjorklund, D. F., & Zeman, B. R. Children's organization and metamemory awareness in their recall of familiar information. *Child Development*, 1982, 53, 799–810.

Borkowski, J. G., & Cavanaugh, J. C. Maintenance and generalization of skills and strategies by the retarded. In N. R. Ellis (Ed.), *Handbook of mental deficiency: Psychological theory and research* (2nd ed.). Hillsdale, NJ: Erlbaum, 1979.

Borkowski, J. G., Peck, V. A., Reid, M. K., & Kurtz, B. E. Impulsivity and strategy transfer: Metamemory as mediator. *Child Development*, 1983, 54, 459–473.

Borkowski, J. G., Reid, M. K., & Kurtz, B. E. Metacognition and retardation: Paradigmatic, theoretical, and applied perspectives. In R. Sperber, C. McCauley, & P. Brooks (Eds.), *Learning and cognition in the mentally retarded*. Baltimore, University Park Press, 1984.

Brown, A. L. The development of memory: Knowing, knowing about knowing, and knowing how to know. In H. W. Reese (Ed.), *Advances in child development and behavior* (Vol. 10). New York: Academic Press, 1975.

Brown, A. L. Knowing when, where and how to remember: A problem of metacognition. In R. Glaser (Ed.), *Advances in instructional psychology*. Hillsdale, NJ: Erlbaum, 1978.

Brown, A. L., & Barclay, C. R. The effects of training specific mnemonics on the metamnemonic efficacy of retarded children, *Child Development*, 1976, 47, 71–80.

Brown, A. L., Bransford, J. D., Ferrara, R. A., & Campione, J. C. Learning, understanding, and remembering. In J. H. Flavell & E. M. Markman (Eds.), *Carmichael's handbook of developmental psychology* (Vol. 1), 1983.

Brown, A. L., & Campione, J. C. Training strategic study time apportionment in educable retarded children. *Intelligence*, 1977, 1, 94–107.

Brown, A. L., Campione, J. C., & Barclay, C. R. Training self-checking routines for estimating test readiness: Generalization from list learning to prose recall. *Child Development*, 1979, 50, 501–512.

Brown, A. L., Campione, J. C., & Murphy, M. D. Maintenance and generalization of trained metamnemonic awareness by educable retarded children: Span estimation. *Journal of Experimental Child Psychology*, 1977, 24, 191–211.

Brown, A. L., & Lawton, S. C. The feeling of knowing experience in educable retarded children. *Developmental Psychology*, 1977, *13*, 364–370.

Brown, A. L., & Smiley, S. S. Rating the importance of structural units of prose passages: A problem of metacognition development. *Child Development*, 1977, *48*, 1–8.

Brown, A. L., & Smiley, S. S. The development of strategies for studying texts. *Child Development*, 1978, *49*, 1076–1088.

Brown, A. L., Smiley, S. S., Day, J., Townsend, M., & Lawton, S. C. Intrusion of a thematic idea in children's recall or prose. *Child Development*, 1977, *48*, 1454–1466.

Brown, A. L., Smiley, S. S., & Lawton, S. C. The effects of expe.ience on the selection of suitable retrieval cues for styding texts. *Child Development*, 1978, *49*, 829–835.

Cavanaugh, J. C., & Borkowski, J. G. The metamemory–memory "connection": Effects of strategy training and maintenance. *The Journal of General Psychology*, 1979, *101*, 161–174.

Cavanaugh, J. C., & Borkowski, J. G. Searching for metamemory–memory connections: A developmental study. *Developmental Psychology*, 1980, *16*, 441–453.

Cavanaugh, J. C., & Perlmutter, M. Metamemory: A critical examination. *Child Development*, 1982, *53*, 11–28.

Chi, M. T. H. Knowledge structures and development. In R. S. Siegler (Ed.), *Children's thinking: What develops?* Hillsdale, NJ: Erlbaum, 1978.

Chi, M. T. H. Representing knowledge and metaknowledge: Implications for interpreting metamemory research. In R. H. Kluwe & F. E. Weinert (Eds.), *Metacognition, motivation, and learning*. Hillsdale, NJ: Erlbaum, in press.

Cooper, H. M. Statistically combining independent studies: A meta-analysis of sex differences in conformity research. *Journal of Personality and Social Psychology*, 1979, *37*, 131–146.

Cooper, H. M., & Rosenthal, R. Statistical versus traditional procedures for summarizing research findings. *Psychological Bulletin*, 1980, *87*, 442–449.

Corsale, K. *Children's knowledge and strategic use of organizational structure in recall.* Paper presented at the biennial meeting of the Society for Research in Child Development, Boston, April 1981.

Corsale, K., & Ornstein, P. A. Developmental changes in children's use of semantic information in recall. *Journal of Experimental Child Psychology*, 1980, *30*, 231–245.

Cox, G. L., & Paris, S. G. *The nature of mnemonic production deficiencies: A lifespan analysis.* Paper presented at the biennial meeting of the Society for Research in Child Development, San Francisco, March 1979.

Danner, F. W. Children's understanding of intersentence organization in the recall of short descriptive passages. *Journal of Educational Psychology*, 1976, *68*, 174–183.

Elliott, S. N. *Sixth grade and college students' metacognitive knowledge of prose organization and study strategies.* Paper presented at the annual meeting of the American Educational Research Association, Boston, 1980.

Ericsson, K. A., & Simon, H. A. Verbal reports as data. *Psychological Review*, 1980, *87*, 215–251.

Eyde, D. R., & Altman, R. *An exploration of metamemory processes in mildly and moderately retarded children.* Unpublished manuscript, University of Missouri—Columbia, 1978.

Flavell, J. H. Cognitive monitoring. In P. Dickson (Ed.), *Children's oral communication skills.* New York: Academic Press, 1981.

Flavell, J. H. First discussant's comments: What is memory development the development of? *Human Development*, 1971, *14*, 272–278.

Flavell, J. H. Metacognition and cognitive monitoring: A new area of cognitive-developmental inquiry. *American Psychologist*, 1979, *34*, 906–911.

Flavell, J. H. Metacognitive development. In J. M. Scandura & C. J. Brainerd (Eds.), *Structural/process theories of complex human behavior*. Alphen a.d. Rijn: Sijthoff & Noordhoff, 1978.

Flavell, J. H., Friedrichs, A., & Hoyt, J. Developmental changes in memorization processes. *Cognitive Psychology*, 1970, *1*, 324–340.

Flavell, J. H., & Wellman, H. M. Metamemory. In R. V. Kail, Jr. & J. W. Hagen (Eds.), *Perspectives on the development of memory and cognition*. Hillsdale, NJ: Erlbaum, 1977.

Gage, N. L. *The scientific basis of the art of teaching*. New York: Teachers College Press, 1978.

Glass, G. V. Primary, secondary, and meta-analysis of research. *Educational Researcher*, 1976, *5*, 3–8.

Glass, G. V. Integrating findings: The meta-analysis of research. In L. S. Shulman (Ed.), *Review of research in education* (Vol. 5). Itasca, IL: Peacock, 1978.

Glass, G. V., McGaw, B., & Smith, M. L. *Meta-analysis in social research*. Beverly Hills: Sage, 1981.

Hagen, J. W. Commentary. *Monographs of the Society for Research in Child Development*, 1975, *40*(1, Serial No. 159).

Justice, E. M. *The development of metamemory concerning memory strategies and its relationship to memory behavior*. Unpublished manuscript, Old Dominion University, Norfolk 1981.

Justice, E. M., & Bray, N. W. *The effects of context and feedback on metamemory in young children*. Paper presented at the biennial meetinng of the Society for Research in Child Development, San Francisco, March 1979.

Kee, D. W., & Bell, T. S. The development of organizational strategies in the storage and retrieval of categorical items in free recall learning. *Child Development*, 1981, *52*, 1163–1171.

Kelly, M., Scholnick, E. K., Travers, S. H., & Johnson, J. W. Relations among memory, memory appraisal, and memory strategies. *Child Development*, 1976, *47*, 648–659.

Kendall, C. R., Borkowski, J. G., & Cavanaugh, J. C. Metamemory and the transfer of an interrogative strategy by EMR children. *Intelligence*, 1980, *4*, 255–270.

Kluwe, R. H. Cognitive knowledge and executive control: Metacognition. In D. Griffin (Ed.), *Human mind—animal Mind*. New York: Springer, 1982.

Knopf, M., Körkel, J., Schneider, W., Vogel, K., Weinert, F. E., & Wetzel, M. Die Entwicklung von Metakognition, Attributionsstilen und Selbstinstruktion. The development of metacognition, attributional style, and self-instruction. Preliminary research report, University of Heidelberg, August 1981.

Kobasigawa, A. Retrieval strategies in the development of memory. In R. V. Kail, Jr., & J. W. Hagen (Eds.), *Perspectives on the development of memory and cognition*. Hillsdale, NJ: Erlbaum, 1977.

Kramer, J. J., & Engle, R. W. Teaching awareness of strategic behavior in combination with strategy training: Effects on children's memory performance. *Journal of Experimental Child Psychology*, 1981, *32*, 513–530.

Kreutzer, M. A., Leonard, C., & Flavell, J. H. An interview study of children's knowledge about memory. *Monographs of the Society for Research in Child Development*, 1975, *40*(1, Serial No. 159).

Kurtz, B. E., Reid, M. K., Borkowski, J. G., & Cavanaugh, J. C. On the reliability and validity of children's metamemory. *Bulletin of the Psychonomic Society*, 1982, *19*, 137–140.

Lange, G. Organization-related processes in children's recall. In P. A. Ornstein (Ed.), *Memory development in children*, Hillsdale, NJ: Erlbaum, 1978.

Levin, J. R., Yussen, S. R., DeRose, T. M., & Pressley, M. Developmental changes in assessing recall and recognition memory capacity. *Developmental Psychology*, 1977, *13*, 608–615.

Markman, E. M. *Factors affecting the young child's ability to monitor his memory.* Unpublished doctoral dissertation, University of Pennsylvania, 1973.

Masur, E., McIntyre, L., & Flavell, J. H. Developmental changes in apportionment of study time among items in a multi-trial free recall task. *Journal of Experimental Child Psychology*, 1973, *15*, 237–246.

Meichenbaum, D., Burland, S., Gruson, L., & Cameron, R. Metacognitive assessment. In S. Yussen (Ed.), *The growth of reflection in children.* New York: Academic Press, in press.

Moely, B. E. Organizational factors in the development of memory. In R. V. Kail, Jr., & J. W. Hagen (Eds.), *Perspectives on the development of memory and cognition.* Hillsdale, NJ: Erlbaum, 1977.

Monroe, E. K., & Lange, G. The accuracy with which children judge the composition of their free recall. *Child Development*, 1977, *48*, 381–387.

Moore, M. J., & Haith, M., *Executive processes during memory retrieval.* Paper presented at the biennial meeting of the Society for Research in Child Development, San Francisco, March 1979.

Moynahan, E. D. The development of knowledge concerning the effect of categorization upon free recall. *Child Development*, 1973, *44*, 238–246.

Moynahan, E. D. The development of the ability to assess recall performance. *Journal of Experimental Child Psychology*, 1976, *21*, 94–97.

Moynahan, E. D. Assessment and selection of paired-associate strategies: A developmental study. *Journal of Experimental Child Psychology*, 1978, *26*, 257–266.

Neimark, E., Slotnick, N. S., & Ulrich, T. Development of memorization and strategies. *Development Psychology*, 1971, *5*, 427–432.

Paris, S. G. Coordination of means and goals in the development of mnemonic skills. In P. Ornstein (Ed.), *Memory development in children.* Hillsdale, NJ: Erlbaum, 1978.

Paris, S. G., & Lindauer, B. K. The development of cognitive skills during childhood. In B. Wolman (Ed.), *Handbook of developmental psychology.* Englewood Cliffs, NJ: Prentice–Hall, 1982.

Paris, S. G., Newman, R. S., & McVey, K. A. Learning the functional significance of mnemonic actions: A microgenetic study of strategy acquisition. *Journal of Experimental Child Psychology*, 1982, *34*, 490–509.

Posnansky, C. J. Age and task related differences in the use of category size information for retrieval of categorized items. *Journal of Experimental Child Psychology*, 1978, *26*, 373–382.

Pressley, M., & Levin, J. R. Developmental differences in subjects' associative-learning strategies and performance: Assessing a hypothesis. *Journal of Experimental Child Psychology*, 1977, *24*, 431–439.

Ringel, B. A., & Springer, C. J. On knowing how well one is remembering: The persistence of strategy use during transfer. *Journal of Experimental Child Psychology*, 1980, *29*, 322–333.

Rogoff, B., Newcombe, N., & Kagan, J. Planfulness and recognition memory. *Child Development*, 1974, *45*, 972–977.

Salatas, H., & Flavell, J. H. Behavioral and metamnemonic indicators of strategic behaviors under remember instructions in first grade. *Child Development*, 1976, *47*, 81–89.

Stein, N. L., & Glenn, C. G. An analysis of story comprehension in elementary school children. In R. O. Freedle (Ed.), *Discourse processing: Multidisciplinary perspectives.* Norwood, NJ: Ablex, 1979.

Tenney, Y. J. The child's conception of organization and recall. *Journal of Experimental Child Psychology*, 1975, *19*, 100–114.

Waters, H. S. Memory development in adolescence: Relationships between metamemory, strategy use, and peformance. *Journal of Experimental Child Psychology*, 1982, 33, 183–195.

Wellman, H. M. *The role of metamemory in memory behavior: A developmental demonstration.* Unpublished manuscript, University of Michigan, 1979.

Wellman, H. M. Tip of the tongue and feeling of knowing experiences: A developmental study of memory monitoring. *Child Development*, 1977, 48, 13–21.

Wellman, H. M. Metamemory revisited. In M. T. H. Chi (Ed.), *Trends in memory development research.* Basel, Switzerland, Karger, 1983.

Wimmer, H., & Tornquist, K. The role of metamemory and metamemory activation in the development of mnemonic performance. *International Journal of Behavioral Development*, 1980, 3,. 71–81.

Wippich, W. Metagedächtnis und Gedächtniserfahrung [Metamemory and memory experience]. *Zeitschrift für Entwicklungspsychologie und Pädagogische Psychologie* 1980, 12, 40–43.

Wippich, W. Verbessert eine Einkaufssituation die Vorhersage der eigenen Behaltensleistungen im **Vorschulalter?** [Does a shopping situation improve the prediction of memory in preschool children]. *Zeitschrift für Entwicklungspsychologie und Pädagogische Psychologie*, 1981, 13, 280–290.

Worden, P. E., & Sladewski-Awig, L. J. Children's awareness of memorability. *Journal of Educational Psychology*, 1982, 74, 341–350.

Yussen, S. R., & Berman, L. Memory predictions for recall and recognition in first-, third-, and fifth-grade children. *Developmental Psychology*, 1981, 17, 224–229.

Yussen, S. R., Levin, J. R., Berman, L., & Palm, J. Developmental changes in the awareness of memory benefits associated with different types of picture organization. *Developmental Psychology*, 1979, 15, 447–449.

Yussen, S. R., & Levy, V. M. Developmental changes in predicting one's own span of short-term memory. *Journal of Experimental Child Psychology*, 1975, 19, 502–508.

Yussen, S. R., Matthews, S. R., Buss, R. R., & Kane, P. T. Developmental changes in judging important and critical elements of stories. *Developmental Psychology*, 1980, 16, 213–219.

CHAPTER 4

Children's Metamemory and the Teaching of Memory Strategies*

Michael Pressley, John G. Borkowski, and Julie O'Sullivan

Introduction

In 1970, a comprehensive chapter about memory in children could have been written with little effort. There were very few research programs on memory development, and the ones that did exist extended ideas from adult cognition in a straightforward fashion; see Hagen, Jongeward, & Kail, (1975) for examples. Since then, however, there has been an explosion of interest in children's memory, focussing on spontaneous strategic processing (e.g., Kail & Hagen, 1977), teaching memory strategies (e.g., Pressley, Forrest-Pressley, Elliott-Faust, & Miller, 1985; Pressley, Heisel, McCormick, & Nakamura, 1982), and metamemory (e.g., Flavell & Wellman, 1977; Pressley, Borkowski, & O'Sullivan, 1984).

This chapter proposes an interface between two of these subareas of memory development, metamemory and the teaching of memory strategies. In doing so, a review of the construct of metamemory is presented, with a discussion on metamemory–memory behavior relationships. A multicomponent model of metamemory about strategies is then presented, followed by a description of three strategy instructional approaches that

*The writing of this chapter was supported by a grant to the first author from the Natural Sciences and Engineering Research Council of Canada. John Borkowski's participation was supported in part by NIE Grant G-81-0134 and in part by NIH Grant No. HD 17648.

111

have a metacognitive component. Throughout the presentation, relevant research is reviewed. When all of the evidence discussed here is considered, it is apparent that the successful teaching of memory strategies is critically dependent on metamemory about those strategies.

The Concept of Metamemory

Flavell and Wellman (1977) provided an important perspective on the nature and function of children's metamemory. For a general definition we cite their original statement about the properties and attributes of metamemory:

> [An] individual's knowledge of and awareness of memory, or of anything pertinent to information storage and retrieval . . . [For example,] a person has metamemory if he [or she] knows that some things are easier to remember than others, is aware that one item is on the verge of recall, while another is wholly irretrievable at present. (p.4)

Flavell and Wellman (1977) assumed that someone with mature metamemory would recognize that (1) some situations require memorization efforts and others do not; (2) large individual differences exist in memory skills; (3) intraindividual differences in memory competence are common across tasks and settings; and (4) monitoring cognitive performance is often useful in the deployment of encoding and retrieval strategies. This final category of metamemorial knowledge—information about the judicious use of strategies—is an extremely important part of metamemory, as documented by the large number of studies directed specifically at instructing children to be more strategic (see Pressley, Heisel, McCormick, & Nakamura, 1982).

A memory strategy on the part of the learner is a course of action or plan, often but not always undertaken with the *goal* of remembering (Brown, 1975; Flavell, 1970; Meacham, 1972; Pressley, Forrest-Pressley, & Elliott-Faust, in press). Such activities can be aimed at encoding, storing, or retrieving information (Brown, 1975). The intelligent adult possesses a variety of memory strategies, with strategy development continuing into adulthood (e.g., Poon, Foxard, Cermak, Arenberg, & Thompson, 1980; Pressley, 1982; Pressley, Heisel, McCormick, & Nakamura, 1982; Pressley, Levin, & Bryant, 1983). Strategies entail basic cognitive processes organized in specific ways (see Borkowski & Büchel, 1983; Pressley, Heisel, McCormick, & Nakamura, 1982). An additional, essential aspect of strategic action is the knowledge that a learner must have about the *value* of a strategy, its *range* of applicability, and *mode* of execution. From this perspective, specific strategy knowledge—a major component of metamemory—may be enhanced by providing strategy-relevant information, either before or after training of the strategy.

Fundamental to the theoretical validation of metamemory is the demonstration of causal linkages between metamemory and memory behavior, specifically between metamemory and the appropriate execution of a strategy. It might be added as well that this causality is assumed to be bidirectional (Brown, 1978), with metamemory directing strategy deployment and, conversely, strategy encounters producing changes in knowledge about memory. A preliminary step to the firm establishment of causal linkages involves correlation research—documenting the existence of metamemory–memory connections in specific situations (e.g., Underwood, 1975). However, the discovery of metamemory–memory connections has been elusive (see Flavell, 1978).

Metamemory researchers have tended to focus on one or two situations in which causal linkages between metamemory and memory performance might exist followed by a single test of the hypothesis, with limited operational specification of the metamemory dimension. Salatas' and Flavell's (1976) examination of the interrelationship of children's knowledge about and use of categorization strategies is an example of research of this type. Another problem of metamemory research is that issues of reliability have been ignored; for instance, the definition of metamemory has often been confined to a single inquiry about a memory state or process (e.g., Cavanaugh & Borkowski, 1980). In general, single metamemory items are unreliable (Kurtz, Reid, Borkowski, & Cavanaugh, 1982). Thus, low correlations with other variables are not surprising (see Rushton, Brainerd, & Pressley, 1983, for a complete analysis of this problem). Despite these methodological problems, recent reviewers have concluded with some confidence (largely unjustified, in our opinions) that there is little evidence in support of a memory–metamemory relationship (e.g., Cavanaugh & Perlmutter, 1982; Chi, 1984).

There are several reasons why a more positive view about the importance of metamemory for memory behavior is tenable:

1. Many of the studies that are cited frequently as contributing to the negative evaluation have methodological shortcomings, including the unreliability of metamemory measures, limited scope, and narrow range of memory tasks (see Rushton et al. 1983; Schneider, Chapter 3, this volume).

2. Strong, positive relationships between aspects of metamemory and memory behavior have been generated, especially (1) when *process* rather than performance measures have been recorded; (2) when tasks have been

challenging; and (3) when strategy modification and reinstatement have been required rather than strategy regurgitation. For example, good memorizers are more aware of their memories and limitations than are bad memorizers (e.g., Levin, Yussen, DeRose, & Pressley, 1977; Yussen & Berman, 1981). Children who transfer a complex elaboration strategy have more mature memory knowledge prior to strategy training than do children who do not (Kurtz et al., 1982). There have been consistent relationships observed between children's knowledge of the retrievability of items in memory and the amount of effort necessary to retrieve that information (e.g., Lachman, Lachman, & Thronesbury, 1979; Posnansky, 1978; Read & Bruce, 1982; Wellman, 1982). Also, strategy use during study of text is related to knowledge of the structure of text (Baker & Brown, 1983; Brown & Smiley, 1978).

3. In an impressive summary of the evidence bearing on the metamemory–memory relationship, Schneider (Chapter 3, this volume) conducted a meta-analysis based on Glass's (1978) recommendations, involving 47 individual metamemory–memory correlations. Across studies correlations averaged .41 (SD = .18). It should be noted that some aspects of metamemory, such as monitoring of memory performance, contributed more heavily to the overall correlation; aspects of declarative metamemory knowledge, such as knowledge of the value of categorization, had a lesser impact. Evidence of a relationship between metamemory and memory processes on difficult transfer tasks provides the initial justification for proceeding to build a model of strategy training and transfer that includes metamemory as a critical component.

Metamemory and Its Relationship to Strategy Use

The fact that not all aspects of metamemory are implicated in memory behavior to the same degree (Schneider, Chapter 3, this volume) suggests that the concept needs to be more highly differentiated. Although a systematic delineation of metamemory in its entirety is beyond the scope of this chapter, we provide an outline of metamemory components that are associated with memory-strategy use in various contexts. By providing a more articulated model of metamemory about strategies, we can present a more complete discussion of the role of metamemory during strategy training and transfer than has been possible to date. The hope is to generate more analytical studies of metamemory and strategy use. At the same time readers are cautioned that the model is not exhaustive. It merely provides a framework with initial components that are likely to remain as major aspects of metamemory. Empirical scrutiny of these fundamental components and their interactions needs to occur before a more intricate theory of metamemory–memory strategy functioning can be advanced.

Metamemory about Strategies

Part of metamemory, which we refer to as metamemory about strategies (MAS), specifically relates to memory strategies. MAS is in a constant state of flux, changing with each new memory experience. It is assumed that MAS is a mixture of procedural knowledge (i.e., strategies and "how-to" knowledge about strategies) and declarative knowledge (i.e., factual knowledge about strategies). This procedural–declarative distinction was recently introduced by Chi (1984). It is a distinction that may prove useful in the analysis of existing research on metamemory. For instance, Schneider (Chapter 3, this volume) and Wellman (1983) have presented data showing higher metamemory–memory correlations for procedural than for declarative knowledge. The procedural and declarative knowledge that makes up MAS can be divided into at least six separate components:

(1) **Learner's Strategies.** The most fundamental elements in metamemory about strategies are the learner's strategies (see Figure 1). It is assumed that a sophisticated learner knows a number of strategies or processing rules, such as the following:

- a. *Single Item Repetition:* Repeating material over and over, one item at a time.
- b. *Cumulative Rehearsal:* Repeating material over and over in a cumulative fashion, rehearsing old items along with new ones (e.g., Flavell, 1970).
- c. *Meaningful Organization:* Looking for meaningful, semantic relationships among items. (e.g., Moely, 1977).
- d. *Hierarchical Allocation:* Studying information in order of its importance, with more important information studied first (e.g., Brown & Smiley, 1978).
- e. *Differential Effort Allocations:* Expending more effort to study the material that is not yet learned (e.g., Brown & Smiley, 1978).
- f. *Imagery Elaboration:* Making up interactive images that include the to-be-learned items (e.g., Pressley, 1977).
- g. *Verbal Elaboration:* Making up a story to include the to-be-remembered items (e.g., Rohwer, 1973).
- h. *Keyword Method:* Transforming unfamiliar items (e.g., foreign

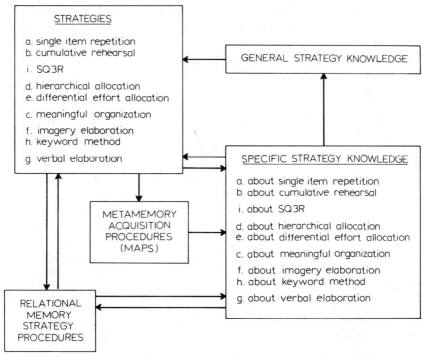

FIGURE 1. Metamemory about strategies: Arrows indicate how subcomponents interact to produce additional metamemory that affects deployment of strategies.

words) to more familiar ones (e.g., sound-alike English words) and then putting them into relational images with other information (e.g., Pressley, Levin, & Delaney, 1982).

i. SQ3R: Surveying what is to be learned; questioning oneself; reading the material; reciting it; reviewing all important information (e.g., Robinson, 1961).

Some of these strategies share subprocesses. For instance, cumulative rehearsal and SQ3R include simple repetition. Imagery and verbal elaboration depend on meaningful relationships, but differ in the modes of representation that they tap. The keyword method includes imagery elaboration. Even though processes overlap among various strategies, it is assumed that a learner can possess strategy rules but not always recognize the processing redundancies among strategies. This knowledge of the relationships among cognitive strategies, especially among their components, needs to be considered as an aspect of metamemory separate from the knowledge of the rules in isolation. The relational aspect of MAS results in the ordering of strategies (such as those depicted in Figure 1); a more complete discussion of relational memory strategies is taken up after discussion of two other components, general and specific strategy knowledge. In general, the principal components of MAS determine the effectiveness of strategy deployment.

(2) **General Strategy Knowledge.** An important aspect of MAS is a set of general principles relevant to all memory strategies. These principles are labelled general strategy knowledge and include information such as (a) it takes effort to apply strategies and (b) if properly applied, strategies aid learning. Because most research on memory strategies has focused on only single strategies, there has been very little work on this type of general, nonspecific knowledge that cuts across strategies. Figure 1 represents general strategy knowledge as serving to direct strategy use and as being derived from specific strategy knowledge, which is considered next.

(3) **Specific Strategy Knowledge.** Each strategy has associated with it unique specific strategy knowledge, although the categories of stored declarative knowledge are probably similar across strategies. For each strategy a proficient memorizer is expected to have knowledge about when to use the strategy, including the type and amount of material that can be learned with the strategy and the retention interval appropriate to the strategy. An especially important piece of specific strategy knowledge is knowing whether a strategy was helpful in the past in learning content similar to that under study. A proficient memorizer knows how to modify the strategy to fit various types of materials. Motivational information is probably also stored, such as how much effort is required to use the strategy and how much fun is associated with its use. There is episodic information associated with strategies such as when, where, and how a strategy was acquired, as well as specific occasions when it was used successfully and unsuccessfully. In this sense, specific strategy knowledge directs the use of strategies (see Figure 1).

The amount of specific strategy knowledge undoubtedly differs tremendously from learner to learner, even among proficient learners. A memory expert has finely tuned notions about how to use imagery strategies, much more highly differentiated than the metamemories of most college students. Nonetheless, if given a paired-associate list, students who learned about imagery in introductory psychology might appear as proficient as the expert, because their metamemory about imagery elaboration would be above the threshold necessary to execute the strategy for paired-associate learning. On the other hand, in other situations, such as predicting the success of 3-year-olds attempting to use imagery strategies, the expert would outperform college students because they have knowledge about the age-appropriateness of the imagery strategy.

(4) **Relational Memory Strategy Procedures** and (5) **Relational Memory Strategy Knowledge.** We hypothesize that there is a set of relational memory strategy procedures that detects commonalities among strategies and produces relational memory strategy knowledge. Relational memory strategy procedures are metarules (Chi, 1984) in that they take other rules as input. In particular, relational memory strategy procedures analyze strategies and group them as similar on the basis of shared processes. Thus, single item repetition, cumulative rehearsal, and SQ3R (described earlier) could be considered similar based on the rehearsal component, as might imagery elaboration, verbal elaboration, and keyword method based on the elaboration component. Within this latter cluster, the version of the keyword method described earlier might be perceived as more similar to imagery elaboration than to verbal elaboration based on the imagery component. The richnesss of declarative knowledge about strategy similarities depends on the extent that the relational memory strategy procedures are executed. Once relationships are established, the memory strategy representations and specific strategy knowledge components are reordered so that the more similar the strategies, the more closely the strategy representations are located. Thus, representational memory strategy knowledge is strategy proximity information, resulting in clusters of strategy representations at varying distances from one another. Although this information is definitely multidimensional, Figure 1 partially represents (in two dimensions) the clusters specified earlier in this paragraph. Thus, there is no box for relational memory strategy knowledge in Figure 1; such knowledge is evidenced in the way strategy representations and specific strategy knowledge components are arranged. That is, the strategies presented earlier in an a, b, c . . . order are rearranged and grouped in Figure 1 by relational memory strategy procedures.

As it turns out, there is no research to date on relational memory strategy knowledge or relational memory strategy procedures, let alone on the issue of how this information is relevant to strategy instruction. We included this component because of our intuitions (based on interviews with children about their use of strategies) that there are important changes in the knowledge about similarities in learning strategies as a function of familiarity with the specific study skills and strategies. To determine whether these intuitions have a basis in fact, multidimensional scaling procedures could be used to index children's representations about different memory strategies as a function of direct experience with those strategies.

(6) **Metamemory Acquisition Procedures.** A final category of MAS is procedural knowledge for acquiring specific strategy knowledge, hereafter referred to as metamemory acquisition procedures (MAPs). MAPs are also similar to Chi's (1984) metarules, or rules that take as input other

rules, with the output being an appropriate evaluation resulting in new knowledge. MAPs include self-testing to determine if a new strategy is helpful or not and knowing how to compare performance after using different strategies to determine relative strategy efficacy. MAPs can greatly aid in the development of other aspects of the MAS, as will become obvious in the subsequent discussion. Figure 1 depicts MAPs as taking strategies as input, with the MAPs operating on that input to produce specific strategy knowledge, which in turn can affect other parts of MAS.

Interaction in the MAS. Declarative knowledge in MAS is tightly linked to procedural components that are also a part of MAS. It should be emphasized that MAS procedures are similar to processes that contribute to the growth of knowledge in general (Kail & Bisanz, 1982). According to the developmental information-processing model developed by Kail and Bisanz, inconsistency detectors monitor cognitive processes and compare the outcomes produced by those processes with outcome expectancies. When inconsistencies are detected, processes are set in motion to reduce them. Similarly in MAS, some of the MAPs are designed to find inconsistencies—to determine if memory outcomes are consistent with efficacy beliefs about strategies, to determine if strategies work as expected with various types of learners, and to determine if strategies work as well with types of materials different from those used during training. The developmental information-processing model also includes regularity detectors, detectors that search for common processes in cognitive routines (Kail & Bisanz, 1982). The relational memory strategy procedures function analogously in our model of MAS.

Interaction rather than isolation characterizes the states of the various components in MAS. For instance, if a child is thinking about deploying strategy X, a thought that might be triggered by a match between the to-be-learned materials and information in specific strategy knowledge about X, she or he might then think of general strategy knowledge, such as the notion that strategies often aid learning. Other pieces of specific strategy metamemory about X might be triggered as well, including that X is appropriate for the types of materials currently presented but that X takes a lot of effort to execute and is not much fun. Finally, the child might realize that strategy Y would be as appropriate as strategy X in this situation because X and Y are represented closely together because of the operation of the relational memory strategy procedures. It might also be noted that Y's specific strategy metamemory includes information that Y is an easy strategy to use. The child might then elect to use Y instead of X. This scenario pictures the components of MAS as *dynamic* and *interactional.*

Unfortunately, it is not possible here to consider in detail each of the interactions diagrammed in Figure 1. Also, there are probably relation-ships not depicted (e.g., Might MAPs feed directly into general strategy knowledge?). In short, Figure 1 is a preliminary version of MAS. It should be noted that the focus of most studies discussed in this chapter are what we refer to as specific strategy knowledge rather than other aspects of MAS. Even investigations of MAPs are largely concerned with specific strategy knowledge, because strategy knowledge is produced by MAPs. The focus for the remainder of this chapter is on the role of specific strat-egy knowledge in the training and use of strategies.

Specific Strategy Knowledge: Correlational Data
Supporting Metamemory–Memory Linkages

It is assumed that the components of MAS in interaction are the pri-mary determinants of memory strategy deployment. In a mature learner, MAS is complete enough to permit the learner to make a strategy exe-cution decision given a particular learning task, as well as to make modi-fications of the strategy, as necessary. In short, all of the fundamental executive machinery is housed in a special kind of system—MAS. Cor-relational support for the presumed linkage between metamemory about strategies and strategy use has been provided by the review of Schneider (Chapter 3, this volume). Thus, we highlight here only a few of the studies that have provided support for a MAS–strategy use association. We do so in order to illustrate the types of designs used to study this problem, as well as to illustrate the outcomes that have been obtained.

Metamemory and Memory in Normal Children

Cavanaugh and Borkowski (1979) studied the relationship between specific strategy knowledge and memory performance in third-grade chil-dren across five sessions. The first and fifth sessions were metamemory assessments tapping knowledge of a cumulative-clustering strategy for free recall of word lists consisting of categorizable items (e.g., toys, animals, and body parts were three of the categories used). In one condition, chil-dren participated only in the metamemory assessments (Phases 1 and 5). During Sessions 2 and 3, children in a strategy-training condition were taught to rehearse the items cumulatively within categories, starting a new cumulative rehearsal sequence when a new category began. Control sub-jects were presented the same lists during Session 2 and 3, but were asked only to learn them, without the benefit of strategy instructions. During a fourth session (2 weeks after training) children were presented a blocked, categorized list, structurally similar to the ones used during training but differing in the specific items; in both conditions they were simply instructed to learn the list. This task constituted a strategy maintenance test for children in the experimental condition. The experimental group learned the strategy and maintained it, as evidenced by pause patterns in their study-time profiles (see Butterfield & Belmont, 1977). However, not all experimental subjects showed strategy use during Session 4, especially if they did not have good prior sepcific strategy knowledge. There was a significant correlation between the pretest knowledge of clustering strategies (i.e., specific strategy knowledge) and the eventual use of the strategy at maintenance.

Kurtz et al. (1982) studied second-grade children who were either taught to use an interrogative elaboration procedure (e.g., Pressley & Bryant, 1982; Turnure, Buium, & Thurlow, 1976) or were left to their own devices to learn a paired-associate list. Before the pairs were presented, a seven-item test of strategic metamemory was given. The assessment tapped specific strategy knowledge about the to-be-trained strategy as well as other strategic information. Children were asked about their awareness of elaboration efficacy, their understanding that planning for retrieval can enhance memory, their knowledge of retrieval, their understanding that gist recall is easier than rote recall, their memory-monitoring capacity, their knowledge of how to allocate study time to familiar versus unfamiliar materials, and their ability to match output demands with input strategies. After the metamemory assessment, experimental subjects were trained to use an interrogative–elaborative strategy during three sessions. Control subjects spent an equivalent amount of time with the experimenter, but were given no strategy instructions. One week later all children were given maintenance and generalization tests with no mention of the strategy. The maintenance task consisted of picture paired associates, a task identical to the ones used during training except for the new items; the generalization task was learning associations between sets of three pictures.

When accuracy was considered, experimental subjects outperformed control subjects on both the maintenance and generalization tasks, with substantially more elaboration occurring as a result of training. There was considerable variability within the experimental condition in the amount of strategy use on both the maintenance and generalization tasks and, furthermore, this variability was related to the variability in the metamemory pretest. That is, knowledge about memory strategies positively correlated with strategy usage at maintenance even when the effect of general intelligence was removed. The relationship between metamemory and elaborative use at generalization was not as strong although still positive. Consistent with other research on elaboration (see Pressley, 1982), higher recall was associated with greater use of elaborations.

Metamemory–Memory Relationships with Special Populations

Relationships between metamemory and the use of strategies have also been obtained with special populations. Kendall, Borkowski, and Cavanaugh (1980) assessed the metamemory in educable mentally retarded (EMR) children at the beginning and end of an interrogative–elaborative strategy training study. The metamemory assessment was a subset of the items used in Kurtz et al. (1982). The training, maintenance, and generalization tasks were also similar to those used by Kurtz and her colleagues. Elaborative strategy use and recall performance were highly related during training, maintenance, and generalization tests. More importantly, there were significant correlations between metamemory and strategy use on both maintenance and generalization tests.

Borkowski, Peck, Reid, and Kurtz (1983) studied metamemory and strategy transfer in impulsive and reflective children. It was hypothesized that impulsive children have a knowledge base that is deficient regarding information about when and how to use strategy skills. Thus, metamemory rather than cognitive tempo might determine strategic behaviors in impulsive children. To address relationships between cognitive tempo, strategy usage, and metamemory, Borkowski et al. (1983) used the 20-item Matching Familiar Figures Test (MFFT) to identify 80 first- and third-grade children as impulsive or reflective. No significant pretraining differences existed between impulsive and reflective children in Wechsler Intelligence Scale for Children vocabulary or achievement scores. These children were given a metamemory questionnaire designed to assess their knowledge of memory processes and other mental operations. Children were then presented a sequence of sort-recall readiness tasks that provided the context for training an organizational strategy. After 3 weeks, maintenance and generalization were examined with a cognitive cuing task that shared components with the sort-recall readiness task, but not identical to it.

Prior to training, impulsive and reflective children did not differ in their use of organizational strategies. In contrast, strategy scores on maintenance and generalization tests were significantly higher for reflective than for impulsive children. These data suggest that reflective children profited more from the strategy training on tests of strategy transfer than did impulsive children. Also, significant but moderate correlations were found between metamemory and strategy usage. More importantly, the correlation between metamemory and strategy use remained significant when impulsivity–reflectivity was partialled out, but the cognitive tempo–strategy transfer correlation became nonsignificant when metamemory effects were removed. This finding takes on greater importance in light of the fact that children were preselected on the basis of wide variation in cognitive tempo. These data are consistent with the interpretation that metamemorial processes in impulsive and reflective children serve as a mediational base during strategy maintenance and generalization.

Aspects of metamemory theory are also consistent with data on cognitive processes in gifted children. Peck and Borkowski (1983) contrasted gifted and average children on a wide variety of tasks assessing perceptual efficiency, strategy usuage, general knowledge, and metacognitive knowledge. Sizable between-group differences emerged on all tasks, except those measuring strategic behaviors. Of interest was the fact that extensive differences in metamemorial knowledge of second-grade gifted versus average children were observed.

In a subsequent longitudinal study with the same children, Peck and Borkowski (1983) traced the emergence of strategic behaviors in gifted and average children following differing degrees of strategy training. It was expected that the learning strategies for gifted and average children would be differentiated according to type of strategy training administered. Given extensive strategy training, gifted and regular children should perform equally well on maintenance and generalization tasks. Performance differences should emerge, however, when children were given minimal strategy training. More specifically, gifted children with their superior metamemories should need little task-specific feedback about the appropriateness of a strategy before they would retain and use it effectively at transfer. Competing explanations of strategy transfer were contrasted following different amounts of strategy training: metamemory versus general knowledge versus perceptual efficiency (as measured by reaction time, Posner memory search, and digit-span tasks). For instance, does metamemory in gifted and average children predict strategy transfer on a minimally trained task when perceptual efficiency is ruled out?

All children in Session 1 received a pretest metamemory battery, the perceptual efficiency tasks, tests of general knowledge, and two recall tasks. After Session 1, gifted and regular children received varying degrees of strategy training on paired-associate and sort-recall readiness tasks; the former was the task given maximal training, the latter minimal training. Children in the control group received the same tasks without strategy instruction. Sessions 2 and 3 were strategy training sessions for the experimental children. An elaboration strategy was taught after the administration of the paired-associate task in Session 2, and again prior to its administration in Session 3. All children were given a paired-associate maintenance task in Session 4, and a generalization task (learning associations between triads of words) in Session 5. Recall measures were obtained in all four sessions, and strategy-elaboration scores were obtained on the maintenance and generalization sessions.

Following the third administration of the sort-recall readiness task in Session 3, the experimental gifted and average children received a brief explanation of a clustering strategy. A sort-recall readiness maintenance test was given in Session 4; in Session 5 a generalization task occurred, which involved components of the sort-recall task, but was not identical to it. For all administrations of the sort-recall readiness and generalization tasks, separate measures of input and output strategies were obtained, as well as measures of recall performance. In Sessions 2, 3, and 5 an alphabet-search task, designed to measure organized retrieval, was given to all children. No strategy training was given with the alphabet-search task. A posttest metamemory battery was administered in Session 6.

The major results were the following: (1) Both gifted and average children showed stable transfer following maximal training on the paired-associate task. (2) Little transfer, in terms of recall accuracy, occurred for either group on the untrained alphabet-search task. However, gifted children exhibited more organized search strategies during the final session. (3) Significant strategy transfer was found on the minimally trained sort-recall readiness task. Gifted children displayed more organization and better recall than average children. (4) Metamemory predicted strategy transfer on all tasks better than perceptual efficiency and appeared to be the best explanation of the superior strategy transfer of the gifted children following minimal strategy instruction. In short, the emergence of organizational encoding and decoding strategies among gifted children on the sort-recall readiness task was predated by metamemorial differences. Preexisting metamemory provided the context in which new specific strategy knowledge took on a more general, durable character. These data are suggestive that the development of mature metamemory is an antecedent to successful strategy training and its transfer to more general contexts.

The pattern of findings with learning-disabled (LD) children is consistent with the outcomes obtained with impulsive and gifted children. Specific learning deficits in LD children are, in part, attributable to failures in the implementation of task-appropriate strategies, rather than deficits in memory or attention per se. In turn, these deficiences in strategic behaviors are paralleled by slow metamemorial development in LD children (Douglass, 1981; Trepanier, 1981).

In summary, correlational evidence with normal and special children buttresses the argument that specific strategy knowledge—one part of MAS—and the deployment of strategies are related. The nature of these relationships, such as unambiguous interpretation of cause and effects, are not revealed by correlational analyses. Other research tactics are more informative about how prior knowledge states cause changes in strategy use as well as whether new memory behaviors produce specific changes in MAS. These studies are taken up in the next section, which deals with the main focus of this chapter, metamemory and the training of strategies.

Metacognitive Approaches to Strategy Instruction

One possibility implied by the correlational data, and consistent with metamemory theory (e.g., Flavell, 1981), is that specific and general strategy knowledge direct strategy deployment. That is, when production deficiencies occur, they are due largely to deficient strategy knowledge (Chi, 1984). If this is so, an important issue for instructional psychologists is determining how to modify strategy knowledge so as to influence positively the deployment of appropriate strategies to meet the demands of different tasks.

There have been three tactics used by investigators to date: (1) The first approach represents a laissez-faire position. In the normal course of cognitive activity, strategy knowledge grows through a variety of metacognitive experiences (Flavell, 1981). There is no need during strategy instruction to attend explicitly to strategy knowledge states. Metacognition will arise spontaneously with the use of trained strategies. (2) Declarative knowledge about specific strategies can be provided directly by teachers. (3) Learners can be taught procedures that will themselves generate strategy knowledge. They can be taught MAPs. The presence of MAPs increases the likelihood that day-in, day-out cognitive experiences become metacognitive experiences in an explicit manner.

Next we consider briefly each of the three tactics, along with supporting data. Before beginning this discussion, however, we should reemphasize that intervention research to date has been limited to the analysis of only two aspects of MAS, specific strategy knowledge and MAPs. Our failure to consider further other aspects of MAS, such as strategy relational knowledge, is due to limitations in the available data.

Laissez-Faire Position

While navigating the world, people acquire many cognitive goals, from learning the changes in the tax laws (to minimize payments) to commiting to memory a short speech that is to be made to a church youth group.

These cognitive goals are accomplished through cognitive actions and strategies that depend heavily on stored metacognitive knowledge (Flavell, 1981). As depicted in Figure 2, the effects of these components on one another are not unidirectional.

The metacognitive experience component is the most important one to consider in the present context. Metacognitive experiences are conscious experiences about cognitive goals, cognitive actions, and/or metacognitive knowledge. These experiences can lead to changes in both cognitive goals and cognitive actions, such as when goal abandonment occurs after realization that a task is beyond one's capabilities or when strategy change occurs after realizing that the previously activated strategy was ineffective. Also, metacognitive knowledge can affect future cognitive behavior:

> [Metacognitive experiences] can add to, delete or revise [metacognitive] knowledge, and can thus play an important role in its development. We can notice and store as metacognitive knowledge what cognitive actions and outcomes co-occur with what metacognitive experiences. (Flavell, 1981, p. 50)

Flavell (1981) made the case that metacognitive experiences are not rare, occurring more frequently in some circumstances than others. His list of probable occasions for metacognitive experiences included the following:

> They are most likely to occur whenever you do a lot of conscious cognition, thereby providing many cognitive events and contents about which to have meta-

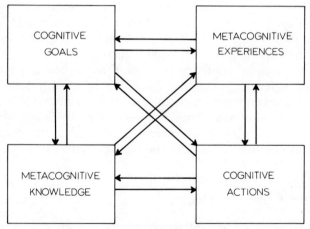

FIGURE 2. Flavell's (1981) model of cognitive processing. From "Cognitive monitoring," by J. H. Flavell, in W. P. Dickson (Ed.), *Children's oral communication skills*, 1981, p. 40, figure 2.1. Copyright 1981 by Academic Press and reprinted by permission.

cognitive experiences . . . where you have to think, speak, or otherwise behave in new and unaccustomed ways (e.g., when trying to communicate with someone from a very different culture . . .). Metacognitive experiences are also likely to occur whenever your cognitions seem to have something wrong with them. . . . You are more likely to have these experiences when attention and memory resources permit (e.g., when you have sufficient time to think about your cognitions, when you are not in a highly emotional state and the like). (Flavell, 1981, p. 49)

Although intuitively appealing, there is little in the way of systematic data documenting metacognitive growth as an accompaniment to strategy execution. The remainder of the discussion of the laissez-faire position is devoted to describing a study in which documented changes in metamemory occurred as a function of strategy usage. Furthermore, the specific strategy knowledge that arose during strategy usage apparently affected subsequent strategy deployment.

Pressley, Levin, and Ghatala (1984) asked adults to try two different learning strategies for vocabulary learning. As a result, a particular type of metacognitive experience occurred, producing knowledge about the relative efficacy of the two strategies. In the first three experiments in the Pressley et al. series, adults were presented a list of Latin and Spanish words to learn. They were informed that after study, a vocabulary test would be given, which would require recall of the meanings. Two different learning strategies were described: (1) Rehearsal consisted of saying the words and their meanings over and over; (2) The keyword strategy involved using part of the vocabulary words that sounded like a known English word as a keyword (e.g., *art* would be a good keyword for the Latin word *artopta*, which means baker), with the keyword placed in an interactive image with the word's meaning (e.g., a baker making a piece of *art* for *artopta*). This method is more effective for vocabulary learning than rehearsal (Pressley, Levin, & Delaney, 1982).

The first experiment included six conditions—the first six listed in Table 1. In the three choice conditions, the adult subjects selected either the repetition or the keyword–elaboration strategy without opportunity to practice the two methods. Before making a strategy choice in the other three conditions (study-test-choice conditions) subjects practiced the two strategies on a 24-item list of vocabulary words. The processing of the practice list was tightly controlled in these study-test-choice conditions so that every other item was learned using rehearsal, with the remaining items learned using the keyword-elaboration method. After studying the practice list, study-test-choice subjects were given a test on the 24 vocabulary words, but no feedback was provided about test performance. Subjects in one choice condition and one study-test-choice condition were told by the experimenter that the rehearsal method was the more effective technique

Table 1

Proportion of Subjects Choosing the Keyword Strategy by Condition and Experiment[a]

	Adults			Children
Condition[b]	Experiment 1	Experiment 2	Experiment 3	Experiment 4
E/choice	.875	—	—	.812
R/choice	.125	.125	—	.188
C/choice	.625	.500	—	.688
E/study-test-choice	1.000	—	—	1.000
R/study-test-choice	.867	.750	.867	.357
C/study-test-choice	1.000	.938	.938	.846
R/study-choice-test	—	.000	.163	—
C/study-choice-test	—	.500	.650	—

[a]From Pressley, Levin, and Ghatala 1984.

[b]E designates that keyword–elaboration strategy was recommended; R designates that rehearsal strategy was recommended; C designates that no strategy was recommended.

(designated as R conditions); subjects in one choice and one study-test-choice condition were told that the keyword method worked better (designated as E conditions); and subjects in one choice and one study-test-choice condition were given no strategy recommendation by the experimenter (C conditions).

The main dependent variable of interest was the strategy that each subject elected to use to learn a list of vocabulary words (first list for choice subjects, second list for study-test-choice conditions). The practice list experience clearly affected whether subjects followed the experimenter's advice or not. The strategy selections in choice conditions of Experiment 1 were determined largely by the recommendations of the experimenter regarding strategy efficacy (see Table 1). The preponderance of study-test-choice subjects selected the keyword strategy regardless of the experimenter's recommendations.

The effect of the practice list experience was most apparent in the differences in strategy selections in the R/choice and R/study-test-choice conditions. That the experimenter's repetition recommendation was ignored by R/study-test-choice subjects, but dramatically increased rehearsal selection in the R/choice condition is powerful evidence that something happened during practice that created an overriding impression that the keyword strategy was more effective than the repetition strategy. The practice list was a metacognitive experience (Flavell, 1979, 1981). That is, knowledge about the two strategies was acquired during practice study–testing that produced changes in the learner's choice of strategic behaviors. Follow-up experiments were conducted with adults, to specify precisely the changes in knowledge that occurred.

During the course of the study just discussed, the adult subjects offered many remarks about how effective the keyword method was, but this occurred only during the testing phase of the experiment. This observation prompted Pressley and his colleagues to hypothesize that monitoring of strategy effectiveness occurred during testing. To assess this possibility, a second experiment included six conditions, four of which were procedurally identical to the R/choice, C/choice, R/study-test-choice, and C/study-test-choice conditions used in the previous experiment. In addition, two conditions were added that were identical to the R/study-test-choice and C/study-test-choice conditions except that subjects in these conditions made their strategy choices after studying the 24-item practice list, but before taking a test on the list (thus, these conditions are labelled R/study-choice-test and C/study-choice-test conditions in Table 1). If realization of keyword method efficacy occurred during testing, knowledge that mediated strategy choice, then strategy selections in the two study-choice-test conditions should have resembled the stategy selections in the choice conditions rather than those made in the study-test-choice conditions. The results were exactly as predicted and are displayed in Table 1. Although the strategy choice data of this second experiment were consistent with the position that during the test learners came to understand that the keyword method is more effective than repetition, a third experiment was conducted to document more directly the acquisition of such knowledge.

The third experiment included conditions procedurally similar to C/study-choice-test, R/study-choice-test, C/study-test-choice, and R/study-test-choice conditions, with subjects asked to estimate their total recall and then their recall of elaboration versus repetition items at the point in the experiment when they made their strategy choices. The strategy choice data (displayed in Table 1) were extremely similar to those obtained in Experiment 2. Most notably, choice of the keyword strategy was low in the R/study-choice-test condition, but not in the R/study-test-choice condition. The most important aspect of the recall estimation data was that when subjects estimated their recall before taking the practice test, they were not aware that the keyword strategy was more effective than the rehearsal strategy. After taking the practice test, subjects indicated that more keyword items than rehearsal items had been learned.

What happened in the Pressley et al. (1984) study in terms of Flavell's model (see Figure 2)? Subjects pursued the cognitive goal of learning a list of vocabulary words, with two cognitive actions to choose from, rehearsal or keyword elaboration. Presumably, their strategy selections were mediated by their knowledge of the differential effectiveness of the two strategies, a piece of specific strategy knowledge. At the outset of the experiment, subjects knew little about the relative effectiveness of the two strategies, as reflected by pretest estimates of the recall levels of keyword versus rehearsed items. When provided a test on a list of practice items, however, subjects realized that they were doing better on keyword items. The test was a metacognitive experience resulting in the modification of specific strategy knowledge. This new knowledge in turn directed subsequent strategy choices. In short, the data in Pressley et al. (1984) are compatible with Flavell's analysis of how metacognitive experiences produce metacognitive knowledge. Flavell (1981) also hypothesized increases "with age in the tendency to notice and attend to metacognitive experiences, and to evaluate their meaning, importance, trustworthiness, and possible implications for cognitive actions" (p. 50). This theoretical position was examined as well by Pressley and his associates in two additional experiments with children.

The fourth experiment in Pressley et al. (1984) was procedurally identical to the first study except that children in Grades 5 and 6 served as subjects. The main finding of Experiment 4 was that children's strategy choices were similar in the study-test-choice and in the choice conditions. Most striking, and in distinct contrast to the results of Experiment 1 with adults, keyword choice was low in the R/study-test-choice as well as in the R/choice condition. Importantly, the magnitude of the difference in actual recall of the keyword-elaborated and rehearsed items in Experiment 4 was roughly comparable to the size of the actual recall differences in the adult studies, so that both children and adults had a comparable objective basis, favoring the keyword strategy, for strategy choice.

Following the practice list–test, why did children continue to follow the experimenter's recommendation that the repetition strategy was more effective? A possibility, consistent with Flavell's (1981) model, is that the children did not monitor the differential effectiveness of the strategies and/or did not use this information in their strategy choice decisions. Alternatively, children might simply value the opinion of the experimenter more than adults did, a position consistent with other data (e.g., Bixenstine, DeCorte, & Bixenstine, 1976; Dweck, Hill, Redd, & Steinman, 1976; Miller, 1976; Rubin, 1976). A final experiment with children in Grades 5–7 showed that both factors were operating. One of the more interesting outcomes in the experiment was the determination that the children did realize that keyword was more effective than rehearsal, although they underestimated the magnitude of the effect. When children were provided explicit information about their learning with the two strategies and thus, it was assured that they knew how great the keyword advantage was, they consistently selected the keyword strategy. It appears that knowledge gained by children as a function of strategy experience is less accurate than knowledge gained by adults from those same experiences; as well, such knowledge seems less certain to influence children's subsequent cognitive behaviors. This tentative conclusion provides motivation for investigating other types of educational interventions that might generate specific strategy knowledge. It is to research on these interventions that we now turn.

Supplying Metamemory Information Directly during Instruction

Metamemory and the Incompleteness of Instruction

When strategy training procedures are examined, it becomes immediately apparent that strategy instructions usually do not include more than a description of how to execute the component processes of a strategy. Little information is provided about when the strategy can be used profitably, how the strategy can be modified to fit various types of materials, or what benefits will accrue to the user. In short, strategy instruction is often deficient with respect to MAS. Although a thorough review of the problem is beyond the scope of this chapter, the procedures in three strategy-training studies help concretize the problem. The particular studies selected as examples have what we consider to be typical instructions, similar in explicitness to instructions in most studies on teaching strategies (see Pressley, Heisel, McCormick, & Nakamura, 1982).

Rehearsal is one of the most frequently studied strategies for simple list learning. The procedures used by Naus, Ornstein, and Aivano (1977) were typical of those used in research on rehearsal. Children instructed to rehearse were simply told to practice the presented word aloud with any two other words in the list. They were encouraged to do this for the entire presentation interval. Notably lacking from the directions was any information about why the rehearsal strategy was appropriate for list learning, how the rehearsal strategy was linked to the goal of memory, or how the rehearsal strategy might be varied and in what circumstances.

No strategy for paired-associate learning has received as much attention as elaboration (Pressley, 1982). The directions used by Pressley and Levin (1977) in their research on children's use of elaboration were a bit more specific than directions provided by Naus et al. (1977) to their participants, but they were still vague. All subjects in Pressley and Levin (1977) were told that their task was to remember that the paired items go together. The imagery subjects were told to generate mental images of the paired items interacting and that these images would aid learning. Thus, the Pressley and Levin directions included specific strategy knowledge about learning gains associated with strategy use. However, the instructions used by Pressley and Levin still included little specific, detailed information about the strategy.

The final example is drawn from the prose learning literature and represents a thorough attempt to train imagery in a reading context (see Brown & Smiley, 1978; Guttmann, Levin, & Pressley, 1977; Levin & Pressley, 1981). Children in the experimental condition of Pressley's (1976) study were instructed to construct images representing the contents of a concrete story that they were to read. Before presentation of the story, subjects in the experimental condition were told that making up pictures in the head is a good way to remember things. The experimental subjects practiced using the strategy with simple and complex sentences, paragraphs, and parts of a short story. Throughout training, subjects were shown pictures of good images after attempting to construct their own representational images on practice materials. Again, as in the aforementioned paired-associate study, the positive effects of the imagery strategy were highlighted by the experimenter. Also, the subjects in this study were shown how the strategy could be applied to a variety of different materials. This illustrates the training of greater specific strategy knowledge than occurred in the two studies discussed previously. However, Pressley (1976) did not explicitly inform subjects that the strategy was most applicable to concrete stories, nor was any information provided to subjects as to how to modify the strategy for abstract materials. In short, specific strategy information that could have been included in the instructions was omitted.

Training Specific Strategy Knowledge

Does including specific strategy information in strategy instruction increase the use of a strategy or improve its effectiveness? Experimenters have directly manipulated specific strategy knowledge in only a very few studies; those studies are summarized in Table 2. The conclusions that follow from these experiments are extremely limited for three reasons:

1. Most of the studies included children only, usually 9 years of age or younger.
2. In all but one of the studies cited in Table 2, provisions of one specific type of information was investigated—that is, information about the strategy's effectiveness for the trained task.
3. Most of the studies focused on maintenance of the strategy, rather than generalization or on other processing changes that might be produced by appropriate specific strategy information.

The one general conclusion that follows from these studies is that providing information about a strategy's specific utility for the training

Table 2

Studies Manipulating Specific Strategy Knowledge

Study	Participants	Strategy/task and specific strategy knowledge manipulated	Effects of manipulation
Black & Rollins (1982)	6½- to 7½-year-olds	Category organizational strategy for categorizable lists; information about the utility of the strategy.	Utility information positively affected use of strategy and recall on 2- to 3-week delayed post-test.
Borkowski, Levers, & Gruenen-felder (1976)	4- to 5-year-olds & 6- to 7-year-olds	Elaboration of paired-associates; awareness of strategy's value.	Two-week maintenance positively affected by awareness information.
Cavanaugh & Borkowski (1979)	8- to 9-year-olds	Clustering-rehearsal strategy for recall of categorizable list; information about the value of the strategy for recall.	Value information produced higher metamemory for strategy-specific information; no reported effects on memory behaviors.
Kennedy & Miller (1976)	6- to 7-year-olds, nonrehearsers	Rehearsal for serial recall; feedback about strategy's value.	Feedback positively affected maintenance.
Kramer & Engle (1981)	8-year-olds, mildly retarded and normals	Rehearsal for list recall; awareness of the strategy's effectiveness.	Strategy maintained even without awareness instruction; appeared to use strategy on transfer task, but no effect on transfer performance level (possible ceiling effect).
Lawson & Fuelop (1980)	Retarded adults, mean IQ = 55	Cumulative rehearsal for serial recall; information about the strategy's value.	1-week maintenance of strategy increased.

(Continued)

Table 2 (*Continued*)

Study	Participants	Strategy/task and specific strategy knowledge manipulated	Effects of manipulation
Paris, Newman, & McVey 1982	7- to 8-year-olds	Rehearsal and category organizational strategies for list recall; feedback about the strategy's usefulness	Feedback positively affected maintenance.
Posnansky (1978)	5-year-olds and 8-year-olds	Use of category information at retrieval for recall of categorizable lists; either informed or not informed at testing about size of each category in list.	Recall of 5-year-olds positively affected by information; use of categories was efficient in 8-year-olds without supplementary information.
Ringel & Springer (1980)	7-, 9-, and 11-year-olds	Category sorting procedure for recall of categorizable lists; feedback about the effect of sorting strategy on recall levels.	9-year-olds experienced greatest benefit from feedback; no maintenance in any conditions with 7-year-olds; 11-year-olds maintained strategy even without awareness information.

task positively affects strategy maintenance, at least with young, grade-school children. In the one published study that attempted to determine whether information about a strategy's specific utility affected generalization (Kramer & Engle, 1981), children appeared to use the strategy on a transfer task, as evidenced by pause-time analyses (e.g., Butterfield & Belmont, 1977). However, there were no significant effects on memory performance.

In reviewing Kramer and Engle (1981), O'Sullivan and Pressley (1984) noted that it was not at all obvious how knowing a strategy's specific utility for training task X would be sufficient to increase transfer of the strategy

to a new learning domain. Throughout the 20th century it has been assumed that in order for transfer to occur, learners must know the critical
attributes of situations that call for use of a particular skill or strategy (see
Mann, 1979, for a historical overview; Campione, Brown, & Ferrara, 1982;
Gagné, 1977; House, 1982). Thus, based on long-standing analyses of transfer, O'Sullivan and Pressley (1984) reasoned that adding information to
instruction about when a strategy can be employed should enhance transfer—that is, provision of more general utility information than the specific
utility information manipulated in previous studies.

All of the subjects in O'Sullivan and Pressley (1984) were given two
memory tasks, first learning city–product pairing and then acquiring Latin
vocabulary–definition linkages. The keyword method can profitably be applied to both of these tasks (Pressley & Dennis-Rounds, 1980). The first
experiment of the study involved fifth- and sixth-grade children. Control
subjects were presented both of the memory tasks with no instruction in
keyword usage. In each of the other four conditions of the experiment,
subjects were instructed in keyword method usage for the city–product
task. In the instruction condition the subjects were given keyword method
instruction much as it has taken place in other studies. The instruction
subjects were told to use a part of each town's name that sounded like a
familiar English word as a keyword (e.g., bell could be a keyword for *Belleville*), and then to place the keyword referent and the town's product in
an interactive image (e.g., the stones pulled out of Belleville's quarries
might have been visualized as hitting a bell).

In addition to receiving strategy training, subjects in the elaborated
instruction condition were also provided information about the general
utility of the keyword strategy while they were instructed in keyword usage
for city–product recall. The general utility information consisted of informing subjects that use of the keyword strategy would enhance their
learning and informing them (1) that the keyword "works well when you
have to remember that *two* things go together" (p. 278), and (2) that
when they had to remember that two words went together, they should
look for a keyword for one of the pair members and construct an interactive image between the keyword and second item for the pair. The experimenter then demonstrated how the method could be adapted to
learning a list of men and their professions and a list of country–food pairings. The experimenter also demonstrated how the method was inappropriate for verbatim learning of prose material.

In the experience condition, children received strategy training on
city–product pairs combined with subject practice in applying the technique to the men–professions task, learning of passages, and the country–
foods list. After trying the strategy with each material type, the experi-

menter informed the subjects whether the method was helpful for each particular task or not, but no prescription about the general usefulness of the method was provided. In the elaborated instruction plus experience conditions, subjects received strategy training as well as elaborated instructions and experience.

Following instruction appropriate to their conditions, subjects were asked to learn 15 city–product pairings and were subsequently tested on their memory of the products given the town names. The results for that task can be summarized succinctly. All four conditions that received keyword strategy training performed at comparable levels and better than control subjects. After the city–product task, children were presented a list of 21 Latin nouns. At this point, children in all conditions were simply instructed to try hard to remember what each Latin word meant. After presentation of the 21 Latin words, subjects were tested on the meanings and subsequently were quizzed on the strategies they had used during learning. During this posttest interview, subjects were provided with Latin words and were required to demonstrate how they had learned the items. Although Latin learning was higher in each of the four conditions that included keyword instruction than in the control condition, there were striking performance differences between these four conditions (see Table 3). Adding the elaborated instruction to training significantly increased transfer over that observed in the instruction condition. Experience produced transfer recall intermediate between that obtained in the instruction condition and recall in the two conditions that included elaborated instruction. Reported keyword strategy use on the Latin task was higher in all four conditions that included keyword training for city–product learning; in general, reported strategy-use correlated with recall, with significantly greater strategy-use reported in the elaborated instruction and elaborated instruction plus experience groups than in the instruction group. The level of strategy use reported by experience subjects was intermediate between strategy use in strategy training and elaborated instruction conditions. Thus, in general, with children as subjects there was evidence that elaborated instructions increased strategy transfer.

A question that remained after Experiment 1 was whether elaborated instructions produced maximum transfer. Pressley and Dennis-Rounds (1980) argued that the limit of transfer is the performance level of subjects directly instructed to use the strategy for the task under consideration. Following that line of reasoning, a second experiment was carried out with Grade 5 and Grade 6 subjects, which included elaborated instruction and instruction conditions, as well as an explicit reinstruction condition in which subjects were told to use the keyword method for learning Latin vocabulary and were given detailed instructions on how to do so. Elabo-

Table 3

Percentage Recall of Latin–English Pairs on the Transfer Task in O'Sullivan and Pressley (1982) by Condition and Experiment

	Children[a]				Adults[b]	
	Experiment 1		Experiment 2		Experiment 3	
Condition	Trial 1[c]	Trial 2	Trial 1	Trial 2	Trial 1	Trial 2
Control	8.8	24.1	—	—	32.4	55.2
Instruction	24.8	39.5	31.7	52.9	63.4	84.0
Experience	27.9	43.8	—	—	62.3	89.4
Elaborated instruction	45.2	66.2	54.8	77.1	68.7	88.7
Elaborated instruction plus experience	35.5	57.9	—	—	61.8	88.1
Explicit reinstruction	—	—	54.5	79.1	64.2	85.7

[a]Children were presented a total of 21 items.

[b]Adults were presented a total of 31 items.

[c]There were 10 study-test trials in the study. Patterns of results are the same when the data are averaged across all 10 trials. That is, the patterns obtained on Trials 1 and 2 well illustrate the outcomes in the experiment.

rated instruction subjects once again outperformed instruction subjects at transfer, with no significant differences in transfer recall between the elaborated instruction and explicit reinstruction conditions (see Table 3). In summary, adding elaborated instructions, which included information about when to use the keyword strategy (i.e., general utility information), increased children's transfer performance to levels obtained when subjects were given an explicit instruction to use the keyword method on the transfer task.

Is elaborated instruction necessary to maximize transfer with more mature students? With adults as subjects, O'Sullivan's and Pressley's (1984) Experiment 3 included all of the conditions of their Experiment 1 as well as an explicit reinstruction condition, so that the comparisons made in Experiment 1 could be made and the issue of maximum transfer could be addressed in a single experiment. The transfer results of Experiment 3 are depicted in Table 3. In all of the conditions provided with strategy training, recall at transfer was high and statistically comparable to the performance in the explicit reinstruction condition. Also, on the posttest questionnaire, subjects in all conditions that included strategy training indicated use of the keyword method to learn the Latin vocabulary, with reported use roughly comparable in these conditions. Briefly, with adults, elaborated instruction was not critical for maximum transfer, whereas with children, transfer task performance was improved by provision of a form of specific strategy knowledge (i.e., general utility information). Thus, O'Sullivan and Pressley (1984) succeeded in showing that provision of specific strategy knowledge could affect transfer, but that the effects of provision of metamemorial interventions interact with developmental level. More research on the provision of specific strategy knowledge is required before a final evaluation can be made about the potency of providing specific strategy information during instruction. Research with a greater range of manipulations and a greater age range of subjects is required (see Table 2). On that note we turn to an alternative way to increase learners' knowledge of strategies—by teaching them to generate such knowledge directly.

Metamemory Acquisition Procedures (MAPs)

Suppose that you have been taught the keyword strategy. What could you do to increase your metacognitive knowledge about it? First of all, you could conduct tests of your vocabulary knowledge when you use the method versus when you try some other strategy. You could try to adapt the technique to a variety of vocabulary words, even trying to extend the method to new materials. You could test yourself a few days after studying to determine if use of the method produced long-term effects on your vocabulary knowledge. Also, you might assess how much effort the method required and try to monitor whether the effort requirement might tempt you to use another strategy. You might see if you could teach the method to children in order to gauge whether the method's utility is developmentally constrained. All of these suggestions are what we refer to as *metamemory acquisition procedures* (MAPs).

The study of strategies for acquiring metacognitive information is in the embryonic stage. Even those authors who argue for the importance of these higher-order strategies have difficulty pointing to research that unambiguously documents the phenomenon (e.g., Brown, Campione, & Day, 1981; Chi, 1984). We think that the study of MAPs should be a high priority because learners who possess such strategies are likely to be more autonomous and effective in a variety of situations requiring cognitive strategy interventions.

In this section, we address a study that succeeded in demonstrating the efficacy of one strategy for acquiring metamemory information about memory strategies. Then, we review two other approaches to the training of memory strategies that included MAPs. In reviewing these research projects, the "fuzzy" concept of MAPs should become clarified.

The Lodico, Ghatala, Levin, Pressley, and Bell Study

The purpose of a study by Lodico, Ghatala, Levin, Pressley, and Bell (1983) was to determine if training 7- to 8-year-old children about general principles of strategy monitoring influences subsequent strategy choices. The focus of the training was to teach children to monitor their performance under different strategies, and to explain changes in their performance in terms of strategic behavior. During training, children practiced these skills in the context of tasks that were quite different from the memory tasks to which they were subsequently exposed.

At the outset, children in the experimental condition were told that there are many ways to play games and that some ways are better than others. They were also told that good game-playing requires that they select the method that allows them to do better in the game. The children then executed two different tasks and were required to try two different methods of execution for each task. For the first task, the children drew a circle freehand and then traced one with a circular cookie cutter. After drawing the two circles they were asked to evaluate which circle was better and why they thought they did better. After making the evaluation, the children were asked how they would draw a circle if they were required to do it again and wanted to draw the best possible circle. Throughout the session, feedback was provided; a second round with the task was given to those few children who could not provide the correct responses on the first trial.

For the second task, children were required to remember a list of letters, which were first presented in a random order. After study, they were tested on the letters. Children were then told to rearrange the letters so that they could spell their name (each child had been given a different set of letters) and were tested. As on the circle task, children were asked when they performed better, why, and what they would do if they were to play the game again. Again, feedback was provided, and the game was repeated for those who had difficulty.

Control children spent an equal amount of time playing the game with the experimenter. They practiced the same strategies on the same tasks as the experimental children. Control children, however, did not receive instructions about the value of monitoring, were not instructed to assess their performance when using the strategies, and were not told to select the more effective strategy. After training, all children were informed that they were going to play some more games. Consistent with training, experimental children were reminded of the importance of keeping track of their performance so that they could determine the best way to play the games. After that point, however, the experimental and control children were treated identically.

Immediately after training, children were given two memory tasks, a paired-associate task and a free recall task, with their order of presentation counterbalanced across the experimental and control conditions. For each task, there were three study-test trials, each involving a different list of items. On the first two trials, children were instructed to use two different acquisition strategies, with the order of the strategies counterbalanced within each task. For the paired-associate task the two strategies were verbal elaboration, which is known to be effective in associative learning relative to the other strategy taught, repetition of the pairs as they were presented. For the free-recall task, the more effective strategy was multiple-item repetition, and the less effective strategy was single-item repetition. After the children had completed the second study-test trial and, thus, had completed practice with both of the strategies for a task, they were presented the lists from the first two study lists with the question, "Do you think you remembered more when you learned these words the first time, or the second time when you learned these words?" After the children made their choice, they were asked, "Why were you better at remembering that time?" After answering this second question, the children were given a third study-test trial. They were told that they could use either of the two strategies in order to remember as many words as possible. Following the third test trial, the children were asked why they chose one strategy over the other. The procedures were identical for the other task. No feedback was provided at any time during either paired-associate or free recall learning.

Elaboration generally produced better associative learning than repetition. For most children, multiple repetition produced better free recall than single-item repetition. Those who did not conform to this pattern were dropped so that more unambiguous interpretations of the strategy-monitoring data could be made, although the results were largely unaffected by this exclusion. The majority of children in both experimental and control conditions accurately assessed which of the two lists were remembered better. Of the children who made such strategy efficacy estimates accurately, the proportion attributing their performance to the more effective strategy was calculated. A greater proportion of experimental than control subjects explained their improved performance by referring to the more effective strategy. For both tasks, a higher proportion of experimental than control children utilized the more effective strategy when given a forced choice between the strategies on the third trial. Most impressively, when experimental children chose the more effective strategy, they justified their choice by saying that they thought that use of the strategy would enhance their performance. Most control subjects either could not explain their choice or gave reasons unrelated to optimization of performance.

Lodico et al.'s (1983) study provides unequivocal support for the position that children as young as 7 to 8 years of age can be taught to monitor their strategy performance and then use the information to make subsequent strategy-choice decisions. This study reflects the training and testing of a MAP. That monitoring was not critically deficient was evident from the fact that even control children knew which lists they had learned better. What was lacking was an understanding that the differential performance was due to the use of the two strategies. When the data in Lodico et al. (1983) and those produced by Pressley et al. (1984 child data) are considered together, the case is compelling that children can possess metamemory knowledge about relative strategy efficacy, without integrating that information with other metamemory information and using the composite to direct subsequent cognitive activity.

The Lodico et al. (1983) study represents an approach to how MAPs can be studied, without confounding the MAP with a particular memory strategy. It has usually been the case that when MAPs have been taught together with a specific strategy, there has been neither (1) intraexperimental manipulation that would allow determination of whether the MAP actually enhanced the use of the memory strategy, nor (2) an assessment of whether the MAP would be transferred to a new learning task.

Two studies that have included MAPs as part of their training are reviewed here to provide readers with additional examples of the application of MAPs. We also point out how slight modifications in the designs of these studies would have allowed determination of whether the MAPs contributed to the effects observed in the studies, as well as comment on how experiments might be designed to determine if children can learn to transfer MAPs from one specific memory strategy to another.

The Brown and Barclay (1976) Study

Brown and Barclay (1976) included two groups of EMR children (MA = 6 years [MA6] and MA8). Each subject was taught one of three strategies for learning a list for serial recall. In the labeling condition, subjects were trained to expose the items in a serial order, labeling each one in turn. Subjects were trained to repeat this procedure for four cycles through the list. More complex strategies, which were anticipated to be more effective, were taught in the anticipation and rehearsal conditions:

> In both the anticipation and rehearsal groups the subjects were trained to pass once through the list, exposing the labeling each item in turn. On the remaining three compulsory list exposures [rehearsal or anticipation was induced]. The anticipation strategy was to attempt to name each item before exposing it to view. The rehearsal procedure trained was a cumulative rehearsal strategy in which Ss where trained to rehearse items in groups of three. In all groups Ss were encouraged to continue with

the strategy (after the fourth compulsory viewing) until they were sure they knew the whole set. (p. 75)

Three posttests were given to subjects after the completion of training. On the day after training, three new lists were presented; children were prompted to use the trained strategy. Next, three new lists were presented, but this time without prompting. Two weeks later another unprompted maintenance test was given on three new lists.

The results can be described as follows: The MA6 children in the anticipation and rehearsal conditions recalled significantly more items than children in the label conditions on the prompted posttest, but did not do so on the unprompted tests. However, recall of MA8 children in the anticipation and rehearsal conditions exceeded that of MA8 children in the label condition on all three posttesting sessions. Nonetheless, Brown and Barclay (1976) noted that on all posttests both the younger and older EMR children appeared to use the trained strategy. Brown and Barclay explained this pattern of results by suggesting that the younger children had a monitoring deficiency:

> Both younger and older Ss appear to maintain the strategy as indexed by observation of their overt behavior, even though objective measures [i.e., recall] indicated that the younger Ss failed to maintain the improvement shown on posttest 1. Thus, the younger Ss did not abandon their efforts entirely after the initial prompted posttests; rather they failed to monitor the efficient use of the trained strategy in a way that would encourage them to continue its use until recall readiness was achieved. (p. 78)

Of course, the explanation presented by Brown and Barclay (1976) of their results is ad hoc. Without an external measure of monitoring, it is not possible to determine whether the problem with the younger children was with their monitoring of recall readiness or in their execution of other aspects of their anticipation and rehearsal procedure. A better methodological approach would be to manipulate the amount of memory monitoring carried out in conjunction with anticipation or rehearsal strategies. This seems especially appropriate in the case of cumulative rehearsal. One can imagine a condition in which children would be taught to perform cumulative rehearsal on a list with instructions to self-test between trials. These children would be taught to continue study of the list until they could say all items to themselves without error. During training, yoked control subjects would be given as many cycles through the list as trained subjects elected, with the instruction to rehearse the items cumulatively on each cycle. The control condition would differ from the experimental condition only in that control subjects would neither decide nor be trained how to decide whether to select another presentation of the list. It would be expected that if monitoring added something to the rehearsal strategy, trained subjects would do better than control subjects on some dependent measures but not others. For instance, if subjects were instructed to study until they knew all of the items, performance of trained subjects would be expected to exceed that of control subjects because trained subjects would presumably keep track of whether they were ready for a test and not elect a test until they were ready. On the other hand, recall after one cumulative rehearsal cycle would not be expected to differ between the two conditions because both groups would have had equal practice at cumulative rehearsal per se.

Tests could be devised to determine if subjects would transfer the monitoring strategy. For instance, what would occur if participants in the preceding two conditions were given a list of paired associates with the instruction to study using elaboration until they could remember all of the associations (i.e., not requesting a test from the experimenter until all items were learned)? If the monitoring strategy was transferred by the experimental subjects, it would be expected that they would be better prepared for recall when they asked for the test than would control subjects.

In closing the discussion of Brown and Barclay's (1976) study, we emphasize that the type of monitoring that they presumed occurred in their rehearsal and anticipation conditions (i.e., self-testing to determine if one is ready for a test) is an instance of a MAP. However, the Brown and Barclay study did not permit an unambiguous separation of the effects of the MAP from the specific memory strategies studied. The type of MAP hypothesized—recall readiness—is important and general enough that we hope future experiments will evaluate its scope and power.

The Asarnow and Meichenbaum (1979) Study

Meichenbaum's (1977) general self-instructional approach as adapted to memory strategy development was examined by Asarnow and Meichenbaum (1979). Self-instructions, as Meichenbaum trains it, includes MAPs. Unfortunately, for purposes of this chapter, MAPs were presented in conjunction with other self-instructional components. Thus, it is impossible to reach clear conclusions about the efficacy of MAPs from Asarnow and Meichenbaum's (1979) data. Nevertheless, given the widespread usage of self-instructional approaches to self-regulation (e.g., Meichenbaum, 1977; Pressley, 1979; Pressley, Reynolds, Stark, & Gettinger, 1983), discussion of the Asarnow and Meichenbaum experiment highlights the fact that MAPs are not really newcomers to the cognitive theory and application, even if the evaluation of their impact on instructional packages has largely been ignored.

Asarnow and Meichenbaum (1979) first identified kindergarten children who either showed no tendency to rehearse in preparation for a serial recall task or rehearsed inconsistently. Children were assigned to one of three instructional conditions.

During training in the self-instructional training condition, subjects were presented an instructional sequence similar to that used in studies of self-instructional training in other domains (Meichenbaum, 1977):

> This procedure involved a) the experimenter modeling a cognitive strategy [rehearsal] for performing the serial recall task; b) the child performing the task while the experimenter instructed the child; and c) the child instructing herself or himself aloud while performing the task. In order to enable the experimenter to gradually fade support the cognitive strategies were presented in a question and answer format. At the outset of the training the experimenter supplied both questions and answer. As training progressed the experimenter waited before responding and encouraged the child to respond. This fading procedure was employed until the child was answering all questions and occasionally asking them as well. The modeled cognitive strategies included a) questions concerning the nature and demands of the task; b) answers to these questions which described the behaviors involved in the production of a rehearsal strategy; c) answers to the questions providing feedback concerning the value of employing a rehearsal strategy on the task; d) rehearsal on the task; and e) self-reinforcement.

That Asarnow and Meichenbaum (1979) trained the self-instructional training children to ask themselves questions about the task and then to answer the questions makes the procedure a MAP. Presumably, by formulating the questions and seeking out answers, children would increase their understanding of the strategy. Performance in the self-instructional training condition was contrasted with that in an induced rehearsal condition that included procedures approximating those used in traditional rehearsal-training studies (e.g., Keeney, Cannizzo, & Flavell, 1967), as well as with performance in a no-strategy control condition. The most pronounced effects of training occurred with children who had not produced rehearsal strategies on the pretest. On the immediate posttest the recall levels of non-producers in the self-instructional training and nonproducers in the induced rehearsal conditions were comparable and greater than performance in the control condition. On a 1-week follow-up, however, the self-instructional nonproducing children maintained the strategy, but the induced rehearsal children did not.

As enthusiasts for MAPs, we would like to conclude that the self-questioning component accounted for the increased maintenance in the self-instructional training condition. Unfortunately, this condition also included self-reinforcement, fading, and other components not found in the induced rehearsal condition. It is impossible to draw unequivocal conclusions about the effects of MAPs on strategy maintenance. Future experiments should include self-instructional packages that vary the amount and style of self-questioning procedures. This would allow evaluation of the importance of the self-questioning strategy for the self-instructional package. It would be interesting to test whether subsequent strategy learning would be affected positively by including the self-questioning component in the training of an earlier-acquired strategy. If self-questioning is a general MAP, the efficiency and completeness of learning subsequent strategies should covary with the degree of generality of self-questioning training during the initial strategy training. This research has profound bearing both on the theoretical position that metamemory is a general regulator of mnemonic activity and on practical issues concerned with clinical implementation of strategies. The potential application of self-questioning procedures with MAPs can be seen in studies by Short and Ryan (1984) and Wong and Jones (1982). Unfortunately, these studies suffer from analytical difficulties similar to those present in Brown and Barclay (1976) and Asarnow and Meichenbaum (1979)—a confounding of MAPs with specific strategies.

Future MAP Research

In this section we have reviewed general strategies for acquiring information about cognitive processes that are appropriate for specific tasks and purposes. The power of training MAP components lies in their generality. They should prove useful in developing knowledge about a wide variety of strategies in diverse problem areas. To date, the MAP most prominently cited in the literature has been memory monitoring. We hope that in the near future, researchers will begin investigating other MAPs such as (1) trying strategies with lots of different to-be-learned content, which presumably produces knowledge about the limits imposed by materials on a strategy; (2) trying the strategy out with friends, which should provide information about the populations who can and cannot use the strategy effectively; (3) comparing the strategy with other strategies, which might sharpen the distinctions among strategies, allowing subjects to make more fine-grained distinctions in their deployment of strategies; and (4) fooling around with the strategy to see what happens when a strategy is modified, leading the child toward the act of strategy invention.

Limitations on the Training of MAPs

It is unclear whether all of the MAPs we have discussed produce changes in memory behaviors. We suspect that training MAPs with young children may not automatically produce positive benefits unless they are induced shortly preceding occasions on which they might prove useful, as in the Lodico et al. (1983) study. These suspicions arise in part because of the results of a study conducted by Borkowski and his colleagues.

Kurtz and Borkowski (1984) included first- and third-grade children as subjects in a metamemory and strategy training study. In the first phase, children were assessed for their (1) general metamemorial knowledge, (2) use of strategic behaviors on cognitive cuing, paired-associate, and alphabet-search tasks, and (3) general world knowledge as measured by the vocabulary subtest of the WISC. Then children were randomly assigned to conditions. In the two most relevant conditions, subjects were either given MAP training or they were not.

Training in the MAP condition consisted of instructing children about the dynamic and creative properties of the mind. Rehearsal, clustering, and checking were described and modeled as examples of deliberate strategic behaviors; encoding and retrieval aspects of these strategies were discussed. The importance of matching input tactics with output demands was stressed. Strategy selection, monitoring, and modification were described and illustrated. Examples of learning situations were presented by the trainers; children were encouraged to select the most useful strategies. Feedback on the efficiency of the strategies was included at several points. New examples were given of nonacademic and academic strategies. In the final metamemory training session relatively less time was devoted to the description of processes and more time was given to children's applications of knowledge and information about superordinate, executive processes. Each training session lasted approximately 25 minutes.

Subjects in the control condition did not receive MAP training; they spent an equal amount of time with the experimenters during the second phase of the study, engaging in dialogue that covered topics similar to those used in metamemory training, but without reference to cognitive self-awareness or increased efficiency of cognitive functioning. In all three sessions the experimenters presented material to be learned and encouraged student participation in problem solving.

During the third and fourth phases of the study, one-half of the subjects in the metamemory condition and all subjects in the control condition received extensive training in the use of specific strategies—clustering-rehearsal, interrogative elaboration, and exhaustive search—appropriate for each of the three tasks (cognitive cuing, paired-associate learning, and alphabet search). In the fifth phase of the study, children were given two memory tasks that were slightly different from the tasks used during training, but ones for which the trained strategies would be appropriate. These tasks served as near generalization tests.

The results can be summarized briefly. MAP training did not increase metamemory for trained versus untrained subjects. Also, there were no group differences in strategy use for metamemory-trained versus un-trained subjects on the generalization tests. However, there were significant correlations between pretest metamemory and strategy generalization only in the MAP training condition. High initial levels of metamemory seemed to be essential for capitalizing on MAP training in order to achieve good strategy generalization.

The lesson to be learned from the Kurtz and Borkowski (1984) study is that the training of MAPs does not guarantee changes in metamemory or memory behaviors. Fine-grained analyses are needed to determine the sufficient and necessary conditions for MAPs to produce changes in metamemory, as well as analyses of what must occur for newly acquired metamemory to be used in the service of future strategy deployment. Lodico et al. (1983) demonstrated that one particular MAP can result in changes in memory strategy usage, but other experiments need to be conducted in order to specify the boundary conditions for MAP training.

General Discussion and Conclusions

Teaching a person a strategy is one thing. Teaching the person a strategy so that they can use that strategy broadly is quite another. Logically, it makes very good sense to assume that specific strategy knowledge is necessary for a strategy to be generally useful. After all, strategy-specific metamemory includes information about when and where the strategy can be used, the utility of the strategy relative to other approaches, the modifiability of the strategy, as well as more episodic information such as the context in which the strategy was learned and whether or not it was fun to use the strategy. There does not seem to be any way for a child to deploy a strategy in a situation not identical to the training situation without at least some of these specific strategy knowledge components.

Only rarely has training of MAS components been included in strategy instruction. It has been assumed that normal experiences with a strategy are sufficient to cultivate specific strategy knowledge. For instance, in trying to apply a strategy learned as an aid for study in context X to another context, Y, the learner might discover that the strategy is more applicable for content X than content Y or that with slight modification the strategy works better with Y than with X. The problem with this laissez-faire approach is its inefficiency. A great deal of time might be spent with content Y before realizing the relevance of the strategy to situation X. In addition, children are not necessarily sensitive to metacognitive experiences or their importance, as illustrated by the fifth through seventh graders in the study of Pressley et al. (1984). These children failed to use their realization that one strategy was better than the other to direct future strategy deployment. Fortunately, there are alternatives to leaving the learner adrift in a sea of metacognitive experiences that may surround the individual and yet never be understood or abstracted into metamemory.

When complete strategy instructions are given, the learner is provided with specific strategy knowledge. To the extent that explicit training in metamemory has been tried, it has proven successful. There is ample documentation that providing subjects with information about a strategy's utility increases subsequent usage, at least in situations similar to the training task. In the most extensive study to date about the effects on generalization of providing specific strategy knowledge, O'Sullivan and Pressley (1984) were able to increase the generalized usage of the keyword method through provisions of general utility information about the strategy; that study, however, is only a modest beginning. Analysis of the effects of many different types of metamemory contents are needed. Research in this area has fixated on the problem of strategy utility. It is time to move on to other aspects of specific strategy knowledge.

The third approach, the teaching of MAPs, is much more ambitious than the simple teaching of specific strategy knowledge. With this approach, the learner is taught to form personalized metacognitive experiences and to make the most of them. For instance, Lodico et al. (1983) taught children to compare the efficacy of strategies and to use that information to make strategy decisions. This skill does not normally develop until adulthood (Pressley et al., 1984). There are obviously many other potential MAPs. We hope that their development in instructional packages and subsequent evaluation will be forthcoming. It is important that MAPs not be thought of as tied to any particular strategy. Past research has generally confounded what we call MAPs with specific memory strategies (e.g., Brown & Barclay, 1976; Brown, Campione, & Barclay, 1979; Paris, Newman, & McVey, 1982; Wong & Jones, 1982). The Lodico et al. (1983) study provided a model of how the effects of MAPs can be separated from the effects of cognitive strategies.

Metamemory has traditionally been thought of as a fuzzy concept (see Wellman, 1983). Throughout this chapter we have tried to present a framework for clarifying its potential role vis-a-vis strategy use and, especially, the importance of metamemory training for improving the effectiveness of strategy training. Positive results have been obtained when spectific strategy knowledge has been provided and when children have been taught MAPs. These data can be viewed as validating parts of Flavell's (1981) model of metamemory: Adding specific strategy knowledge or MAP components enhances strategy use.

The data presented in this chapter are of relevance to both the validation of metamemory theory and the implementation of strategies in applied contexts. We hope that additional interventions based on specific strategy knowledge and MAPs will be developed and tested. We anticipate that this research will lead to theoretical refinements in the concept of metamemory and technological advancement in its educational utility. At the same time it seems imperative to begin validation work on relational memory strategy knowledge and general knowledge about memory strategies, as well as research on the effects of these two components on memory strategy usage in combination with other components. We have attempted to provide a scaffolding, parts of which are supported by bits and pieces of data. We hope that this framework might be turned into a more complete theoretical structure in the near future.

References

Asarnow, J. R., & Meichenbaum, D. Verbal rehearsal and serial recall. *Child Development*, 1979, *50*, 1173–1177.

Baker, L., & Brown, A. L. Metacognitive stills and reading, In D. Pearson (Ed.), *Handbook of Reading Research*. New York: Longman, 1984.

Bixenstine, V. E., DeCorte, M. S., & Bixenstine, B. A. Conformity to peer-sponsored misconduct at four grade levels. *Developmental Psychology*, 1976, *12*, 226–236.

Black, M. M., & Rollins, H. J., Jr. The effects of instructional variables on young children's organization and free recall. *Journal of Experimental Child Psychology*, 1982, *33*, 1–19.

Borkowski, J. G., & Büchel, F. P. Learning and memory strategies in the mentally retarded. In M. Pressley & J. R. Levin (Eds.), *Cognitive strategy research: Psychological foundations*. New York: Springer-Verlag, 1983.

Borkowski, J. G., Levers, S. R., & Gruenenfelder, T. M. Transfer of mediational strategies in children: The role of activity and awareness during strategy acquisition. *Child Development*, 1976, *47*, 779–786.

Borkowski, J. G., Peck, V., Reid, M. K., & Kurtz, B. Impulsivity and strategy transfer: Metamemory as mediator. *Child Development*, 1983, *54*, 459–473.

Brown, A. L. The development of memory: Knowing, knowing about knowing, and knowing how to know. In H. W. Reese (Ed.), *Advances in child development* (Vol. 10). New York: Academic Press, 1975.

Brown, A. L. Knowing when, where, and how to remember: A problem of metacognition. In R. Glaser (Ed.), *Advances in instructional psychology*. Hillsdale, NJ: Erlbaum, 1978.

Brown, A. L., & Barclay, C. R. The effect of training specific mnemonics on the metamnemonic efficiency of retarded children. *Child Development*, 1976, *47*, 71–80.

Brown, A. L., Campione, J. C., & Barclay, C. R. Training self-checking routines for estimating test readiness: Generalization from list learning to prose recall. *Child Development*, 1979, *50*, 501–512.

Brown, A. L., Campione, J. C., & Day, J. D. Learning to learn: On training students to learn from text. *Educational Researcher*, 1981, *10*, 14–21.

Brown, A. L., & Smiley, S. S. The development of strategies for studying text. *Child Development*, 1978, 49, 1076–1088.

Butterfield, E. C., & Belmont, J. Assessing and improving the executive cognitive functioning of mentally retarded people. In I. Bialar & M. Sternlicht (Eds.), *Psychological issues in mental retardation*. Chicago: Aldine, 1977.

Campione, J. C., Brown, A. L., & Ferrara, R. A. Mental retardation and intelligence. In R. J. Sternberg (Ed.), *Handbook of human intelligence*. Cambridge, England: Cambridge University Press, 1982.

Cavanaugh, J. C., & Borkowski, J. G. The metamemory–memory connection: Effects of strategy training and maintenance. *Journal of General Psychology*, 1979, 101, 161–174.

Cavanaugh, J. C., & Borkowski, J. G. Searching for metamemory–memory connections: A developmental study. *Developmental Psychology*, 1980, 16, 441–453.

Cavanaugh, J. C., & Perlmutter, M. Metamemory: A critical examination. *Child Development*, 1982, 53, 11–28.

Chi, M. T. H. Representing knowledge and meta-knowledge: Implications for interpreting metamemory research. In R. H. Kluwe & F. E. Weinert (Eds.), *Metacognition, motivation, and learning*. Hillsdale, NJ: Erlbaum, 1984.

Douglass, L. C. *Metamemory in learning disabled children: A clue to memory deficiency*. Paper presented at the annual meeting of the Society for Research in Child Development, Boston, April 1981.

Dweck, C. S., Hill, K. T., Redd, W. H., & Steinman, W. M. The impact of social cues on children's behavior. *Merrill-Palmer Quarterly*, 1976, 22, 83–123.

Flavell, J. H. Cognitive monitoring. In W. P. Dickson (Ed.), *Children's oral communication skills*. New York: Academic Press, 1981.

Flavell, J. H. The development of mediated memory. In H. W. Reese & L. P. Lipsitt (Eds.), *Advances in child development and behavior* (Vol. 5). New York: Academic Press, 1970.

Flavell, J. H. Metacognition and cognitive monitoring: A new area of cognitive-developmental inquiry. *American Psychologist*, 1979, 34, 906–911.

Flavell, J. H. Metacognitive development. In J. M. Scandura & C. J. Brainerd (Eds.), *Structural/process theories of complex human behavior*. Alphen a. d. Rijn: Sijthoff & Noordhoff, 1978.

Flavell, J. H. & Wellman, H. M. Metamemory. In R. V. Kail, Jr., & J. W. Hagen (Eds.), *Perspectives on the development of memory and cognition*. Hillsdale, NJ: Erlbaum, 1977.

Gagné, R. M. *The conditions of learning* (3rd ed.). New York: Holt, Rinehart, & Winston, 1977.

Glass, G. V. Integrating findings: the meta-analysis of research. *Review of research in education* (Vol. 5). Itasca, IL: Peacock, 1978.

Guttman, J., Levin, J. R., & Pressley, M. Pictures, partial pictures, and young children's oral prose learning. *Journal of Educational Psychology*, 1977, 69, 473–480.

Hagen, J. W., Jongeward, R. H., & Kail, R. V. Cognitive perspectives on the development of memory. In H. W. Reese (Ed.), *Advances in child development and behavior* (Vol. 10). New York: Academic Press, 1975.

House, B. J. Learning processes: Developmental trends. In J. Worell (Ed.), *Psychological development in the elementary years*. New York: Academic Press, 1982.

Kail, R. V., & Bisanz, J. Information processing and cognitive development. In H. W. Reese & L. P. Lissitt (Eds.), *Advances in child development and behavior* (Vol. 17) (pp. 45-82). New York: Academic Press, 1982.

Kail, R. V., & Hagen, J. W. (Eds.) *Perspectives on the development of memory and cognition*. Hillsdale, NJ: Erlbaum, 1977.

Keeney, T. J., Cannizzo, S. R., & Flavell, J. H. Spontaneous and induced verbal rehearsal in a recall task. *Child Development*, 1967, 38, 953–966.

Kendall, C. R., Borkowski, J. G., & Cavanaugh, J. C. Metamemory and the transfer of an interrogative strategy by EMR children. *Intelligence*, 1980, 4, 255–270.

Kennedy, B. A., & Miller, D. J. Persistent use of verbal rehearsal as a function of information about its value. *Child Development*, 1976, 47, 566–569.

Kramer, J. J., & Engle, R. W. Teaching awareness of strategic behavior in combination with strategy training: Effects on children's memory performance. *Journal of Experimental Child Psychology*, 1981, 32, 513–530.

Kurtz, B. E., & Borkowski, J. G. (1984). Children's metacognition: Exploring relations among knowledge, process, and motivational variables. *Journal of Experimental Child Psychology*, 37, 335–354.

Kurtz, B. E., Reid, M. K., Borkowski, J. G., & Cavanaugh, J. C. On the reliability and validity of children's metamemory. *Bulletin of the Psychonomic Society*, 1982, 19, 137–140.

Lachman, J. L., Lachman, R., & Thronesbery, C. Metamemory through the adult life span. *Developmental Psychology*, 1979, 15, 543–551.

Lawson, M. J., & Fuelop, S. Understanding the purpose of strategy training. *British Journal of Educational Psychology*, 1980, 50, 175–180.

Levin, J. R., & Pressley, M. Improving children's prose comprehension: Selected strategies that seem to succeed. In C. Santa & B. Hayes (Eds.), *Children's prose comprehension: Research and practice.* Newark, DE: International Reading Association, 1981.

Levin, J. R., Yussen, S. R., DeRose, T. M., & Pressley, M. Developmental changes in assessing recall and recognition memory capacity. *Developmental Psychology*, 1977, 13, 608–615.

Lodico, M. G., Ghatala, E., Levin, J. R., Pressley, M., & Bell, J. A. Effects of meta-memory training on children's use of effective memory strategies. *Journal of Experimental Child Psychology*, 1983, 35, 263-277.

Mann, L. *On the trail of process.* New York: Grune & Stratton, 1979.

Meacham, J. A. The development of memory abilities in the individual and in society. *Human Development*, 1972, 15, 205–228.

Meichenbaum, D. *Cognitive behavior modification.* New York: Plenum Press, 1977.

Miller, S. A. Extinction of Piagetian concepts: An updating. *Merrill-Palmer Quarterly*, 1976, 22, 257–281.

Moely, B. E. Organizational factors in the development of memory. In R. V. Kail & J. W. Hagen (Eds.), *Perspectives on the development of memory and cognition.* Hillsdale, NJ: Erlbaum, 1977.

Naus, M. J., Ornstein, P. A., & Aivano, S. Developmental changes in memory: The effects of processing time and rehearsal instructions. *Journal of Experimental Child Psychology*, 1977, 23, 237–251.

O'Sullivan, J., & Pressley, M. (1984). The completeness of instruction and strategy transfer. *Journal of Experimental Child Psychology*, 38, 275–288.

Paris, S. G., Newman, R. S., & McVey, K. A. Learning the functional significance of mnemonic actions: A microgenetic study of strategy acquisition. *Journal of Experimental Child Psychology*, 1982, 34, 490–509.

Peck, V., & Borkowski, J. G. *The emergence of strategic behavior and metamemory in gifted children.* Paper presented at the biennial meeting of the Society for Research in Child Development, Detroit, April 1983.

Poon, L. W., Fozard, S. L., Cermak, L. S., Arenberg, D., & Thompson, L. W. (Eds.) *New directions in memory and aging.* Hillsdale, NJ: Erlbaum, 1980.

Posnansky, C. J. Age- and task-related differences in the use of category-size information for the retrieval of categorized items. *Journal of Experimental Child Psychology*, 1978, 26, 373–382.

Pressley, G. M. Mental imagery helps eight-year-olds remember what they read. *Journal of Educational Psychology*, 1976, 61, 355–359.

Pressley, M. Elaboration and memory development. *Child Development*, 1982, 53, 296–309.

Pressley, M. Imagery and children's learning: Putting the picture in developmental perspective. *Review of Educational Research*, 1977, 47, 485–522.

Pressley, M. Increasing children's self-control through cognitive interventions. *Review of Educational Research*, 1979, 49, 319–370.

Pressley, M., Borkowski, J. G., & O'Sullivan, J. T. Memory strategy instruction is made of this: Metamemory and durable strategy use. *Educational Psychologist*, 1984, 19, 84–107.

Pressley, M., & Bryant, S. L. Does answering questions really promote associative learning? *Child Development*, 1982, 53, 1258–1267.

Pressley, M., & Dennis-Rounds, J. Transfer of a mnemonic keyword strategy at two age levels. *Journal of Educational Psychology*, 1980, 72, 575–582.

Pressley, M. Forrest-Pressley, D. L., & Elliott-Faust, D. How to study strategy instructional enrichment. Illustrations from research on children's prose memory and comprehension. In F. Weinert & M. Perlmutter (Eds.), *Development of memory*. Hillsdale, NJ: Erlbaum, in press.

Pressley, M. Forrest-Pressley, D. L., Elliott-Faust, D., & Miller, G. E. Children's use of cognitive strategies, how to teach strategies, and what to do if they can't be taught. In M Pressley & C.J. Brainerd (Eds.), *Cognitive learning and memory in children*. New York: Springer-Verlag, 1985.

Pressley, M., Heisel, B. E., McCormick, C. B., & Nakamura, G. V. Memory strategy instruction with children. In C. J. Brainerd & M. Pressley (Eds.), *Progress in cognitive development research* (Vol. 2): *Verbal processes in children*. New York: Springer-Verlag, 1982.

Pressley, M., & Levin, J. R. Task parameters affecting the efficacy of a visual imagery learning strategy in younger and older children. *Jounal of Experimental Child Psychology*, 1977, 24, 53–59.

Pressley, M., Levin, J. R., & Bryant, S. L. Memory strategy instruction during adolescence: When is explicit instruction needed? In M. Pressley & J. R. Levin (Eds.), *Cognitive strategy research: Psychological foundations*. New York: Springer-Verlag, 1983.

Pressley, M., Levin, J. R., & Delaney, H. D. The mnemonic keyword method. *Review of Educational Research*, 1982, 52, 61–91.

Pressley, M., Levin, J. R., & Ghatala, E. S. Memory-strategy monitoring in adults and children. *Journal of Verbal Learning and Verbal Behavior*, 1984, 23, 270–288.

Pressley, M., Reynolds, W. M., Stark, K. D., & Gettinger, M. Cognitive strategy training and children's self-control. In M. Pressley & J. R. Levin (Eds.), *Cognitive strategy research: Psychological foundations*. New York: Spring-Verlag, 1983.

Read, J. D., & Bruce, D. Longitudinal tracking of difficult memory retrievals. *Cognitive Psychology*, 1982, 14, 280-300.

Ringel, B. A., & Springer, C. J. On knowing how well one is remembering: The persistence of strategy use during transfer. *Journal of Experimental Child Psychology*, 1980, 29, 322-333.

Robinson, F. P. *Effective study* (Rev. ed.). New York: Harper & Row, 1961.

Rohwer, W. D., Jr. Elaboration and learning in childhood and adolescence. In H. W. Reese (Ed.), *Advances in child development and behavior* (Vol. 8). New York: Academic Press, 1973.

Rubin, K. H. Extinction of conservation: A life-span investigation. *Developmental Psychology*, 1976, *12*, 51–56.

Rushton, J. P., Brainerd, C. J., & Pressley, M. Behavioral development and construct validity: The principle of aggregation. *Psychological Bulletin*, 1983, *94*, 238-247.

Salatas, H., & Flavell, J. H. Behavioral and meta-mnemonic indicators of strategic behaviors under remember instructions in first grade. *Child Development*, 1976, *47*, 81–89.

Short, E. J., & Ryan, E. B. Metacognitive differences between skilled and less skilled readers: Remediating deficits through story grammar and attribution training. *Journal of Educational Psychology*, 1984, *76*, 225–235.

Trepanier, M. L. *Learning disabled children's understanding of their memory ability*. Paper presented at the annual meeting of the American Educational Research Association, Los Angeles, April 1981.

Turnure, J. E., Buium, N., & Thurlow, M. The effectiveness of interrogatives for prompting verbal elaboration productivity in young children. *Child Development*, 1976, *47*, 851–855.

Underwood, B. J. Individual differences as a crucible in theory construction. *American Psychologist*, 1975, *30*, 128–134.

Wellman, H. M. Metamemory revisited. In M. T. H. Chi (Ed.), *Contributions to human development*, Vol. 9. *Trends in memory development research*. Basel: S. Karger, 1983.

Wong, B. Y. L., & Jones, W. Increasing metacomprehension in learning-disabled and normally achieving students through self-questioning training. *Learning Disabilities Quarterly*, 1982, *5*, 228–240.

Yussen, S. R., & Berman, L. Memory predictions for recall and recognition in first-, third-, and fifth-grade children. *Developmental Psychology*, 1981, *17*, 224–229.

CHAPTER 5

How Do We Know When We Don't
Understand? Standards for Evaluating
Text Comprehension

Linda Baker

Introduction

An important metacognitive skill in reading is evaluating the current
state of one's ongoing comprehension. This evaluation is one of the two
component activites involved in comprehension monitoring. The other
component, regulation, comes into play when the reader has evaluated his
or her understanding and found it inadequate. At such time, a competent
reader selects and deploys some sort of remedial strategy. Several papers
have examined the concept of comprehension monitoring in some depth
and have presented empirical evidence of its usefulness (Baker, 1982; Baker
& Brown, 1984a; Baker & Brown, 1984b; Flavell, 1981; Markman, 1981;
Wagoner, 1983). However, our understanding of the processes involved in
either evaluation or regulation is rather incomplete, in part because most
of the investigations of comprehension monitoring have been primarily
concerned with demonstrating its existence (or lack thereof) among selected populations. Moreover, it is difficult to draw generalizations across
studies because of the large variations in the way comprehension monitoring has been operationalized.

The most popular operationalization has focused on the evaluation
phase and involves introducing problems of some sort into otherwise intact text. Success at identifying these problems is taken as evidence that

155

subjects evaluated their understanding during reading. However, what most researchers have ignored is that success at identifying a particular type of problem, such as a nonsense word, requires the use of a particular standard or criterion against which to evaluate one's understanding. And success at identifying another type, such as a logical inconsistency, requires a very different type of standard. In other words, researchers have tended to regard comprehension monitoring as a unitary phenomenon; a reader is either good at it or not. It is my contention that this approach to comprehension monitoring is inadequate. A reader may be quite successful at evaluting personal understanding of individual words yet quite unsuccessful at evaluating the ideas within a text for internal consistency.

The purpose of this chapter is to offer a new framework within which to integrate the existing research that is either directly or indirectly relevant to comprehension monitoring. This framework focuses on the different kinds of standards that readers use to evaluate their understanding. The specific standards included in this framework have been derived from both theoretical and empirical work on the cognitive processes involved in comprehension and comprehension monitoring.

An Overview of the Framework

There are three basic types of standards that readers use to evaluate their understanding: lexical, syntactic, and semantic. Successful application of these standards requires increasingly thorough processing of the text. The lexical standard operates at the level of individual words, and surrounding context can be completely ignored. Examples of its use include realizing that a string of letters is not a real word or that the meaning of a particular word is not known. The syntactic standard requires sensitivity to the grammatical constraints of the language, a sensitivity that is acquired relatively early in the course of language acquisition. An example of its use is realizing that a string of words is in a scrambled sequence. The semantic standard requires consideration of the meanings of individual sentences and the text as a whole. Standards of this type are most crucial to effective comprehension and are therefore discussed in greatest depth.

The semantic standards have been classified into five categories: (1) *propositional cohesiveness,* checking that the ideas expressed in adjacent propositions can be successfully integrated; (2) *structural cohesiveness,* checking that the ideas expressed throughout the text are thematically compatible; (3) *external consistency,* checking that the ideas in the text are consistent with what one already knows; (4) *internal consistency,* checking that the ideas expressed in the text are consistent with one another; and (5) *informational clarity and completeness*, checking that the text clearly states all of the information necessary to achieve a specific goal.

Plan of the Chapter

Each standard of evaluation is discussed in sequence. Direct and indirect evidence for its use is presented, drawing on research examining both cognitive and metacognitive aspects of comprehension. Whenever possible, differences in development and in reader proficiency are considered. It should be noted that some of the research evidence comes from listening tasks. Although there are of course several important differences between reading and listening, the standards used to evaluate comprehension are probably quite similar. It is in the regulation phase that differences arise. For example, a reader can go back to a previously read sentence if a difficulty arises, whereas a listener cannot. And a listener often can interrupt the speaker and request clarification, whereas a reader cannot.

The fact that each standard is considered separately is not meant to imply that readers use only one standard when evaluating their understanding. The separation is in part an expository convenience and in part a reflection of the literature. That is, most studies have used paradigms that reveal the use of one specific type of standard. Nevertheless, readers frequently use multiple standards during a single encounter with a text. Data supporting this claim are presented in the section on multiple evaluation standards.

Most of the research paradigms either implicitly or explicitly call for the reader to evaluate the comprehensibility of the text rather than his or her own comprehension. However, the standards one should use are the same in either case. It makes little difference during the evaluation phase of comprehension monitoring whether the difficulty is text-based or reader-based. It is during the regulation phase that the distinction becomes important because the steps a reader should take to deal with the problem differ depending on its source.

As noted earlier, the most common method for assessing comprehension monitoring has been to manipulate the to-be-read material in such a way that readers should experience difficulty *if* they were evaluating their understanding. In this chapter, the type of manipulation used is the basis for inferring the type of standard required. So, for example, if readers rate text as more difficult to understand when it contains difficult vocabulary, we can infer they were using a lexical standard. And if they spend more time reading a sentence that is inconsistent with a preceding sentence, we can infer an internal consistency standard. In general, the researchers themselves did not interpret their studies from the perspective of the standard used.

A central theme throughout the chapter includes the problems of interpretation that arise when comprehension monitoring is regarded as a unitary phenomenon—that is, when a researcher concludes that subjects did not evaluate their understanding on the grounds that they failed to notice the intended problems. Having learned through personal experience the fallacy of this conclusion, I am perhaps more inclined than most to argue against it. Let me give an illustration.

In an unpublished study, I asked college students to evaluate a passage about Renaissance artists containing the following segment:

> Within daVinci's notebooks can be found sketches of war machines and flying machines—including a tank and a parachute—as well as accurate drawings on anatomy and optics. These sketches lacked any future practicality but have become well-known to many people.

The segment was intended to be inconsistent: daVinci's drawings were remarkably prescient; how could one say they lacked practicality? A surprisingly large number of students did not report this inconsistency. My initial conclusion was that the subjects did not monitor their comprehension as they read. However, subsequent questioning of the students revealed an alternative explanation. Students explained it was *true* that the drawings lacked practicality. They went on to explain that they had seen pictures of those drawings and knew that the airplanes could not possibly fly because they were aerodynamically unsound. In other words, the students used an *external* consistency standard, evaluating the text with respect to what they already knew, rather than an *internal* consistency standard, which had been my implicit criterion for comprehension monitoring. The students' interpretation of the passage was different from what I intended to convey, yet it was certainly plausible. Not only does the example illustrate the importance of considering comprehension monitoring with respect to specific standards, but also it demonstrates the value of obtaining multiple response measures. If I had simply scored as an error the subjects' failure to identify the inconsistency, I would have been left with a very misleading impression of their comprehension monitoring activities. When trying to understand these cognitive activities, "wrong" answers can be at least as revealing as "correct" answers, as Piaget so long ago observed.

We now turn to a consideration of the standards themselves, beginning with the lexical standard.

Lexical Standards of Evaluation

Lexical standards involve evaluation of one's understanding of individual words. These standards can be applied without regard to surrounding context and so, although they may be necessary for comprehension, they are not sufficient. In other words, an immature reader who decides he or she understands a passage because the meaning of each individual word is known may regard a passage containing randomly arranged words to be as comprehensible as an intact passage. Although it is often possible to get the gist of a passage without understanding the meaning of every word, some words are obviously more crucial to comprehension than others. A reader could still be said to understand the preceding sentence even if unsure of the meaning of *obviously*; the same cannot be said about the word *comprehension*. An efficient reader should have some heuristics available for distinguishing between those words that are central to the main point and those that modify or embellish it (e.g., knowing that unknown adjectives can usually be safely ignored, nouns cannot). In other words, once the lexical standard has been applied and a problem noted, it is not always necessary to go on to the regulation phase of comprehension monitoring. The reader instead may make a strategic decision that the word comprehension failure need not be remedied.

In this section we first consider evidence regarding children's use of the lexical standard while listening and while reading. We then consider evidence that some readers overrely on this particular standard. Finally, we show that the standard is frequently used with regard to surrounding context.

Children's Use of the Lexical Standard

Although the research evidence is somewhat contradictory, it is apparent that under optimally structured task demands, children of 4 and 5 years of age evaluate their understanding of individual words. For example, Flavell, Speer, Green, and August (1981) found that 4- and 5-year-old children were quite aware of failures to understand a difficult vocabulary word (*hypotenuse*) when listening to directions to assemble block buildings, and they recognized that a word that was inaudible because it was obscured by a sneeze posed an obstacle to carrying out the task. Baker (1984a) asked children to find the "words that aren't real words" as they listened to a set of simple stories. Five-year-old children correctly reported almost 60% of the two-syllable nonsense words that had been substituted for nouns in some of the stories. By 7 years of age, the detection rate for these nonsense words was above 90%.

Other studies using reading tasks have not found such positive evidence. Miller and Isaksen (1978) introduced nonsense words into passages and asked first and third graders to read the passages aloud. The younger children gave no indications that they noticed the nonsense words. Paris and Myers (1981), using this same paradigm, found that both good and poor readers in fourth grade showed little awareness of the nonsense words. In a second task, Paris and Myers asked the children to underline words or phrases they did not understand. Fewer than half of the nonsense words were underlined by the good readers and even fewer by the poor readers. Though these failures to notice nonwords suggest that even the good readers did not evaluate their understanding carefully, an alternate explanation is possible. The children may have assumed that the nonwords were simply words whose meaning they did not know and were reluctant to admit their ignorance. If the children had been told to expect nonsense words, their performance may have been much better.

Baker (1984b) has provided some evidence in support of this explanation. Good and poor readers in the fourth and sixth grades read expository passages and were asked to find problems that had been embedded within them. Half of the children were specifically told that nonsense words would be one of the problems present in the passages; the remaining children were simply told to try to find the problems. Those children who received specific instructions identified 58% of the nonsense words; those receiving general instructions identified 44%. Additional details about this study are provided in the section on multiple standards of evaluation. The important point here is that reliable increases in identification resulted when the children knew that nonsense words would be present.

Note, however, that even with specific instructions, children missed 42% of the nonsense words. Clearly additional factors are involved. One possibility that may apply to poorer readers in particular is the following: Rather than evaluate word *understanding*, perhaps they evaluate word *decodability*. There is evidence that some younger and poorer readers believe that good reading is saying all the words correctly (e.g., Canney & Winograd, 1979; Myers & Paris, 1978). This immature conception of reading would give children the illusion of being successful readers if they could pronounce all of the words. Because the nonwords in both Paris and Myers

(1981) and Baker (1984b) were easy to decode, they posed no obstacle. Had these readers encountered a word they could not pronounce, perhaps they would have been blocked. Paris and Myers (1981) obtained evidence supporting this interpretation in a third task. Subjects were asked to read a passage containing several difficult vocabulary words and were encouraged to look up words they did not know in a dictionary. While the good readers tended to look up the difficult words, the poor readers sought assistance in pronouncing them.

The decoding interpretation also runs into difficulty, however, when we consider the results of a study by Baker (in press), involving college students differing in verbal ability. Whereas the high-ability group (mean SAT-Verbal score = 599) identified 92% of the nonsense words embedded in college-level texts when specifically instructed to seek them, the lower-ability group (Mean SAT-Verbal score = 388) identified only 63% under similar instructions. (When nonspecific instructions were given, the high-ability group reported 64% and the low-ability group 54%.) Surely one would not wish to argue that the reason these college students did not identify more nonsense words was because the words were decodable!

Exclusive Use of the Lexical Standard

There is some evidence that less-able readers may use the lexical standard of evaluation exclusively. For example, Canney and Winograd (1979) reported that poor readers in fourth grade judged a passage composed of rearranged clauses as being as comprehensible as an intact passage. These children failed to evaluate using either syntactic or semantic standards. Garner (1981) introduced either difficult vocabulary items or internal inconsistencies into passages and asked fifth-grade poor readers to rate the comprehensibility of the passages. Passage ratings were consistently lower when difficult words were present, even though these words were adjectives whose meanings were not crucial to comprehension. The ratings for inconsistent passages did not differ from normal passages.

More direct evidence for the exclusive use of the lexical standard among poorer readers was provided in the Baker (1984b) study. For many of the poorer readers, the *only* type of problem mentioned concerned individual word meanings, even though inconsistencies and prior knowledge problems were also present. However, the tendency to use only the lexical standard was much less pronounced when the children were given specific instructions as to the types of problems they should seek (59% vs. 18%). Thus, it appears that although many poorer readers, when left on their own, rely exclusively on a lexical standard of evaluation, they can be in-

duced to apply other standards. By the time poorer readers reach adulthood, this overreliance on the lexical standard is seldom observed; Baker
(in press) found that fewer than 10% of the low verbal ability college students used the lexical standard exclusively.

Using the Lexical Standard in Context

Although the lexical standard can be used out of context, it is more
common for readers to take into account the local context in which the
word occurs. Thus, judgments of word understanding are frequently mediated by the semantic and/or syntactic constraints of the surrounding
text. Readers may make judgments about the meanings of individual words
on the basis of only partially correct visual information. Words that are
misspelled, for example, are often assigned a meaning compatible with the
surrounding context, even when the misspellings create real words that
are anomalous in that context (e.g., changing the "u" in "house" to an
"r," resulting in "horse"). When the context is predictive, both children
(Ehrlich, 1981) and adults (Ehrlich & Rayner, 1981) are less likely to notice
the misspellings than when the context is neutral. It is not that subjects
failed to process the misspelled words; analysis of eye movements revealed
longer fixations on and more regressions to these words. In the Ehrlich
and Rayner study, 75% of the adults were subsequently able to report the
misspellings. These data suggest that the readers evaluated their understanding of the word, found it did not fit with the context, and revised
their interpretation.

Similarly, readers may believe they understand a given word, but subsequent context may require them to revise their interpretation. Carpenter and Daneman (1981) had college students read sentence pairs in which
the first sentence biased a particular meaning of a homograph presented
in the second sentence. The meaning was either compatible or incom-
patible with the biasing context. Consider the set: "Cinderella was sad she
couldn't go to the dance. There were big tears in her brown dress (eyes)."
The word "sad" biases the interpretation of "tears" consistent with the
word "eyes." Subjects who encountered the word dress showed increased
fixation times because they had to assign a new meaning to the word
"tears."

In summary, the research reveals that both children and adults evaluate their understanding by checking that the meanings of individual
words are known. However, it seems that demand characteristics of the
task affect the likelihood that failures to understand will be reported. For
example, both children and adults are more likely to identify nonsense

words in expository passages when they are specifically told they will be present (Baker, 1984b; Baker, in press). There also seem to be differences in the sophistication with which readers respond to their realization that a word understanding failure has occurred. Less effective readers tend to perceive such problems as more detrimental to overall comprehension than more effective readers. Similarly, they tend to overrely on the lexical standard to the exclusion of other standards of evaluation. This overreliance is probably a major underlying factor in their comprehension difficulties.

We return to a discussion of issues involving the use of the lexical standard in a later section, where the studies examining multiple standard use are considered in more detail. We turn now to a discussion of syntactic standards.

Syntactic Standards of Evaluation

Syntactic standards involve judgments as to the grammaticality of a string of words or the recognition that a particular word is not syntactically acceptable given the surrounding context. By definition, syntactically anomalous text is also semantically anomalous, so it may be difficult to tell whether syntactic or semantic evaluation leads to detection of the anomaly. For example, a reader may realize that the string, "John to store went the big" is incomprehensible either because it violates rules of grammar or because it has no coherent interpretation. Researchers have devoted relatively little attention to readers' use of syntactic standards of evaluation, perhaps on the assumption that oral language fluency entails a grasp of syntactic principles sufficient for reading. There is evidence, however, that poor readers are less likely to evaluate syntactic acceptability than good readers.

For example, Paris and Myers (1981) disrupted the comprehensibility of short passages by rearranging the words within clauses, as in the sentence, "He must be very brave to train lions and wants do to what he tigers." Fourth-grade good and poor readers were audiotaped as they read the passages aloud and the tapes were analyzed for hesitations and substitutions. The flow of reading was disrupted by the anomalous phrases for both the good and poor readers, but more so for the good readers. Similar findings were obtained in a second task, in which children were instructed to underline phrases they did not understand as they were reading. Good readers were twice as likely to underline the syntactic anomalies as the poor readers.

Isaksen and Miller (1976) also violated syntactic constraints by substituting intransitive verbs for transitive verbs (e.g., "The farmer planted the beans" was changed to "The farmer went the beans.") Fourth-grade good readers were more likely to detect the anomalies during oral reading than were fourth-grade poor readers.

Several studies of oral reading of nonmanipulated text have also revealed differences between good and poor readers in their sensitivity to syntactic constraints. Weber (1970) reported that good and poor readers in the first grade did not differ in the extent to which they corrected errors that were grammatically acceptable to the sentence context, but good readers were twice as likely to correct errors that were grammatically inappropriate. Beebe (1980) found that among fourth-grade boys, those identified as poor readers were less likely to correct their unacceptable substitutions than good readers. The same pattern has been obtained for poorer readers in seventh grade (Kavale & Schreiner, 1979).

Among adult readers, syntactic evaluation has been examined using more subtle manipulations. The focus here has been more on discovering when during reading adults evaluate syntactic acceptability than on whether such evaluation occurs. For example, Frazier and Rayner (1982) examined college students' processing of *garden path sentences* that lead the reader to incorrect interpretation of meaning by being initially structurally ambiguous. Consider the sentence, "Tom heard the latest gossip about the new neighbors wasn't true." For most people, the initial interpretation needs to be revised when the final two words are encountered. Frazier and Rayner found that subjects immediately attempted reanalysis of such sentences as indicated by fixation duration and regressive eye movements. In other words, on first encountering the word that did not fit with their initial syntactic parsing, readers initiated error correction procedures. Further evidence of ongoing syntactic evaluation has been reported by Tyler and Marslen-Wilson (1977). Subjects were presented with syntactically ambiguous phrases preceded by a clause that biased a particular interpretation of the phrase. They were then asked to name probe words that were either consistent with this interpretation or inconsistent. Naming latencies were longer for the inconsistent probes.

In summary, although there have been few investigations directly implicating syntactic standards, we do know that readers can and do evaluate the text for syntactic appropriateness. Better readers are more sensitive to syntactic constraints than poorer readers, although this often may be the result of semantic rather than syntactic evaluation. However, the following provides some evidence that syntactic and semantic standards are separable: good readers are more likely to self-correct oral reading errors that violate syntactic constraints than those that do not, whereas poor readers are not likely to notice either type. Nevertheless, syntactic evaluation probably plays a less central role in monitoring comprehension than does either lexical or semantic evaluation. The reason for this is that, in general, syntactic parsing occurs automatically as part of the effort to comprehend. It may not be necessary to evaluate syntax per se; problems at the syntactic level become apparent when semantic interpretation is difficult (e.g., Frazier & Rayner, 1982). We turn now to a consideration of standards involved in the evaluation of the semantic interpretation of a text.

Semantic Standards of Evaluation

Thus far we have discussed two standards of evaluation that can be applied with relatively superficial processing of the text. Decisions that one *has* understood ought to be based on more than the fact that all of the individual word meanings are known and the sentences are grammatically acceptable. But decisions that one *has not* understood similarly should not be made on the basis of lexical and syntactic criteria only. Because comprehension entails the construction of a semantic representation of the text as a whole, evaluation of one's comprehension must be based on standards sensitive to broader semantic considerations. Five such standards have been identified and are discussed in this section of the chapter. The first two standards involve evaluation of the cohesiveness of text at the propositional and structural levels, respectively. The second two involve evaluation of the consistency of the text with respect to prior knowledge (external consistency) and with respect to the ideas within the text itself (internal consistency). The fifth standard involves evaluating whether the text is sufficiently complete and clear to enable one to achieve a specific goal, whether it is a concrete goal such as following instructions or a more abstract goal such as extracting the gist. In a sense, this fifth standard serves as the residual, encompassing the semantic dimensions that cannot be subsumed under any of the other headings.

Propositional Cohesiveness

As people read, they attempt to construct an integrated representation of the text as a whole. Individual ideas or propositions are combined to form larger meaningful units. Successful integration requires that the relationships between and among propositions is clear. These relationships are often signalled by what Halliday and Hasan (1976) term cohesive ties. Examples include pronouns, definite descriptions, and logical connectives. These devices serve to connect successive propositions or sentences in a text and in fact are what distinguish text from a disconnected set of sentences. Researchers concerned with cognitive processes in comprehension have extensively documented that propositional cohesiveness plays an important role in comprehension. The fact that text manipulations that decrease cohesiveness affect on-line response measures such as reading times and eye movements provides evidence that people evaluate text for propositional cohesiveness during reading. Two of the more common types of cohesive devices are considered in this section: anaphora and logical connectives.

Anaphora

Anaphora is the process of referring back to a previously mentioned person, object, or situation. It is most explicitly signalled by pronouns. In fact, Hirst and Brill (1980) suggest that pronouns serve as a signal to the reader to integrate the text. Empirical evidence suggests that pronouns are indeed given an assignment as soon as they are encountered in the text. Carpenter and Just (1977) have collected eye movement data showing that subjects, upon encountering a pronoun, pause and frequently look back at the antecedent noun in the text. Repetition of the same lexical item is also often an indication that an anaphoric reference is intended, although in some cases, the word may refer to a new instance of the concept (Yekovich & Walker, 1978). The distinction is often signalled by the definiteness of the article: Definite noun phrases indicate referential ties whereas indefinite noun phrases do not. As Clark and Sengul (1979) note, "In most circumstances, we do not feel we have understood a sentence until we have identified the objects, events, and states referred to by the definite noun phrases it contains" (pp. 39–40). Several factors influence the ease or difficulty of this referent identification. For example, the distance between the anaphoric referent and its antecedents affects comprehension time (Cirilo, 1981; Clark & Sengul, 1979; Frederiksen, 1981; Garrod & Sanford, 1977). When the distance is short, the antecedent presumably is still present in working memory; however, when the distance is greater, the reader needs to search long-term memory and reinstate the appropriate referent for integration.

When referential continuity cannot be established directly, either by making a match with existing short-term memory contents or by searching long-term memory, "bridging" inferences (Clark & Haviland, 1977) are required. This type of integration puts the greatest demands on the comprehension process, although context usually constrains the interpretation sufficiently that bridging inferences are relatively easy to make. Consider the sentences: "John stood watching while Henry fell down some stairs. He tripped over a skate." Although the referent of "he" is not specified, the reader readily infers that it was Henry who tripped over the skate and this is what caused him to fall down the stairs. Not surprisingly, readers require more time to identify referents when there is less contextual constraint (Hirst & Brill, 1980).

When pronoun assignment is left intentionally ambiguous, readers frequently draw inferences to resolve the ambiguity. For example, Baker (1979b) had college students read and recall expository passages containing ambiguous referents. Many of the students recalled the passages as though there had been no ambiguity. When they were later told that ambiguities were present and were instructed to reread the passages to order to find them, 93% of the students identified an ambiguity involving the main point of a passage but only 70% reported noticing it during reading. These results suggest that readers may detect ambiguities (evaluate) and draw bridging inferences (regulate) without being aware of having done so. All of the preceding processing studies clearly show sensitivity to ambiguous referents, yet this sensitivity may be below the level of awareness.

Studies of children's processing of anaphoric referents in text are surprisingly scarce, despite the fact that comprehension of anaphora is crucial to text integration. (Children's awareness of ambiguity in *oral* messages has been extensively studied within the referential communication tradition. See the section on informational clarity and completeness.) Some insight into early processing strategies was provided in a study by Wykes (1981). Five-year-olds were presented with sentence pairs describing two actors and an action and the children were required to act out the action with props. The second sentence contained a pronoun whose referent could either be identified by gender cues (e.g., "Jane found John's ball. She gave it to him.") or require an inference (e.g., "Jane needed Susan's pencil. She gave it to her.") Children had more difficulty assigning correct referents when inferences were required than they did when gender cues were available. Wykes also found, not surprisingly, that the number of pronouns in the sentences affected their comprehensibility. On the basis of the errors the children made, Wykes concluded that the children assigned reference on the basis of the subject or focus of the previous sentence and they failed to revise the assignment if subsequent information showed it was inappropriate.

This immature processing strategy has also been found among poorer readers at the high school level (Frederiksen, 1981). These students tend to select the grammatical subject as the preferred referent, regardless of whether it was the focus of the sentence. Efficient readers, in contrast, are very sensitive to violations of the given–new contract: When the subject of a sentence introduces new information rather than information already given, comprehension is delayed by the difficulty of establishing propositional cohesiveness (Clark & Haviland, 1977; Carpenter & Just, 1977; Yekovich, Walker & Blackman, 1979). Such violations have also been found to interfere with readers' ability to detect disruptions of structural cohesiveness (Williams, Taylor, & Ganger, 1981).

In conclusion, the available research indicates that the presence of anaphora slows down the comprehension process. However, as long as the referents can be established, whether directly or inferentially, comprehension proceeds smoothly; there is little evidence of detrimental effects on *product* measures of comprehension (cf. Freebody & Anderson, 1983; Irwin, 1982). Perhaps as a consequence, readers typically are unaware of the processing operations they carry out to establish cohesiveness; it is only when they are unable to integrate the text that their efforts become conscious. It may be that the propositional cohesiveness standard is spontaneously applied as part of the effort to comprehend rather than deliberately invoked to evaluate the success of the effort. Additional research is needed to examine this possibility.

Logical Connectives

A second major way in which writers establish cohesion is by using transition words or connectives. These connectives link propositions by indicating the nature of the relationship between them. For example, the connectives *however* and *although* signal a change in the direction of thought, whereas *additionally* and *moreover* indicate that more of the same is coming. Logical connectives, like pronouns, can be used as stopping points for evaluating one's understanding. If readers are unable to grasp the relationship signalled by the connective, then they should have difficulty integrating the propositions. These theoretical arguments led Markman (1981) and Baker (1979b) to suggest that mature readers probably use connectives as a standard in comprehension monitoring. However, empirical evidence suggests that connectives may not be very important to many readers. Baker (1979b) introduced inappropriate connectives into expository passages and assessed college students' ability to identify them. Surprisingly, only 14% of the problems were identified, even when the students were informed that the passages contained inappropriate connectives.

This apparent insensitivity to the role of connectives was further examined in an unpublished study I conducted. Short expository passages were selected from several college-level textbooks and were presented to students with selected connectives deleted. The students' task was to fill in the appropriate connective. Responses were scored loosely, such that any word expressing the same general meaning as the target word was accepted. In only 58% of the cases were students able to supply the appropriate type of completion. Contrast this figure with the 94% average of several graduate students and faculty members.

Similar results were reported in a recent study by Bridge and Winograd (1982). Ninth graders were asked to supply the missing words in an expository passage and to explain why they had selected those words. The missing words involved three different types of cohesive relationships, one of which was connectives. The outcome of significance here is that both good and poor readers had the most difficulty supplying connectives and explaining their choices.

Thus, although countless study skills guides recommend paying particular attention to connectives or transition words (e.g., Adams & Spira, 1978; Wood, 1978), students do not seem to do so. Nevertheless, several studies have shown that connectives do facilitate comprehension. For example, Pearson (1974–1975) asked fourth-graders to read and recall sentences where the causal connectives were present (explicit) or deleted (implicit). Most of the time the subjects included causal connectives in their recall even when they were absent in the text. If they did not do this, there was a 50% chance of not recalling the information at all. Explicit connectives have also been found to facilitate recall among community college students, but not among regular college students (Marshall & Glock, 1978–1979). The authors interpreted this finding as indicating that better readers are capable of inferring the connectives and so do not require them to be explicitly stated in the text. However, this interpretation is difficult to reconcile with the evidence that students are frequently unable to infer missing connectives.

In summary, our present knowledge about the extent to which readers use logical connectives as a means of keeping track of their understanding is rather limited and inconclusive. Connectives are important in theory; perhaps instructional change is needed to make them important in practice.

Structural Cohesiveness

Structural cohesiveness is a second major characteristic of text that influences comprehension and comprehensibility. It differs from propositional cohesiveness in that its evaluation requires a global, top-down (general-to-specific) analysis of the text as opposed to a local, bottom-up (specific-to-general) analysis. A reader judges propositional cohesiveness in the effort to link each incoming proposition with recently encountered propositions. A reader judges structural cohesiveness in the effort to identify the main theme of the text and relate incoming information to that theme. The distinction between structural and propositional cohesiveness is analogous to Kintsch and van DijK's (1978) distinction between macrostructure and microstructure processing.

In this section, several different aspects of structural cohesiveness are examined. We begin by considering some of the conventions for writing structurally cohesive text and reader's sensivity to these conventions, first for expository prose and then for narrative. Much of the relevant information derives from studies focusing on cognitive aspects of comprehension as opposed to metacognitive. We then address more directly evidence for the use of a structural cohesiveness standard. This evidence comes primarily from the comprehension monitoring literature.

Structural Cohesiveness of Expository Prose

Just as writers make use of certain techniques to establish propositional cohesiveness, so too do they capitalize on certain conventions to establish structural cohesiveness. For example, paragraphs are typically structured with the main topic identified in the initial sentence. Kieras (1980) demonstrated that mature readers are sensitive to this convention, being more accurate at identifying main ideas when they are expressed in the initial sentence of a technical passage than when embedded within the passage. When the topic sentence appears first, the reader's task is simplified. Because the macrostructure has already been identified, the subsequent sentences can immediately be evaluated with respect to their relationship to the theme. When the topic sentence is not presented first, or when the topic must be inferred, the reader has to build up his or her own conception of the macrostructure. This interferes with comprehension because the difference is not as obvious between important information and supporting detail within the passage.

Evidence from a number of studies suggests that good readers attend to the macrostructure of a text in order to determine what should be remembered. The recall protocols of better readers tend to reveal a closer correspondence to the text macrostructure than do those of poorer readers in college (Eamon, 1978–1979), ninth grade (Meyer, Brandt, & Bluth, 1980), sixth grade (Taylor, 1980), and fifth grade (McGee, 1982). Moreover, when asked to judge the importance of ideas in passages, good readers at both the college level (Eamon, 1978–1979) and junior high level (Smiley, Oakley, Worthen, Campione, & Brown, 1977) are better than poor readers at making distinctions between those ideas most central to the theme and those that are more incidental. Similar differences in importance judgments have been observed among elementary school children of different ages (Brown & Smiley, 1977).

When conventional rhetorical structure is violated, readers recall less information from the text. This is true for adults (Kieras, 1978; Kintsch & Yarbrough, 1982) as well as for children, even those as young as 8 years of age (Danner, 1976). Variations in structural organization also influence the amount of time required to read text. Kieras (1978) and Greeno and Noreen (1974) found that subjects take longer to read individual sentences within poorly organized passages than they do to read the same sentences presented in a conventional paragraph organization. (It should be noted that disruptions in structural cohesivenes frequently create disruptions in propositional cohesiveness. Such was the case in Kieras's (1978) study, where changes in paragraph organization resulted in changes in the number of sentences that expressed totally new information. Thus, not only was it more difficult to identify the macrostructure of the passage, it was also more difficult to integrate each new sentence with the preceding one.)

Structural Cohesiveness of Stories

In addition to the conventions for writing structurally cohesive expository passages, there are also conventions for writing structurally cohesive stories. These conventions have been formalized in several different story grammars (e.g., Mandler & Johnson, 1977; Rumelhart, 1975; Stein & Glenn, 1978), which specify the categories of information in a well-formed story and the order in which these categories should appear. Numerous studies have demonstrated that deleting or reordering some of these categories impairs both children's and adults' recall of stories (e.g., Mandler, 1978; Stein & Nezworski, 1978; Thorndyke, 1977). Moreover, as Pratt, Luszcz, MacKenzie-Keating, and Manning (1982) have shown, the story schema plays an important role in adults' judgments about their comprehension of stories. For example, when major story categories were disrupted, subjects' ratings of overall comprehensibility were lower than when minor categories were disrupted.

It has been suggested that one of the first standards of evaluation a child may use concerns the structural cohesiveness of a story (Markman, 1981). Although we lack empirical evidence directly relevant to this suggestion, a number of studies have shown that elementary school children do have knowledge about the kinds of information that should appear in stories. For example, Whaley (1981) found that third graders were able to fill in missing categories and predict subsequent information as competently as sixth and eleventh graders. If this knowledge does play an important role in evaluating one's comprehension, then training children in story structure should improve their evaluation abilities.

Two studies independently addressed this possibility. Short and Ryan (1982) taught fourth-grade boys who had been identified as less-skilled readers to ask themselves five "wh" questions (who, what, why, when, where) about the setting and episode categories of a story. The training did facilitate the children's comprehension, as reflected in subsequent recall measures, but it had no effect on the children's ability to detect and correct errors in the story components. Contrary results were found by Capelli and Markman (1982), who trained third and sixth graders to use five similar "wh" questions. Subsequently, the children were given passages containing inconsistent information and were instructed to use the trained strategy as they read. Later, when probed for their awareness of the inconsistencies, subjects in both grades identified more inconsistencies than untrained children. The reason for the different outcomes in the two studies is unclear.

Evaluation of Structural Cohesiveness

Readers' ability to evaluate the structural cohesiveness of expository and narrative text has been directly examined in a few studies. For example, Williams, Taylor, and Ganger (1981) presented simple expository paragraphs to children in fourth, fifth, and sixth grade, as well as to college students, and asked them to find the sentences that did not fit with the topic. These anomalous sentences varied along several dimensions that were assumed to affect the ease of detection.

1. **Relationship to the macrostructure.** Some of the the sentences were unrelated to the macrostructure of the passage. For example, the unrelated sentence in a passage about how insects build homes was "Birds sit on their eggs to keep them warm." The related sentence in the same passage was "Insects are harmful and can be killed by special chemicals." It was expected that such sentences would be easier to detect as anomalous than those dealing with the same general topic.

2. **Referential cohesiveness.** Some of the sentences used a canonical topic/comment format, with given information in the subject portion of the sentence and new information in the predicate, while some of the sentences used a noncanonical format. The previously quoted sentence about insects is in canonical order; the noncanonical version is "Special chemicals can be used to kill harmful insects." It was expected that anomalous sentences that preserved referential continuity would be harder to identify.

3. **Presence or absence of collocational ties.** Some of the sentences expressed ideas that were semantically associated with the rest of the paragraph on the basis of prior knowledge. For example, the previously quoted sentence about birds is collocationally tied to the passage about insects because birds and insects are associated, but a sentence about school being out for the summer would have no such ties with a passage about insects. It was expected that anomalous sentences would be harder to detect when collocational relationships were present.

4. **Serial position within the paragraph.** Because readers must gradually build up a conception of the text macrostructure, it was expected that detection would be better when the anomaly appeared later rather than earlier.

5. **Presence or absence of an explicit topic sentence.** It was expected that an explicit topic sentence would facilitate detection because it provides a cue to the macrostructure.

Williams et al. found that all four variations of the anomalous sentences themselves (within a given context) affected ease of detection in the expected directions. Adults had higher detection rates than the children, as one would expect, but there were no differences among the children of different ages. The one factor that did not show the expected effect was presence or absence of a topic sentence; only the adults benefitted from its presence. However, a subsequent experiment by the authors revealed that when the salience of the topic sentence was increased, children did use it effectively, leading to better detection of anomalous sentences when it was present rather than absent. In sum, the data indicate that children can evaluate the structural cohesiveness of expository text when explicitly instructed to do so. However, it is clear that many different factors affect the success with which they do so.

It was somewhat surprising that Williams et al. did not find differences in the evaluation skills of the fourth and sixth graders. However, there is evidence that among children in this age range, there are differences in their ability to detect structurally anomalous sentences. This evidence was provided in a study by Harris, Kruithof, Terwogt and Visser (1981). Harris et al. constructed narrative passages that could be interpreted in either of two ways and the appropriate interpretation was signalled by the title. One sentence in each passage was thematically anomalous. For example, in a story entitled "At the Hairdressers," all of the sentences were consistent with the hairdresser theme except for the sentence, "Luckily there are no cavities this time." The same passage also appeared under the title "At the dentists." Again, all of the sentences except one were consistent with the dentist theme. The anomalous sentence, "He sees his hair getting shorter," is, of course, consistent with the hairdresser theme. The passages were presented to 8- and 11-year-old children sentence by sentence, and reading times were recorded. After reading each passage, the children were asked to identify the line that did not fit with the rest of the story and were permitted to inspect the story in order to do so. Harris et al. found that the 11-year-olds were more likely to identify the anomalous lines than the 8-year-olds. However, both age groups were equally likely to read the anomalous lines more slowly than the appropriate lines.

This latter finding indicates that the 8-year-olds were sensitive to the anomalies during reading. Why, then, did they not report them as frequently as the older children? This discrepancy between verbal and nonverbal indices of comprehension monitoring has been observed in several studies (e.g., Flavell et al., 1981; Patterson, Cosgrove, & O'Brien, 1980) and seems more common among younger children than older. Harris et al. deal with the discrepancy by making a distinction between *constructive* processing, as reflected in modulations of reading rate, and the monitoring of that processing, as indicated by detection of anomalies. In other words, they do not regard reading-time modulations as on-line evidence of comprehension monitoring, in contrast to the approach taken in this chapter. According to Harris et al., children of both ages seem to generate an internal signal that an obstacle to comprehension has been encountered; however, older children seem to have more capacity to notice or interpret the signals.

The two studies just discussed have been interpreted as evidence that readers attend to the macrostructure of a passage as they read, identifying the theme and evaluating the extent to which each new sentence can be integrated with this theme. However, the data could also be interpreted as evidence that readers process text by activating a particular schema (see the following section, regarding external consistency) and matching the text information with appropriate slots in the schema. So, for example, in the Harris et al. study, children may have activated their knowledge about dentists when they encountered the title, and then they recognized in the sentence about hair getting shorter a violation in their mental script for what typically happens at a dentist's office.

This schema-activation interpretation was adopted by Winograd and Johnston (1982), who examined whether children would be more likely to notice anomalous sentences when they were given an orienting task designed to activate the appropriate schema. Good and poor sixth-grade readers read two narrative passages containing thematically anomalous sentences and were later probed for their awareness of the sentence that did not fit. The orienting task consisted of showing subjects a picture depicting the outside of a place of entertainment (e.g., two children outside a circus tent) and asking them to imagine what might be seen inside. The children then read the passage dealing with that theme (e.g., a circus). Contrary to expectations, the children were no more likely to notice the anomalies with schema activation than without, although the good readers were somewhat better overall than the poorer readers. Winograd and Johnston attribute their null finding to problems with the error-detection paradigm.

Though such problems may have been a factor, it does seem that provision of an appropriate context within which to evaluate a passage should facilitate detection of discrepancies. Perhaps the schema-activation task itself was ineffective; the authors do not present data relevant to this possibility. We know that schema activation does have a strong influence on comprehension and memory. This has been shown most dramatically when ambiguous passages are presented with or without disambiguating titles (e.g., Bransford & Johnson, 1972; Schwarz & Flammer, 1981). Moreover, when the title is inappropriate, recall is even worse than when no relevant context is supplied (Townsend, 1980). These effects hold for children as well as adults. Harris, Mandias, Terwogt, and Tjintjelaar (1980) reported that 8- and 10-year old children remember more information and judge passages to be more comprehensible when a relevant setting context is provided than when it is not. Thus, even 8-year-olds "realize there is a suprasentential level of comprehension and notice its absence or disruption" (Harris et al., 1980; p. 170).

Thus far, the research pertaining to the use of a structural cohesiveness standard has involved children as subjects. Williams et al. (1981) included adults in their study, but because the materials were appropriate for upper elementary children, the data provided little insight as to whether adults routinely evaluate structural cohesiveness. One study has provided evidence that adults are sensitive to thematically anomalous information during text processing and that they can very rapidly identify such discrepancies. The study was carried out by Green, Mitchell, and Hammond (1981). College students were presented with a passage a few words at a time. They read the segments at their own pace and initiated presentation of the subsequent segments. In one version of the passage, an anomaly was embedded within a single segment. The critical sentence, with slashes delineating the segments, was "The general immediately ordered/his staff to prepare/a lavish formal ball/and Andrei was asked to lead/the first dance/with the commander's daughter." In the anomalous version, "a full council of war meeting" replaced the segment "a lavish formal ball." Note that the incongruity is not apparent until the reader encounters the segment "the first dance." Reading times were greater on this segment for subjects who received the anomalous version than for those who read the standard version. In addition, eight subjects were given explicit instructions to press a special button as soon as they identified "something odd in context and fairly gross." Seven of the eight subjects pressed the button on first encountering the dance segment, and the eighth pressed the button in the next segment, reportedly having tried and failed to resolve the incongruity. The fact that subjects noticed the discrepancies during initial processing demonstrates effective use of a structural-cohesiveness standard of evaluation.

To summarize, this section has examined several different dimensions of structural cohesiveness and their effects on comprehension. When text lacks structural cohesiveness, comprehension is impaired because it is difficult for the reader to identify a thematic framework within which to integrate the material. It is difficult to make distinctions as to what is most important and what is less so. It is difficult to activate relevant prior knowledge because it is not apparent what is relevant and what is not. A specific type of structural cohesiveness is important for adequate story comprehension; the story should conform to the rules of a story grammar by including certain kinds of information in a specific sequence. Efforts are underway to teach children these rules, which essentially serve as one type of standard for evaluating comprehension. Finally, studies have examined readers' evaluation of structural cohesiveness in expository and narrative text. Williams et al. identified several factors that affect the success with which this standard can be applied by both child and adult readers. Harris, Kruithof, Terwogt, and Visser (1981) and Winograd and Johnston (1982) demonstrated that older and better readers are more sensitive to structurally anomalous sentences than are younger and poorer readers, whereas Green et al. (1981) showed effective use of the standard among adults.

External Consistency

There is no doubt that comprehension involves a continual interaction between the reader's prior knowledge and the printed page. Both children and adults routinely activate prior knowledge about a topic and incorporate it into their memory representation of a passage (e.g., Brown, Smiley, Day, Townsend & Lawton, 1977; Ceci, Caves & Howe, 1981; Koblinsky and Cruse, 1981; Landis, 1982; Spiro, 1980; Sulin & Dooling, 1974). Accordingly, it has been necessary to introduce the role of prior knowledge and expectation into the discussion of other standards of evaluation. This section, however, focuses on the use of prior knowledge as a standard in its own right, called upon to evaluate information in the text for consistency with what is known. We first consider evidence that external consistency (or the lack thereof) affects comprehension. We then consider the extent to which children evaluate their comprehension with respect to external consistency, followed by a consideration of some adult data.

External Consistency and Comprehension

Information that is inconsistent or incongruent with past experience is more difficult to recall, as Owings, Peterson, Bransford, Morris, and Stein (1980) found for both better and poorer fifth-grade students. Despite these effects on recall, however, only the better students identified less-congruent passages as difficult to learn and adjusted their study times accordingly. This suggests that the poorer readers did not use an external consistency standard as they were reading. Nevertheless, these poorer students were quite capable of deciding whether the passages made sense when specifically asked to evaluate them with respect to their own experiences. Under these circumstances they recognized, for example, that it is much less sensible for a hungry boy to go to bed than to eat a hamburger. Recently, an extensive series of studies by Bransford and his colleagues has shown that poorer students can be trained to draw on prior knowledge to render arbitrary information more meaningful and memorable (see Bransford, Stein, Vye, Franks, Auble, Mezynski, & Perfetto, 1982).

Additional evidence of the effects of external consistency on comprehension was provided in Ceci, Caves, and Howe's (1981) study of children's long-term memory for information that was inconsistent with their prior knowledge. Seven- and 10-year-olds listened to passages containing descriptions of television characters that were inconsistent with their televised attributes. For example, the Six-Million-Dollar Man was described as too weak to carry a can of paint. When tested 3 weeks later, the children's memory for the characters had shifted in the direction of their prior knowledge. In other words, they were more likely to say that they remembered the Six-Million-Dollar Man as strong rather than weak. However, the older children showed less distortion in their long-term recall than the younger children, leading Ceci et al. to suggest, "It is as if the 10 year olds during the course of listening to the story *made a mental note to themselves* that certain characters were completely opposite to their expectations" (p. 449, italics mine).

Children's Use of the External Consistency Standard

Several direct examinations of children's use of external consistency standards have been undertaken. These studies have involved listening and reading tasks, with expository and narrative texts. Those studies involving multiple standards (Baker, in press, 1984a, 1984b; Markman & Gorin, 1981) are only briefly mentioned here (see the section addressing this topic for details). Pace (1979) constructed short stories containing script-inconsistent information, such as a mother making sandwiches with peanut butter and ice cream rather than jelly. Children in kindergarten were asked to identify the inconsistencies after listening to the passages and children in second, fourth, and sixth grade were asked to do the same after either reading or listening. Only 25% of the kindergartners reported the mistakes. Interestingly, second graders performed at this same low level when listening, but on the reading task the detection rate rose to 66%. The older children had considerably better detection of the inconsistencies for both reading and listening. Further research would be helpful to elucidate the reasons for the reading–listening discrepancy among the second graders. In a subsequent study with kindergartners, Pace (1980) found that by explicitly instructing the children to listen for incongruities and by increasing the blatency of the violations (e.g., peanut butter and shoe polish sandwiches), the children's detection rate was much better. However, it is not possible to tell whether the improvement was due to the instructional set, the saliency, or both.

Baker (1984a) has also found that 5-year-olds were capable of identifying more than 60% of the prior-knowledge violations embedded in simple narratives when they were set to find the mistakes. Moreover, the detection rate for 7-year-olds rose to 83% and for 9-year-olds, 97%. In contrast to these high levels of problem detection found among older elementary school children, Markman and Gorin (1981) found that 8- and 10-year-olds reported an average of 34% and 47%, respectively. Children reported more falsehoods when they were specifically instructed to listen for them (39% and 61%, respectively), but these levels were still well below those of Baker's subjects. One reason for the difference may be that Baker's subjects were given immediate feedback and a second opportunity to identify any problems missed in the first attempt, a manipulation that led to large gains.

One factor that may mediate the likelihood of noticing an inconsistency with prior knowledge is based on an intriguing finding by Erickson and Mattson (1981). When college students were asked to answer the question, "How many animals of each kind did Moses take on the ark?" most answered "two," even though they knew that Noah sailed the ark and were warned that some questions might contain incorrect names. Follow-up experiments revealed that the "Moses illusion" only occurs when the substituted name shares semantic features with the correct name. For example, subjects never made a mistake when "Nixon" replaced "Moses" in the question. The authors conclude, "The fewer semantic features of a word that fit into the description, the likelier it is that the inconsistency will be noticed" (p. 550).

This explanation can be applied to Pace's finding that kindergarteners were more likely to notice a "peanut butter and shoe polish" violation than a "peanut butter and ice cream" violation. Ice cream shares many more semantic features with jelly than does shoe polish. It may also be a factor in the differences in problem detection reported by Baker (1984a) and by Markman and Gorin (1981). One of the violations in the former study was, "Every morning Jack chopped wood with a baseball bat." One of the violations in the latter study was "They [koala bears] sleep on the tree tops where cool soft grass grows." *Grass* and *leaves* (the correct word) share more semantic features than *baseball bats* and *axes*. Given the powerful effects of semantic relatedness in lexical decision tasks, even when the target itself is anomalous in context (Kleiman, 1980), it should not be surprising to find a similar relatedness effect in other aspects of text processing. Recall also the Williams et al. (1981) finding that readers are better able to identify contextually anomalous sentences when there are no collocational ties with the theme of the passage, in other words, when there are no semantic features in common.

Not only do children differ with age in their evaluation of external consistency, as indicated in the studies of Baker (1984a), Markman and Gorin (1981), and Pace (1979), they also differ with reading ability. Baker (1984b) found that better fourth- and sixth-grade readers identified 48% of the prior-knowledge violations embedded in short expository passages, whereas poorer readers identified only 28%. Note that even the detection rates for the better readers are considerably lower than those reported by Baker (1984a). In part, this results from collapsing over age, which had a significant effect, and in part from collapsing over instruction type. When the children were specifically instructed to evaluate the text for information that conflicted with what they knew to be true, problem detection was better than when simply instructed to look for nonspecified problems (49% vs. 27%). Nevertheless, children still failed to identify a substantial proportion of prior-knowledge violations, failures for which lack of relevant prior knowledge was ruled out in subsequent questioning. Several possible reasons remain for the discrepancy with Baker (1984a). One reason may simply be that feedback and second opportunities were not provided in the second study. Another possible reason is that one task involved listening and the other reading. However, Baker's (1984a) replication experiment involving 11-year-old children in a reading situation revealed a pattern of performance that was virtually the same as that of the 9-year-old children who participated in the listening task. A third, potentially more important, reason may be that one task used expository text while the other narrative. Perhaps children are less likely to evaluate textbook-like material with respect to external consistency: they assume that the author is always correct and so never question the facts.

Adults' Use of the External Consistency Standard

There is little evidence regarding the extent to which adults evaluate their understanding with respect to what they already know. The Erickson and Mattson (1981) study cited earlier provides some indirect evidence that adults do not always test for propositional truthfulness. A more direct indication the adults do not consistently evaluate text for congruence with prior knowledge was provided in Baker's (in press) study of multiple-standard use. One of the problems embedded within expository passages were violations of prior knowledge. Students who were specifically alerted to look for these problems identified more than those who were not (32% vs. 12%), and those with higher verbal ability identified more than those with lower ability when given these specific instructions (39% vs. 25%). Subsequent questioning revealed that the students generally did have the relevant prior knowledge needed to identify the problems. Unexpectedly, several of the students, most of whom were in the lower verbal ability group, did not have the relevant prior knowledge to reject the fact that Ronald Reagan had been governor of Montana. (The materials had been pretested with a group of older students who did have the relevant prior knowledge.) Nevertheless, even if we correct for lack of prior knowledge, the detection rates were quite low.

One additional study bears on adults' evaluation of external consistency. This study provided both verbal and nonverbal measures of problem identification and was carried out by Soviet psychologists, Tikhomirov and Klochko (1981). A narrative passage was constructed that contained three separate propositions that violated basic laws of physics (e.g., rivers flowing *up* mountains). The passage was presented to three groups of subjects: high school students, undergraduate physics majors, and faculty and graduate students in the physics department. The subjects were first asked to check the passage's grammaticality and after doing so, they were asked to recall the passage. They were then asked to read the passage aloud in preparation for a second retelling. After recall, they were asked whether they had noticed any problems. If they had not, they were given the specific task of searching for the violations, using a think-aloud procedure. Throughout the session, the subjects' galvanic skin responses (GSRs) were recorded. The results revealed that only 1 of the 45 subjects noticed the prior-knowledge violation while checking for grammaticality. The outcome is not too surprising given that the subjects were set to carry out relatively superficial processing of the text. More surprising, especially because many of these subjects qualified as subject matter experts, was that only 2 people reported the problems after the second task, which presumably required deeper processing. However, with specific directions to find the problems, the detection rate rose to 84%. The GSR data provide important information to supplement these verbal reports. They suggest that some of the subjects who did not report the problems initially may have noticed them subconsciously. The GSR recordings of these subjects fluctuated sharply when they read the contradictory information. Moreover, all of the skin-responsive subjects went on to report the problems when directed to seek them. In contrast, none of the subjects whose GSR recordings were stable reported the problems subsequently. The implications of this intriguing finding are discussed in the conclusions section, within the context of verbal–nonverbal discrepancies in evaluation activities.

In conclusion, the external consistency standard is one that has high ecological validity in the sense that it is a central component of critical reading. Readers must evaluate what they read for its truth, validity, and plausibility in order not to be swayed by propaganda (Baker, 1979a). Nevertheless, we have seen that many children do not spontaneously evaluate for external consistency (Baker, 1984b; Markman & Gorin, 1981), although when they are specifically instructed to do so in a simple situation, they seem quite capable (Baker, 1984a; Pace, 1980). The implication here is that children would benefit from more explicit instruction and practice in evaluating for external consistency in order to make it a routine component of their text processing. Our knowledge about adults' use of an external consistency standard is limited. Both Baker's (in press) and Tikhomirov and Klochko's (1981) data suggest that adults rarely spontaneously adopt a standard of external consistency. This disconcerting finding may be symptomatic of a general lack of critical reading.

Internal Consistency

In the preceding section we examined the extent to which readers consider whether the ideas expressed within the text are consistent with what they already know. In this section, we examine the extent to which readers consider whether the ideas expressed within the text are consistent with one another. One prerequisite to testing for internal consistency is the integration of textual propositions. Accordingly, the section begins with a discussion of information integration and factors limiting its occurrence. We then consider evidence directly relevant to the use of an internal consistency standard, first among children and then among adults. Because a substantial proportion of the comprehension monitoring studies have used internal inconsistencies as their embedded errors, we already know quite a bit about circumstances influencing the effectiveness and/ or likelihood of the use of this standard. These circumstances are also considered.

Integration as a Prerequisite to Evaluation

An essential prerequisite to evaluating text for internal consistency is the integration of separate propositions in the text. This integration occurs when readers establish referential cohesiveness, and it also occurs when non-coreferential text propositions are combined. These combined propositions yield new, implicit information that may be as crucial to understanding a passage as the explicitly stated content. Numerous studies have shown that this semantic integration occurs in both children and adults (e.g., Blachowicz, 1977–1978; Bransford, Barclay, & Franks, 1972; Danner & Mathews, 1980; Johnson & Smith, 1981; Liben & Posnansky, 1977; Paris & Carter, 1973; Small & Butterworth, 1981; Walker & Meyer, 1980). There is some question as to whether the related propositions are integrated during initial processing or at the time of test. However, studies using verification latencies suggest that the information is integrated during reading, for both second and sixth graders (Danner & Mathews, 1980) and for adults (Walker & Meyer, 1980). Such a finding is of course crucial to the hypothesis that readers evaluate text for internal consistency during reading. If they did not compare and combine propositions as they were reading, they could hardly be expected to notice inconsistencies among the propositions.

There do seem to be limitations on the circumstances under which propositions are spontaneously integrated. Walker and Meyer (1980) presented college students with the to-be-integrated propositions presented either in adjacent sentences or separated in different paragraphs with 10 or so intervening sentences. Subjects were faster at verifying inferences based on premises that were contiguous than those that were not, suggesting that propositions close together in the text were integrated during reading while those further away were not. The effects of premise separation were also examined in a developmental study by Johnson and Smith (1981). Children in third and fifth grades read a story requiring integration of premises appearing at different distances from each other. The children were later tested both for their memory of the premise information and for their ability to answer inferential questions. Although the fifth graders' inferential responses were not affected by premise separation, the third graders only integrated the premises when they were contained within the same paragraph. This pattern held even given memory for the premise information.

Taken together, the results of these studies suggest that information integration is more likely to occur spontaneously when the premises are both active simultaneously in working memory. Younger readers do not seem to retrieve from long-term memory the information that is necessary for integration. While older readers are capable of doing so, they probably only do so after reading, if specifically questioned. This suggests that readers may not test widely separated propositions for internal consistency as they read. Empirical tests of this suggestion are discussed subsequently.

Evaluating Text for Internal Consistency

We turn now to consideration of the studies directly concerned with evaluating text for internal consistency. Our discussion of these studies is brief because most have been reviewed extensively elsewhere (e.g., Baker & Brown, 1984a; Baker & Brown, 1984b; Wagoner, 1983). Again, the multiple standard studies are discussed more thoroughly in that section. The seminal investigation was carried out by Markman (1979). Children in third, fifth, and sixth grades listened to short essays containing inconsistent information, and then they were probed for their awareness of the inconsistencies. Some of the inconsistencies could only be noticed if the child made an inference, while others were quite explicit. Children in all grades tested were equally poor at reporting the inconsistencies, though they were somewhat more successful with the explicit problems. Garner (1980, 1981) has shown that junior high students, particularly those identified as poor readers, are also poor at evaluating text for internal consistency. The students were asked to rate brief passages for ease of understanding and to justify whatever low ratings they gave. Poor readers were less likely to rate inconsistent text as difficult to understand, though good readers were by no means proficient at this task either. Even college students frequently fail to report inconsistencies, as noted by Baker (1979b) and by Baker and Anderson (1982).

These often-reported detection failures need to be interpreted with caution, however, as Baker (1979b) and Winograd and Johnston (1982) have argued. Many failures to report inconsistencies may not be caused by the failure to monitor comprehension but rather by the use of strategies for resolving comprehension problems. Retrospective reports and recall protocols collected by Baker (1979b) revealed that students frequently made inferences to supplement the information explicitly presented in the text, having decided that some relevant information had been omitted.

Moreover, some students occasionally failed to detect inconsistencies because they had assigned alternative interpretations to the text, feeling that they had understood when in fact they did not get the intended meaning.

Another explanation for failures to notice inconsistencies is that the subjects used a different standard for evaluating their understanding. Rather than focusing on the consistency of the facts *within* the text, they focused on an isolated fact and asked "Is it true?" (Osherson & Markman, 1975). In other words, they evaluated the information for external consistency rather than internal consistency. Baker (1984a), Markman (1979), and Markman and Gorin (1981) found that this occurred frequently, especially among younger children, and Baker (1979b) and Baker and Anderson (1982) observed that many college students who failed to report inconsistencies did report perceived violations with their prior knowledge.

Nevertheless, even when the experiments are designed to take into account these alternative interpretations, the data still suggest that readers are not very effective at evaluating expository text for internal consistency. In Baker's (1984b) multiple standard study, sixth graders identified more inconsistencies than fourth graders (46% vs. 27%) and better readers identified more than poorer readers (51% vs. 22%). But note that about half of the inconsistencies went unreported. Even less effective evaluation of internal consistency was observed among college students reading fairly lengthy expository passages (Baker, in press); higher verbal ability students identified only 20% of the problems, lower ability students 4%.

As yet little evidence regarding the use of an internal consistency standard has been obtained during the reading process. To my knowledge, no studies have collected processing measures from children. Baker and Anderson (1982) did so with adults as subjects. They presented college students with expository passages containing inconsistent information. Subjects read through the passages sentence by sentence at their own pace and were encouraged to reread previous sentences whenever they wished. A computer automatically recorded reading times on each exposure to a sentence and the pattern of movement through the text. As expected, subjects spent more time on sentences containing information that conflicted with information presented elsewhere, and they looked back more often at inconsistent sentences. These modifications in processing indicate that the subjects monitored their comprehension as they were reading, evaluating whether the ideas expressed in the text were consistent with one another. Several postreading measures provided additional support for this conclusion. Surprisingly, the expected relationships between changes in on-line processing and inconsistency detection were weak. Subjects who spent more time on the inconsistent target sentences during reading were no more likely to identify the inconsistency later than those who did not. However, we did uncover the following complex relationship: Subjects who spent more time on an inconsistent sentence and later pointed out the inconsistency in the passage when asked to do so were more likely to report they had noticed the problem as they were reading. In other words, increased exposure time reflects awareness of an inconsistency, as originally hypothesized, but the converse is not true; the absence of longer exposure times does not indicate that subjects failed to notice the problems.

Factors Influencing the Use of an Internal Consistency Standard

Several factors apparently affect the ease of application of an internal consistency standard. One of these is the degree of separation of the inconsistent information, as suggested earlier. Markman (1979) presented third and sixth graders with passages containing inconsistent information either in contiguous or noncontiguous sentences. The older children were more likely to notice inconsistencies in the adjacent than in the nonadjacent sentences, though there were no differences for the younger children. Garner and Kraus (1981–1982) also examined whether the contiguity of inconsistent information would affect the likelihood of detection. Inconsistent facts were either placed four sentences apart or contained within a single (long) sentence. Good readers in junior high were more likely to report the inconsistencies when they were contained within a single sentence, but poor readers were not. These studies suggest that one common shortcoming in children's comprehension monitoring is a failure to consider the relationships across noncontiguous sentences in a text. Though they may be capable of evaluating consistency of single sentences, they still need to develop the skills to integrate and evaluate information across larger segments of text.

A second obvious factor affecting the use of an internal consistency standard is the nature of the instructions given to the subjects. Markman (1979) found that when children were specifically warned in advance that a problem might be present in the text, both third and sixth graders were more likely to report the inconsistency. In addition, the sixth graders were as likely to report the implicit problems as the explicit when they were given this warning. Markman and Gorin (1981) extended this finding by giving some subjects explicit instructions to listen for inconsistencies and some a general warning that a problem might be present. Both 8- and 10-year-olds benefitted from the specific instructions, with the older children showing greater benefit. Baker (1984b) also showed a strong effect of instructions on the success with which fourth- and sixth-graders could identify inconsistencies in expository prose (52% for specific instructions and 21% for general). The effect also obtained for college students as well (Baker, in press): 21% versus 4%, respectively.

A different type of intervention was tried by Garner and Taylor (1982). Fourth, sixth and eighth graders read a brief passage with an inconsistency and then were provided with increasingly more specific hints as to the source of difficulty. Even after the experimenter underlined the two sentences that conflicted with one another and told the child they did not make sense, fourth-graders and older poor readers were rarely able to report the exact nature of the problem. However, the intervention did increase the likelihood that better readers would notice the inconsistency.

There is additional evidence that when task demands are simple and explicit, children show much greater awareness of inconsistencies than previously reported. Baker (1984a) had 5-, 7-, and 9-year-old children evaluate short narrative passages for "mistakes," one type of which was an inconsistency. If the children did not report the mistake after the first presentation of the passage, they were re-presented with it and asked to try again. Under these circumstances, the 9-year-olds identified 95% of the inconsistencies, the 7-year-olds reported 74%, and the 5-year-olds identified 45%. Studies by Ackerman (1981, 1982) and by Stein and Trabasso (1982) have shown that 6-year-olds are quite sensitive to inconsistencies between events in simple stories. In addition, Wimmer (1979) found that inducing children to evaluate the consistency of events in a story had a significant effect on detection. When so induced, 92% of the 6-year-olds and 50% of the 4-year-olds noticed the inconsistent act, as compared to 50% and 0%, respectively, who were not induced. It is clear that even very young children are capable of evaluating the internal consistency of a passage. The tremendous differences in detection rates that have been reported in the literature illustrate the importance of careful specification of the text and task characteristics that can affect performance.

To summarize, evaluation for internal consistency requires that the reader or listener integrate and compare text propositions that are frequently nonadjacent. Several studies have shown that students of all ages and ability levels are surprisingly unlikely to carry out those processing activities spontaneously. The initial interpretation of these data was that the students did not monitor their comprehension. This interpretation has been revised in light of subsequent evidence that students do, in fact, evaluate their understanding, but they often use standards other than the internal consistency standard. Additionally, it has become clear that children do have the competence to evaluate for internal consistency. When the task demands are very explicit and the to-be-evaluated materials are simple narratives, even 5-year-olds can apply the internal consistency standard adequately, though not yet proficiently.

Informational Clarity and Completeness

The fifth semantic standard involves evaluating whether the text contains information that is sufficiently clear and complete. This standard is perhaps most crucial in the context of reading directions in order to act, as opposed to reading to learn. Directions of all sorts, for example, ought to be evaluated for completeness prior to their execution. Of course, a reader may realize the instructions are inadequate upon failing to reach the desired goal, but time and money can often be saved by evaluating them first. Evaluating text for clarity and completeness is a standard with high ecological validity because instructions are notorious for their omissions, misprints, and ambiguities. An incident reported in the Baltimore Sunpapers illustrates this point. The newspaper published the recipes for a luncheon that had been served to President Reagan during a visit to Baltimore. One of the recipes was for a mustard sauce. Several readers attempted to make the sauce, failing to realize that the primary ingredient, mustard, was not mentioned anywhere but in the title. So they ended up with a rather peculiar-tasting mustard sauce. In this section, we first considerer evidence for ineffective evaluation of informational completeness, followed by evidence of a more positive nature.

Evidence Suggesting Ineffective Use of the Standard

There is a large body of literature examining children's ability to evaluate messages for clarity and completeness. Most of this research has involved listening tasks within a referential communication paradigm, but the findings are certainly relevant in the present context. Somewhat surprisingly, there appear to be few studies examining the use of this standard among adults. Riesbeck (1980), however, has presented a case study of adults' judgments of the clarity of directions for getting to a particular location. He noted that the directions, which contained ambiguities and required inferences, seldom appeared problematic to the adults when simply asked to read them over. It was not until they were asked to draw a pictorial layout of a crucial intersection that they realized there was a problem. Riesbeck concludes that directions typically are not fully worked out until execution time.

In light of Riesbeck's findings, it should hardly be surprising that children often fail to evaluate messages for completeness and clarity. Patterson and Kister (1981) review numerous studies showing that young elementary school children frequently indicate that they have understood a message even when it was ambiguous or incomplete and that they often fail to question the speaker or seek additional information when their understanding is poor.

In an empirical analog of Riesbeck's task, Markman (1977) had children in first and third grades judge the adequacy of instructions for playing a card game or performing a magic trick. In both sets of instructions, crucial information had been omitted. Although the third graders were usually aware of the omission, it was often not until the first graders actually tried to carry out the instructions that they realized there was a problem. In other words, they did not evaluate the text for completeness as they were listening.

An alternative paradigm for examining the use of a completeness standard is to ask children to judge when they have been given sufficient information to be able to carry out a task. For example, Kotsonis and Patterson (1980) presented rules for a game one at a time until their subjects indicated that they knew how to play. Differences between normal-achieving and learning-disabled 8- and 10-year-olds were found in that the learning-disabled children evaluated informational completeness less effectively.

Evidence Suggesting Effective Use of the Standard

Thus far, the portrayal of young children's ability to evaluate for clarity and completeness has been rather negative. Several studies have shown, however, that under certain conditions, their skills are actually quite good. For example, Patterson, O'Brien, Kister, Carter, and Kotsonis (1981) varied the stimulus complexity and degree of message ambiguity in a referential communication task and found strikingly better evaluation of message clarity by first graders when the stimuli were of low complexity and the messages were very clearly ambiguous. Similarly, Pratt and Bates (1982) found that 5-year-olds were more likely to detect ambiguities in messages when they were provided with pictures depicting the situation described in the message. These results were taken as support of Shatz's (1978) claim that as long as processing demands are sufficiently light, message monitoring and evaluation activities can be found at any point in development.

A second line of evidence that young children are sensitive to message inadequacies comes from studies that have used nonverbal measures of problem detection. Children as young as 4 years take more time to respond to inadequate than to adequate messages (Bearison & Levey, 1977; Ironsmith & Whitehurst, 1978; Patterson et al. 1980). They also exhibit signs of puzzlement in their body and eye movements, as well as in facial expressions (Beal & Flavell, 1982; Flavell et al., 1981; Patterson et al., 1981).

The nonverbal indicants are not always accompanied by verbal indicants, however, and this is particularly true for younger children. The study by Flavell et al. illustrates this discrepancy well. Kindergarten and second-grade children were instructed to construct block buildings identical to those described on tape by a child. Some of the instructions contained ambiguities, unfamiliar words, insufficient information, or unattainable goals. Children were encouraged to replay the tape as often as necessary in order to construct the buildings. The children were videotaped as they attempted to carry out the instructions, and the videotapes were analyzed for nonverbal signs of problem detection (e.g., looking puzzled or replaying the tape). The children later were asked if they had succeeded in making a building exactly like the instructor's and whether they thought the instructor did a good job in conveying the instructions.

As expected, the older children were more likely to notice the inadequacies in the messages than the younger. Even though both kindergartners and second graders showed nonverbal signs of puzzlement during the task, the kindergartners were less likely to report later that some of the messages were inadequate. A subsequent study by Beal and Flavell (1982) ruled out the possibility that the kindergartners' failure to identify the instructions as inadequate occurred because they forgot their initial uncertainty. The authors conclude that young children do not know how to interpret their feelings of puzzlement, even when they are made aware of the ambiguities. This conclusion is similar to that of Harris et al. (1981): younger children generate the same signals of comprehension failure as older children, but they do not know their significance.

In conclusion, the informational completeness standard is most crucial in the evaluation of one's understanding of instructions that require some sort of overt response. At any rate, it is under these conditions that it has most frequently been examined. There are, however, situations where it is important to evaluate expository text for completeness—for example, when a concept is introduced without explanation. A lexical standard is insufficient here; a reader may know perfectly well what certain words mean, but does not grasp their significance in that context. To my knowledge, this dimension of informational completeness has not been directly examined, although Baker (in press) found that many adults spontaneously adopted this standard. The existing research has made it quite clear that there are developmental differences in the effectiveness with which children apply the standard. But perhaps more importantly, it is clear that preschool children have the ability to use the standard; adequate performance depends on the appropriate selection of the task.

Multiple Standards of Evaluation

As noted in the introduction, the organization adopted for this chapter was not meant to suggest that readers use only a single standard of evaluation during any one encounter with a text. To the contrary: because comprehension is multidimensional, evaluation of that comprehension must also be multidimensional. Most investigators of comprehension monitoring, however, have either ignored or chosen to overlook this important point. They operationalize comprehension monitoring as success at identifying a particular type of problem. Failure to find the problem is interpreted as failure to monitor comprehension, rather than as failure to use a particular standard of evaluation. It is important to recognize that readers who do not seem to be using one particular criterion for evaluating their understanding may well be using others. In this section, we focus on this possibility, first by examining evidence for the spontaneous adoption of two or more standards and, then by considering data on the instructed use of multiple standards in comparison to spontaneous use.

Spontaneous Adoption of Multiple Standards

Some of the studies introduced in previous sections are reconsidered here. These studies have manipulated their materials in such a way that subjects must use more than one standard in order to notice all of the problems. In none of these studies were subjects informed prior to reading that problems would be present; thus, the focus is on spontaneous adoption of standards.

Lexical and syntactic standards of evaluation were required in a study by Paris and Myers (1981). These investigators examined fourth-grade good and poor readers' skill at evaluating their understanding of passages that contained two nonsense words and two rearranged clauses each. Examples of each type, respectively, are "He saw a black wolf and a red fox in their kales." and "He must be very brave to train lions and wants do to what he tigers." Two different measures of comprehension monitoring were obtained: (1) oral reading hesitations and self-corrections, and (2) underlined words or sentences that the child did not understand. On the oral reading measure, both groups of readers showed significantly more hesitations on the scrambled phrases than on the nonsense words. Although this suggests that the subjects were more successful at using a syntactic standard than a lexical standard, it is important to bear in mind that the nonsense words were in fact short and pronounceable. It is not necessary to know the meaning of a word, or even recognize a string of letters as a word, in order to read it aloud.

A better indication of the standards the children used is provided by the directed underlining task. Good readers were more likely to underline both types of anomalous information than poor readers; scrambled phrases were more frequently underlined than nonsense words; and good readers differed more from the poor readers on the scrambled phrases than on the nonsense words. The fact that only 25% of the nonsense words were underlined by good readers and 18.8% by the poor readers seems inconsistent with the idea that lexical standards should be easy to apply. Surely these fourth-grade children knew they did not know the meaning of words like *kales, leets,* and *klids.* However, when given the instructions to underline things they did not understand, they probably assumed they *should* know what these apparently simple words meant and so were reluctant to admit their ignorance. Despite these problems in interpretation, the relative ordering of the two standards makes sense. Comprehension should be more disrupted by a multiword segment of text that is both syntactically and semantically anomalous than by a single unfamiliar word whose meaning can be inferred from context.

Other studies have shown that lexical standards can in fact be used very effectively, especially in comparison to some of the semantic standards of evaluation. It is reasonable to expect this outcome, given that lexical evaluation requires only the consideration of an individual word, without regard to context, whereas semantic standards require the integration of longer segments of text or the integration of text and prior knowledge.

The Flavell et al. (1981) study, discussed earlier, provides an illustration. One of the instructions for constructing a block building contained an unfamiliar vocabulary word: *hypotenuse.* Because it was impossible to carry out the instructions without understanding this word, virtually all of the kindergartners and second graders in the study noticed this problem. In contrast, when contextual information in the instruction was inconsistent with the action to be performed, children seldom noticed the problem. For example, very few of the children were bothered by these instructions: "Both blocks in this building are the same shape. Put the round block on top of the blue square." They simply carried out the directed action, without evaluating the consistency of the two sentences.

The lexical standard took precedence over the internal consistency standard among a different population of subjects as well. Garner (1981) had poor readers in the fifth and sixth grade read short passages containing either two difficult words each (e.g., multifarious, expeditiously) or contradictory facts (e.g., in one sentence a departure time of 7:00 was mentioned; in a subsequent sentence the time was given as 5:00). Each child read one passage containing difficult vocabulary, one containing a contradiction, and a third that was intact. Subjects were asked to rate each passage on a 3-point scale as to ease of understanding and then to explain their ratings. The children rated the passages with the unfamiliar words as hardest to understand, and the contradictory passages were given ratings similar to the intact passages. All of the children explained that the low ratings were given because of the words they did not know; none of them mentioned the contradictions.

The study provides very clear evidence that the children used word understanding as the standard against which to evaluate their understanding. It could be argued, in fact, that the children overrelied on this standard, because in all cases the difficult words were modifying adjectives whose meaning was not central to the passage. This finding raises two additional questions: (1) Would good readers at this grade level give similar ratings or would they be more sensitive to the fact that the words were not crucial to comprehension? (2) What characteristics of the vocabulary words mediated this response? For example, was it that the words were multisyllabic and somewhat difficult to pronounce, in contrast to the simple one-syllable pseudowords used by Paris and Myers?

The final study to be considered actually bridges the two parts of this section in that multiple standards were required, but subjects were only instructed to use one of them. The investigation, which focused on the internal consistency and external consistency standards, was carried out by Markman and Gorin (1981). Two versions of eight short passages were constructed, one version containing a final sentence that violated prior knowledge, the other version having a similar final sentence that was inconsistent with an earlier sentence. For example, in a passage about koala bears, the prior knowledge violation was in the sentence, "They sleep on the tree tops where cool, soft, grass grows" and the inconsistency was in the sentence, "They sleep on the ground in the cool, soft grass" which conflicts with the earlier sentence, "They will sleep only high up on the tops of trees."

Eight- and 10-year-old children were instructed to listen to a set of passages and report the problems. Each set had an equal number of inconsistencies and prior-knowledge violations as well as several intact "filler" passages. Some of the children were told that the essays would contain falsehoods; some were told they would contain inconsistencies; a third group was simply told that some of the essays had problems with them. Of interest to the investigators was whether the children would adjust their standards of evaluation in accordance with their instructional set. Results indicated that they did; children of both ages were more likely to identify falsehoods when they were alerted to look for falsehoods and the same was true for the inconsistencies. Although inconsistencies were generally better detected than prior-knowledge violations, Markman and Gorin argue that this difference is uninterpretable because the problem types are noncomparable. This argument obviously has profound implications for any effort to make comparisons among standards; I therefore address it in the concluding section of the paper. For now, suffice it to say that the difference is difficult to interpret because no children were specifically instructed to use *both* standards of evaluation.

Instructed Adoption of Multiple Standards

Three studies by Baker (1984a, 1984b, in press) are considered in this section. The first is concerned with instructed standard use under optimally structured conditions. The second two involve comparisons of instructed and noninstructed use under more typical conditions.

Baker (1984a) examined children's ability to use the lexical standard and two semantic standards—external consistency and internal consistency—under very explicit instructions to find the mistakes. Five, 7-, 9-, and 11-year-old children were presented with short narrative passages, each containing two different types of mistakes. The problems consisted of (1) two-syllable nonsense words (e.g., welkins, brugen) that replaced nouns as the last word in a sentence; (2) inconsistencies in which two sentences, separated by one intervening sentence, contained conflicting information (e.g., one sentence described a rabbit's fur as brown, a subsequent sentence as white); and (3) violations of prior knowledge, where events were described that are inconsistent with what is true or possible (e.g., that ice cream grows in gardens, that dogs purr). The oldest children read the passages on their own (Experiment 2); the younger children listened as the passages were read aloud (Experiment 1). The children were given careful instructions and practice in finding the problems, and they were given feedback throughout the session. If they did not report all of the problems after the first exposure to the passage, they reread or relistened to it. If they still did not report a problem, it was identified for them. In other words, care was taken to maximize performance.

Not surprisingly, older children identified more problems than younger children and, in both experiments, nonsense words and prior-knowledge violations were more likely to be identified than internal inconsistencies. (The mean identification rates attained by the second trial were presented earlier under discussion of individual standards.) Perhaps the most important aspect of the study was its demonstration that children across a wide age range indeed can evaluate their understanding quite effectively using at least these three different standards. Granted, children do not typically encounter situations in which they are specifically told what criteria they should use to decide whether they understand, nor are they given explicit feedback about their efforts. Yet the results make it clear that children possess better evaluation skills than are apparent in most investigations of comprehension monitoring.

The value of having the criteria specified explicitly was put to a more direct test in a second study by Baker (1984b). Half of the subjects were given the specific instructions; half were only generally informed that problems would be present. This study used expository materials similar to materials that children encounter in their content-area texts, and the task involved reading rather than listening. Again, passages were modified to contain the following problem types: nonsense words, prior knowledge violations, and internal inconsistencies. Three passages had one of each problem type and an additional three passages had no problems. Subjects were fourth and sixth graders identified as better and poorer readers on the basis of their reading scores on the California Achievement Test (mean stanine scores = 7.7 and 4.2, respectively). The subjects were instructed to underline anything they thought was a problem as they were reading and then they were to explain what, if anything, was problematic about the passage. After they finished reading all passages, they were questioned about missed problems in order to find out how they had interpreted the information.

Identification of intentionally introduced problems was but one of several dependent measures and is not considered in detail here. Briefly, more nonsense words were identified than either prior-knowledge violations or inconsistencies, which did not differ. Sixth-graders identified more problems than fourth-graders only if they were in the better reading group. All children identified more problems when given specific instructions as to the types of standards they should use. Finally, neither grade, reading level, nor type of instruction interacted with problem type.

Children's response protocols were also examined for their use of different standards of evaluation *throughout* the testing session. All evaluative comments the children made were taken as evidence of using a standard, regardless of whether they pertained to intentionally introduced problems. One analysis revealed that the frequency with which the different standards were used differed as a function of reading level and instruction type. Poorer readers applied the external consistency standard and the lexical standard more often than better readers (3.96 vs. 3.40 and 3.02 vs. 2.54, respectively); and they applied the internal consistency standard less often (.67 vs. 2.0). Subjects receiving specific instructions applied the external consistency and internal consistency standards more than twice as often as those receiving general instructions (5.02 vs. 2.29, and 1.94 vs. .96, respectively). The difference for the lexical standard, though still statistically significant, was of much smaller magnitude (3.13 vs. 2.36). Children receiving general instructions were more likely to apply the lexical and external consistency standards than they were to apply the internal consistency standard, implicating differences in the likelihood of spontaneous adoption. Qualitative differences in the children's standard repertoires were also revealed. For example, many more younger and poorer readers, in contrast to older and better readers, *never* used the internal consistency standard. Moreover, many of these same children relied exclusively on the lexical standard. In other words, they never identified problems other than those at the individual word level.

The final study directly concerned with multiple standards was carried out by Baker (in press) with college students. The materials were 12 200-word passages adapted from college-level textbooks in animal behavior, local governments, and current environmental issues. No attempt was made to change the style or structure of the original material, thus affording ample opportunities for subjects to apply multiple standards of evaluation. Within each topic area, one passage each was modified to contain a nonsense word, a prior knowledge violation, and an internal inconsistency. The subjects (introductory psychology students) were preselected on the basis of their SAT-Verbal (Scholastic Aptitude Test) scores; only those with scores above 580 or below 420 were invited to participate (actual mean scores were 599 and 388). Half of the subjects within each group received very specific instructions as to the types of problems they should seek; the other half received only general instructions to look for problems. The subjects read each passage at their own pace, underlining anything problematic and then explaining the problem to the experimenter. After reading all passages, the subjects were questioned about the problems they had missed in order to ascertain their interpretations.

Identification of intentionally introduced problems are commented upon only briefly here. Nonsense words were most likely to be identified, prior knowledge violations much less so, and even less detectable were internal inconsistencies. Both verbal ability level and type of instruction influenced performance and the two factors interacted. Thus, the higher-ability students who received specific instructions were superior to the three remaining groups. The higher-ability group who received general instructions was intermediate to the two lower groups. There were no interactions of problem type with either of the other two factors.

As in the previous study, *all* of the students' comments were classified as to the type of standard they revealed, and several additional analyses were conducted. Frequency of application of specific standards did not differ as a function of verbal ability level, but did differ with instruction type. Students receiving general instructions used the lexical standard and the structural cohesiveness standard most often (3.53 and 3.48); the informational completeness standard next most frequently (1.21); and the remaining four standards were used less than once each throughout the testing session. Students receiving specific instructions used the external consistency and lexical standards most often (3.45, 4.0), followed by internal consistency, structural cohesiveness, and informational completeness (1.72, 1.55, 1.52). Least frequently used were the propositional cohesiveness and syntactic standards (.45, .07). The lexical standard was applied equally often by subjects in the general instruction condition and in the specific. Qualitative analyses revealed that there were more students in the low-verbal-ability group than in the high group who never used the internal consistency standard. In addition, more students receiving general instructions than specific never used the external consistency and internal consistency standards. The fact that the lexical standard was the only one of the three that students adopted spontaneously with any frequency is somewhat disconcerting. The students were told that there were problems, yet they seldom focused on any other dimensions of the text. The data differ from those collected from the children (Baker, 1984b) in that the external consistency standard was not applied by the college students as frequently as the lexical. This may be indicative of a decreasing tendency, as one progresses through school, to challenge the truth of what one is reading, an unfortunate byproduct of the "answer is in the book" school of instruction (Goodman, 1976).

In summary, this section of the chapter dealt with the use of multiple standards of evaluation. Studies reviewed in this section incorporated tasks that required readers or listeners to evaluate their understanding with respect to more than one standard. Sometimes the subjects were specifically told which standards to use; other times they were left to adopt them spontaneously. The research shows quite clearly that children as young as five years of age can evaluate their understanding using more than one standard. However, it also shows that both children and adults tend to apply fewer *different* standards of evaluation when they are not given specific instructions as to what standards to use (Baker, in press, 1984b). Nevertheless, instructions to adopt particular standards are quite effective.

A number of important questions arise from this concern with multiple standard use. Unfortunately, the existing data base is still too small to afford answers. Attempts to generalize across studies are difficult because of variations in the standards tested, variations in task demands, and of course variations in materials. Moreover, no single study was designed to examine the use of more than three standards. Future research, therefore, should seek more definitive answers to such questions as the following: Are some standards more likely to be applied than others? Do children develop proficiency with some standards sooner than others? Do better readers apply certain standards more effectively than poorer readers? Are some standards more essential to comprehension monitoring than others?

Conclusions

The primary purpose of this chapter was to present a conceptualization and a documentation of the different dimensions along which readers may evaluate their own comprehension. The conceptualization
consisted of a set of standards, classified as to whether their application
required primarily lexical, syntactic, or semantic processing. The documentation consisted of evidence culled from the empirical literature on
both comprehension *per se* and comprehension monitoring. It should be
apparent, but perhaps bears mentioning, that there was some circularity
involved in realizing the goal of the chapter. That is, the framework was
initially derived on the basis of empirical data, data that in turn lent cred-
ibility to the framework. Nevertheless, data collected since the framework
was developed (Baker, in press) indicate that mature readers do in fact
evaluate text comprehensibility using criteria that can reliably be classified
into the seven identified categories. Though there were individual differences in the particular standards used, all seven standards were represented in the sample with no residual of unclassifiable responses.

Most of the chapter was devoted to a discussion of each standard of
evaluation in turn, with a final section on multiple standards. Relevant
research was reviewed and, whenever possible, tentative conclusions were
drawn regarding developmental and reading proficiency differences in the
use of the standard. Not surprisingly, there were both quantitative and
qualitative differences in the literature relevant to the various standards.
For example, we know a great deal more about children's use of the internal consistency standard than we do about their use of the propositional
cohesiveness standard. For this reason, I do not attempt to provide a general summary here. Rather, I focus on a few general issues, with particular
attention to the questions that remain to be answered.

One such issue concerns the discrepancy between verbal and performance measures of comprehension monitoring. Several different investigators have found that performance indicators reflect ongoing evaluation
of one's comprehension while subsequent verbal reports indicate a lack of
awareness of comprehension difficulties (e.g., Flavell et al., 1981; Harris
et al., 1981; Tikhomirov & Klochko, 1981). Such data suggest that at least
certain standards of evaluation are applied automatically, as intrinsic components of the comprehension process. Just what determines whether detected problems reach the level of consciousness remains an important
empirical question. Certainly the classic metacognitive variables of person,
task, and strategy will be relevant here, and there is some evidence that

the child's developmental level must be taken into account. Both Flavell et al. and Harris et al. found the verbal-performance discrepancy more common among younger children than older. But in the former study, the younger children were 6 years old and the older were 8, whereas in the latter the younger were 8 years old and the older 10. Therefore, it is unlikely that anything as simple as an explanation based on young children's verbal report difficulties would suffice. Moreover, Tikhomirov and Klochko reported the discrepancy among highly educated adults. In sum, the available evidence suggests, as Flavell et al. have argued, that subjects may generate internal signals of comprehension failure but for some reason do not interpret them correctly. Further research is needed to elucidate the reason or reasons.

A second issue concerns the distinction between spontaneous versus instructed evaluation of one's comprehension. Many of the earlier studies on comprehension monitoring were concerned with children's ability to notice problems when they were not given any clue that problems would be present. The approach seemed perfectly reasonable, because the intent was to generalize to situations where such clues are not typically provided. However, it became clear that children's comprehension monitoring skills were being underestimated, primarily because children, as well as adults, expect that the messages they encounter will be true, informative, consistent, and so forth. If they are told otherwise, they show considerably more competence at identifying the problems.

My point here is not that studies that focus on spontaneous evaluation are of little value, but rather that they are based on an overly optimistic conception of comprehension outside of the laboratory. Children are *not* typically taught how to evaluate and regulate their own comprehension; hence they do so ineffectively if at all. They are not encouraged to critically evaluate what they read; hence they accept text as given. These same shortcomings frequently carry over into adulthood. However, the effectiveness is encouraging of interventions as simple as instructing a child to consider how the text relates to what he or she already knows so that it becomes possible to find embedded mistakes. Full-scale classroom interventions such as that carried out by Paris and his colleagues (Paris, Lipson, Jacobs, Oka, DeBritto, & Cross, 1982) hold considerable promise. It is clear that children can evaluate their own understanding; that they do not do so spontaneously is at least partially attributable to the way they have been taught.

The final issue to be considered is a problem alluded to earlier but dismissed temporarily for lack of a simple resolution. Markman and Gorin (1981) argued that it was inappropriate to make comparisons among problems that require the use of different standards, because the problems were generated on noncomparable bases. In other words, how can we be sure that a particular prior knowledge violation is as difficult to detect using an external consistency standard as a particular internal inconsistency is to detect using an internal consistency standard? We already know that within problem types, some problems are easier to detect than others. For example, increasing the salience of prior-knowledge violations increases their detectability (Pace, 1980). And manipulating the amount of information intervening between the component premises of an internal inconsistency also affects detection (Garner & Kraus, 1981–1982; Markman, 1979). It is quite likely that, with judicious manipulations, an experimenter could show that *any* standard can be applied both more effectively and less effectively than any other. Because of this problem, the section on mulitple standards concluded with a number of questions still unanswered. Without some metric for establishing comparability of problems, generalization is dangerous.

This difficulty notwithstanding, there are still meaningful ways to examine differences in the extent to which readers apply different standards. For example, a prime concern in Baker (1984b, in press) was with *all* of the comments readers made in response to the task demands to identify portions of the text that were hard to understand. Thus, I was less interested in problem detection per se than I was in the standards that were used for evaluating the entire text. Differences were found as a function of age, reading level, and instruction condition in the types of standards used, the number of different standards used, and the relative frequencies of individual standard applications. The fact that many students, both children and adults, identified problems in nonproblematic material might be regarded by some as inappropriate standard use (i.e., false alarms). However, I wish to argue very strongly against this position. In a naturalistic reading task, such misapplications of the standards are in fact healthy signs. They indicate, for example, that a reader knows she or he does not know the meaning of a particular word, and so should take steps to remedy the situation. Similarly, if she or he detects an inconsistency with prior knowledge, this should indicate that either (1) there is a problem in her or his knowledge base, or (2) there is a problem in the text. In other words, the comments reflect the students' assessment of their own comprehension and are informative in their own right.

In conclusion, the literature discussed in this chapter has illustrated that there are many different standards for evaluating one's comprehension. Differences in the facility with which these standards can be used depend on a number of complex factors, most of which are not at present well understood. Future investigations of comprehension monitoring should attempt to take some of these factors into account. If our ultimate goal is to improve readers' abilities to decide for themselves when they understand and when they do not, it is essential that we provide them with concrete guidelines on how to make those decisions.

Acknowledgements

Preparation of this chapter and some of the research reported herein was supported in part by the National Institute of Education under grant number NIE-G-81-0100. I wish to thank Ruth Garner, Bruce Lombardi, Susan Sonnenschein, and the editors of this volume for their helpful comments on earlier versions of the manuscript.

References

Ackerman, B. P. Children's use of contextual expectations to detect and resolve comprehension failures. *Journal of Experimental Child Psychology*, 1982, 33, 63–73.

Ackerman, B. P. Young children's understanding of a speaker's intentional use of a false utterance. *Developmental Psychology*, 1981, 17 472–480.

Adams, W. R., & Spira, J. R. *Reading beyond words*. New York: Holt, Rinehart, & Winston, 1978.

Baker, L. Children's effective use of multiple standards for evaluating their comprehension. *Journal of Educational Psychology*, 1984, 76, 588-597 (a)

Baker, L. Comprehension monitoring: Identifying and coping with text confusions. *Journal of Reading Behavior*, 1979, 11, 363–374. (b)

Baker, L. Differences in the standards used by college students for evaluating their comprehension of expository prose. *Reading Research Quarterly*, in press.

Baker, L. *Do I understand or do I not understand: That is the question*. (Reading Education Report #10). Champaign, IL: University of Illinois, Center for the Study of Reading, July, 1979. (a)

Baker, L. An evaluation of the role of metacognitive deficits in learning disabilities. *Topics in Learning and Learning Disabilities*, 1982, 2, 27–36.

Baker, L. Spontaneous versus instructed use of multiple standards for evaluating comprehension: Effects of age, reading proficiency, and type of standard. *Journal of Experimental Child Psychology*, 1984, 38, 289-311.(b)

Baker, L., & Anderson, R. I. Effects of inconsistent information on text processing: Evidence for comprehension monitoring. *Reading Research Quarterly*, 1982, 17, 281–294.

Baker, L., & Brown, A. L. Cognitive monitoring in reading. In J. Flood (Ed.), *Understanding reading comprehension*. Newark, DE: International Reading Association, 1984.

Baker, L., & Brown, A. L. Metacognitive skills and reading. In P. D. Pearson, M. Kamil, R. Barr, & P. Mosenthal (Eds.), *Handbook of reading research*. New York: Longman, 1984.

Beal, C. R., & Flavell, J. H. Effect of increasing the salience of message ambiguities on kindergartners' evaluations of communicative success and message adequacy. *Developmental Psychology*, 1982, 18, 43–48.

Bearison, D. J., & Levey, L. M. Children's comprehension of referential communication: Decoding ambiguous messages. *Child Development,* 1977, *48,* 716–720.

Beebe, M. J. The effect of different types of substitution miscues on reading. *Reading Research Quarterly,* 1980, *15,* 324–336.

Blachowicz, C. Z. Semantic constructivity in children's comprehension. *Reading Research Quarterly,* 1977–1978, *13*(2), 188–199.

Bransford, J. D. *Human cognition: Learning, understanding and remembering.* Belmont, CA: Wadsworth, 1979.

Bransford, J. D., Barclay, J. R., & Franks, J. J. Sentence memory: A constructive versus interpretive approach. *Cognitive Psychology,* 1972, *3,* 193–209.

Bransford, J. D., & Johnson, M. K. Contextual prerequisites for understanding: Some investigations of comprehension and recall. *Journal of Verbal Learning and Verbal Behavior,* 1972, *11,* 717–726.

Bransford, J. D., Stein, B. S., Vye, N. J., Franks, J. J., Auble, P. M., Mezynski, K. J., & Perfetto, G. A. Differences in approaches to learning: An overview. *Journal of Experimental Psychology: General,* 1982, *111,* 390–398.

Bridge, C. A., & Winograd, P. N. Readers' awareness of cohesive relationships during close comprehension. *Journal of Reading Behavior,*1982, *14,* 299–312.

Brown, A. L. Metacognitive development and reading. In R. J. Spiro, B. C. Bruce, & W. F. Brewer (Eds.), *Theoretical issues in reading comprehension.* Hillsdale, NJ: Erlbaum, 1980.

Brown, A. L., & Smiley, S. S. Rating the importance of structural units of prose passages: A problem of metacognitive development. *Child Development,* 1977, *48,*1–8.

Brown, A. L., Smiley, S. S., Day, J., Townsend, M., & Lawton, S. C. Intrusion of a thematic idea in children's recall of prose. *Child Development,* 1977, *48,* 1454–1466.

Canney, G., & Winograd, P. *Schemata for reading and reading comprehension performance.* (Tech. Rep. #120). Champaign, IL: University of Illinois, Center for the Study of Reading, April, 1979.

Capelli, C. A., & Markman, E. M. Suggestions for training comprehension monitoring. *Topics in Learning and Learning Disabilities,* 1982, *2,* 87–96.

Carpenter, P. A., & Daneman, M. Lexical retrieval and error recovery in reading: A model based on eye fixations. *Journal of Verbal Learning and Verbal Behavior,* 1981, *20,* 137–160.

Carpenter, P. A., & Just, M. A. Reading comprehension as eyes see it. In M. A. Just & P. A. Carpenter (Eds.), *Cognitive processes in comprehension.* Hillsdale, NJ: Erlbaum, 1977.

Ceci, S. J., Caves, R. D., & Howe, M. J. A. Children's long-term memory for information that is incongruous with their prior knowledge. *British Journal of Psychology,* 1981, *72,* 443–450.

Cirilo, R. K. Referential coherence and text structure in story comprehension. *Journal of Verbal Learning and Verbal Behavior,* 1981, *20,* 358–367.

Clark, H. H., & Haviland, S. E. Comprehension and the given-new contract. In R. O. Freedle (Ed.), *Discourse production and comprehension.* Norwood, NJ: Ablex, 1977.

Clark, H. H., & Sengul, C. J. In search of referents for nouns and pronouns. *Memory and Cognition,* 1979, *7,* 35-41.

Danner, F. W. Children's understanding of intersentence organization in the recall of short descriptive passages. *Journal of Educational Psychology,* 1976, *68,* 174–183.

Danner, F. W., & Mathews, S. R. When do young children make inferences from prose? *Child Development,* 1980, *51,* 906–908.

Eamon, D. B. Selection and recall of topical information in prose by better and poorer readers. *Reading Research Quarterly,* 1978–1979, *14,* 243–257.

Ehrlich, S. F. Children's word recognition in prose context. *Visible Language,* 1981, *15,* 219–244.

Ehrlich, S. F., & Rayner, K. Contextual effects on word perception and eye movements during reading. *Journal of Verbal Learning and Verbal Behavior*, 1981, *20*, 641–655.

Erickson, T. D., & Mattson, M. E. From words to meaning: A semantic illusion. *Journal of Verbal Learning and Verbal Behavior*, 1981, *20*, 540–551.

Flavell, J. H. Cognitive monitoring. In W. P. Dickson (Ed.), *Children's oral communication skills.* New York: Academic Press, 1981.

Flavell, J. H., Speer, J. R., Green, F. L., & August, D. L. The development of comprehension monitoring and knowledge about communication. *Monographs of the Society for Research in Child Development*, 1981, *46*, (5, Whole No. 192).

Frazier, L., & Rayner, K. Making and correcting errors during sentence comprehension: Eye movements in the analysis of structurally ambiguous sentences. *Cognitive Psychology*, 1982, *14*, 178–210.

Frederiksen, J. R. Understanding anaphora: Rules used by readers in assigning pronominal referents. *Discourse Processes*, 1981, *4*, 323–347.

Freebody, P., & Anderson, R. C. Effects of vocabulary difficulty, text cohesion, and schema availability on reading comprehension. *Reading Research Quarterly*, 1983, *18*, 277–294.

Garner, R. Monitoring of passage inconsistency among poor comprehenders: A preliminary test of the "Piecemeal Processing" explanation. *Journal of Educational Research*, 1981, *74*, 159–162.

Garner, R. Monitoring of understanding: An investigation of good and poor readers' awareness of induced miscomprehension of text. *Journal of Reading Behavior*, 1980, *12*, 55–64.

Garner, R., & Kraus, C. Good and poor comprehender differences in knowing and regulating reading behaviors. *Educational Research Quarterly*, 1981–1982, *6*, 5–12.

Garner, R., & Taylor, N. Monitoring of understanding: An investigation of the effects of attentional assistance needs at different grade and reading proficiency levels. *Reading Psychology*, 1982, *3*, 1–6.

Garrod, S., & Sanford, A. Interpreting anaphoric relations: The integration of semantic information while reading. *Journal of Verbal Learning and Verbal Behavior*, 1977, *16*, 77–90.

Goodman, K. S. Behind the eye: What happens in reading. In H. Singer & R. B. Ruddell (Eds.), *Theoretical models and processes of reading.* Newark, DE: International Reading Association, 1976.

Green, D. W., Mitchell, D. C., & Hammond, E. J. The scheduling of text integration processes in reading. *Quarterly Journal of Experimental Psychology*, 1981, *33A*, 455–464.

Greeno, J. G., & Noreen, D. L. Time to read semantically related sentences. *Memory and Cognition*, 1974, *2*, 117–120.

Halliday, M. A. K., & Hasan, R. *Cohesion in English.* London: Longman, 1976.

Harris, P. L., Kruithof, A., Terwogt, M., & Visser, T. Children's detection and awareness of textual anomaly. *Journal of Experimental Child Psychology*, 1981, *31*, 212–230.

Harris, P. L., Mandias, F., Terwogt, M. M., & Tjintjelaar, J. The influence of context on story recall and feelings of comprehension. *International Journal of Behavioral Development*, 1980, *3*, 159–172.

Hirst, W., & Brill, G. A. Contextual aspects of pronoun assignment. *Journal of Verbal Learning and Verbal Behavior*, 1980, *19*, 168–175.

Ironsmith, M., & Whitehurst, G. J. The development of listener abilities in communication: How children deal with ambiguous information. *Child Development*, 1978, *49*, 348–352.

Irwin, J. W. The effects of coherence explicitness on college readers' prose comprehension. *Journal of Reading Behavior*, 1982, *14*, 275–284.

Isaksen, R. L., & Miller, J. W. Sensitivity to syntactic and semantic cues in good and poor comprehenders. *Journal of Educational Psychology*, 1976, *68*, 787–792.

Johnson, H., & Smith, L. B. Children's inferential abilities in the context of reading to understand. *Child Development*, 1981, *52*, 1216–1223.

Kavale, K., & Schreiner, R. The reading processes of above average and average readers: A comparison of the use of reasoning strategies in responding to standardized comprehension measures. *Reading Research Quarterly*, 1979, *15*, 102–128.

Kieras, D. E. Good and bad structure in simple paragraphs: Effects on apparent theme, reading time, and recall. *Journal of Verbal Learning and Verbal Behavior*, 1978, *17*, 13–28.

Kieras, D. E. Initial mention as a signal to thematic content in technical passages. *Memory and Cognition*, 1980, *8*, 345–353.

Kintsch, W., & van Dijk, T. A. Toward a model of text comprehension and production. *Psychological Review*, 1978, *85*, 363–394.

Kintsch, W., & Yarbrough, J. C. Role of rhetorical structure in text comprehension. *Journal of Educational Psychology*, 1982, *74*, 828–834.

Kleiman, G. M. Sentence frame contexts and lexical decisions: Sentence-acceptability and word-relatedness effects. *Memory and Cognition*, 1980, *8*, 336–344.

Koblinsky, S. A., & Cruse, D. F. The role of frameworks in children's retention of sex-related story content. *Journal of Experimental Child Psychology*, 1981, *31*, 321–331.

Kotsonis, M. E., & Patterson, C. J. Comprehension monitoring skills in learning disabled children. *Developmental Psychology*, 1980, *16*, 541–542.

Landis, T. Y. Interactions between text and prior knowledge in children's memory for prose. *Child Development*, 1982, *53*, 811–814.

Liben, L. S., & Posnansky, C. J. Inferences on inferences: The effects of age, transitive ability, memory load, and lexical factors. *Child Development*, 1977, *48*, 1490–1497.

Mandler, J. M. A code in the node: The use of a story schema in retrieval. *Discourse Processes*, 1978, *1*, 14–35.

Mandler, J. M., & Johnson, N. S. Remembrance of things parsed: Story structure and recall. *Cognitive Psychology*, 1977, *9*, 111–151.

Markman, E. M. Comprehension monitoring. In W. P. Dickson (Ed.), *Children's oral communication skills*. New York: Academic Press, 1981.

Markman, E. M. Realizing that you don't understand: A preliminary investigation. *Child Development*, 1977, *46*, 986–992.

Markman, E. M. Realizing that you don't understand: Elementary school children's awareness of inconsistencies. *Child Development*, 1979, *50*, 643–655.

Markman, E. M., & Gorin, L. Children's ability to adjust their standards for evaluating comprehension. *Journal of Educational Psychology*, 1981, *73*, 320–325.

Marshall, N., & Glock, M. Comprehension of connected discourse: A study into the relationships between the structure of text and information recalled. *Reading Research Quarterly*, 1978–1979, *16*, 10–56.

McGee, L. M. Awareness of text structure: Effects on children's recall of expository text. *Reading Research Quarterly*, 1982, *17*, 581–590.

Meyer, B. J. F., Brandt, D. M., & Bluth, G. J. Use of top-level structure in text: Key for reading comprehension of ninth-grade students. *Reading Research Quarterly*, 1980, *16*, 72–103.

Miller, J. W., & Isaksen, R. L. Contextual sensitivity in beginning readers. *The Elementary School Journal*, 1978, *78*, 325–331.

Myers, M., & Paris, S. G. Children's metacognitive knowledge about reading. *Journal of Educational Psychology*, 1978, *70*, 680–690.

Osherson, D., & Markman, E. Language and the ability to evaluate contradictions and tautologies. *Cognition*, 1975, 3, 213–226.

Owings, R. A., Peterson, G. A., Bransford, J. D., Morris, C. D., & Stein, B. S. Spontaneous monitoring and regulation of learning: A comparison of successful and less successful fifth graders. *Journal of Educational Psychology*, 1980, 72, 250–256.

Pace, A. J. *The effect of inconsistent information on children's comprehension of stories about familiar situations.* Paper presented at the American Educational Research Association meetings, San Francisco, April 1979.

Pace, A. J. *Further explorations of young children's sensitivity to world-knowledge-story information discrepancies.* Paper presented at the meeting of the Southeastern Conference on Human Development, Alexandria, April, 1980.

Paris, S. G., & Carter, A. Y. Semantic and constructive aspects of sentence memory in children. *Developmental Psychology*, 1973, 9, 109–113.

Paris, S. G., Lipson, M. Y., Jacobs, J., Oka, E., DeBritto, A. M., & Cross, D. *Metacognition and reading comprehension.* A symposium presented at the International Reading Association Meeting, Chicago, April, 1982.

Paris, S. G., & Myers, M. Comprehension monitoring, memory, and study strategies of good and poor readers. *Journal of Reading Behavior*, 1981, 13, 5–22.

Patterson, C. J., Cosgrove, J. M., & O'Brien, R. G. Nonverbal indicants of comprehension and noncomprehension in children. *Developmental Psychology*, 1980, 16, 38–48.

Patterson, C. J., & Kister, M. C. The development of listener skills for referential communication. In P. Dickson (Ed.), *Children's oral communication skills.* New York: Academic Press, 1981.

Patterson, C. J., O'Brien, C., Kister, M. C., Carter, D. B., & Kotsonis, M. E. Development of comprehension monitoring as a function of context. *Developmental Psychology*, 1981, 17, 379–389.

Pearson, P. D. The effects of grammatical complexity on children's comprehension, recall, and conception of certain semantic relations. *Reading Research Quarterly*, 1974–1975, 10, 155–192.

Pratt, M. W., & Bates, K. R. Young editors: Preschoolers' evaluation and production of ambiguous messages. *Developmental Psychology*, 1982, 18, 30–42.

Pratt, M. W., Luszcz, M. A., MacKenzie-Keating, S., & Manning, A. Thinking about stories: The story schema in metacognition. *Journal of Verbal Learning and Verbal Behavior*, 1982, 21, 493–505.

Riesbeck, C. K. "You can't miss it!": Judging the clarity of directions. *Cognitive Science*, 1980, 4, 285–303.

Rumelhart, D. E. Notes on a schema for stories. In D. G. Bobrow & A. Collins (Eds.), *Representation and understanding: Studies in cognitive science.* New York: Academic Press, 1975.

Schwarz, M. N. K., & Flammer, A. Text structure and title—effects on comprehension and recall. *Journal of Verbal Learning and Verbal Behavior*, 1981, 20, 61–66.

Shatz, M. The relationship between cognitive processes and the development of communication skills. In B. Keasey (Ed.), *Nebraska Symposium on Motivation.* Lincoln: University of Nebraska Press, 1978.

Short, E. J., & Ryan, E. B. *Metacognitive differences between skilled and less skilled readers: Remediating deficits through story grammar and attribution training.* Unpublished manuscript. Chapel Hill, NC: University of North Carolina, 1982.

Small, M. Y., & Butterworth, J. Semantic integration and the development of memory for logical inferences. *Child Development*, 1981, 52, 732–735.

Smiley, S. S., Oakley, D. D., Worthen, D., Campione, J. C., & Brown, A. L. Recall of thematically relevant material by adolescent good and poor readers as a function of written versus oral presentation. *Journal of Educational Psychology*, 1977, *69*, 381–387.

Spiro, R. J. Accommodative reconstruction in prose recall. *Journal of Verbal Learning and Verbal Behavior*, 1980, *19*, 84–95.

Stein, N. L., & Glenn, C. G. An analysis of story comprehension in elementary school children. In R. Freedle (Ed.), *New directions in discourse processing*. Norwood, NJ: Ablex, 1978.

Stein, N. L., & Nezworski, T. The effects of organization and instructional set on story memory. *Discourse Processes*, 1978, *1*, 177–193.

Stein, N. L., & Trabasso, T. What's in a story: An approach to comprehension and instruction. In R. Glaser (Ed.), *Advances in instructional psychology* (Vol. 2). Hillsdale, NJ: Erlbaum, 1982.

Sulin, R. S., & Dooling, D. J. Intrusion of a thematic idea in retention of prose. *Journal of Experimental Psychology*, 1974, *103*, 225–262.

Taylor, B. M. Children's memory for expository text after reading. *Reading Research Quarterly*, 1980, *15*, 399–411.

Thorndyke, P. W. Cognitive structures in comprehension and memory of narrative discourse. *Cognitive Psychology*, 1977, *9*, 77–110.

Tikhomirov, O. K., & Klochko, V. E. The detection of a contradiction as the initial stage of problem formation. In J. Wertsch (Ed.), *The concept of activity in Soviet psychology*. Armonk, NY: M. E. Sharpe, 1981.

Townsend, M. A. R. Schema activation in memory for prose. *Journal of Reading Behavior*, 1980, *12*, 49–53.

Tyler, L. K., & Marslen-Wilson, W. D. The on-line effects of semantic context on syntactic processing. *Journal of Verbal Learning and Verbal Behavior*, 1977, *16*, 683–692.

Wagoner, S. A. Comprehension monitoring: What it is and what we know about it. *Reading Research Quarterly*, 1983, *18*, 328–346.

Walker, C. H., & Meyer, B. J. F. Integrating different types of information in text. *Journal of Verbal Learning and Verbal Behavior*, 1980, *19*, 263–275.

Weber, R. M. A linguistic analysis of first-grade reading errors. *Reading Research Quarterly*, 1970, *5*, 427–451.

Whaley, J. F. Readers' expectations for story structures. *Reading Research Quarterly*, 1981, *17*, 90–114.

Williams, J. P., Taylor, M. B., & Ganger, S. Text variations at the level of the individual sentence and the comprehension of simple expository paragraphs. *Journal of Educational Psychology*, 1981, *73*, 851–865.

Wimmer, H. Processing of script deviations by young children. *Discourse Processes*, 1979, *2*, 301–310.

Winograd, P., & Johnston, P. Comprehension monitoring and the error detection paradigm. *Journal of Reading Behavior*, 1982, *14*, 61–74.

Wood, N. V. *College reading and study skills*. New York: Holt, Rinehart & Winston, 1978.

Wykes, T. Inference and children's comprehension of pronouns. *Journal of Experimental Child Psychology*, 1981, *32*, 264–278.

Yekovich, F. R., & Walker, C. H. Identifying and using referents in sentence comprehension. *Journal of Verbal Learning and Verbal Behavior*, 1978, *17*, 265–277.

Yekovich, F. R., Walker, C. H., & Blackman, H. S. The role of presupposed and focal information in integrating sentences. *Journal of Verbal Learning and Verbal Behavior*, 1979, *18*, 535–548.

CHAPTER 6

A Metacognitive Framework
for the Development of First
and Second Language Skills*

Ellen Bialystok and Ellen Bouchard Ryan

Introduction

Such uses of language as literacy and metalinguistic performance require higher levels of skill than are required by conversational uses of language. Researchers have accumulated a variety of problems and tasks that
not only discriminate between levels of skill for each of these language
uses but also track the development of that skill by children in the process
of gaining proficiency with the language (Dale, 1976; Gibson & Levin,
1975; Sinclair, Jarvella, & Levelt, 1978). Yet, the cognitive bases underlying
the development of literacy and of metalinguistic skills and their relationships to learning to talk remain to be specified.

The study of the relationship of metalinguistic skills to literacy is particularly in need of theoretical clarification. There is considerable evidence
linking the development of metalinguistic ability with the onset of literacy,
or learning to read (e.g., Ehri, 1979). Typically, children who do well in
metalinguistic tasks also learn to read quickly and easily, although it is not
clear how to interpret such correlations. Results from metalinguistic tasks

*Preparation of this chapter was partially supported by grant 6-81-0134 from the Na-
tional Institute of Education and by a grant from the Social Sciences and Humanities Research Council, Canada.

METACOGNITION, COGNITION,
AND HUMAN PERFORMANCE
VOL. 1
207

themselves show diversity and change across the measures used and the children sampled, making the concept of metalinguistic ability appear vague and undefined (e.g., Ryan & Ledger, 1983). Moreover, bilingual children often perform differently from monolinguals on literacy and metalinguistic tasks (e.g., Cummins, 1979). The interaction between the development of these skills and second language learning, therefore, also needs to be considered. Finally, the relationship between the specialized language skills demonstrated on reading and metalinguistic tests must be related to the conversational uses of language from which they developed. In this chapter, we discuss these issues within the context of an integrative structure of the cognitive bases underlying language proficiency.

Dimensions of Language Skill

The present framework is an attempt to understand the development of language proficiency across a variety of situations that differ in difficulty and exhibit some developmental sequence. The types of situations examined, which we call language-use domains, are *conversational* or interactive uses; *literacy* uses, including reading and writing; and *metalinguistic* tasks. The study of the interrelationship of these language-use domains addresses issues such as the reasons for their observed developmental ordering, their patterns of correlation, and their interaction with proficiency in other languages. In addition, the framework addresses the internal structure of each of these domains. Accordingly, issues that concern the development of one of these abilities, such as learning to read, are examined from the same theoretical perspective.

The framework consists of two skill components which are considered to develop along continuous dimensions. These dimensions are theoretically orthogonal although pragmatically parallel and interrelated in complex ways. Both these dimensions appear in numerous developmental descriptions, although usually in a slightly different form and rarely in combination with each other. The two skill components represented along these dimensions are *analyzed knowledge* and *cognitive control*. The first is essentially derived from a concern with the epistemology and mental representation of knowledge and the second with the executive procedures tapped in the deployment of knowledge. Clearly, then, all tasks require both aspects; and the development of these skill components for representing and using information cannot proceed totally independently.

This two-dimensional framework evolved from an analysis of the cognitive skills that differentiate metalinguistic awareness from ordinary linguistic communication. Some past definitions of *metalinguistic performance* have emphasized structured knowledge of the language: awareness of syntactic and semantic properties of language (Gleitman, Gleitman & Shipley, 1972), self-consciousness about language (Gleitman & Gleitman, 1979), knowledge of features and functions of language (Downing, 1979). Other definitions have focused on control over language form: ability to attend to language forms in and of themselves (Cazden, 1974) and ability to shift attention from meaning to form (Hakes, 1980, 1982; Lundberg, 1978). In addition, many definitions of metalinguistic awareness have incorporated both aspects: speaking about language (Jakobson, 1971), thinking about language and commenting on it (Papandropoulou & Sinclair, 1974; Read, 1978), conscious awareness of and ability to manipulate language as an object (Ehri, 1975), and reflection (usually conscious) upon the nature and properties of language (Clark, 1978; Van Kleeck, 1982). Highlighting the developing interrelationships between these two features, Vygotsky (1934/1962) spoke of controlled knowledge of language in the sense that reflecting upon language yields structured knowledge, which in turn frees the individual to use that knowledge deliberately.

We argue that distinguishing between these two interrelated aspects of metalinguistic performance is not only valuable for clarifying the nature of metalinguistic development but also for providing a clearer understanding of the full range of linguistic, literate, and metalinguistic developments in both first and second languages. Moreover, treating both analyzed knowledge and control as linear dimensions allows us to go beyond dichotomies (e.g., *meta* vs. *non*, analyzed vs. unanalyzed, deliberate control vs. situationally determined) to the characterization of both tasks and abilities in terms of degrees of control and analyzed knowledge. It should be noted that the more general term metacognition was initially reserved for conscious (i.e., highly analyzed) knowledge (Flavell & Wellman, 1977), but it has now been extended to include executive control (Brown, 1980).

The assumption of the framework is that a minimal but common set of underlying cognitive skills constitutes the mental underpinnings of language proficiency. Hence, elaboration of the skill components along these two dimensions by children is reflected in increased performance in a variety of problems. The approach has an economy in that the same dimensions serve to describe the structure of particular language abilities and to relate different language abilities to each other. The progression from novice to expert levels of skill within a domain can be explained for adult second language mastery as well. Moreover, because the dimensions are derived from ordinary cognitive mechanisms, their development is consistent with the principles of development used to explain a variety of emerging abilities.

In this chapter we begin by explicating the nature of the two skill components, the specific patterns of interaction that occur between the dimensions, and the factors responsible for the development of each. The development of skill in each of the three language-use domains—conversation, literacy, and metalinguistic tasks—is then interpreted within this framework. Finally, some further implications of the framework are suggested. Ultimately, the goal is to understand the nature and development of language proficiency as a function of these two cognitive dimensions.

Dimension of Analyzed Knowledge

While young children are clearly operating from an understanding of the grammatical structure of English in order to produce grammatical utterances, their knowledge of that structure or even awareness that it exists is much later in appearing. Different levels of knowledge of a particular rule of grammar are required in order to use the rule spontaneously for communication than to retrieve the rule deliberately in response to specific code-directed needs (e.g., to write a sentence or to judge its grammaticality). We consider the difference in these two uses of the rule to be in the explicitness with which the rule must have been encoded by the learner. This difference is reflected in the relative placement of knowledge of that rule along the dimension of analyzed knowledge. Information that appears as unanalyzed knowledge is used routinely, with little or no awareness of the structure of that information, and is not subject to intentional manipulation. Information that appears as analyzed knowledge is used creatively, with attention to the structural properties of information, and deliberately participates in transformations.

The distinction between analyzed and unanalyzed knowledge follows from a long tradition in both epistemology and psychology. Polanyi (1958), for example, distinguishes objective from personal knowledge; and, in a similar manner, Scheffler (1965) distinguishes knowledge from belief. Piaget's (1954) distinction between operative and figurative knowledge is similar in that the transformational functions he attributes to operative knowledge are possible, in our terms, only with analyzed knowledge. Finally, Pylyshyn (1981) elaborates a model for the propositional representation of information in which an important component of the system comprises tacit knowledge that is functionally equivalent to nonanalyzed knowledge. In all these distinctions, there is a difference between the forms in which knowledge may be represented and, hence, the situations in which that knowledge may be used. In our terms, most ordinary cognitive activities may proceed on the basis of nonanalyzed knowledge; but more difficult problems require analyzed representations of knowledge. Our system contrasts with these distinctions, however, in that we consider values along a dimension, rather than dichotomous categories, to reflect this aspect of representation.

If we assume a propositional representation of information consisting of a predicate argument structure (see Miller & Johnson-Laird, 1976), then for both analyzed and nonanalyzed knowledge the proposition is the same (e.g., knowledge about subject–verb agreement). The difference between the two is whether or not the learner also has access to the structure of the proposition—what is the predicate, what are the arguments, and the like. It is this access to structure that permits the construction and manipulation of the representations (e.g., ability to correct sentences with incorrect subject–verb agreement or to state the rules). Predicates, for example, can be deliberately assigned to construct specific, often novel propositions; and similarities among propositions in terms of these structures can be detected and also understood.

Our knowledge of the language system (including rules of grammar, semantics, phonology, and discourse) varies along the dimension of the degree to which it is analyzed. Access to the structure of analyzed representations is essential to the solution of certain linguistic problems (Bialystok, in press). For language, the objective representations of the code permit the relationships between the forms and the meanings and among the language forms themselves to be examined separately and manipulated for various purposes. At many points along the dimension, the information may be the same; the learner, that is, can generate grammatical sentences. But as the learner moves toward an analyzed representation of that information, the knowledge of the structure of the system and of the relationships between forms and meanings permits the deliberate utilization of that system for specific purposes. At the analyzed extreme of this dimension, the learner can verbalize the rules governing these form–meaning relationships. Thus, Cazden's (1974) distinction between access and conscious knowledge can be dealt with in terms of different degrees of analyzed knowledge.

The dimension of analyzed knowledge applies functionally to descriptions of language proficiency; that is, certain uses are possible only for certain levels of analyzed knowledge (Ehri, 1979). For example, if a structural regularity of a language is known, then the learner may use that structure in new contexts, decipher language, especially written forms that make use of that structure, and modify or transform that structure for other literary or rhetorical purposes. If an aspect of the language is nonanalyzed, then it is understood more as a routine or pattern (Hakuta, 1974) and has limited application to new contexts or new purposes. Only a very minimal degree of analysis is necessary to use language creatively in the generation of novel grammatical utterances. At the same time, however, young children who overgeneralize the inflectional morphemes of English, as in the overextension of -*ed* to irregular verbs, demonstrate slightly more analyzed knowledge of the language than do children in the previous stage who correctly imitate the irregular forms.

The extent to which language tasks require analyzed representations of knowledge for their solution tends to be inversely correlated with the amount of context given with the problem. Thus, the dimension of embedded–disembedded context (Donaldson, 1978) roughly specifies the degree of analyzed knowledge that would be required by tasks or situations at various points along that dimension. This relationship is a reflection of the availability of alternative routes to meaning. The more the language is redundant with the concrete or conceptual context, the less need there is to extract the meaning directly from the language. Thus, for contextualized uses, it is less important for the learner's representation of the language to be objective and analyzed.

Development occurs along this analyzed-knowledge dimension with general cognitive maturity. In Piagetian terms, the ability to analyze a domain of knowledge into explicitly structured categories and to draw inferences from that structure is a feature of concrete operational thought (Inhelder & Piaget, 1964). Problems such as class inclusion and seriation have provided illustrations of this point. In a study of children's ability to draw deductive inferences on a Piagetian task, Bryant and Trabasso (1971) have shown the child's knowledge to be a major contribution to the solution. Typically, preoperational children fail problems of the type: If A > B and B > C, then A ? C. Bryant and Trabasso argued that the failure was not due to lack of inference-making skills, as traditionally explained, but to lack of (analyzed) knowledge of the relationship between the pairs. By assuring that young children had not only remembered but also understood the relational information, they found that 4-year-old children performed the inference task easily.

Specific language experiences, too, are relevant to growth along this dimension. In the process of learning to read, the child is presented with concrete cues concerning language structure (i.e., letter–sound patterns, spaces between words, capitalization, punctuation.) Because languages share aspects of structure, at least to the degree that there are language universals, those structures are applicable to the analysis of the code for any language. Hence, knowledge of the structure of one language confers an important advantage in the analysis of a subsequent language. Even for the construction of language-specific principles, the experience gained from the activity in the context of another language should facilitate the construction of analyzed linguistic knowledge. In a study by Scribner and Cole (1981) of Vai speakers in Africa who were either literate, biliterate, or schooled, the literate and especially biliterate subjects performed significantly better than nonliterate subjects on tasks requiring high analyzed knowledge, for example, stating the source of error in syntactically deviant sentences. Such findings support the claim that learning to read not only requires adequate levels of analyzed knowledge but also results in the attainment of still higher levels of such knowledge.

Finally, the structured representation of the code for a language can be promoted through instruction. If the learner is at a sufficient point of cognitive maturity and analyzed knowledge to accept the statement of language structure, then explicit information about the structure of the code can result in a more analyzed representation of that code for the learner. However, just as instructional procedures for promoting development through the Piagetian stages are restricted by the child's current level of cognitive development and are therefore effective only for children about to advance spontaneously (Flavell, 1963), so too are instructional statements regarding knowledge effective only for learners on the verge of insight.

Dimension of Cognitive Control

The cognitive-control dimension represents an executive function that is responsible for selecting and coordinating the required information within given time constraints. If the relevant information is not obvious, then selection becomes difficult; if a variety of sources must be consulted, then coordination becomes difficult; if a number of processes are interdependently involved, then speed or fluency becomes difficult. For example, because the usual purpose of language is communicative, and because children's early experiences with language are virtually confined to this function, the aspect of the linguistic message that spontaneously appears most relevant to the child is the meaning. If a language problem requires some attention to form, as in reading and writing, then the child must deliberately or intentionally focus on form in order to supplement, derive, or override the meaning. And the more compelling the meaning, the more control is required to retrieve formal information. There is a tendency, therefore, for increased values along the control dimension to be correlated with an increase in the proportion of attention that must be directed to form in order to succeed on the task. The selection of appropriate information in these cases is more demanding. Similarly, the control to coordinate information becomes more important where monitoring procedures are required to oversee several facets of a problem, such as form and meaning, or meaning and context, and so on. Information-processing or limited-capacity views suggest the importance of processing fluency in these cases to accommodate the necessary operations. The specific ways in which control is affected are discussed separately for each language domain.

The basis of control is a cognitive ability similar to those described by Piaget as constituting operational thought. Piaget's notion of decentering, for example, involves ignoring a salient attribute in order to direct attention elsewhere and consider multiple cues for problem-solving purposes (Inhelder & Piaget, 1964). For example, in the conservation of liquid problem, only the height of the liquid in the beaker seems relevant to the problem, and so the child is initially unable to focus on other perceptual features of the display, such as the relative width of the two beakers. The fact that the two beakers *look* different is sufficiently compelling to judge that they *are* different, and the child is able neither to decenter nor to coordinate other information into the solution.

A similar problem can be seen in the three-mountain task. The child is asked to select the picture that represents the appearance of three colored mountains from another viewpoint. Typically, preoperational children select their own viewpoint, an error that has been called egocentric by Piaget and his followers. The explanation is that the child does not realize that the display must look different from another position. A variety of evidence, however, indicates that the child does indeed know that the appearance changes but is simply unable to calculate the correct appearance of the display from the new perspective (Salatas & Flavell, 1976). To solve the problem, one must coordinate the information from the viewer's own perspective with the features that can provide landmarks from the new perspective. The systematic integration of these two viewpoints will yield the correct answer, and the child's difficulty in various kinds of perspective-taking tasks can be predicted on the basis of the complexity of that integration (Olson & Bialystok, 1983). Thus, the child will not commit egocentric errors if the display has objects with nameable features, or one object instead of three, and so on. The child's difficulty with the problem then can be described in terms of the need to select and coordinate information.

The selection and coordination of information impose similar restrictions on the child's ability to solve problems with language. The child, for example, must be able to deliberately examine either the form or the meaning of the language in accordance with the task demands, irrespective of the saliency of one or the other. Further, these linguistic aspects must be coordinated with each other and integrated with the context, knowledge of the world, and so on in order to succeed in certain language problems.

The *automaticity component* of cognitive control has a crucial role in determining task difficulty, even when the required levels of control and analyzed knowledge are not altered. The fluency with which the selection and coordination operations may be executed determines the extent to which the learner can reduce the specific demands for control and knowledge inherent in any task. High levels of automaticity permit the learner to display more skilled performance, even with no apparent increase in knowledge.

The fluent processor, for example, has an advantage of performing tasks that carry a time restriction. Such time restrictions may be imposed in three ways: *naturally*, as in the need for fluency and spontaneity in conversation; *cognitively*, as in the need to decode words sufficiently quickly to allow space in working memory for storing the meanings of sentences in reading; or *artificially*, as in the imposition of a time constraint on a metalinguistic or reading task. Such restrictions, regardless of their origin, increase the burden on the control dimension, in that the operations must be executed under more stringent conditions. Thus, whether the task requires attention to meaning or to form, control problems are introduced when efficiency and speed become criteria for success. The effect of automaticity requirements on task difficulty becomes especially apparent for conversation because the need to focus on meaning generally keeps the other demands on the control dimension fairly low. If the retrieval of those meanings is not fluent (e.g., for second-language learners), the amount of control necessary for success is increased. In all these situations, automaticity of the control functions is an overriding determinant of success.

As learners become more skilled or fluent in performing a given task, the demands of the cognitive control dimension, such as controlling the direction of search for information, are reduced. As Shiffrin and Schneider (1977) have demonstrated with perceptual and learning processes, increased automaticity in the execution of basic operations expands the cognitive capacity for higher-level processing. Relatedly, Case, Kurland and Goldberg (1982) have shown that increased speed of counting is strongly correlated with developmental increases in the working memory span for the products of counting. The important dependence of working memory upon automaticity was established by having adults count with nonsense labels. The span was reduced to that of 6-year-olds, the level predicted by the speed with which they could count using the unfamiliar names. Again, improving the automaticity of control carried important implications for general improvement in skill.

Advanced levels of selection and automaticity in the control function allow the learner to compensate for gaps in either control or knowledge in order to meet the task requirements. Thus, the difficulty posed by lack of appropriate knowledge may be sidestepped through adoption of particular control strategies with which other sources are searched for information. Similarly, highly elaborated knowledge can sometimes be traded off against various other strategies for solving a task. A learner, that is, may adjust the strategies being used to compensate for deficits in control or analyzed knowledge. Such adjustments, which result in the deliberate manipulation of task demands, reflect a fluency that is part of cognitive control. In more general terms, however, this strategic ability may be applied to tasks where situations indicate the necessity for slightly different approaches, creating a flexibility in problem solving. Such flexibility is particularly important in domains such as reading, where different goals (e.g., gist vs. detail recall) may require strategically different control procedures (Brown, 1980).

The increased automaticity of fluency which accompanies skilled performance has usually been attributed to a factor more similar to our knowledge than to our conception of control. Shiffrin and Schneider (1977), for example, conflate the nature of the representation and the automaticity of its retrieval in their model. Similarly, Anderson (1982) assumes that automaticity is a feature of the procedural representations of knowledge associated with skilled performance. In our model, however, the mechanisms for retrieving information are relatively content-free and separate from the representations of knowledge. Control processes, that is, are required to retrieve any knowledge, whether analyzed or nonanalyzed; and the development of this focusing and retrieval mechanism proceeds separately and in response to different experiences than does the development of analyzed representations of knowledge. The common association between these two, however, is a reflection of the contingency that in most tasks requiring advanced proficiency, high levels of both control and knowledge are implicated. Moreover, the experiences that promote one for the child typically promote the other. In the study by Scribner and Cole (1981), however, schooling was a significant predictor of success on tasks that appear to require high levels of control, such as syllogistic reasoning with counterintuitive premises, whereas literacy was not. Thus, it may be that schooling is particularly important in the development of the control function.

An important factor governing improvement along the control dimension is the increasing cognitive maturity that leads to operational thought. Initially, such abilities include those of selection and coordination associated with concrete operational thought as outlined previously for the conservation and perspective tasks, but ultimately include the logicodeductive abilities essential to formal operational thought (Gallagher, 1978). At this stage, operations may be performed not only on the world, but also on other operations. The cognitive skills necessary to accomplish such tasks are similar, we claim, to the cognitive skills that characterize increasing values along the dimension of cognitive control.

Other descriptions of cognitive development are those that assume a more quantifiable view of growth. Pascual-Leone (1970, 1983), for example, argues that development through the Piagetian stages may be explained in terms of an expansion in the size of the child's working memory. Such an expansion would be particularly necessary for the control responsible for coordinating information. Case (in press), too, argues that coordination of existing schemes allows a child to overcome a limited span, hence forming the foundation of cognitive growth.

The advance along the control dimension as it applies to language task, however, is also guided by more specific experiences. Using more than one language may alert the child to the structure of form–meaning relation and promote the ability to deliberately consider these separate aspects of propositions. Some more specific experiences that serve to promote the control functions are discussed in the context of the separate language domains.

Interaction of the Two Dimensions

The combination of the analyzed knowledge and cognitive control dimensions yields a coordinate system into which three language-use domains can be placed and related to each other. The values along these dimensions are considered only in the most general quantitative terms— low, moderate, and high. The three domains placed into this system are the conversational uses of language, the literacy skills of reading and writing, and the ability to solve metalinguistic problems. The regions circumscribed to represent each domain are proposed to correspond only to approximate typical values on the two major dimensions. Notice that the domains overlap in their values on these dimensions.

Because the three domains described in this framework are all reflections of developing language ability, it has seemed reasonable to assume that there is some connection among them. Yet, apart from a general sequencing in which conversational uses of language typically precede metalinguistic ones, for example, there has been no precise way in which

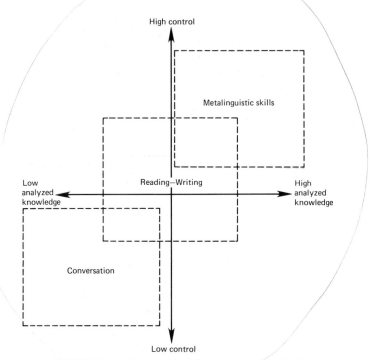

FIGURE 1. A Metacognitive Model of Language Skills

to describe these relationships. The problem of their interrelationship becomes especially crucial, however, when examining the development of reading and of metalinguistic ability in young children.

The general finding in the literature is that there is a correlation in the development of metalinguistic ability and learning to read. Some researchers have interpreted this relationship causally: metalinguistic ability is a prerequisite for learning to read (e.g., Rozin & Gleitman, 1977; Ryan, 1980). Other interpretations reverse this order and indicate the relevance of reading to the solution of metalinguistic tasks (e.g., Ehri, 1975). In our framework, however, neither metalinguistic skills nor literacy skills are taken causally. Rather, both are promoted through development along the same two underlying skill components, namely cognitive control and analyzed linguistic knowledge. Consequently, the relationship between them is a reflection of their shared cognitive basis. This approach accounts as well for bidirectional relationships in which it is found that an advance in each of these domains, either naturally or through instructional intervention, has an effect on the advancement of the other (Goldstein, 1976).

The separation of the two skill components by means of the dimensions has been difficult partly because other factors obscure the commonality of various language tasks. The differences between conversation and reading, for example, would appear to be greater than their relative placements on two dimensions. Moreover, the development of more advanced language mastery from conversational uses of language to literate and metalinguistic uses of language confounds the two dimensions in that each of these domains requires an increase on both dimensions. The effect of this confounding is to give the appearance of a linear development that connects these domains, rather than improvement along two dimensions. Our claim, however, is that two dimensions nonetheless account for a substantial part of the description of the cognitive underpinnings of language skills.

Two sources of evidence provide a rationale for the separation of the dimensions. First, it is possible to independently manipulate the analyzed knowledge and cognitive control demands of a variety of tasks within a domain. For example, reading technical text is more difficult than reading familiar text primarily because the former requires higher levels of analyzed knowledge of language in order to reconstruct the meanings. Similarly, reading a particular passage for gist as opposed to specific fact, for example, requires different control procedures. The process of reading, then, can be shown to vary as a function of the analyzed knowledge and control demands of the particular task. Further examples of the separation of the two dimensions for various tasks are provided in the sections addressing the different language domains.

The second indication that the two dimensions are separate follows from the problems of first- and second-language learning by children and adults. There is a compelling temptation for researchers to compare processes responsible for first- and second-language learning (Cook, 1969; Ervin-Tripp, 1974; Krashen, 1981). Clearly, the fact that both refer to the internalization of a linguistic system makes the comparison natural, although most analyses go on to reveal inherent differences rather than emphasize similarities between the two. If the comparison focuses on the relationship between adult second-language and child first-language learning, then the incomparability of the two learner groups in terms of cognitive and linguistic sophistication undermines any reasonable comparison. Yet a decidedly unparsimonious view of cognition emerges from the position that the processes of acquiring a first and second language are fundamentally different. How then can we resolve the apparent similarities and differences?

What is similar between the two, we suggest, is that they are based on the same two cognitive dimensions we have described. Both require adequate facility with control and analyzed linguistic knowledge to perform in particular language domains. What is different about the two, however, is that the learner enjoys a different degree of competence with control and analyzed linguistic knowledge when dealing with the two languages. The major challenge for children learning a first language is the development of cognitive control to permit the child to enter more difficult domains of language use. The main control problem for a second-language learner is to execute the established operations with sufficient automaticity to meet the local task demands. Thus, if control has been mastered for a first language, the main control need for second-language learning is to develop automaticity. The major challenge for second-language learning, and in particular, adult second-language learning, is in the development of analyzed linguistic knowledge. This dimension is more specific to a particular language and as such is less transferable to a second language.

The Conversation Domain

The general placement of conversation skills in the framework is at a relatively low value for both the control and the analyzed knowledge dimensions. Variations in conversation types can be charted along these two dimensions to illustrate both the structure of the requisite skills and the development of the ability to participate in more challenging conversations by both first- and second-language learners.

Within conversation, we include all the uses of language that engage at least two interlocutors in an exchange of information. The overlapping area between reading–writing and conversation represents the range of language functions that are relatively informal but may involve written forms. Examples of these functions are personal letters, notes, and other accounts that are characterized more as written speech than as text per se. Although they typically presuppose a shared context, the absence of an interlocutor excludes these as conversation.

Analyzed Knowledge and the Need for Context

The extent of contextualization of a conversation varies as a function of the type of conversation and the relative status and familiarilty of the interlocutors. The decontextualization of conversation as a result of technical, unfamiliar, or academic topics, or unfamiliar interlocutors, tends to increase the linguistic demands for analyzed knowledge. The most contextualized conversation, and therefore the least demanding on analyzed linguistic knowledge, is said to represent children's early uses of language. In these situations, a sympathetic interlocutor interacts with a child about familiar topics in the *here and now* (Snow, 1979; Snow & Ferguson, 1977). The language is largely redundant to the meaning or intention being conveyed. Macnamara (1972) argued that such redundancy was critical to child language acquisition and that it was impossible to account for the child's formal progess with the language if the child did not first understand what utterances meant in their given context.

Language development, on this view, involves incorporating a relatively greater use of linguistic cues (Donaldson, 1978; Wells, 1981). Empirical evidence for the role of context in the child's early language comprehension has been demonstrated by studies in which linguistic and contextual information conflict with respect to meaning. Under these conditions, children interpret the meaning through nonlinguistic means (Clark, 1973; Donaldson & McGarrigle, 1974).

The opposite extreme of contextualization is reflected in an increased demand for analyzed linguistic knowledge. For conversations between strangers who (possibly) share no knowledge of the world or perspective, any commonality or mutual comprehensibility that emerges must be established by primarily linguistic means. Similarly, in discussion about abstract issues (e.g., philosophy or religion), theoretical concerns (e.g., the theories of language learning), or largely unfamiliar topics (e.g., nuclear physics) less can be assumed to be true, or to be shared. Correct interpretation of meanings in these cases is unlikely to be provided by contextual, or situational factors. The language, in short, must accurately represent the meaning. Thus, the code needs to be understood in such a way that particular meanings and shades of meaning can be created or interpreted through the manipulation of that code. The effect of using a conditional instead of a simple present tense verb, for example, might have serious consequences if the topic of conversation is political or religious convictions.

The general relationship between the amount of context provided in the situation and the amount of analyzed knowledge required by the learner is that a decrease in context requires an increase·in analyzed knowledge as a route to meaning. As the language becomes less redundant to the meaning, a more analyzed description of that language is necessary for the recovery of that meaning.

Control and the Need for Automaticity

The dimension of control makes a more uniform demand on conversation than does analyzed knowledge. Irrespective of the degree to which the conversation requires analyzed knowledge, similar constraints are imposed on a learner's control procedures. Conversations, that is, must be meaningful, and fluent interaction between the participants must be achieved. The selection and coordination of information is largely oriented to meaning although the meaning may incorporate a number of nonlinguistic sources. This focus on meaning is not typically difficult to achieve because that is likely to be the natural direction of attention in language use. The problem for the control dimension in conversation, rather, is the achievement of automaticity.

For adult fluent speakers of a language, the demand for automaticity is not often apparent, as the challenge for fluency is easily met. It is only in situations in which retrieval is temporarily disrupted that we can appreciate the usual ease with which the process is executed. The familiar tip-of-the-tongue experience illustrates this point (Brown & McNeill, 1966). In these cases, sufferers can often recover an enormous amount of detail about the word or the name sought (e.g., the number of syllables, the first letter, and the intonation pattern) without being able to retrieve the target word. With this wealth of linguistic description, the problem cannot be lack of analyzed linguistic knowledge; the problem can only be attributed to retrieval of existing knowledge. This interpretation is supported by the observation that such words or names are often effortlessly retrieved at a later time. Such special cases of control breakdown provide further evidence for the separability of the dimensions in conversation.

Similarly, temporary speech disfluencies sometimes reported for preschool children (Dalton & Hardcastle, 1977; Van Riper, 1972) can be interpreted in terms of the inadequacy of the control dimension. Although children may have sufficient linguistic and nonlinguistic knowledge to participate in certain complex conversations and indeed, want to participate in such exchanges, their control over that knowledge is not sufficiently automatic to produce fluent speech. The problem, then, is one of retrieval of knowledge. This disparity between cognitive intention and procedural execution of those intentions manifests itself as disfluent speech.

Conversations in a Second Language

The necessity to achieve automatic control is particularly evident for second-language learners. In the early stages of using a new language, the effort to retrieve existing knowledge of that language is great; responses require time to formulate, words are not always available on demand, structures do not emerge naturally. Practice using the language improves the learner's access to knowledge, and this improvement is reflected in greater fluency. The important distinction here is that fluency need not require any new or different information; rather, it requires more auto-maticity in the retrieval of existing information. Thus, a conversation is a particularly demanding task for an early second-language learner because of these demands for automatic retrieval. McLaughlin, Rossman, and McLeod (1982) have discussed the development of such automaticity for conversations in a second language from an information-processing per-spective.

Krashen (1981) distinguishes formal learning of the code of a second language from unconscious natural acquisition. He claims that the infor-mation gained through learning is useful only as a monitor to edit output emanating from acquired knowledge. He argues that over- or underuse of the monitor during conversation is detrimental to the interaction. Too little use may leave the utterance too poorly formed to be interpretable whereas too much use may simply take too long. Accordingly, he identifies three kinds of language learners—monitor overusers, monitor optimal-users, and monitor underusers. In our terms, optimal monitor-users select appropriately from information about both form and meaning. The mon-itor overuser who focuses excessively on form sacrifices automaticity and must direct attention back to the meaning. Accordingly, such a learner increases the metalinguistic component of an essentially linguistic con-versational task. The underuser, by contrast, needs to look more closely at the language. The problem in both cases is to deliberately focus atten-tion to one or the other as required. This selectivity and coordination is the responsibility of cognitive control. Hulstijn (1982) illustrates the effects exerted upon second-language monitoring by external manipulations of control requirements.

Language learners participating in conversations have at their dis-posal a number of strategies for overcoming their limitations in control or analyzed knowledge. While deficiencies in either of these dimensions may be remediated, the strategies themselves are applied primarily as a func-tion of control procedures. The learner compensates for gaps in fluency or knowledge by focusing elsewhere, involving other information, or ex-ecuting other routines. Research with adult second-language learners has shown the consistency and variety of these strategies in attempting to communicate information beyond their competence (Bialystok, 1983; Tar-one, 1980). The effect of such strategies is to allow language learners to communicate in situations that exceed their mastery of the language in terms of one of the underlying dimensions. While such strategies are cer-tainly germane to native language conversations, even by children, second-language learners should enjoy an advantage in that the requisite control procedures governing their use should be more advanced as a result of experience.

If conversations vary along these two dimensions, then increased skill with the cognitive-control and analyzed-knowledge aspects of the language should be reflected in the ability to participate in more-difficult conversations. In a study of adult learners of English as a second language (Bialystok, 1982), language tasks were assessed for their demands on high or low analyzed linguistic knowledge and high or low automaticity (control). This classification produced four groups of tests, three of which were conversational. These were administered to learners at two levels of study—intermediate and advanced. The results showed clear progression in the ability to solve the various tasks as a function of their placement in this classification. The advanced learners performed well on tasks requiring low analyzed knowledge, low automaticity, and those requiring a high value on one of the two dimensions but low on the other. They did poorly on tasks for which high levels of both analyzed knowledge and control were required. The intermediate learners could deal only with the tasks requiring low levels of skill on both dimensions. Thus, second-language learners demonstrated developing competence with the language in a manner consistent with the interpretation that the increased difficulty in tasks is describable by the two underlying dimensions. Which of the two dimensions is relatively more advanced for a particular learner likely varies as a function of method of instruction, opportunity for language use, and a variety of individual characteristics.

Conversations in both first and second languages, then, can be shown to vary along these two dimensions. More importantly, however, the learner's ability to perform skillfully in these conversational situations progresses in terms of increased values for the skill components on these two underlying dimensions.

The Reading–Writing Domain

Reading and writing, as we have argued, typically require higher degrees of cognitive control and analyzed linguistic knowledge than does conversation. The claim that these two requirements are the specific cognitive barriers to the acquisition of literacy skills is an elaboration of more general statements made earlier by researchers such as Cazden (1974), Mattingly (1972), and Vygotsky (1934/1962). Both reading and writing involve directing attention to linguistic forms and coordinating linguistic analysis with a meaning goal. Moreover, the absence of an interlocutor importantly distinguishes these activities from conversations (Bereiter & Scardamalia, 1982).

The primary difference between the two activities is that writing depends on more-detailed analyzed knowledge. The required degree of analyzed knowledge about sound–spelling relationships is greater when expressively spelling words than when receptively recognizing them. Similarly, vague notions of discourse structure may be adequate to interpret written text but are decidedly inadequate to produce it (Bereiter & Scardamalia, 1982).

Even though writing makes more demands on coordination as a productive task, the automaticity burden is less. While lower-level knowledge, such as spelling, quickly becomes automatized, higher-order aspects of language structure may be exploited with little pressure on automaticity. Further, advanced writing of lengthy, organized text tends to draw more on the strategic, coordinating, and monitoring aspects of control than does skilled reading. Nonetheless, while reading may generally demand slightly higher levels of control and writing slightly higher levels of knowledge, there is evidence that both are centrally implicated in these tasks. Bereiter and Scardamalia (1982) have offered a similar analysis for writing by arguing that two prerequisites for skilled writing are "having knowledge coded in ways that make it accessible, which would mean having it coded in some hierarchical way" and having "an executive procedure for bringing this knowledge into use at the right times and in the proper relation to other resource demands of the task" (p. 43). In our terms, the first condition is analyzed knowledge and the second is cognitive control. Their research has produced a variety of evidence documenting the special contribution of each to the attainment of skilled writing.

We assume that, apart from different levels of analyzed knowledge and control that are required, reading and writing are essentially equivalent in their cognitive basis. Because most of the interest in the development of language proficiency and metalinguistic awareness has concerned reading, the remainder of this discussion focuses on reading.

Cognitive Control and Analyzed Knowledge in Beginning Reading

With its dependence on structural analysis, the reading process draws on analyzed knowledge of many features of language. First, in order to master reading in an alphabetic script, an accessible concept of the phoneme and knowledge of the complex relationships between phonemes and spellings are necessary. Because the segmentation of speech into phonemes tends to be a relatively late cognitive achievement and because its link with alphabetic reading is so obvious, phonological development has been of central interest to reading researchers (Liberman, Shankweiler, Liberman, Fowler, & Fischer, 1977; Rozin & Gleitman, 1977). Also necessary for reading is an analyzed concept of word, including the arbitrary relationship between a form and its meaning and the separate identity of function words. Similarly, an analyzed concept of sentence is involved in extracting meaning from text. These concepts, too, are poorly established among prereaders and beginning readers (Ehri, 1979; Ryan, 1980; Ryan & Ledger, 1982). Finally, as reading becomes more isolated from concrete experience and familiar contexts, comprehension also involves analyzed knowledge of the typical structure of texts (e.g., narrative vs. expository) and of the manner in which they draw upon world knowledge (Spiro, 1980; Stein & Glenn, 1979).

The control function for the reader is to retrieve the relevant analyzed knowledge of the language forms and coordinate this information in order to reconstruct the meaning of the printed message. Children learning to read appear to progress through three major stages: (1) realizing that print conveys meaning in much the same way as speech; (2) attending to printed features (e.g., letters, letter combinations, spaces between words, capitalization, punctuation), relating these to linguistic features, and interpreting them; and (3) incorporating the attention to forms with the goal of extracting meaning. Stage 1 is analyzed knowledge; Stage 2 involves both analyzed knowledge and control; and Stage 3 is an achievement of cognitive control.

In terms of the three stages, preschoolers who read their storybooks on the basis of book-supported memorization are exhibiting the first important stage of beginning reading. Indeed, the important influence of the home upon early reading in school (Wells, 1981) may largely relate to the effects of home experiences on this first stage. The important discovery for the child in this stage is that the symbols on the page are nonarbitrarily related to the language that can be read from them (Downing, 1979). Vygotsky (1978) in fact, reports that an important development in young preschool children occurs when they record information through what appears to be meaningless squiggles but in fact are systematic and interpretable symbols to the child.

It is all the more important for children to learn the meaningfulness of print in the preschool years because school readiness and beginning reading programs concentrate on Stage 2. This second stage, in which the linguistic features of print are examined (Downing, 1979), remains significant for beginning or mature readers whenever difficulty is encountered, as in sounding out new words. The essential feature is that form is the centre of attention. Inadequate automaticity in this aspect of control and, to anticipate Stage 3, inadequate attention to meaning, result in breakdowns such as the inability to blend sounds into words.

Stage 3 is often considered to be a natural consequence of Stage 2—the reader, that is, automatically focuses back on meaning. Yet, the existence of poor comprehenders, whose understanding of text falls far short of their ability to identify all the forms (Golinkoff, 1976; Ryan, 1981), and the tendency of poor readers to describe reading as form-oriented rather than meaning-oriented (Canney & Winograd, 1979; Paris & Myers, 1981) attest to the difficulty of Stage 3.

The automaticity of control is also crucial for reading. Readers not only must coordinate attention to forms and the reconstruction of meanings, but also must process the forms sufficiently quickly and smoothly to allow space in working memory for retaining the evolving meanings (LaBerge & Samuels, 1974; Perfetti & Hogaboam, 1975). Hence, readers may be hampered in their achievement of Stage 3 (i.e., real reading) by nonautomatic recognition of the forms, by lack of awareness of the need to relate forms back to meaning, or by difficulty in coordinating forms with meaning.

Application to Readiness and Beginning-Reading Instruction

Subskills instruction for prereaders as well as readiness assessments tends to emphasize analyzed linguistic knowledge of sound–symbol relationships and attention to linguistic forms. Continuing the emphasis on Stage 2, many beginning-reading programs focus on knowledge of and attention to these formal relationships rather than on the coordination of forms and meanings. The long-standing debate about whether to teach beginning reading via the look–say, controlled vocabulary, or phonics methods centers around this issue (see Chall, 1967). The first approach bypasses the problem by providing analyzed knowledge of word–sound relationships, thus requiring little control but restricting considerably the size of the vocabulary. In contrast, the latter two methods stress building up children's analyzed knowledge about spelling–sound relationships but require greater control procedures to use that knowledge to generate words.

Because explicit language rules can only be incorporated if the child's knowledge base is sufficiently structured, the latter two methods additionally place a greater burden on analyzed knowledge. Thus, explicit phonics instruction for very young learners often yields only rote learning of the rules. Usually the application of phonics-rule knowledge to reading requires extensive control because the phonic learning context is often unrelated to meaning. Texts composed so that the sound–spelling regularities can easily be inferred, however, are more like word-learning exercises than reading. In all of these approaches, decoding words is the focus while the coordinating aspect of reading represented by Stage 3 is assumed to follow automatically.

As with conversations, increased contextualization assists decoding by guiding the recognition of words and interpretation of the text with less need for analyzed linguistic knowledge. The language-experience approach, in which children learn to read texts that they have dictated, provides such familiar context and language that reading for meaning can be achieved without much attention to form or dependence on analyzed knowledge. As such, the approach promotes the development of a Stage 1 understanding of the reading process.

Although pictures are generally thought to provide helpful supporting contexts for reading, some research suggests that young and poor readers show less accurate word recognition and comprehension for text with accompanying pictures than without (see discussion by Schallert, 1980). These findings have been interpreted in terms of an attentional hypothesis—the more readily understood pictures distract these less-skilled readers from the text. Therefore in the presence of compelling pictures, poor readers do not achieve the Stage 2 level of focus on forms. This point is further considered in the discussion of poor readers in the following section. Good readers, or those with Stage 3 skills, may benefit from pictures, in that they promote the coordination of forms and meanings.

The transition between Stages 2 and 3 levels of control can be examined by the use of text composed of word symbols such as pictographs or logographs rather than traditional spellings. These have been employed to assess and teach the coordinating skills normally associated with Stage 3 reading before the sound–spelling relationships have been learned (Farnham-Diggory, 1967; Woodcock, Clark, & Davies, 1969). Ryan and collaborators have developed a pictograph-sentence memory task that requires children to notice that a sequence of pictograph symbols forms a meaningful sentence and to process its meaning for later recall. This task provides the opportunity to examine whether prereaders and young beginning readers have sufficient analyzed knowledge of words and sentences and sufficient control over these units to integrate the meanings of nonalphabetic symbols. Moreover, brief strategy training procedures permit enhancement of Stage 3 cognitive control without any modification of analyzed knowledge (Ledger & Ryan, 1982; Ryan & Ledger, 1982). This paradigm illustrates the potential for examining analyzed knowledge and control skills separately.

Application to Poor Readers

The present framework has implications for the problems of poor readers with respect to four issues: (1) causal links between metalinguistic deficiencies and poor reading; (2) overuse versus underuse of linguistic context; (3) deficiencies of control versus knowledge in story recall; and (4) study skills. Finally, the failure of advanced readers to become speed readers is addressed.

Comparisons of good and poor readers have consistently revealed striking differences in phonological skills. Although control and knowledge have not been systematically differentiated in previous research, deficiencies among poor readers along both dimensions seem to be involved (Fox & Routh, 1980; Liberman et al., 1977; Tallal, 1980). Although smaller in magnitude, similar contrasts in orally presented metalinguistic tests of lexical and syntactic awareness have also been observed (Ehri, 1979; Forrest-Pressley & Waller, 1984; Ryan & Ledger, 1983). Although these metalinguistic differences have often been assigned causality for reading problems, we interpret them in terms of the overlapping demands upon analyzed knowledge and control for the two domains. Thus metalinguistic exercises that promote clear development along either of these dimensions should enhance reading, and successful reading experiences should further promote development, particularly in analyzed knowledge (see Goldstein, 1976).

The comprehension difficulties of poor readers for text composed of relatively easy words has been explained both as overuse of semantic and syntactic cues (Perfetti & Hogaboam, 1975) and underuse of these contextual cues (Ryan, 1981). In terms of the three stages in control of the reading process, overuse of linguistic context to compensate for weak decoding skills would be viewed as a reversion to Stage 1, in which attention to linguistic forms is insufficient, whereas underuse would be viewed as failure to progress from Stage 2 to Stage 3.

Research on listening and reading shows developmental differences in children's sensitivity to the typical components of simple stories (i.e., story grammar), as well as deficit in this area among poor readers as compared to good readers (Dickenson & Weaver, 1979; Short & Ryan, in press; Stein & Glenn, 1979). As with all group comparison studies, one cannot determine whether weaker story comprehension performance of the less-skilled readers is due to less analyzed knowledge of story structure or to less ability to utilize that knowledge appropriately. However, studies that manipulate either the amount of knowledge or the degree of control can illuminate reasons for the performance differences. For example, Short &

Ryan (1984) have shown that three sessions of training in a self-instructional strategy based on story grammar can enable less-skilled readers to achieve the level of story comprehension exhibited by skilled readers, presumably by having increased cognitive control. In contrast, a study training students in analyzed knowledge of discourse markers allowed those students to write texts containing more such markers than used by a control group, but the texts of the trained group were no more coherent. That is, they had increased knowledge but not increased control (Scardamalia & Paris, in press).

Some important study skills require levels of analyzed linguistic knowledge greater than that of the typical poor reader. For example, noting that good readers spontaneously use underlining and notetaking when asked to study a text, Brown and Smiley (1978) instructed poorer readers to underline or to take notes on the important information while studying texts. However, recall for the important ideas was not facilitated; indeed, examination of the underlining and notes indicated that the students did not focus on the important information. Other studies (e.g., Smiley, Oakley, Worthen, Campione, & Brown, 1977) have supported the conclusion that less-skilled readers are not proficient in discriminating important from unimportant information. Without this analyzed knowledge, control support conditions that presume it (e.g., underlining, notetaking, outlining, and skimming) can have only minimal impact.

Whereas the cognitive control aspects of skimming are readily teachable to readers with adequate knowledge to identify important information, training in speed reading alone rarely yields long-term benefits, even for readers with advanced linguistic knowledge (Geva, 1980; Harris & Sipay, 1980). In contrast to other advanced study skills, speed reading is difficult because of control demands. The adoption of apparently unnatural strategies to extract information from unexpected places in the text is required. Old habits of directing attention from word to word or according to the meaning must be dismantled, and new habits of directing attention according to a meaning-irrelevant pattern (e.g., following one's finger along a zig-zag pattern down the page) must be developed. Because the focus is upon speed, the new habits must be practiced to a high level of automaticity as well. Few readers practice speed-reading skills sufficiently to achieve the automaticity necessary for maintenance of this new approach to reading.

In summary, it is generally difficult to isolate the responsibility of either cognitive control or analyzed knowledge in problem reading. Descriptions that trace the source of difficulty to some type of accessing problem, for example, studies reported by Barron (1981), remain ambiguous with respect to the cause of the difficulty. Failure to retrieve the necessary information at any level (phonological, lexical, conceptual) may be due either to an inadequately analyzed representation of that information, or to the absence of necessary control procedures to either search in the appropriate knowledge source or retrieve the knowledge that exists. In both cases, failure would be attributed to the inability to access the relevant information, but in each case, that failure has a very different origin.

Reading in a Second Language

According to the analysis offered in the present framework, a child must progress through three stages to become a reader. Once this has been accomplished, the application of the process to a new language presents no serious challenge. To the extent that adequate control may be assumed, reading in a second language requires only that the learner establish adequate analyzed knowledge of the language structure—in particular, phoneme–grapheme correspondences and grammatical structures. While this admittedly is a far higher level of analyzed linguistic knowledge of the second language than that necessary for conversation, a learner who has already mastered reading in one language does not have the initial problem of establishing such analyzed concepts as phonemes, words, and sentences.

In the absence of fully elaborated analyzed knowledge of a language, a skilled reader learning to read a second language may find contextualization useful in simplifying the task, in that it reduces the role of analyzed linguistic knowledge as the route to meaning. Similarly, the lack of adequate automaticity may introduce problems in control and may revert the reader to Stage 2 in the reading process (e.g., Favreau, Komoda, & Segalowitz, 1980). The reversion to Stage 2 would presumably be more likely in reading languages that use a different script (alphabet) from that characterizing the learner's first language. In these cases, decoding requires more attention to form, and the possibility of losing track of meaning is increased. Thus, while there may be initial setbacks in both cognitive control and analyzed knowledge, a skilled reader should have little difficulty in becoming biliterate if she or he is bilingual.

Children learn to read in two languages in a variety of educational programs, but for our purposes, two are particularly pertinent: immersion programs for language majority children and vernacular programs for language minority children. In both these cases, the development of reading skills in the child's home language and in the school language is relevant to our framework.

In French immersion programs in Canada, children whose home language is English are instructed for all or part of their education in French (see Swain & Lapkin, 1982). Thus, reading and literacy skills in general are introduced in French, although the child's usual language for communication is English. English is not introduced as a subject until approximately Grade 3, at which time reading in English begins. Achievement in French reading skills, for these students, is equivalent to the achievement reported for monolingual French students who have learned to read French in regular school programs (Cziko, 1976; Tucker, 1975).

The more interesting problem, however, is the transfer of these skills to English when it is introduced as a subject. Results of evaluation studies have shown that by Grade 4 the English literacy skills of French immersion students are equivalent to those of the English monolingual students of the same age (Cziko, 1976; Lambert & Tucker, 1972; Tucker, 1975). Thus, although reading and indeed, all academic uses of language, have been acquired through French, immersion students read English as well as students educated in English.

Our interpretation of this finding follows from the relative command by the immersion students of both the cognitive control and analyzed knowledge dimensions. First, because they could already read in French, we claim that their control processes were adequate to support reading in general. Further, it is likely the case that learning to read in a second language additionally boosted their control. Second, although their education has been conducted in French, their analyzed knowledge of English was adequate to support reading. Two factors are likely responsible for the sophistication of their analyzed knowledge of English. First, basic linguistic principles and universal aspects of language (e.g., the concepts of phoneme and word) would have easily transferred from French to English. Second, their home background is typically middle-socioeconomic status (SES), where education and literacy are highly valued. Home experience in which parents read to children and in which written language is a means of interpersonal communication (Wells, 1981) tends to promote higher literacy skills in children because, we would argue, it develops analyzed knowledge of the language.

A controversial issue in immersion education at present is the treatment of slow or learning-disabled students. One view suggests that these students are better educated in English-only programs where literacy skills are developed in their first language (Trites & Price, 1978). The opposite approach claims that (1) literacy skills are developed to approximately the same level of competence in second-language instruction, but students have the benefit of some mastery of an additional language and (2) the exclusion or expulsion of these students from immersion programs is potentially damaging for social and psychological reasons (Bruck, 1978). From our perspective, the development of the control procedures needed for reading can proceed for any language in which there is adequate analyzed linguistic knowledge and then can be easily transferred to other languages. Thus, the specific language in which literacy is expected or taught is less important than the attempt to promote the required cognitive control.

The second kind of bilingual education is for children whose home language differs from the usual school language, but the school language is the socially valued language. Immigrant children, for example, are typically in this position of home–school language conflict. Such children have often experienced poor school success and relatively low levels of literacy.

Recently, programs have been developed to educate such children in the vernacular (e.g., Skutnabb-Kangas & Toukomaa, 1976). In one program, Navajo-speaking children in New Mexico have been introduced to reading through Navajo, rather than English, as had traditionally been the case (Rosier & Holm, 1980). English was introduced as a subject later in school. The results have shown not only that Navajo skills were well-developed, but also that English reading skills were at grade norm level by the end of elementary school. This contrasts sharply with the traditional patterns of low literacy skills in either language that have consistently been reported for Navajo children in English-language schools.

How, then, can we reconcile the apparent contradiction between the effects of home–school language switch in the French immersion and the Navajo situation? Why, that is, does learning to read in the school language create no difficulty for French immersion students but serious problems for Navajo students? An important difference between the two groups is in their initial mastery of the two dimensions—the Navajo students had little analyzed knowledge to appreciate the value of printed text and little experience manipulating language to develop control. Thus, the first task was to establish these minimal values, and this was achieved more easily in the language with which they were most familiar. French immersion students had already advanced beyond this point for both dimensions, thus they were more ready to learn to read.

To summarize, reading requires moderate levels of both cognitive control and analyzed linguistic knowledge. If one or both are not developed to this level, then the student will experience problems in learning to read. This is the case with the poor readers in both regular programs and bilingual programs. If development along these two dimensions is adequate, then reading is not only easy to learn, but also easy to transfer to other languages for which adequate analyzed knowledge is available.

The Metalinguistic Domain

Within the present framework, metalinguistic tasks are those language tasks that demand high values both for analyzed linguistic knowledge and for control to direct deliberate attention to language forms. As with the definitions of metalinguistic ability given earlier, tasks used to assess metalinguistic awareness are highly diverse. This diversity creates the impression of conceptual confusion and impedes the construction of a coherent concept of metalinguistic skill or the development of a prototypical test of its presence. Scribner and Cole (1981) conclude that metalinguistic skill cannot be considered a "general orientation to language or a unitary set of skills" but rather a "highly diversified array of knowledge and skills" (p. 156). The two skill components have the potential for systematizing the variety of metalinguistic tasks that have been used and for consolidating a more coherent concept of the nature of metalinguistic ability.

Classification of Metalinguistic Tasks within the Framework

The value of the present model is illustrated here with the array of tasks used to assess and promote awareness of sentence structure. Even though all of these tasks tap relatively high levels of analyzed knowledge and control, they can be divided into three major categories on the basis of their relative emphasis: (1) analyzed knowledge; (2) cognitive control; and (3) coordination of both knowledge and control. Within each of these categories, examples are provided of task manipulations that place further burdens on either control or analyzed knowledge. The same type of analysis could be conducted for lexical and phonological tasks.

Evaluation and Explanation: Emphasis on Analyzed Linguistic Knowledge

Evaluating sentences and providing explanations about grammatical structure are activities that focus on specific aspects of analyzed linguistic knowledge. The most typical tests of grammatical sensitivity have been those involving judgments of sentence acceptability and corrections of unacceptable sentences (Gleitman et al., 1972; Hakes, 1980; Ryan & Ledger, 1983). Most researchers using these tasks have focused on the knowledge dimension. The following tasks can be ranked in terms of their demands for analyzed knowledge from moderate to very high: (1) judgment of acceptability, (2) location of an unacceptable part of a sentence, (3) correction, and (4) explanation. Performance on all of these tasks presupposes the same degree of control—that is, the basic ability to focus attention on the structure rather than the meaning of sentences. Once children have developed sufficient cognitive control to perform the task, then they can display their analyzed knowledge on any of these tasks.

The control demands of the judgment and correction tasks can be enhanced by increasing the saliency of meaning as a competitor for attention. A real-world example of this manipulation involves the difference between proofreading an unfamiliar text and proofreading a paper that we have just written. Proofreading for spelling and typing errors is always difficult because it violates the usual search for meaning. However, such proofreading for our own papers poses a special difficulty because our attention is so strongly drawn to judgments of meaning. Presentation of meaningful and anomalous sentences for judgment of grammatical acceptability similarly increase the difficulty of maintaining attention to sentence form. The same change in control demands can be achieved with a correction task in which anomalous, ungrammatical sentences (e.g., "All the day long, the cat bark in the yard.") can be made either meaningful or grammatical (Bialystok, 1984).

Other types of sentence evaluation address ambiguity, synonymy, and paraphrase. Judgments of ambiguity and the ability to provide two different paraphrases for deep- and surface-structure ambiguities require both analyzed knowledge and control (Hirsh-Pasek, Gleitman, & Gleitman, 1978; Kessel, 1970; Shultz & Pilon, 1973). Compared to the usual grammaticality judgments, ambiguity tasks involve more cognitive control, in that the first meaning found must be ignored while the structure is analyzed for another meaning. Judgments of synonymy (Beilin, 1975; Hakes, 1980) involve ignoring superficial differences in structure to examine structural relationships, whereas paraphrase (Menyuk, 1981) involves selection of alternative surface forms to express precisely the meaning of a given sentence. Even though all these tasks focus on meaning, they are metalinguistic in requiring specific attention to structure in the solution of the task. Yet, the strong support of meaning for paraphrase and synonymy suggests that these tasks may only be interesting for learners with limited cognitive control (e.g., children below the age of 8) or with limited analyzed knowledge of the language (e.g., second-language learners).

At the level of explanation, traditional school grammar has assumed the ability to attend to structure and has emphasized analyzed knowledge in tasks such as learning definitions of parts of speech, identifying the subject and predicate within a sentence, and sentence diagramming. Other types of school tasks that stress analyzed knowledge are defining a sentence, producing a sentence, and producing instances of particular structures, such as a passive sentence or a dangling participle. As well, explicit rules are often involved in second-language and literacy instruction. Finally, the discipline of linguistics is devoted to the articulation of systematic rules of language structure.

Sentence Repetition and Substitution: Emphasis on Cognitive Control

The grammatical activities presented here focus on the control dimension. Manipulating sentences can vary in control difficulty from the relatively low burden involved in repeating meaningful sentences to the rather high burden involved in making anomalous substitutions in sentences for grammatical purposes.

Repeating individual sentences makes only limited demands on either knowledge or control because attention to meaning supports the repetition of grammatical structures. Yet, various manipulations can raise the need for control and/or analyzed knowledge. For example, verbatim repetition of slightly deviant sentences is more difficult (Beilin, 1975; Menyuk, 1969; Scholl & Ryan, 1980) because control is required to suppress the natural tendency to normalize and because specific knowledge of that grammatical feature is also tapped. Similarly, using grammatical structure to recall nonsense sentences or anomalous sentences (Entwisle & Frasure, 1974; Weinstein & Rabinovitch, 1971) stresses the control dimension (i.e., attending to structure in the absence of meaning) while depending on knowledge of typical sentence structures.

Representing the other end of the control dimension from sentence repetition, a task developed by Ben-Zeev (1977) requires much attentional control. In her word-substitution task, one must substitute a given word for a target word in a sentence even though the resulting string may violate semantic and syntactic rules (e.g., substitute "spaghetti" for "they" in "They are good children."). A task similar in format (i.e., substituting words in sentences) but quite different in its emphasis on analyzed knowledge is the kind of part-of-speech task found on language-learning aptitude tests (Carroll & Sapon, 1959, 1967). In these tasks, one must identify the word or phrase in one sentence that plays the same role as a target within another sentence (e.g., identify the word serving the same role in "Children like dogs" as "potatoes" in "Farmers grow potatoes").

Given the contrast between these two types of difficult tasks, we can generate variations that alter the burdens on control and knowledge. For example, some knowledge about parts of speech can be required in a sentence-substitution task by asking that a child substitute "helpful" for the appropriate word in a target sentence (e.g., "They are good children."). The more that the resulting sentence deviates from semantic rules or world knowledge, the more control would be involved. Moreover, in the original task, comparison of reasonable substitutions with nonsense substitutions would provide specific information about the locus of a child's control difficulties. Control difficulties could be further increased by providing a compelling alternative location for the new word within the target sentence (e.g., substitute "smart" for "long" in "The cat has long legs."). These modifications illustrate the value of separating the control and analyzed knowledge dimensions.

Within this category also, we can place school tasks that involve changing sentences to meet particular structural constraints. In the pattern practice exercises used in second language instruction, the student must ignore the present sentence meaning while making substitutions which maintain the grammatical structure. In transformational exercises (such as changing a declarative into an interrogative or a passive into an active sentence), the student must maintain most of the meaning while altering the structure. Likewise, sentence combining exercises require students to preserve meaning, but the structural alteration involves integrating several sentence meanings into the structure of a single sentence.

Sentence Completion: Coordinating Form and Meaning

The tasks within this category require participants to create a well-formed sentence from some sentence ingredients. Task difficulty is a function of the distance between the presented information and the target sentence. These activities require the coordination of analyzed linguistic knowledge and attention to grammatical structure. Consequently, these are the metalinguistic tasks most like reading and writing.

Sentence segmentation (Klein, Klein, & Bertino, 1974; Ryan, Mc-Namara, & Kenney. 1977) involves identifying word boundaries in a sentence printed without spaces. This task requires some limited attention to sentence structure as a means of identifying the hidden sentence. The frequently used cloze task necessitates slightly more attention to structure as well as coordination of structure and meaning to complete the partial sentence.

At a more challenging level, solving a sentence anagram (i.e., reordering a set of words to form a meaningful sentence) requires substantial knowledge about the possible structures and possible roles of particular words. Also, a moderate degree of control is involved in coordinating attention to the forms and meanings of the words, the possible structures, and the possible sentence meanings. The analyzed knowledge requirement can be reduced by providing cues to the sentence structure of the target sentence (e.g., by having all the sentences with the same structure or by priming the structure of each sentence with a practice sentence). On the other hand, support for the control aspects can be provided through interspersed hints regarding the need to find a likely verb, to try out various subject nouns, to check the meaningfulness of evolving sentence parts, and to reconsider previous decisions if an evolving sentence is nonsense or in training a systematic strategy to follow these steps (Weaver, 1979). The control burden could be increased by presenting ambiguous words in different parts of speech across successive problems (e.g., *fair* as noun vs. *fair* as adjective). Solving a sentence anagram for an anomalous or nonsense sentence increases the burden primarily on structural knowledge.

This classification serves to clarify the nature and variation of metalinguistic skills by describing the ways in which the three task groupings draw on the two underlying dimensions differently. Moreover, our discussion has highlighted the ways in which new tasks can be constructed so that individual differences along these two dimensions can be examined more carefully. Finally, this organizational scheme permits more-specific predictions regarding relationships between metalinguistic skills and other linguistic and cognitive achievements. For example, particularly strong relationships would be expected for (1) formal learning of a foreign language and those tasks emphasizing analyzed linguistic knowledge, (2) cognitive measures of decentering and attentional control and those tasks emphasizing cognitive control, and (3) reading–writing skills and coordination tasks. Van Kleeck's (1982) analysis of metalinguistic tasks in terms of cognitive strategies does provide an elaboration of the control requirements of diverse tasks consistent with our framework. However, it does not address developmental increases in analyzed knowledge that occur simultaneously.

Awareness of a Second Language

If metalinguistic ability is considered in terms of the control required to examine a structured representation of language, then aspects of that ability should override its application to a particular language. Moreover, the process involved in learning a second language should promote a learner's placement along both these dimensions, increasing again the basis of metalinguistic ability. Thus, metalinguistic skill should be higher for two types of learners. First, competent (presumably adult) speakers of one language who are in the process of learning another language should find metalinguistic problems in that new language fairly easy to solve. The primary restriction is the extent to which the learner has analyzed knowledge of the new language. Second, learners who know two languages should solve metalinguistic problems more effectively than monolingual speakers of either language. This effect should be especially apparent for children who are becoming bilingual at the same time that they are initially developing along the control and analyzed-knowledge dimensions.

Studies have examined the ability both of adults and of children to make metalinguistic judgments in a second language. Some, notably those with children, also compare performance to that of monolingual peers, providing an opportunity to better isolate the influence of bilingualism on the developing metalinguistic function.

Studies of adult metalinguistic ability include judgments both of an artificial language and of a language being learned. For the first, adults were exposed to an artificial language comprising letter strings generated from a complex grammar (Reber, 1976). Although subjects had very little knowledge of the grammar, and indeed, in most experimental conditions were not aware that it existed, high accuracy was reported both for judging grammaticality (Reber, 1976) and for solving anagrams (Reber & Lewis, 1977). The ability to generate any of the rules of the system, however, was very poor, even when performance indicated that the learners had in fact been using the correct rules implicitly. In our terms, the two tasks, judgment–anagram and rule articulation differ in the amount of analyzed knowledge required, the latter being more demanding. The adult subjects, however, had established adequate control procedures to perform well in the metalinguistic tasks to the extent permitted by their degree of analyzed knowledge.

The second series of studies elicited grammaticality judgments from adult native speakers of English in the early stages of learning French as a second language (Bialystok, 1979). Three types of judgments were required: (1) distinguish correct from incorrect sentences, (2) locate the form class containing the error (e.g., the adjective is wrong), and (3) identify the rule violated (e.g., adjective should follow the noun). While control demands are similar, the conditions differ in the extent of analyzed knowledge required. The results indicated significant differences in learners' ability to succeed in these three conditions, even though errors in all conditions were based on precisely the same rules. Learners' knowledge of those rules was not sufficiently analyzed to provide the solutions for the more demanding knowledge conditions.

These results show that in spite of being at fairly low levels of formal study in a new language, the learners could nonetheless make difficult metalinguistic judgments. In fact, in the study using an artificial language, there was no formal learning at all. The extent to which such judgments could be made depended on the amount of analyzed knowledge required for the solution.

Finally, in the study by Bialystok the learners of French who knew at least one other language performed better in the judgment tasks than did the learners who knew only English. This advantage is likely a reflection of our claim that experience with other languages increases cognitive control. No doubt some advantage in analyzed linguistic knowledge from greater exposure to language universals also occurred. The more important test of this effect, however, is in the examination of bilingual and monolingual children for their ability to solve metalinguistic problems.

In our discussion of the transfer of metalinguistic ability for adults, we have assumed that the task is easy because adults have achieved sufficient cognitive control to solve the problems and are limited primarily by their restricted analyzed knowledge of the new language. Children, however, have two problems to overcome: (1) analyzed knowledge, as for the adults, but also (2) establishment of the control procedures to deal with the task. The experience of learning a second language in childhood may have its greatest impact on cognitive control. As Vygotsky (1962/1934) argued, bilingual children learn earlier about the arbitrariness that connects words with meanings, and so should be better equipped to retrieve only one or the other of these as required by the task. Thus, children learning two languages may have greater cognitive control than monolingual children, thereby providing the foundation for metalinguistic ability before it is evident in their monolingual peers. If so, then the particular advantage for bilingual children should be in those metalinguistic tasks requiring high cognitive control.

Studies examining the relative metalinguistic proficiency of monolingual and bilingual children have reported mixed results. For example, evidence of the superiority of bilingual children on metalinguistic tasks has been reported for middle-SES (socioeconomic status) children by Ben-Zeev (1977) and Ianco-Worrall (1972). A study of lower-SES bilingual children performing the same tasks indicated a weaker bilingual advantage (Ben-Zeev, 1977).

The explanation of this interaction between SES and metalinguistic ability may lie in the relative levels of control and analyzed knowledge for the two populations. Middle-SES children, as we claimed earlier for reading, likely have a fairly analyzed conception of language because of their home experiences. The effect of bilingualism for these children, then, is to promote cognitive control to the point where they are able to solve metalinguistic problems. Thus, all else being equal, bilingual children perform better than monolingual children when their analyzed knowledge is sufficient to allow the cognitive control to advance. The lower-SES children, however, likely did not have adequate analyzed knowledge on which to base the possibility of enriched cognitive control, so little advantage of bilingualism was evident. This lack of analyzed knowledge makes the tasks difficult for these children in much the same way that the adults in the studies reported earlier found certain tasks difficult when the demands on analyzed knowledge were excessive.

This interaction stresses the need to consider two dimensions as the foundation of these special language skills. The solution to metalinguistic problems requires high levels of both cognitive control and analyzed linguistic knowledge. As we have seen for both adults and children learning two languages, the inadequacy of one of these prevents the solution to certain kinds of problems. Advantages of bilingualism disappear for learners who have not developed sufficient analyzed knowledge of any language to form the basis for the ability to develop, or for problems that require a high level of language-specific analyzed knowledge for their solution.

Summary and Conclusions

Value of the Framework

The framework we have described posits that two cognitive skill components, each of which develops along a continuous dimension, are required to solve a variety of problems. We have argued that the elaboration of these skill components is responsible for the systematic development of language skills for both first and second languages. We expect that similar analyses could indicate the extent to which their development is also responsible for an increasing ability to solve other types of cognitive problems.

The two dimensions used to construct the framework are based on ordinary developmental factors that are included in a variety of theoretical perspectives. By abstracting these common dimensions, it is possible to relate such disparate developmental paradigms as Piagetian, neo-Piagetian, and information-processing views. Each of these paradigms includes a crucial developmental ability that is at least to some degree captured by our two dimensions. Piagetian views, for example, require structured (analyzed) knowledge for operational thought and the development of control procedures to permit decentering from a single perspective and coordinating information. Neo-Piagetian views stress the importance of automaticity in working memory as well as the eleaboration of knowledge to support solutions to problems. Information-processing models assume an executive function (control) that is responsible for selecting and coordinating information in problem solving, and they emphasize the role of automaticity in facilitating higher levels of control.

An important implication of the framework is that it confers a systematicity upon a variety of seemingly unrelated tasks. By abstracting two common cognitive underpinnings of language tasks, it is possible to examine the structure of these tasks in general and to understand the interrelationships among particular tasks. Thus, rather than assume a moderate but equivalent relationship to exist among tests of various language skills, the framework makes more precise predictions about which tasks are indeed more similar.

The structure of language skill has been particularly controversial in two areas: (1) the relationship between literacy and metalinguistic skills and (2) the relationship between first- and second-language performance. For the former, the framework obviates the difficult causality issue by attributing responsibility for both skills to common developmental factors. In view of mixed evidence for the primacy of one domain or the other, an underlying factor explanation appears more parsimonious. The advantage of the present framework is that the two factors not only provide a basis for these two relatively sophisticated language skills but also incorporate the skills required for the informal or conversational uses of language.

An adequate description of the relationship between first and second language skills has been equally evasive. The literature reports instances of facilitation, nonfacilitation, and even, in some cases, interference of one language upon performance in another language. Here, too, interpretation of the variety of findings has been hindered by the lack of a clear understanding of the relationships among the various tasks. Again, more specific predictions can be made by approaching the question of the interaction between languages in the solution to specific linguistic problems in terms of the relationships among the problems. The structure of language problems in terms of the two underlying dimensions suggests, for example, that high control skills should transfer quite readily to other languages whereas tasks based on highly analyzed knowledge are likely to remain more language specific. Thus, language learners should benefit most directly from previous language experience when operating in domains requiring high control.

A second implication of the framework is that it provides a means of analyzing the concept of language skill. By identifying two components of that skill, it is possible to state more precisely the nature of that skill and possibly its relationship to other skills. Thus, instead of an abstract or vague notion of verbal ability, which is apparently implicated in all language tasks and presumably improves with age, it is possible to state at least two components of that ability. The improvement of verbal ability in these terms is a reflection of cognitive achievements along two dimensions. Explanations of language (and cognitive) development are enhanced when the global concept of ability is explicated into precise cognitive constituents. In addition, this analytic concept of ability serves again to discriminate among language tasks, in that the components of this verbal ability are differentially implicated in their solution.

Finally, the framework provides a coherent means of explaining improvement or development. As we have seen, each of the dimensions is consistent with a well-established tradition of developmental psychology. The spirit of the dimensions captures essential aspects of both cognitive and information-processing views of development. The elaboration of Piagetian-type schemata, for example, provides an important part of the description of the development of analyzed knowledge. Similarly, the development of executive functions as described by Flavell, Piaget, and others is central to the development of the control function. Thus, the assumption that the child improves in the two directions indicated by the dimensions is supported by a wealth of developmental literature that documents just such improvement. Accordingly, the nature and means by which the development necessary to the operation of the framework proceeds is compatible with current developmental principles.

Directions for Future Research

Certain research directions are suggested because the framework clarifies the interrelationships that exist among language tasks. Moreover, because of the cognitive underpinnings of the framework, the ways in which the framework may be applied to the study of cognitive problems are also outlined. Because the framework defines the relationships among tasks in terms of two underlying dimensions, it should be possible to make precise predictions about the relative difficulty of particular tasks. Tasks that require more control, for example, should be more difficult than those that place lower demands on this dimension. The hypotheses concerning relative task difficulty, therefore, should be tested. Such studies, which could yield a coherent description of a variety of tasks, would appear especially valuable in the area of metalinguistic skills.

The study of tasks with respect to the framework can incorporate important task characteristics such as modality and means of presentation.

Alternative modes of presenting tasks can be seen to have differential effects upon control and knowledge. For example, modality primarily affects control—oral presentation stresses automaticity and meaning more than written presentation, which more naturally elicits attention to structure. Manipulating factors such as explicitness of instructions, degree of practice, and kinds of hints reduces the burden on control, but typically does not affect the need for analyzed knowledge. Multiple-choice format for responding, on the other hand, taxes knowledge less than does a more open-ended format. Likewise, receptive tasks generally call upon less-analyzed knowledge than do corresponding productive ones. Such differences should be explored programmatically.

In addition to studying the relationships among specific tasks in the context of the framework, the relationships among more general skills should also be examined. For example, while language clearly incorporates phonological, lexical, and grammatical content, their interrelationships have not been systematically explored. This is particularly evident at the level of metalinguistic knowledge where studies of each of these aspects of language has proceeded somewhat independently. Examining their development in terms of the same two cognitive dimensions should yield a more integrated description of metalinguistic development.

Similarly, reading and writing have not typically been studied from the same prespective. Much fruitful research in both areas has revealed important aspects of the cognitive prerequisites of each; a study of their possible interrelationship could proceed in terms of the hypotheses generated from this framework.

Finally, the interrelationships that define skills in a first and second language can also be examined in these terms. Second-language programs differ in emphasis on one or the other of these dimensions. Structural language programs, for example, stress the acquisition of analyzed linguistic knowledge, while immersion programs promote the control and automaticity functions of language use. These differences may be reflected in the level or type of achievement attained with respect to these two dimensions. Development of the control functions, for example, may permit greater generalizability to first-language skills because this is less language-specific than the knowledge dimension. Accordingly, we would predict, for instance, that French immersion programs promote the development of metalinguistic and reading skills in English. Similarly, the age of the learner and the particular aptitude of the learner would be influential in determining the benefit of particular programs because of the levels of control and analyzed knowledge required.

The framework suggests, as well, directions for intervention and remediation in the improvement of metalinguistic and metacognitive performance. External manipulations in the task, which affect the control and/or the knowledge requirements, may enhance performance for some learners. Instructions that break the task into components, for example, reduce the requirement for coordination and therefore simplify the control burden. Similarly, manipulation of time constraints would also be expected to affect the control demands. The requirements for analyzed knowledge in a particular task can be modified by the amount of contextualization provided. Structurally identical problems presented in a more relevant context should be easier to solve than their abstract counterparts because of their differential reliance upon analyzed knowledge. Knowledge requirements could be further reduced by simplifying the relevant structures or by providing rules from which to choose.

Improvement may also be accomplished by dealing directly with the learner, rather than by modifying the task demands. Control may be promoted through strategy training that emphasizes attention and coordination skills. In addition, automaticity may be trained for the problem components. If reading is problematic, perhaps the establishment of automatic word-recognition procedures would contribute to the attainment of the target skill. Structured knowledge, too, can be imparted in a componential way so that the learner at least knows all the relevant pieces of information for the problem.

Training in these skills would apply directly to language problems, but it also would be interesting to examine the extent to which they promote the solution of other metacognitive problems. If, indeed, the skills underlying both sets of problems are similar, then such strategy training should prove valuable in the development of metacognitive skills (see Belmont & Butterfield, 1977; Borkowski & Cavanaugh, 1979). The strongest prediction from the framework would be that there is a stronger relationship between the application of the same dimension to different problem areas than between different dimensions in the same problem area. Thus, the ability to solve a high-control metalinguistic problem should be more related to the ability to solve a high-control metacognitive problem than it is to the ability to solve a low-control (high knowledge) metalinguistic problem. Such predictions should be empirically tested.

Finally, the framework can be applied to the study of individual differences in problem solving. The conventional classifications used to represent individual differences are notoriously nonexplanatory. Difference in ability and styles (such as IQ, field dependence–independence, impulsivity–reflectivity) serve to discriminate approaches to problem solving without identifying the critical source of that difference. The present framework offers a possible explanatory basis for such descriptions. In general it appears that many of the frequently measured individual differences are rooted primarily in one of the two dimensions. Intelligence tests, for example, typically require large amounts of structured knowledge. Questions involving logical deductions and the abstraction of principles, similarities, and the like, are characteristic of highly analyzed knowledge demands. Other individual differences, such as reflective–impulsive and field dependent–independent, are more strongly related to control. Individuals, that is, vary in the extent to which they can focus on aspects of a problem, disregard meaningless information, coordinate parts of the puzzle, and so on. By pursuing an analysis of individual differences in these terms, it would be possible to better understand the nature of those differences and their relationship to problem solving and perhaps to design procedures for overcoming problems that arise from such differences and impair some children in their solution to particular problems.

In conclusion, we have presented an organizational framework for conceptualizing the dual influence of cognitive control and analyzed knowledge in skills ranging from linguistic to metalinguistic. It may be profitable in the future to develop a similar scheme for other domains of metacognition. The relevance of the two dimensions to nonlanguage domains can be illustrated with metamemory. Despite efforts to draw clear boundaries between cognitive and metacognitive processes, we would suggest that memory processes vary in a graduated manner from cognitive to metacognitive to the extent that more cognitive control and more analyzed knowledge are involved. At the high ends of these two dimensions, current assessments can be found to stress one or the other of the two (Cavanaugh & Perlmutter, 1982). For example, metamemory interview questions tend to focus on verbalizable analyzed knowledge of memory processes, whereas adapting an instructed memory strategy to fit an altered task format primarily requires cognitive control. Of course, the specific definitions of these two dimensions would have to be modified for the memory domain, but separation of two such dimensions and examination of their interrelationships may provide a promising approach to model building. Furthermore, specific task manipulations along either the knowledge or the control dimensions may be most helpful in illuminating the actual demands of particular metamemory tasks.

References

Anderson, J. R. Acquisition of cognitive skill. *Psychological Review*, 1982, 89, 369–406.
Barron, J. Reading skill and reading strategies. In A. M. Lesgold & C. A. Perfetti (Eds.), *Interactive processes in reading*. Hillsdale, NJ: Erlbaum, 1981.

Beilin, H. *Studies in the cognitive basis of language development.* New York: Academic Press, 1975.

Belmont, J. M., & Butterfield, E. C. The instructional approach to developmental cognitive research. In R. V. Kail, Jr., & J. W. Hagen (Eds.), *Perspectives on the development of memory and cognition.* Hillsdale, NJ: Erlbaum, 1977.

Ben-Zeev, S. Mechanisms by which childhood bilingualism affects understanding of language and cognitive structures. In P. A. Hornby (Ed.), *Bilingualism: Psychological, social, and educational implications.* New York: Academic Press, 1977.

Bereiter, C., & Scardamalia, M. From conversation to composition: The role of instruction in a developmental process. In R. Glaser (Ed.), *Advances in instructional psychology,* (Vol. 2). Hillsdale, NJ: Erlbaum, 1982.

Bialystok, E. Explicit and implicit judgments of L2 grammaticality. *Language Learning,* 1979, 29, 81–103.

Bialystok, E. On the relationship between knowing and using linguistic forms. *Applied Linguistics,* 1982, 3, 181–206.

Bialystok, E. Some factors in the selection and implementation of communicative strategies. In C. Faerch & G. Kasper (Eds.), *Strategies in interlanguage communication.* London: Longmans, 1983.

Bialystok, E. Cognitive dimensions of metalinguistic awareness. Paper presented at the annual meeting of the Canadian Psychological Association, Ottawa, 1984.

Bialystok, E. Psycholinguistic dimensions of second language proficiency. In C. N. Candlin & M. P. Breen (Eds.), *Interpretive strategies in language learning.* Oxford: Oxford University Press, in press.

Borkowski, J. G., & Cavanaugh, J. C. Maintenance and generalization of skills and strategies by the retarded. In N. R. Ellis (Ed.), *Handbook of mental deficiency: Psychological theory and research.* Hillsdale, NJ: Erlbaum, 1979.

Brodzinsky, D. M. Children's comprehension and appreciation of verbal jokes in relation to conceptual tempo. *Child Development,* 1977, 48, 960–967.

Brown, A. L. Metacognitive development and reading. In R. J. Spiro, B. Bruce, & W. F. Brewer (Eds.), *Theoretical issues in reading comprehension.* Hillsdale, NJ: Erlbaum, 1980.

Brown, A. L., & Smiley, S. S. The development of strategies for studying texts. *Child Development,* 1978, 49, 1076–1088.

Brown, R., & McNeill, D. The 'tip of the tongue' phenomenon. *Journal of Verbal Learning and Verbal Behavior,* 1966, 5, 325–337.

Bruck, M. Switching out of French immersion. *Interchange,* 1978, 9, 86-94.

Bryant, P. E. & Trabasso, T. Transitive inferences and memory in young children. *Nature,* 1971, 232, 456–458.

Canney, G., & Winograd, P. *Schemata for reading and reading comprehension performance* (Tech. Rep. No. 120). Champaign, IL: University of Illinois, Center for the Study of Reading, 1979.

Carroll, J. B., & Sapon, S. M. *Modern Language Aptitude Test.* New York: The Psychological Corporation, 1959.

Carroll, J. B., & Sapon, S. M. *Modern Language Aptitude Test—Elementary.* New York: The Psychological Corporation, 1967.

Case, R. *Intellectual development: A systematic reinterpretation.* New York: Academic Press, in press.

Case, R., Kurland, D. M., & Goldberg, J. Operational efficiency and the growth of short term memory span. *Journal of Experimental Child Psychology,* 1982, 33, 386–404.

Cavanaugh, J. C., & Perlmutter, M. Metamemory: A critical examination. *Child Development,* 1982, 53, 11–28.

Cazden, C. B. Play with language and metalinguistic awareness: One dimension of language experience. *The Urban Review*, 1974, 7, 28–39.

Chall, J. S. *Learning to read: The great debate*. New York: McGraw-Hill, 1967.

Chomsky, C. *Consciousness is related to linguistic awareness*. Paper presented at the International Reading Association Seminar on Linguistic Awareness and Learning to Read, Victoria, 1979.

Clark, E. V. Non-linguistic strategies and the acquisition of word meanings. *Cognition*, 1973, 2, 161 182.

Clark, E. V. Awareness of language: Some evidence from what children say and do. In A. Sinclair, R. Jarvella, & W. J. M. Levelt (Eds.), *The child's conception of language*. New York: Springer-Verlag, 1978.

Cook, V. The analogy between first and second language learning. *IRAL*, 1969, 7, 207–216.

Cummins, J. Linguistic interdependence and the educational development of bilingual children. *Review of Educational Research*, 1979, 49, 222–251.

Cziko, G. A. The effects of language sequencing on the development of bilingual reading skills. *Canadian Modern Language Review*, 1976, 32, 534–539.

Dale, P. S. *Language development: Structure and function* (2nd ed.). New York: Holt, Rinehart & Winston, 1976.

Dalton, P. & Hardcastle, W. J. *Disorders of fluency*. New York: Elsevier, 1977.

Dickenson, D. K., & Weaver, P. A. *Remembering and forgetting: Story recall abilities of dyslexic children*. Paper presented at the annual meeting of the American Educational Research Association, San Francisco, April 1979.

Donaldson, M. *Children's minds*. London: Fontana, 1978.

Donaldson, M., & McGarrigle, J. Some clues to the nature of semantic development. *Journal of Child Language*, 1974, 1, 185–194.

Downing, J. *Reading and reasoning*. New York: Springer-Verlag, 1979.

Ehri, L. C. Word consciousness in readers and prereaders. *Journal of Educational Psychology*, 1975, 67, 204–212.

Ehri, L. C. Linguistic insight: Threshold of reading acquisition. In T. G. Waller & G. E. MacKinnon (Eds.), *Reading Research: Advances in theory and practice*. New York: Academic Press, 1979.

Entwisle, D. R. & Frasure, N. E. A contradiction resolved: Children's processing of syntactic cues. *Developmental Psychology*, 1974, 10, 852–857.

Ervin-Tripp, S. Is second language learning like the first? *TESOL Quarterly*, 1974, 8, 111–127.

Farnham-Diggory, S. Symbol and synthesis in experimental reading. *Child Development*, 1967, 38, 223–231.

Favreau, M., Komoda, M. K. & Segalowitz, N. Second language reading: Implications of the word superiority effect in skilled bilinguals. *Canadian Journal of Psychology*, 1980, 34, 370–380.

Flavell, J. H. *The developmental psychology of Jean Piaget*. Princeton, NJ: Van Nostrand, 1963.

Flavell, J. H., & Wellman, H. M. Metamemory. In R. V. Kail, Jr. & J. W. Hagen (Eds.), *Perspectives on the development of memory and cognition*. Hillsdale, NJ: Erlbaum, 1977.

Forrest-Pressley, D. L., & Waller, T. *Cognition, metacognition and reading*. New York: Springer Verlag, 1984.

Fox, B., & Routh, D. K. Phonemic analysis and severe reading disability in children. *Journal of Psycholinguistic Research*, 1980, 9, 115–119.

Gallagher, J. M. The future of formal thought research: The study of analogy and metaphor. In B. Z. Presseisen, D. Goldstein, & M. H. Appel (Eds.), *Topics in cognitive development* (Vol. 2): *Language and operational thought*. New York: Plenum Press, 1978.

Geva, E. *Metatextual notions and reading comprehension.* Unpublished doctoral dissertation, University of Toronto, 1980.

Gibson, E. J., & Levin, H. *The psychology of reading.* Cambridge, MA: MIT Press, 1975.

Gleitman, H., & Gleitman, L. R. *Language and language judgment.* In C. J. Fillmore, D. Kepler, & W. S.-Y. Wang (Eds.), *Individual differences in language ability and language behavior.* New York: Academic Press, 1979.

Gleitman, L. R., Gleitman, H., & Shipley, E. F. The emergence of the child as a grammarian. *Cognition,* 1972, *1,* 137–164.

Goldstein, D. M. Cognitive-linguistic functioning and learning to read in preschoolers. *Journal of Educational Psychology,* 1976, *68,* 680–688.

Golinkoff, R. M. A comparison of reading comprehension processes in good and poor readers. *Reading Research Quarterly,* 1976, *11,* 623–659.

Hakes, D. T. *The development of metalinguistic abilities in children.* New York: Springer-Verlag, 1980.

Hakes, D. T. The development of metalinguistic abilities: What develops? In S. A. Kucsaj (Ed.), *Language development: Language thought and culture.* Hillsdale, NJ: Erlbaum, 1982.

Hakuta, K. Prefabricated patterns and the emergence of structure in second language learning. *Language Learning,* 1974, *24,* 287–297.

Harris, A. J. & Sipay, E. R. *How to increase reading ability* (7th ed.). New York: Longmans, 1980.

Hirsh-Pasek, K., Gleitman, L. R., & Gleitman, H. What did the brain say to the mind? In A. Sinclair, R. Jarvella, & W. J. M. Levelt (Eds.), *The child's conception of language.* New York: Springer-Verlag, 1978.

Hulstijn, J. H. *Monitor use by adult second language learners.* Amsterdam: Krips Repro Meppel, 1982.

Ianco-Worrall, A. Bilingualism and cognitive development. *Child Development,* 1972, *43,* 1390–1400.

Inhelder, B., & Piaget, J. *The early growth of logic in the child.* London: Routledge & Kegan Paul, 1964.

Jakobson, R. Two aspects of language and two aspects of aphasic disturbance. In R. Jakobson, *Selected writings II: Word and language.* The Hague: Mouton, 1971.

Kessel, F. S. The role of syntax in children's comprehension from ages six to twelve. *Monographs of the Society for Research in Child Development,* 1970, *35*(6).

Klein, H. A., Klein, G. A., & Bertino, M. Utilization of context for word identification decisions in children. *Journal of Experimental Child Psychology,* 1974, *17,* 79–86.

Krashen, S. D. *Second language acquisition and second language learning.* New York: Pergamon Press, 1981.

LaBerge, D., & Samuels, S. J. Toward a theory of automatic information processing in reading. *Cognitive Psychology,* 1974, *6,* 293–323.

Lambert, W. E., & Tucker, G. R. *Bilingual education of children.* Rowley, MA: Newbury House, 1972.

Ledger, G. W., & Ryan, E. B. The effects of semantic integration training on recall for pictograph sentences. *Journal of Experimental Child Psychology,* 1982, *33,* 39–54.

Liberman, I. Y., Shankweiler, D., Liberman, A. M., Fowler, C., & Fischer, F. W. Phonetic segmentation and recoding in the beginning reader. In A. S. Reber & D. L. Scarborough (Eds.), *Toward a psychology of reading.* Hillsdale, NJ: Erlbaum, 1977.

Lundberg, I. Aspects of linguistic awareness related to reading. In A. Sinclair, R. J. Jarvella, & W. L. M. Levelt (Eds.), *The child's concept of language.* New York: Springer-Verlag, 1978.

Macnamara, J. The cognitive basis of language learning in infants. *Psychological Review*, 1972, 79, 1–13.

Mattingly, I. G. Reading, the linguistic process, and linguistic awareness. In J. E. Kavanaugh & I. G. Mattingly (Eds.), *Language by ear and by eye*. Cambridge: MIT Press, 1972.

McLaughlin, B., Rossman, T., & McLeod, B. Second-language learning: An information-processing perspective. Unpublished manuscript, University of California—Santa Cruz, 1982.

Menyuk, P. *Sentences children use*. Cambridge, MA: MIT Press, 1969.

Menyuk, P. Language development and reading. In J. Flood (Ed.), *Understanding reading comprehension*. Newark, DE: International Reading Association, 1981.

Miller, G. A., & Johnson-Laird, P. N. *Language and perception*. Cambridge, MA: Harvard University Press, 1976.

Olson, D. R., & Bialystok, E. *Spatial cognition: The structure and development of the mental representation of spatial relations*. Hillsdale, NJ: Erlbaum, 1983.

Papandropoulou, I. & Sinclair, H. What is a word? Experimental study of children's ideas on grammar. *Human Development*, 1974, 17, 241–258.

Paris, S. G., & Myers, M. Comprehension monitoring, memory, and study strategies of good and poor readers. *Journal of Reading Behavior*, 1981, 13, 5–22.

Pascual-Leone, J. A mathematical model for the transition rule in Piaget's developmental stages. *Acta Psychologica*, 1970, 32, 301–345.

Pascual-Leone, J. Growing into human maturity. In P. B. Baltes & O. G. Brim (Eds.), *Life-span development and behavior* (Vol. 5). New York: Academic Press, 1983.

Perfetti, C. A., & Hogaboam, T. Relationship between single word decoding and reading comprehension skill. *Journal of Educational Psychology*, 1975, 67, 461–469.

Perfetti, C. A. & Lesgold, A. M. Coding and comprehension in skilled reading and implications for reading instruction. In L. B. Resnick & P. Weaver (Eds.), *Theory and practice in early reading*. Hillsdale, NJ: Erlbaum, 1980.

Piaget, J. *The construction of reality in the child*. New York: Ballantine Books, 1954.

Polanyi, M. *Personal knowledge*. Chicago: University of Chicago Press, 1958.

Pylyshyn, Z. W. The imagery debate: Analogue media versus tacit knowledge. *Psychological Review*, 1981, 88, 16–45.

Read, C. Children's awareness of language, with emphasis on sound systems. In A. Sinclair, R. J. Jarvella, & W. J. M. Levelt (Eds.), *The child's conception of language*. New York: Springer-Verlag, 1978.

Reber, A. S. Implicit learning of synthetic languages: The role of instructional set. *Journal of Emperimental Psychology: Human Learning and Memory*, 1976, 2, 88–94.

Reber, A. S., & Lewis, S. Implicit learning: An analysis of the form and structure of a body of tacit knowledge. *Cognition*, 1977, 5, 333–361.

Rosier, P. & Holm, W. *Bilingual education series*, (Vol. 8): *The Rock Point Experience*. Washington, DC: Center for Applied Linguistics, 1980.

Rozin, P., & Gleitman, L. R. The structure and acquisition of reading II: The reading process and the acquisition of the alphabetic principle. In A. S. Reber & D. L. Scarborough (Eds.), *Toward a psychology of reading*. Hillsdale, NJ: Erlbaum, 1977.

Rubin, A. A theoretical taxonomy of the differences between oral and written language. In R. J. Spiro, B. C. Bruce, & w. F. Brewer (Eds.), *Theoretical issues in reading comprehension*. Hillsdale, NJ: Erlbaum, 1980.

Ryan, E. B. Metalinguistic development and reading. In L. H. Waterhouse, K. M. Fischer, & E. B. Ryan, *Language awareness and reading*. Newark, DE: International Reading Association, 1980.

Ryan, E. B. Identifying and remediating failures in reading comprehension: Toward an instructional approach for poor comprehenders. In G. E. MacKinnon & T. G. Waller (Eds.), *Advances in reading research* (Vol. 3). New York: Acadermic Press, 1981.

Ryan, E. B., & Ledger, G. W. Assessing sentence processing skills in prereaders. In B. Hutson (Ed.), *Advances in Reading/Language Research* (Vol. 1). Greenwich, CN: JAI Press, 1982.

Ryan, E. B., & Ledger, G. W. Learning to attend to sentence structure: Links between metalinguistic development and reading. In J. Downing & R. Valtin (Eds.), *Language awareness and learning to read.* New York: Springer Verlag, 1983.

Ryan, E. B., McNamara, S. R., & Kenney, M. Linguistic awareness and reading ability among beginning readers. *Journal of Reading Behavior,* 1977, 9, 399–400.

Salatas, H., & Flavell, J. H. Perspective taking: The development of two components of knowledge. *Child Development,* 1976, 47, 103–109.

Scardamalia, M., & Paris, P. The function of explicit discourse knowledge in the development of text representations and composing strategies. *Cognition and Instruction,* in press.

Schallert, D. L. the role of illustrations in reading comprehension. In R. J. Spiro, B. C. Bruce, & W. F. Brewer (Eds.), *Theoretical issues in reading comprehension.* Hillsdale, NJ: Erlbaum, 1980.

Scheffler, I. *Conditions of knowledge.* Glenview, IL: Scott, Foresman & Co., 1965.

Scholl, D. M., & Ryan, E. B. The development of metalinguistic performance during the early school years. *Language and Speech,* 1980, 23, 199–211.

Scribner, S., & Cole, M. *The psychology of literacy.* Cambridge, MA: Harvard University Press, 1981.

Shiffrin, R. M., & Schneider, W. Controlled and automatic human information processing (Vol. 2): Perception, learning, automatic attending, and a general theory. *Psychological Review,* 1977, 84, 127–190.

Short, E. J., & Ryan, E. B. Metacognitive differences between skilled and less skilled readers: Remediating deficits through story grammar and attribution training. *Journal of Educational Psychology,* 1984.

Shultz, T., & Pilon, R. Development of the ability to detect linguistic ambiguity. *Child Development,* 1973, 44, 728–733.

Sinclair, A., Jarvella, R. J., & Levelt, W. J. M. (Eds.). *The child's conception of language.* New York: Springer-Verlag, 1978.

Skutnabb-Kangas, T., & Toukomaa, P. *Teaching migrant children's mother tongue and learning the language of the host country in the context of the sociocultural situation of the migrant family.* Helsinki: The Finnish National Commission for UNESCO, 1976.

Smiley, S. S., Oakley, D. D., Worthen, D., Campione, J., & Brown, A. L. Recall of thematically relevant material by adolescent good and poor readers as a function of written versus oral presentation. *Journal of Educational Psychology,* 1977, 69, 381–387.

Snow, C. E. Conversations with children. In P. Fletcher & M. Garman (Eds.), *Language acquisition.* Cambridge: Cambridge University Press, 1979.

Snow, C. E., & Ferguson, C. A. (Eds.) *Talking to children: Language input and acquisition.* Cambridge: Cambridge University Press, 1977.

Spiro, R. Constructive processes in prose comprehension and recall. In R. J. Spiro, B. C. Bruce, & W. F. Brewer (Eds.), *Theoretical issues in reading comprehension.* Hillsdale, NJ: Erlbaum, 1980.

Stein, N. L., & Glenn, C. G. An analysis of story comprehension in elementary school children. In R. Freedle (Ed.), *Discourse processing: Multidisciplinary perspectives.* Hillsdale, NJ: Erlbaum, 1979.

Swain, M., & Lapkin, S. *Evaluating bilingual education: A Canadian case study.* Clevedon, England: Multilingual Matters, 1982.

Tallal, P. Auditory temporal perception, phonics, and reading disabilities in children. *Brain & Language*, 1980, *9*, 182–198.

Tarone, E. Communication strategies, foreigner talk, and repair in interlanguage. *Language Learning*, 1980, *30*, 417–431.

Trites, P. A., & Price, M. A. Specific learning disabilities in primary French immersion. *Interchange*, 1978, *9*, 73–85.

Tucker, G. R. The development of reading skills within a bilingual education program. In S. S. Smiley & J. C. Towner (Eds.), *Language and reading*. Bellingham, WA: Sixth Western Washington Symposium on Learning, 1975.

Van Kleeck, A. The emergence of linguistic awareness: A cognitive framework. *Merrill-Palmer Quarterly*, 1982, *28*, 237–265.

Van Riper, C. *Speech correction* (5th ed.). Englewood Cliffs, NJ: Prentice-Hall, 1972.

Vygotsky, L. S. *Thought and language*. Cambridge: MIT Press, 1962 (original 1934).

Vygotsky, L. S. *Mind in society: The development of higher psychological processes*. Cambridge, MA: Harvard University Press, 1978.

Weaver, P. A. Improving reading comprehension: Effects of sentence organization instruction. *Reading Research Quarterly*, 1979, *15*, 129–146.

Weinstein, R., & Rabinovitch, S. Sentence structure and retention in good and poor readers. *Journal of Educational Psychology*, 1971, *62*, 25–30.

Wells, G. Language, literacy and education. In G. Wells, *Learning through interaction—the study of language development*. Cambridge: Cambridge University Press, 1981.

Woodcock, R. W., Clark, C. R. & Davies, C. O. *The Peabody rebus reading program*. Circle Pines, MN: American Guidance Service, 1969.

CHAPTER 7

The Role of Metacognition
in Contemporary Theories
of Cognitive Development

Steven R. Yussen

Introduction

Metacognition, broadly speaking, is identified as that body of knowledge and understanding that reflects on cognition itself. Put another way,
metacognition is that mental activity for which other mental states or processes become the object of reflection. Thus, metacognition is sometimes
referred to as thoughts about cognition, or thinking about thinking. Examples of this might include (1) contemplating which of two strategies to
use to help remember a list of words (metamemory), (2) considering
whether you have understood a message someone has just given you
(metacomprehension), and (3) considering what conditions might produce
the least distractibility while you are trying to observe something (meta-
attention).

As Cavanaugh and Perlmutter (1982) argued recently, the concept of
metacognition actually is an old one if considered within the context of
ideas in the history of philosophy. However, metacognition has only been
seen as an explicit topic of scholarly interest in psychology since the early
1970s. John Flavell was one of the first scientists to use the term consistently, starting around 1971 (Flavell, 1971), and the focus of his interest,
and that of many others who followed his lead, was memory phenomena
(dubbed "metamemory"). Since that time we have witnessed an explosion

of empirical research on the topic (cf. Brown, Bransford, Ferrara, & Campione, 1983; Flavell, 1979, 1981a), and a host of theoretical propositions relating metacognition to specific domains of inquiry (e.g., *reading*—Baker & Brown, 1982; *comprehension*—Flavell, 1981; Markman, 1979; *memory*—Flavell & Wellman, 1977; *social interaction*—Flavell, 1971; and *attention*—Miller & Weiss, 1981) as well as to cognition considered more generally (e.g., Borkowski, 1984; Meichenbaum, Burland, Gruson, & Cameron, 1984; Sternberg & Powell, 1983). It is clearly a dynamic and lively area of research, judging by a number of critical signs. Many of the leading cognitive theorists have attempted to explain how metacognition intrudes into virtually all cognitive activities; applied researchers have rushed in to argue for the centrality of metacognition in understanding academic deficits (e.g., Hagen, Barclay, & Newman, 1982; Loper, Hallahan, & Lanna, 1982; and its key role in planning successful remediation and intervention efforts (Capelli & Markman, 1982; Loper, 1982; Meichenbaum, 1980); finally, the sheer volume of papers retrieved when conducting a search of abstracts in the psychological literature, attests to the quantitative magnitude of work in the field.[1]

The basic purpose of this essay is to offer a critical look at the concept of metacognition as it now exists in the field of cognitive development and to offer suggestions on how it can be strengthened through efforts both to offer more precise distinctions and demonstrations concerning the concept, as well as to broaden the nature of theoretical discussion about it. The essay is divided into four parts. Each one stresses a theme, which in turn serves to organize a set of related issues. To provide an advanced organizer, the four points are summarized as follows:

1. The use of the term *metacognition* is highly variable in current theory and research, and leads to a broad range of outcomes in its power and utility.

2. Although there have been commendable efforts to offer theories of metacognitive development, with few exceptions most of these have been assimilated into some form of information-processing

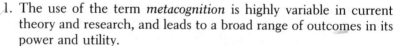

---

[1]In November, 1983, we conducted a search of the American Psychological Association Abstracts (APA) that covers the period from 1967 to the present, abstracting all major journal articles and Ph. D. dissertations that are of a primarily psychological nature. Restricting our retrieval to metacognition, metamemory, & comprehension monitoring, we turned up 142 different abstracts, over 80% of which were publications since 1978. A similar search through the abstracts of the Educational Research Information Clearinghouse (ERIC) produced 209 different abstracts. The ERIC files cover approximately the same period (1966 to present), with a major difference being the fact that ERIC references many more nonjournal papers than the APA abstracts (e.g., final government agency reports, technical reports, professional conference papers).

framework. Other theoretical perspectives should be considered as well.

3. For the most part, metacognitive development has been conceptualized with a clear eye toward childhood. There are important reasons to think about metacognitive phenomena in adults, however, and to consider the nature of change in adults, as well.

4. Finally, the study of metacognition has been trapped by a particular framework for studying cognition and problem solving generally. This might be called the puzzle-solving framework. Puzzle solving is a limited metaphor for understanding many important cognitive phenomena—both in children and adults. And it may be a particularly unfortunate framework for understanding many of the more interesting phenomena of adult, cognitive life.

Let us turn, then, to the main portion of the essay, beginning with the first of these points.

Variability in Meanings

When we want to obtain some clear apprehension of an idea or concept, there are a number of ways to proceed. One approach is to offer a clear definition from which follow some intuitively obvious cases, examples, and demonstrations. Two investigators, John Flavell (Flavell & Wellman, 1977) and Ann Brown (Baker & Brown, 1982), have offered independent and complementary sets of definitions–descriptions of the domain, which help in this regard.

Let us consider Flavell's ideas first. Flavell suggests that we may distinguish between metacognitive *knowledge* and metacognitive *experience*. While engaged in some cognitive activity, such as reading, we may direct what we are doing in response to some knowledge we have stored in memory about the activity in general. For example, I may read over a section quickly, realizing that it covers material I have already mastered. Or I may put my reading material down and search out a dictionary to help understand an unfamiliar word whose meaning seems to be instrumental for understanding many points that are being made in the selection. In each case, I can be said to have acted on the basis of what I already *know* about the act of reading through past learning, experience, and development. Specifically, I used the knowledge that

1. When I encounter something already known well to me while reading, it is most efficient to move through that material quickly.

    2. If I encounter a word or term that is unknown to me, it is best to discover its meaning quickly, before it disrupts further comprehension.

    In contrast, these very same situations may have engendered in me some conscious or semiconscious awareness of my state of knowledge while reading itself. Encountering the familiar material, for example, may have stimulated some in situ reaction such as "Aha, I know this already." Or, getting stuck on the unfamiliar word might have led to a reaction such as "Oh, Oh. I don't know that word. What does the writer mean here?" These reactions are metacognitive experiences—relatively spontaneous reactions or reflections that occur *on line* (during the cognitive process) while the cognitive enterprise is rolling along. Metacognitive *experiences*, then, are here-and-now reactions to the ongoing cognitive activity, whereas metacognitive *knowledge* consists of stored concepts (declarative and procedural knowledge, we might say), which are called up from memory to guide the cognitive activity.

    Flavell goes on to describe the broad classes of knowledge that an individual might acquire about some cognitive activity. The four general classes and examples of each include (1) *tasks*—knowledge about how the nature of the task influences performance on it (e.g., knowing that it is easier to recognize something than to recall it); (2) *self*—knowledge about one's own skills, strengths, and weaknesses as a cognitive being (e.g., knowing that one remembers words better than numbers); (3) *strategies*—knowledge about the differential value of alternative strategies for enhancing performance (e.g., knowing that an interactive visual image will better preserve the association between two words than repeatedly rehearsing the words; and finally, (4) *interactions*—knowledge about ways in which the pairs or trio of preceding categories of knowledge interact with one another to influence the outcome of some cognitive performance (e.g., for the pairing of *tasks* with *strategies*, knowing that it is of some help to repeat items on a list to *remember* them, but of little help to repeat the same message to a listener if the listener fails to *understand* it the first time.)

    Brown's contribution to defining and describing metacognition has been to fine-tune the sense of what we mean by metacognitive knowledge. There are two kinds, she believes—static and strategic. *Static knowledge* is the verbalizable things people state about cognition—many of the things people might state about Flavell's four preceding categories, for example. *Strategic knowledge*, by comparison, consists of those steps that individuals actually take to regulate and modify the progress of a cognitive activity when it actually occurs. There are, no doubt, a host of strategies that peo-

executive thinking

ple use to regulate particular cognitive activities that prove to be specific to those activities alone. However, Brown suggests a list of general strategies which might, conversely, be present in almost all forms of cognitive activity. These general metacognitive strategies include, but are not restricted to, *planning*—figuring out how to proceed; *predicting*—estimating some quantitative aspect of the outcome of the cognitive activity, such as how much will be remembered or understood or how much time a task might take to complete; *guessing*—taking a stab at an answer prior to reaching a complete cognitive solution; and, finally, *monitoring*—taking stock of how well one has progressed toward some goal in the cognitive activity. Brown argues that strategic forms of metacognition offer the most interesting avenue for research and progress in the field and that while static forms of metacognition are interesting, they hold out less promise for scientific manipulation and model building.

These, then, are some of the major ideas that have structured the definition of metacognition as a field. To be sure, there have been other major statements about the nature of metacognition as well (e.g., Borkowski, 1984; Sternberg & Powell, 1983; Yussen & Santrock, 1982). But it is our impression that the distinctions offered by the preceding two investigators have had the greatest collective impact. Therefore, this discussion focuses upon them. But in the interest of assuming collective impact, to ensure that our account is complete, and out of fairness to some of the other theoreticians in the field, we have briefly summarized some of the other statements about metacognition in Table 1.

How well, then, do these definitions and or descriptions offered by Flavell and Brown serve us in studying metacognition? To return to the theme of this section of the essay, our conclusion is that the ideas have led to somewhat variable meanings and uses in the field—a result the investigator's themselves cannot be blamed for, because clear descriptions can become confused in the hands of bad interpretations. But, we believe that part of the problem has stemmed from a failure among many investigators to appreciate that these definitional schemes really cannot be expected to do much more than logically describe the kinds of knowledge and events that exist. Within the definitional categories, for example, we see nothing that could tell us, in advance, where to look, if after having defined a specific metacognition, we wanted to discover the answer to such questions as (1) whether hypothetical metacognitive knowledge develops in children, (2) during what period of time, (3) across what quantitative or qualitative levels of understanding, (4) exhibits individual differences, (5) is related and in what way to metacognitive knowledge Y, (6) is functionally and measurably related to the outcome of cognitive event

Table 1

Other Descriptions of Metacognition

Campione and Brown (1978)
    Theory of Intelligence
        The architectural system
        The executive system
            knowledge
            scheme
            control processes
            metacognition
Yussen and Santrock (1982)

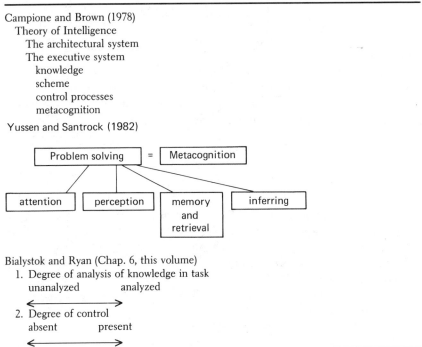

Bialystok and Ryan (Chap. 6, this volume)
    1. Degree of analysis of knowledge in task
        unanalyzed   analyzed

        ←——————————→
    2. Degree of control
        absent   present

        ←——————————→

X, (7) can be taught to children under what conditions, and (8) can be used to intervene, successfully, in improving some specific performance, say, of cognitive event X.

In short, we claim that the definitional schemes do not help us much in answering most of the interesting questions that scholars in the field wish to address. In and of themselves, these schemes do not provide enough information to arrive at specific theoretical predictions about the acquisition and use of specific forms of metacognition. But, on the other hand, we believe it is unfortunate to criticize, prematurely, the whole field of inquiry, as a number of people have, simply because some of the early thinking about it was not sufficiently developed to lead to unambiguous and clear predictions.

Where investigators have been successful in addressing one or more of the preceding eight points, they have seen successful because they recognized (even if implicitly) the limitations of the framework within which they were operating, and they proceeded accordingly. Specifically, they had an appreciation of the importance of the following two points:

1. The existing definitions of metacognition are *open* rather than closed.
2. A key to successful demonstrations is identifying prototypical phenomena. A discussion of each point follows.

1. The existing definitions of metacognition are open rather than closed. An *open definition* is one that suggests possibilities, examples, and cases, but does not place a boundary at a certain point, so that there is a clear sense of what is excluded.

If we focus on the descriptive category—task variables, for example—we see that one of the earliest metacognitive phenomena studied was the child's appreciation that the number of items on a list—its length—influences how successfully one can remember the whole list (e.g., Flavell, Friedrich, & Hoyt, 1970; Yussen & Levy, 1975). Given that a child might learn about task properties of memory while growing up, the length of a list to be remembered seems like an obvious phenomenon to study: The list's length is an obvious property of memory and is demonstrably important in actual memory. However, like many phenomena in psychology, the simple length of a list sometimes is less important than the kind of memory required (recognition versus recall—Levin, Yussen, DeRose, & Pressley, 1977; constructive versus nonconstructive recognition—Yussen & Pacquette, 1978) or one's knowledge of the memorability of particular items on the list (e.g., Kelly, Scholnick, Travers, & Johnson, 1976). Therefore, most of us were not prepared for the complex set of findings that emerged. Developmental changes in a child's accuracy at predicting his or her own span of memory are sometimes obtained and sometimes not, from early childhood to the middle elementary school years. And, sometimes there is a relation between a child's accuracy at predicting span and actual memory and sometimes there is not (Chapter 3, this volume).

The descriptive exhortation to look for task variables in memory and the knowledge that length is an important variable in actual memory was appropriate, and it led to an understandable belief that an important metacognitive acquisition could be documented by examining children's knowledge about length. But the descriptive category simply pointed to a possible line of inquiry. Alone, it did not offer any of the important details concerning what additional task factors, information-processing requirements, or context effects might moderate the acquisition of this knowledge. The object lesson here is that definitions of possible metacognitive acquisitions should not be confused with actual metacognitive acquisitions. And failing to find an acquisition, one should not then dismiss the conceptual domain as trivial. One needs to look harder, with better ideas and techniques.

2. **A key to success in demonstrating the existence and/or development of particular metacognitive knowledge is the identification of prototypical phenomena.** Although formal definitions and descriptions of phenomena are useful, many contemporary students of cognitive psychology believe that we make more progress and arrive at a more penetrating understanding of important concepts when we have prototypical examples of them. Eleanor Rosch (e.g., Rosch, 1973; 1978), for example, has argued that much of our understanding of ordinary concepts in the world is organized around prototypes, rather than formal, exhaustive definitions of concepts. Additionally, because we seem more likely to offer incomplete or open definitions of concepts, prototypes (if they are indeed powerful, organizing forces around which much of our ordinary cognition is framed) offer a more useful alternative. A *prototype* is a specific example of a concept or event. Other cases are compared for their similarity with features of the prototypical case, rather than their identity with it. The more similar are the features of the other cases, the more likely we are to identify them as prototypes.

In the study of metacognitive development, it is useful to identify some of those phenomena that seem, based on evidence now in hand, to be prototypical examples of knowledge acquisitions for which one of the eight key questions can be given a clear answer. The value of this exercise is to direct our scholarship to phenomena with empirical payoff and to avoid further work on phenomena likely to prove unfruitful.

In a review of research examining developmental trends in the relation between metamemory and memory behavior, Schneider (Chap. 3, this volume) pinpointed one nice illustration of this point. He reminds us of the discrepancy between those metamemory studies reviewed by Cavanaugh and Perlmutter (1982) where a dozen empirical studies yielded moderate or low correlations between children's statable knowledge of memory and their performance on certain memory tasks, whereas Wellman (1984), identified a handful of empirical studies where there were more substantial links between metamemory and memory behavior. Schneider's analysis suggests that the Cavanaugh and Perlmutter findings are mostly about knowledge of *organizational strategies* (e.g., grouping, clustering, categorizing), whereas Wellman's review focuses on *memory-monitoring knowledge* (e.g., knowing when one is ready to recall, knowing if an item is in memory). The latter phenomena seem more certain to yield links between knowledge and performance.

Another useful example comes from the field of comprehension research. Investigators have now accumulated a modest body of information on a highly interesting aspect of comprehension monitoring. Simply stated, the question of interest is "Are subjects aware of encountering difficulty in understanding while reading something or listening to oral discourse?" "If so, what do they do about it?" Among developmental psychologists, of course, a further question is "At what age or level of maturity does awareness occur?" Classic studies of this phenomenon have now been conducted by a number of investigators (Baker & Anderson, 1982; Flavell, 1981; Markman, 1977; 1979). There seems to be genuine evidence that the awareness of encountering difficulty does develop with age (e.g., Markman, 1979), although sometimes even adults do not appreciate that they have failed to comprehend something (e.g., Glenberg, Wilkinson, & Epstein, 1982), and the way awareness is measured seems to make a difference. This last point is critical and bears some resemblance to the metamemory example mentioned previously. It turns out that if subjects are queried about having encountered difficulty by being asked questions such as "Did you understand that?" "Was there anything that didn't make sense?" "Was there anything unclear?" and so forth, their verbal responses often suggest ignorance of any problem. However, in the case of reading, subjects virtually always slow down in their speed of processing the text that proves more difficult, whether they seemed verbally cognizant of a problem or not (e.g., Baker & Anderson, 1982; Buss, 1981). Additionally, Flavell and his associates (Flavell, Speer, Green, & August, 1981) have documented a parallel phenomenon in young children's metacognition of an oral (listening) task. They found that, although young children did not always identify an impoverished message as flawed in any way, the children frequently showed spontaneous signs of processing difficulty while the message was being heard—they made funny expressions with their faces, looked bewildered, and produced other body language indicative of puzzlement.

The appropriate research has not accumulated yet, but we suspect that these signs of processing in reading and listening will prove to be powerful predictors of actual comprehension and reliable indicators of stable developmental and individual differences in meta-awareness of comprehension difficulty. We are less certain about the verbal measures.

So, what do we conclude about these two examples (metamemory and metacomprehension) and what do they tell us, in general, about the identification of prototypical phenomena in metacognition? One conclusion is that Ann Brown's hunch may be correct. It may be easier to find solid evidence for reliable metacognitive phenomena when we focus on measures closely linked to metacognitive decisions and processes. The memory-monitoring literature reviewed by Wellman would seem to make closer contact with the acts of studying for retrieval and of gauging one's current state of storage than the knowledge of hypothetical organization strategies stressed by Cavanaugh and Perlmutter (1982). And the striking way that signs-of-processing difficulties crop up in a reader's speed of moving through a text and in a listener's facial expressions and body language suggests the salience of on-line indicators of comprehension problems.

A second, alternative, lesson, is that we have to be particularly careful in what we identify to study as a likely metacognitive acquisition. It may be that some organizational strategies do not engender very salient meta-cognitive insights in the person because the strategies are not sufficiently omnipresent ecologically and/or are not consistently used in everyday en-deavors. By contrast, the state of one's cognitive readiness is a highly sa-lient and general matter to be reckoned with by everyone, in a frequent, routine way. So, the critical dimension may not be that some metacog-nitions are on line, while others are not. It may be, instead, that some metacognitions are central in one's mental life, while other metacognitions are not.

Theoretical Treatment of Metacognition

Within the field of cognitive development, it is possible to identify four major theoretical paradigms that have been major forces in shaping theory and research since the 1960s. These are listed in Table 2. Respec-tively, these can be referred to as the cognitive-structural, the information-processing, the cognitive-behavioral, and the psychometric orientations to development.

I believe that the development of ideas about metacognition has been dominated by patterns and research approaches largely anchored in the paradigm of information processing. The information-processing para-digm has served the study of metacognition well. It has produced a num-ber of heuristically valuable concepts, research approaches, and empirical findings. And, it is perhaps inevitable that the information-processing ap-proach should dominate at this time, because as a general approach to cognitive development it could be said (arguably) to be gaining strength as the central paradigm in the field, while interest in the others is waning (e.g., Brown, Bransford, Ferrara, & Campione, 1983; Siegler, 1983; Yussen & Santrock, 1982). Be that as it may, I confess to being a confirmed ec-lectic in approaching the general theory of cognitive development, and believe that this path holds the most promise for the future study of me-tacognition. Accordingly, in this section, I argue for a serious consideration

Table 2

Contemporary Cognitive Paradigms and Possible Theoretical Treatment of Metacognition

Paradigm	Representative theorists	Theoretical treatment of metacognition
1. Information processing	Siegler, Klahr, Sternberg, Trabasso	1. Description, modeling of control, executive processes 2. Description, modeling of self-regulatory mechanisms 3. Description, modeling of strategy training and generalization
2. Cognitive–structural	Piaget, R. Brown, Feldman	1. Structural descriptions of knowledge about cognitive events, strategic patterns 2. Emphasizes sequences of structural change 3. Model of relation between structural change in metacognitive knowledge and other knowledge
3. Cognitive–behavioral	Bandura, Mischel, Rosenthal and Zimmerman	1. Status of 'metacognition' in repertoire of symbolic events mediating learning 2. Description of model as source of metacognition 3. Role of metacognition in engineering, technology of behavior change
4. Psychometric	Cattell–Horn, Guilford Structure of Intellect, Kaufman Factor, Structure Model of WISC	1. Issues of measurement (e.g., reliability, validity) 2. Identify metacognitive factors or basic processes

of what sorts of ideas and empirical generalizations each of the theoretical paradigms could contribute to the study of metacognition.

Let us begin with the information-processing paradigm, because it is claimed to be on center stage in the field, now. The information-processing perspective has been described as an approach to development that is concerned with (1) the precise specification of the mental processes and steps needed to complete a given cognitive task, (2) the careful analysis of the properties and features of a given cognitive task, and (3) the need to attend closely to what subjects' actual cognitive performances look like in real time. In Table 2, we have listed the names of several investigators whose general work on cognitive development clearly fits this paradigm.

Contemplating the work that has already been done in the field and considering what holds out the most promise for the future, we are led to three focal concerns with which this paradigm can be most illuminating and productive. First, there is the effort to describe and to model executive processes. In any cognitive activity there are some relatively fast-acting decisions made that direct the subsequent course of the cognitive act. These may be automatic and largely outside of our consciousness or we may think about them momentarily in a semiconscious fashion. Examples include (1) deciding which term to look at next in an analogy problem of the form $A:B$ as C is to D_1, D_2, D_3, D_4, (2) deciding what part of a text to read next if the reader is skimming it for a general appreciation of its content, and (3) deciding whether the perceiver has scanned a pattern in some array sufficiently to make a response choice in a setting where quick-paced reactions are called for. These types of decisions are often made in hundredths or tenths of a second, without our conscious knowledge, and with profound consequences for the success and accuracy of the subsequent cognitive act. Some relatively sophisticated techniques have been developed to estimate the kinds of decisions that are made, the factors that influence them, and the presence of developmental and individual differences in these decision processes (e.g., Sternberg & Powell, 1983).

A second effort is the work on relatively more conscious, self-regulatory mechanisms that individuals apply to help direct the ongoing course of a cognitive act. Typically, these mechanisms are more deliberate, take more time than the aforementioned kind of executive decisions, and are amenable both to introspection and to relatively direct experimental manipulation. The categories of planning and of self-monitoring, considered previously, are of this type. For example, if someone were to write a letter, the first thing the writer might do would be to consider what information to include in it, how much time there would be available to complete the task, and what might be done to make the reader of the letter feel entertained. These are all elements of metacognitive planning. Examples of self-monitoring are the internal assessment a subject makes when she or he considers (1) whether a list of items to be remembered has been mastered yet (been studied long enough), or (2) whether academic reading materials have been mastered yet (or more frequently, whether the material has been mastered as well as it can be, given the amount of time left before the test). Work on self-regulatory processes has been particularly rich in the fields of memory (e.g., Flavell & Wellman, 1977; Schneider, Chapter 3, this volume) and comprehension (e.g., Baker & Brown, 1982; Markman, 1981), and there are also a number of provocative ideas about self-regulatory processes being proposed for other cognitive activities (for example, children's writing—Bereiter & Scardamalia, 1982; and personal management skills—Karoly, 1977).

The third and final focus of the information-processing perspective mentioned here is the attempt to describe how a cognitive strategy is acquired and becomes applied successfully to a range of tasks. Those scholars who have been interested in the plight of poor learners (e.g., those children diagnosed as being mentally retarded or those having some type of learning disability) have long recognized the frustration of training these children to perform better on some task (e.g., memory, discrimination learning, or concept formation), only to see the gains disappear rather quickly over time or manifest themselves in a narrow range of tasks very similar to the ones used in training. It is not much of an accomplishment, these investigators realize, if gains are short-lived or "welded" (Ann Brown's term) to specific tasks—not generalized to a range of problems. A number of these same experts have come to believe that a possible remedy for the past shortcoming is to incorporate one or more components of metacognitive knowledge and/or self-regulatory training when these learners are taught a strategy, so that the children have a deep and meaningful understanding of the strategy and its impact on performance. In a very clever analysis of strategy training research, Pressley, Borkowski, and O'Sullivan (Chapter 4, this volume) have demonstrated that there are different degrees to which training programs seem to offer explicit provision of metamemory knowledge and process to subjects, and the programs that provide the most explicit information prove to be most effective. They also discuss techniques by which subjects acquire new, useful metacognitions—they call these metacognitive acquisition procedures (MAPS).

Let us turn, next, to the cognitive structural paradigm. It would seem that the core of structural theory is now concerned with (1) descriptions of the structural nature of some aspect of cognition, (2) qualitative shifts in the nature of this structure, and (3) ordered sequences of structural change unfolding over significant periods of time (e.g., Feldman, 1980; Flavell, 1982; Lapsley & Serlin, 1984). In order to see some value in the structural approach, it is unnecessary to regard either acquisitions as being universal (cf. Feldman, 1980), or structures as explaining everything about cognitive performance in the domain of interest (cf. Rest, 1983).

With a few noteworthy exceptions, metacognitive development has not been conceptualized in structural terms, yet there is reason to be optimistic about efforts to correct this deficiency. The exceptions are worth mentioning first, before our attention is directed to the additional reasons for optimism. In the field of social cognition, a number of structural schemes have been developed, which (often without using the term *meta-*

cognition implicitly refer to the knowledge children have about the cognitions of people and the cognitive bases underlying people's social interactions. These schemes propose a shifting pattern in the structure of these social metacognitions across childhood. Examples of this work include Selman's (1980) and Flavell's (1982) models of role taking, and Enright, Enright, and Lapsley's (1981) research on distributive justice reasoning. There has also been some work on what might be called naive epistemology. Broughton, for example, has developed a scheme to describe structural changes in adolescents' conceptions about what it means to know something (Broughton, 1975, 1978). In the counseling field, the seminal work by Perry (1970, on forms of intellectual and ethical development in the college years) has spawned a great deal of interest in structural changes in a parallel phenomenon (i.e., what is knowledge, what is a true fact) across young adulthood.

There appear to be at least three ways to approach further work on metacognitive development from a structural perspective. One is a pattern already familiar in some of the preceding exceptions. It is to describe a domain of knowledge about cognition (e.g., a cognitive act, a cognitive characteristic in people, an important strategy) in structural terms. A shortcoming of the information-processing approach, particularly the research on metamemory, is that children are generally regarded as knowing something to a greater or lesser extent or with greater or lesser degrees of quantitative precision (e.g., ("How much can I remember?" "Which strategy is best, X, Y, or Z?" and so forth). Yet, with the right kinds of theoretical analyses, we might discover that for many phenomena, children evolve different theories or structural understandings of the phenomena in question. "Amount remembered" or "relative efficacy of strategies, X, Y, and Z" may only capture a fragment of a more global and complex theory the child has about remembering, which may contain propositions altogether different from amount remembered or relative efficacy of the strategies. Such theories might only come into play in the cognitive activity of older, more mature subjects.

A second goal of structural research in this field could be both to describe the sequences of such metacognitive theories or models held by individuals and to explain some of the critical facts about sequential change. For example, at approximately what ages or developmental levels are the different structural models found? What conditions or experiences seem to be most important for promoting movement from one model to the next? What, if any, related aspects of cognition itself are now understood better by knowing what the individual's metacognitive model of the domain looks like? How do cognition and the unfolding metacognitive models interact with one another to produce change on the metacognitive side?

Finally, a third goal might be to specify how metacognitive models about one domain (e.g., memory, understanding, or attending) are related to metacognitive models about one or more additional cognitive domains. In other words, what, if any, is the logical and psychological connection among the several strands of sequential change believed to occur in the metacognitive knowledge that children develop about different domains?

So that the three goals described here do not seem vacuous, I offer one example of what such an endeavor might look like. Suppose that, as structuralists, we want to understand the child's changing conception of mental life. We postulate that the child has some conception of an entity called the *mind* and of some specific things the mind does. For example, the mind understands and it remembers. Suppose, upon further analysis and research, we are able to uncover a general pattern emerging over time in the way children think about each concept—the mind, understanding, and remembering. For each concept, we observe, say, three qualitatively distinct ways of thinking.

The task then becomes to analyze these patterns in many children to determine if they are general qualitative structures having a particular sequential arrangement. Additionally, a general conception of mind might constrain a general conception of the understanding process, which in turn might constrain the general type of conception individuals have about remembering. Such an analysis is of importance in that it provides us with a potentially valuable theoretical description of how metacognition is organized and changes over time. It would be analogous to Kohlberg's conception of how logical stages of thinking are necessary for particular perspectives on the social world, which in turn underlie particular modes of moral thought.

Turning next to the cognitive-behavioral perspective, the third paradigm listed in Table 2, let us consider some prospects for new theoretical work on metacognition in this paradigm. Among other features, the cognitive-behavioral paradigm emphasizes a close examination of changes in observable behavior mediated by symbolic events. In social learning theory versions of this perspective, there is the additional feature of social modeling as a principal vehicle for acquiring new responses (Bandura, 1969, 1977b; Rosenthal & Zimmerman, 1978). It is becoming clear that the symbolic events postulated in theories of cognitive-behavioral change look increasingly like the processes and events invoked by the information processors. However, at least the mediation of behavior by social events and of response acquisition by social modeling must be retained as distinctive if there is really a separate paradigm to pursue. These two features, in turn, suggest what the distinctive approach might be to studying metacognitive change.

One distinctive line of inquiry is to pursue questions about the status of metacognitive occurrences in the range of symbolic events that mediate learning. So, in Bandura's view of learning, for example, what role do metacognitive phenomena play in attention coding, retention, and reproduction processes? In incentive or motivational conditions? And, given the substantial amount of thinking and writing Bandura has been doing on the topic of self-efficacy (Bandura, 1977a, 1978), in what sense is self-efficacy really a particular strand of self-metacognition? Does another symbolic box have to be added to Bandura's flow chart to more fully handle metacognitive processing in learning, or is it subsumed somewhere else? Is metacognition a mental process of equal standing with the others or does it have some superordinate role to play in learning models as it does in information-processing accounts?

A second direction for scholarship is suggested by the fact that cognitive learning models might contribute more to our understanding of how social models transmit or signal metacognitive experiences and knowledge directly. Social models are, after all, people, who in addition to displaying specific behavioral patterns may be transmitting information to the observer about a variety of matters. For example, the observer may learn, as a matter of course, what skills are associated with what people, what skills particular adults deem important to transmit to children, and what social psychological arrangements others typically create in order to transmit new learning or information more effectively. These all seem to me to be metacognitive in nature.

A third and final focus of cognitive-behavioral theory could concern the role of metacognition in engineering change or in providing workable techniques to alter behavior. Some of the work presently being conducted under the rubric of cognitive behavior modification is a good example of this focus (Karoly, 1977). Investigators are increasingly studying the metacognitive foundation of a variety of change techniques such as the think-aloud method, and the technique of verbal self-instruction. The issue is to determine just how crucial it is to provide a cognitive rationale to accompany some mental mediation and to determine just how extensive and complete it must be (Miller, 1982).

The fourth paradigm listed in the table is the psychometric orientation—particularly the extensive models of the development of intelligence. Some efforts have been made recently to incorporate ideas from experimental cognitive psychology into psychometric models of intelligence (Hunt, 1978; Pellegrino & Glaser, 1982; Sternberg & Powell, 1982), even though the efforts may be unsatisfying to many traditional developmentalists. I submit that the concept of metacognition could benefit from the attention of psychometricians in at least three ways.

First, the matter of measurement has plagued the study of this topic from its inception, and we still have few psychometrically sound measures of metacognitive functioning. The press to establish reliable and valid measures of metacognition, even limited aspects of it, would be a real boon to scientific progress in the field.

Second, an argument could be mounted for seeking out proof that metacognitive phenomena are as widespread in children's intellectual life as many developmentalists now claim they are. Our current tests of intelligence essentially ignore this aspect of functioning. There are few, if any, tasks designed to assess either a child's crystallized knowledge about mental life or distinctively strategic ways of doing things, or to assess fluid abilities such as planning, checking, and monitoring activities. Some existing tests such as the Wechsler Intelligence Scale for Children—Revised (WISC—R) (Wechsler, 1974; Sattler, 1981) and the K-ABC (Kaufman & Kaufman, 1983), of course, do claim to have tasks included in their batteries, which measure these processes. However, there is a substantial inferential leap from these processes to the nature of what children are required to do in these tests. Additionally, from inception, the tasks were not explicitly designed to measure these phenomena. If some of the phenomena we are currently discussing are substantial ones, then we should be able to document them in the form of standardized measures that might give evidence of one or more metacognitive factors or processes in general intelligence.

To briefly put closure on the current discussion of how metacognition can be usefully studied in several different paradigms of cognitive development, the following concluding thought is offered. Many different proposals have been made about approaching the study of metacognition from the perspective of different theoretical schools of thought. However, no effort was put forth to evaluate them in any comparative sense. At this point it seems more valuable to consider the variety of ways in which the concept of metacognition can be studied and advanced with theoretical clarity, than to attempt premature prediction of which approach or task is likely to meet with the greatest success.

Metacognitive Development beyond Childhood

The study of metacognition, like many other branches in the study of cognitive development, is governed primarily by concepts and techniques developed for use with children and adolescents. Although there are some commonalities in the way cognition changes during childhood and adulthood, it is becoming increasingly clear that the differences may merit a great deal of our interest and attention (e.g., Baltes & Willis, 1977; Salthouse, 1982; Schaie, 1974). In Table 3 I present a number of features of cognitive life that highlight the differences between children and adults in the basic nature of cognition, the contexts in which that cognition occurs, and its typical goals and uses. Following a brief explanation of each of these features, we examine their implications for the study of metacognition.

First, let us consider what is uniquely important about cognition during childhood in contrast to adulthood and, accordingly, what ought to be the focus of scholarship about each period. We believe that childhood is largely a time of acquiring a considerable amount of symbolic know-how and learned skills. The vast domain of Piagetian concepts and the attendant shifts in how individuals grasp general features of experience such as time, space, causation, and number represent a substantial acquisition of symbolic understanding and reasoning. Whatever one's theoretical approach to explaining the underlying processes (e.g., Feldman, 1980; Siegler, 1983), there is no denying that a substantial amount of acquisition is practically universal among children. Similarly, most children are learning a large number of cognitive skills through the process of schooling and other informal education. They acquire the ability to read, to write, to think with mathematics, to understand the nature of the world they live in, to understand history, and so on. These are not universally acquired skills (Feldman, 1980), but their acquisition is surely guaranteed by many cultures for many children.

Table 3

Unique Features of Studying Cognitive Development in Childhood and Adulthood

Property of the study	Period	
	Childhood	Adulthood
Focus of inquiry	**Acquisition** of skill skill organization level of skill	**Application** of skill types of specialized expertise domains of applying skill tasks selected
Source of change	Maturation and culture	culture (work, family, economy, history, etc.)
Type of cognitive items selected	|universal cultural discipline based idiosyncratic unique|	
Context of study	School	Work, family, community
Cognitive activity	Puzzle solving	Purpose generated activites

A broad look at cognitive life in adults suggests something different. Adulthood seems to be a period in which a large arsenal of symbolic ability and learned skills are already available and many changes take place in how adults apply these skills and ability. What goals and tasks do they set for themselves? What activities do they choose to pursue at work and at home? What do they hope to achieve and accomplish? These are the important questions that dominate change in cognitive life. As Paul Baltes once summarized the difference between children and adults, childhood is a period for acquiring maturity; adulthood is the time when maturity is put to important use (Baltes, 1980). We must be careful to underscore that the distinction being offered here does not imply that adult life is simple or that changes in adult cognition are trivial to describe. Quite the contrary. The description of how adults use their skills (e.g., Schaie, 1974) and acquire increasing levels of expertise (e.g., Salthouse, 1982) may prove to be just as challenging as has been the study of cognitive development in childhood. And, as I argue in a later part of this section of the chapter, it may well be that there are important changes in the acquisition of skills in adulthood as well, if we are willing to reconceptualize the notion of skill or domain of cognitive achievement from the usual way it has been applied in the childhood literature.

A second dimension for contrasting childhood and adulthood is the source of influence operating to cause cognitive change. Both childhood and adulthood experience the impact of culture in many ways. It is possible to investigate how different socializing agents and different social structures shape the acquisition of particular skills (e.g., school—reading) or uses of skills (work—reading and mastering a selected body of knowledge). And, although there are not yet many canonical examples to illustrate the different ways that culture operates, there are compelling logical grounds for believing that important differences exist.

Some change may result from *normative age-graded* effects, as when a culture guarantees that certain tasks are confronted only at certain ages or stages (e.g., 'good penmanship stressed in Grades 1–3, being an apprentice or an assistant when one first learns a trade). Other changes result from *normative historical* effects, as when everyone living through a certain period of time has an aspect of their cognition shaped through some social practices or events unique to that period (e.g., learning to count numbers by watching the popular TV program—"Sesame Street"; learning to compose and think at a keyboard, given the widespread availability and speed of word-processing equipment). Finally, some change occurs in a *nonnormative historical* fashion, as when a particular historical period exposes some individuals to a particular experience, but not others (e.g., the Vietnam combat experience for soldiers versus the absence of it for others). The differences in the operation of cultural forces in childhood versus adulthood are to be found in the different cultural agents and structures likely to be more pervasive in each period, and the modes (e.g., normative age-graded) by which they operate. We return to this theme in a few paragraphs.

However, a second source of change that helps explain the difference between childhood and adulthood cognition is biological maturation. For the most part, cognitive development during childhood has everything to do with the physical maturing of the brain and central nervous system, whereas cognitive development during adulthood has almost nothing to do with it. The central nervous system (CNS) develops to a fairly high level and moves through a number of steps in a short 12 years or so. By contrast, there is no rapid biological process accompanying cognitive change in adulthood.

A third dimension for contrasting childhood and adulthood is the type of cognitive target frequently adopted in experimental research, which is thought to reflect important aspects of subjects' cognitive lives. To the extent that these scholarly practices reflect real differences in the nature of cognitive change, they may help to further elucidate differences in these periods.

We have adopted a scheme developed by Feldman (1980), who suggests that cognitive acquisitions may be universal, cultural, discipline based, idiosyncratic, or unique. Each type of acquisition can be studied within a developmental framework. That is, it very well may exhibit a clear sequence of qualitatively different levels of functioning, with certain transition steps and processes helping to explain the changes that occur. In Table 3 we have purposefully listed these categories of acquisitions in a line to reflect a generalization we will make about them in a few moments.[2]

A brief description of each domain of knowledge and skill is offered here. *Universal acquisitions* are those cognitions that virtually all human beings develop and/or learn regardless of the particular culture or experiential milieu in which they find themselves. The operations in Piaget's theory of intellectual development are of this sort, as are learning to talk, to apprehend time and space, and to form memories. *Cultural acquisitions*, by contrast, are those cognitions that develop in individuals only because the culture at large teaches, informs, or otherwise consciously intervenes

---

[2]This is not a generalization proposed by Feldman. In fact, Feldman does not develop the conceptual framework of different categories of cognitive acquisitions to explain differences between childhood and adulthood. That application is uniquely ours and we accept any blame or praise for it.

in the person's development. By definition, these acquisitions occur in a large number of individuals, because the culture deems them to be necessary. However, not all cultures guarantee acquisition of the same cognitions, and across long periods of historical time there may be fundamental shifts in the particular cognitions that a given culture nourishes. Examples of cultural acquisitions include learning to read, learning to write, and learning mathematics. *Discipline-based* knowledge and skill refers to cognitions in a specific cultural domain that some people, but not others, are expected to acquire. Examples include the knowledge and skill of specialized trades, such as carpentry and electrical work, or of professions, such as medicine and law. *Idiosyncratic* cognition refers to the knowledge and skill required by yet fewer individuals in a culture, usually those who have forms of subspecialties within discipline-based areas (e.g., a carpenter specializing in constructing roofs, a microbiologist, or a patent attorney). Finally *unique* cognition refers to the knowledge and skill acquired and contributed by those rare individuals who revolutionize the thinking and/or practice in a particular discipline or idiosyncratic domain of endeavor. Individuals who would probably qualify are Newton and Einstein in physics, Skinner and Piaget in psychology, and Mark Twain or Ernest Hemingway in American literature.

The generalization, then, about these domains, is as follows: We believe that in childhood, most cognitive acquisitions and change occur in the universal or cultural domains, whereas in adulthood, most are in the discipline-based, idiosyncratic, or (for the very few rare individuals) unique domains.

A fourth dimension for contrasting childhood and adulthood is the primary context within which important changes occur—at least as contemporary theories and research represent the matter. For childhood, the principal locus has, and will continue to be, the academic setting. Although many everyday skills are learned in childhood outside of the context of school (cf. Paris & Cross, 1983), a major cultural context is the school and the cognitive agenda it sets for children. By contrast, in adulthood, individuals apply their cognitions and acquire discipline-based and idiosyncratic knowledge in many contexts other than schools. They work at one or more jobs; they live in and manage the activities of families; and they live in and participate in the affairs of their neighborhood or community, to name several of the more prominent contexts. So the study of adult cognition is likely to be a more varied affair than the study of childhood cognition, with so many more possibilities manifesting themselves in different contexts.

The fifth and final dimension for contrasting childhood and adulthood is the nature of how cognitive activity is conceptualized. In the next

section of this chapter, I distinguish among three very different conceptions of cognition. Two conceptions that are extremely different from one
another are the view that cognition is like puzzle solving, and the view
that considers cognition to be based on purpose-generated activities. The
tasks we set for children in real life and in experimental situations more
often conform to properties of puzzle solving than of purpose-generated
activities. Many of the important cognitive tasks of adulthood, by contrast,
center on purpose-generated activities, although we still mistakenly study
these phenomena in adults within a puzzle-solving framework. The distinction is taken up at some length in the next section.

For now, we would like to conclude this discussion of the differences
between childhood and adulthood cognition by returning to the issue at
hand—metacognition. What do the differences sketched out above imply
about how to proceed in studying metacognition? Several things are implied.

In studying adults, we need to pay more attention to other kinds of
knowledge domains than we have with children. We need to study how
adults choose a particular skill or form of expertise to address a task—how
they select from among alternative domains of expertise. We also could
profit from studying how adults choose the *domains of applications* to
which the skills are addressed. Finally, we have to consider cultural forces
(likely to be at work for long periods of time) that impinge on these cognitive selection activities of adults.

Alternative Frameworks: "Puzzles" and "Purposes"

Few scholars would argue with the premise that our frameworks for
studying cognition significantly shape the nature of our theories about
cognitive development and the kinds of phenomena we are led to study.
An earlier section illustrated this point by describing how the different
contemporary schools of thought about cognitive development could lead
to different insights about metacognitive development by focusing on different questions and phenomena.

There is another sense of framework, however, which is not given
enough attention in our contemporary thinking about cognitive development. The kind of framework we have in mind is an organizing principle that cuts across the familiar theoretical paradigms discussed already.
I describe the framework in this final section of the essay, and consider
its implications for the study of metacognitive development.

The framework in question is the orientation that cognitive phenomena express themselves in the solution of problems. Implicit in a great deal of research on cognitive development is the notion that if a person is successful in negotiating some cognitive activity (remembering, reading, communicating, inferencing, etc.), she or he has solved a problem. I would also argue that although there are several different frameworks for understanding problem solving, most cognitive developmental framework explicitly or implicitly adopt one type—what I have called puzzle solving.

In Table 4, I outline characteristics of three different problem frameworks. The frameworks are named puzzle solving, ill-defined problems, and planning. My contention is that cognitive development entails the acquisition of knowledge and skills to deal with activities encompassed by all three types of frameworks, but that mostly we study puzzle solving in our formal research, thereby cutting off (no doubt, unwittingly) any examination of much else that is important in cognitive life.

Table 4

Alternative Problem Orientations in Studying Cognitive Phenomena

Characteristics	Puzzle solving	Ill-defined problems	Planning
Representative examples	Towers of Hanoi	Writing an essay	Developing a program for study in school
Starting point	Problem definition Quickly done Straightforward	Considering alternative problems Some ambiguity Some time required	Consider purposes Delayed until purposes established
Nature of solution	Highly specified Tight prescriptions	Some specification	Specifications created in process Unique prescription results
Ownership of tasks (role of others)	Individual (minimal)	Individual (minimal)	Group (maximal)
Degree of risks and rewards	Low	Moderate	High
Role of time	Short duration Short-term solution	Short duration Short-term solution	Long-term duration Long-term planning
Revision	Little Done primarily to fit initial specifications	Some Done to fit changing specifications	A lot Planned in advance Done to fit changed purposes or changed solution framework

To help elucidate the three types of problem frameworks, I identify three prototypical cognitive tasks that might be faced by a school-aged child and give a series of characteristics that help to show the differences among the tasks that result from the different problem frameworks each fits. Our implicit models of how these tasks are best done should not be confused with the actual behavior of real subjects tackling them. We believe that in at least one of these frameworks (planning), almost everyone goes about the task incorrectly, because they have not learned (developed) an understanding of planning principles. As stated above, I believe that adults face many more tasks of planning than do children. However, to keep the discussion simple, I have selected prototypical tasks that children could face or that they have faced. Later, I speculate on just how prominent these alternative problem solving frameworks are in childhood as opposed to adulthood.

As an example of *puzzle solving*, consider the Towers of Hanoi problem. It is shown in Figure 1. Given a series of three wooden poles with a set of disks of decreasing size initially arranged on the left pole as shown, the problem is to move all the disks from the left pole to the right pole according to the following rules: (1) you can only move one disk at a time, (2) you can never put a disk on top of a smaller one, and (3) you must keep each of the disks on one of the three poles at any time.

An as example of *ill-defined problems*, consider the task of writing an essay. For the sake of discussion, let us suppose that a teacher has told a child to write an essay about how it feels to live in America (or whatever the native country happens to be). The essay is to be written in school and completed by the end of the week.

As an example of *planning*, consider the task of developing a program for study in school. Suppose that school authorities have told a child entering a new school that she or he must plan his or her program for the next 3 years.

To solve a puzzle, as in the Towers of Hanoi problem, the starting point is the problem definition. Note that the problem has essentially been defined for the subject, in a rather quick and straightforward manner. To solve it, a clearly specified outcome has been offered with very tight prescriptions.

By contrast, note that the ill-defined problem of writing an essay does not begin with a clear definition. On the contrary, it contains a great amount of freedom and uncertainty as to just what to do—what ideas to get across, how to express them, in what order, and so forth. A number of alternatives would probably have to be considered because there is a good deal of ambiguity present, and some amount of time would be required to figure out what to do. Although the writer must produce a so-

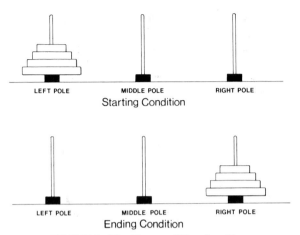

LEFT POLE   MIDDLE POLE   RIGHT POLE
Starting Condition

LEFT POLE   MIDDLE POLE   RIGHT POLE
Ending Condition

FIGURE 1. The Towers of Hanoi problem.

lution (i.e., a finished essay) that has some specifications, there is wide latitude in the final form it may take.

The act of planning, at least as it is practiced by the best planners (e.g., Nadler, 1981; Nadler, Perrone, Seabold, & Yussen, 1984) is altogether different from the two cases just considered. In the case of developing a program for study in school, for example, the starting point in the analysis should not be to figure out what the problem is or what to do, but rather, what one hopes to obtain from school—that is, what are one's purposes. Working out a concrete program is delayed until these purposes are established. The solution would be one uniquely suited to the specific hierarchy of purposes developed for the particular person and situation. It would become specified in the process of establishing the purposes.

Another characteristic that distinguishes among the alternative problem-solving frameworks is what could be called the "ownership" of the task. Who is responsible for the activity and what role is played by others in it? In puzzle solving and ill-defined problems, the answer is usually simple. The individual who is given the puzzle or ill-defined problem to solve bears most or all of the responsibility for completing the task. To the extent that others are involved in helping the individual, we could say that their roles are that of facilitators or expert resources.

In planning, however, a relevant group of people owns the problem, not the individual. In the case at hand, the relevant group is the student's family, teachers, and school administrators. The process of planning is social and collaborative in nature. The solution would be structured by the group. The group is the source from which purposes and values are defined and around which the solution is structured. The group nature of planning is most readily apparent from the fields that spawned it as a perspective in the adult world—for example, architecture, engineering, corporate planning, and government policy making, to name a few. Each discipline typically operates in a setting where solutions are sought by a group for a larger group. However, even in the present example of planning a school program for a student, we can quite easily see the sense in which the process ought to be social–collaborative in nature and involve a group of people. Planning a school program is likely to be linked to one's hopes and aspirations about future employment and/or a career. Fashioning this future is, among other things, likely to involve consideration of financial resources for education and schooling, consideration of one's skills and abilities, and consideration of contributions and obligations to one's family of origin. The other individuals involved in these considerations are central to them, not incidental. Their purposes and values must be integrated into a solution. Thus, ownership of the task differs considerably across the different problem frameworks.

Every cognitive activity involves a certain degree of risk for failure and reward for success. The nature of these risks and rewards differs from one problem-solving framework to another and thus serves as another characteristic that can be used to differentiate among them. In a relative sense, Table 4 suggests that puzzle solving involves a low degree of risk and rewards, ill-defined problems involve a moderate degree, and planning involves a high degree. In solving the Towers of Hanoi problem, not much is invested or at stake, and the consequences for failure or success are slight. The activity is likely to have little lasting impact on one's sense of self-esteem, evaluation by others, or success in school. By contrast, writing the essay involves a bit more cognitive resources, time, reflection, and (perhaps) reward for a job well done. Finally, planning a curriculum requires more time and resources yet and what is at stake is the pattern of success and happiness likely to extend across a significant portion of one's future.

The last two comparisons both touch on the different role of time in the alternative problem-solving frameworks. The message is that the different problem-solving frameworks involve different amounts of time devoted to the activity. However, more than the simple amount of time, the alternative problem-solving frameworks differ in the way that cognitive activity is structured or packaged across time.

In puzzle solving, a solution is often arrived at in a relatively short, circumscribed period of time, and an individual more or less has a solution or does not have one. If one has a solution, there is little or no revision necessary. Ill-defined problems may take a bit longer to solve, and solutions arrived at in circumscribed periods of time may sometimes undergo revision, because often there is confusion about the goal or the nature of a good solution from the outset. But much more than the others, planning assumes that there is no single solution for the circumstance in question and offers only provisional working models (plans). These are tried out for a period of time and then revised as circumstances in oneself and in the world change and the purposes one sets out to achieve meet with differential success. Revision and change are built into planning from the outset and they are not seen as corrective measures but as integral parts of the process.

These, then, are some of the important characteristics by which we can contrast the three alternative problem-solving frameworks. It is my belief that the study of cognitive development is enriched by acknowledging the presence of these three frameworks in human cognitive activity and by developing approaches uniquely suited to the study of each one.

What, then, are the implications for the study of metacognition that seem to flow from the acknowledgement of the existence of these three types of problem-solving frameworks?

One implication is that the nature of the important metacognitive knowledge that individuals acquire may be very different, depending upon which type of problem they are pursuing. Most of the metacognitive theories and processes that have already been proposed (e.g., Brown et al., 1983; Flavell, 1979) would seem to give a good account of puzzle solving and, to some extent, ill-defined problems.

However, a good description of the metacognitive knowledge associated with planning awaits future work. In place of Flavell's scheme of *self, task,* and *strategies,* for example, we might suggest a taxonomy of metacognition for planning that contains knowledge about *human purposes, integrating group desires and values,* and what planners call *time lining.* The focus of knowledge about *human purposes* might entail such things as knowing what people seek to accomplish, knowing that facts and raw information have no meaning in the absence of purposes, that purposes can be hierarchically arranged, and that establishing purpose hierarchies is as much an affective process as an analytic, logical one. The focus of knowledge about integrating group desires and values might entail a recognition that members of a group are quite diverse in desires and values, that desires and values are often hidden in people and require extensive fleshing out, that integration is a synthetic process that must avoid the common pitfall of camouflaging or submerging some members' interests and values to those of others, and that effective group integration requires a group process model in which people work as colleagues with equal status, authority, and importance. The focus of knowledge about time lining might entail an appreciation of how human plans get carried out over years and decades, an understanding of the different phases of a planning cycle, the temporariness of any solution, and the linkage between particular solutions and the historical, social, and economic circumstances existing at the time.

A second implication is that to adequately describe the nature of on-line metacognitive processing might require different levels of analysis for the different kinds of problem frameworks. For example, I firmly believe that it is useful to contemplate an executive processor that engages in fast-acting decisions that are unconscious or semiconscious if the kinds of problems being dealt with are of the puzzle or ill-defined variety. However, I believe there is little of the executive activity present in planning.[3] It is much more of a conscious, deliberative process with key steps evolving over hours and days rather than microseconds. Among the very different metacognitive processes suggested in the planning process are eliciting purposes from people, organizing purposes into hierarchies, and keeping track of diverse steps in planning over time.

A third implication has been stated already. Planning seems to be an activity done mostly by adults, whereas the solving of puzzles and ill-defined problems widely occurs for both children and adults. Elsewhere, we have wondered whether the virtual absence of child-based planning is a necessary feature of childhood, or a failure in our vision as educators of the young (Nadler et al., 1984). If the answer is the former, then our metacognitive theories about planning may open up a truly unique area of research in adult cognitive development. If adult cognitive development is largely about applying skills already acquired or putting one's maturity to use (as opposed to acquiring one's maturity), planning would seem to be a quintessential case of cognitive application to study.

Acknowledgments

This chapter represents a considerable expansion and revision of ideas initially presented in a session at the 1983 meetings of the *Society for Research in Child Development*. The time to read, reflect, and write has been made possible by a continuing grant from the National Institute of Education to the Wisconsin Center for Education Research at the University of Wisconsin-Madison, and by a Fulbright visit to the School of Education at Hebrew University (Jerusalem, Israel)

---

[3]This may seem paradoxical, since the idea of planning is associated with disciplines in which *executives* (people) and *executive planning* abound. However, we believe that in the case at hand, the two senses of *executive activity* diverge and have virtually opposite meanings.

during the Spring semester, 1984. I thank Gerald Nadler for inspiring some of the ideas in here, Karen Rembold for her reactions to an earlier version of the paper, and Dorothy Egener for her professional, trans-Atlantic, manuscript preparation.

References

Baker, L., & Anderson, R. I. Effects of inconsistent information on text processing: Evidence for comprehension monitoring. *Reading Research Quarterly*, 1982, 17, 281–294.

Baker, L., & Brown, A. L. Meta-cognitive skills in reading. In D. Pearson (Ed.), *Handbook of reading research*, 1982.

Baltes, P. *Remarks concluding symposium: "Developmental psychology: History of philosophy and philosophy of history."* American Psychological Association Convention, Montreal, September 1–5, 1980.

Baltes, P. B., & Willis, S. L. Toward psychological theories of aging and development. In J. E. Birren & K. W. Schaie (Eds.), *Handbook of the Psychology of Aging*. New York: Van Nostrand Reinhold, 1977.

Bandura, A. *Principles of behavior modification*. New York: Holt, Rinehart & Winston, 1969.

Bandura, A. Self efficacy: Toward a unifying theory of behavioral change. *Psychological Review*, 1977, 84, 191–215. (a)

Bandura, A. *Social learning theory*. Englewood Cliffs, NJ: Prentice Hall, 1977. (b)

Bandura, A. The self system in reciprocal determinism. *American Psychologist*, 1978, 33, 344–358.

Bereiter, C., & Scardamalia, M. From conversation to composition: The role of instruction in a developmental process. In R. Glaser (Ed.), *Advances in instructional psychology* (Vol. 2). Hillsdale, NJ: Erlbaum, 1982.

Borkowski, J. Signs of intelligence: Strategy generalization and metacognition. In S. R. Yussen (Ed.), *The growth of reflection in children*. New York: Academic Press, 1984.

Broughton, J. The development of natural epistemology in adolescence and early adulthood. Ph. D. dissertation, Harvard University, 1975.

Broughton, J. Development of concepts of self, mind, reality and knowledge. In W. Damon (Ed.), *Social cognition, new directions for child development*. San Francisco: Jossey Bass, 1978.

Brown, A. L., Bransford, J. D., Ferrara, R. A., & Campione, J. Learning, understanding, and remembering. In P. H. Mussen (Ed.), *Handbook of child psychology* (Vol. 3). New York: Wiley, 1983.

Buss, R. R. Development of children's ability to apprehend and distribute attention to important elements in prose. Ph. D. dissertation, University of Wisconsin—Madison, 1981.

Campione, J. E., & Brown, A. L. Toward a theory of intelligence: Contributions from research with retarded children. *Intelligence*, 1978, 2, 279–304.

Capelli, C. A., & Markman, E. M. Suggestions for training comprehension monitoring. *Topics in Learning and Learning Disabilities*, 1982, 2, 87–96.

Cavanaugh, J. C., & Perlmutter, M. Metamemory: A critical examination. *Child Development*, 1982, 53, 11–28.

Enright, R., Enright, W., & Lapsley, D. Distributive justice development and social class: A replication period. *Developmental Psychology*, 1981, 17, 826–832.

Feldman, D. H. *Beyond universals in cognitive development*. Norwood, NJ: Ablex, 1980.

Flavell, J. H. First discussant's comments: What is memory development the development of? *Human Development*, 1971, *14*, 272–278.

Flavell, J. H. Metacognition and cognitive monitoring: A new area of psychological inquiry. *American Psychologist*, 1979, *34*, 906–911.

Flavell, J. H. Cognitive monitoring. In W. P. Dickson (Ed.), *Children's oral communication skills*. New York: Academic Press, 1981. (a)

Flavell, J. H. On cognitive development. *Child Development*, 1982, *53*,(1), 1-10.

Flavell, J. H., Friedrich, A., & Hoyt, J. Developmental changes in memorization processes. *Cognitive Psychology*, 1970, *1*, 324–340.

Flavell, J. H., Speer, J. R., Green, F. L., & August, D. L. The development of comprehension monitoring and knowledge about communication. *Monographs of the Society for Research in Child Development*, 1981, *46*, 1–65.

Flavell, J. H., & Wellman, H. M. Metamemory. In R. V. Kail, Jr., & J. W. Hagen (Eds.), *Perspectives on the development of memory and cognition*. Hillsdale, NJ: Erlbaum, 1977.

Glenberg, A. M., Wilkinson, A. C., & Epstein, W. The illusion of knowing: Failure in the self-assessment of comprehension. *Memory and Cognition*, 1982, *10*(16), 597–602.

Hagen, J. W., Barclay, C. R., & Newman, R. S. Metacognition, self knowledge, and learning disabilities: Some thoughts on knowing and doing. *Topics in Learning and Learning Disabilities*, 1982, *2*, 19–26.

Hunt, E. Mechanics of verbal ability. *Psychological Review*, 1978, *85*, 109-130.

Karoly, P. Behavioral self-management in children: Concepts, methods, issues, and directions. In M. Hersen, R. M. Eisler, & P. Millers (Eds.), *Progress in behavior modification* (Vol. 5). New York: Academic Press, 1977.

Kaufman, A., & Kaufman, N. *K-ABC interpretive manual*. Circle Pines, MN: American Guidance Service, 1983.

Kelly, M., Scholnick, E. K., Travers, S. H., & Johnson, J. W. Relations among memory, memory appraisal, and memory strategies. *Child Development*, 1976, *47*, 648–659.

Lapsley, D. K., & Serlin, R. C. On the alleged degeneration of the Kohlbergian research program. *Educational Theory*, 1984, *34*, 157–169.

Levin, J. R., Yussen, S. R., DeRose, T. M., & Pressley, M. Developmental changes in assessing recall and recognition memory capacity. *Developmental Psychology*, 1977, *13*, 608–615.

Loper, A. B. Metacognitive training to correct academic deficiency. *Topics in Learning and Learning Disabilities*, 1982, *2*, 16–68.

Loper, A. B., Hallahan, D. P., & Lanna, S. O. Meta-attention in learning disabled and normal students. *Learning Disability Quarterly*, 1982, *5*, 29–36.

Markman, E. M. Realizing that you don't understand: A preliminary investigation. *Child Development*, 1977, *48*, 986–992.

Markman, E. M. Realizing that you don't understand: Elementary school children's awareness of inconsistencies. *Child Development*, 1979, *50*, 643-655.

Markman, E. Comprehension monitoring: In W. P. Dickson (Ed.), *Children's oral communication skills*. New York: Academic Press, 1981.

Meichenbaum, D. Cognitive behavior modification with exceptional children: A promise yet unfulfilled. *Exceptional Education Quarterly*, 1980, *9*, 83–88.

Meichenbaum, D., Burland, S., Gruson, L., & Cameron, R. Metacognitive assessment. In S. R. Yussen (Eds.), *The growth of reflection in children*. New York: Academic Press, 1984.

Miller, G. E. Improving comprehension-monitoring performance during reading through self-instruction. Ph. D. dissertation, University of Wisconsin—Madison, 1982.

Miller, P. H., & Weiss, M. G. Children's attention allocation, understanding of attention, and performance on the incidental learning task. *Child Development*, 1981, *52*, 1183–1190.

Nadler, G. *The planning and design approach.* New York: Wiley, 1981.

Nadler, G., Perrone, P., Seabold, D., & Yussen, S. Planning and design in education. Unpublished manuscript, University of Wisconsin—Madison, 1984.

Paris, S., & Cross, D. Ordinary learning. In J. Bisanz, G. Bisanz, & R. Kail (Eds.), *Learning in children.* New York: Springer-Verlag, 1983.

Pellegrino, J. W., & Glaser, R. Analyzing aptitudes for learning: Inductive reasoning. In R. Glaser (Ed.), *Advances in instructional psychology* (Vol. 2.). Hillsdale: Erlbaum, 1982.

Perry, W. O. *Forms of intellectual and ethical development in the college years: A scheme.* New York: Holt, Rinehart, and Winston, 1970.

Rest, J. Morality. In P. H. Mussen (Ed.), *Handbook of child psychology* (Vol. 3). New York: Wiley, 1983.

Rosch, E. H. On the internal structure of perceptual and semantic categories. In T. E. Moore (Ed.), *Cognition and the acquisition of language.* New York: Academic Press, 1973.

Rosch, E. H. Principles of categorization. In E. H. Rosch & B. B. Lloyd (Eds.), *Cognition and categorization.* Hillsdale, NJ: Erlbaum, 1978.

Rosenthal, T. L., & Zimmerman, B. J. *Social learning and development.* New York: Academic Press, 1978.

Salthouse, T. A. *Adult Cognition.* New York: Springer-Verlag, 1982.

Sattler, J. M. *Assessment of children's intelligence and special abilities* (2nd ed.). Boston: Allyn, 1981.

Schaie, K. W. Translation in gerontology—from lab to life: Intellectual functioning. *American Psychologist,* 1974, *29,* 802–807.

Selman, R. *The growth of interpersonal understanding.* New York: Academic Press, 1980.

Siegler, R. H. Information processing approaches to development. In P. H. Mussen (Ed.), *Handbook of child psychology* (Vol. 1). New York: Wiley, 1983.

Sternberg, R. J., & Powell, J. S. The development of intelligence. In P. H. Mussen (Ed.), *Handbook of child psychology* (Vol. 3). New York: Wiley, 1983.

Wechsler, D. *Manual for the Wechsler intelligence scale for children* (rev. ed.). New York: Psychological Corporation, 1974.

Wellman, H. M. A child's theory of mind: The development of conceptions of cognition. In S. R. Yussen (Ed.), *The growth of reflection in children.* New York: Academic Press, 1984.

Yussen, S. R., & Levy, V. M. Developmental changes in predicting one's own span of short-term memory. *Journal of Experimental Child Psychology,* 1975, *19,* 502–508.

Yussen, S. R., & Pacquette, N. S. Developmental changes in predicting recognition memory for semantically related and unrelated sentences. *Developmental Psychology,* 1978, *14,* 107–113.

Yussen, S. R., & Santrock, J. W. *Child Development: An Introduction* (2nd ed.). Dubuque: Wm. C. Brown. 1982.

Author Index

285

Subject Index

860026897